Reconciling Truths

Law and Society Series
W. Wesley Pue, Founding Editor

We pay tribute to the late Wes Pue, under whose broad vision, extraordinary leadership, and unwavering commitment to socio-legal studies our Law and Society Series was established and rose to prominence.

The Law and Society Series explores law as a socially embedded phenomenon. It is premised on the understanding that the conventional division of law from society creates false dichotomies in thinking, scholarship, educational practice, and social life. Books in the series treat law and society as mutually constitutive and seek to bridge scholarship emerging from interdisciplinary engagement of law with disciplines such as politics, social theory, history, political economy, and gender studies.

Recent books in the series:

Daniel Rück, *The Laws and the Land: The Settler Colonial Invasion of Kahnawà:ke in Nineteenth-Century Canada* (2021)

Suzanne Bouclin, *Women, Film, and Law: Cinematic Representations of Female Incarceration* (2021)

Amanda Nelund, *A Better Justice? Community Programs for Criminalized Women* (2020)

Trevor C.W. Farrow and Lesley A. Jacobs, eds., *The Justice Crisis: The Cost and Value of Accessing Law* (2020)

Jamie Baxter, *Inalienable Properties: The Political Economy of Indigenous Land Reform* (2020)

Jeremy Patrick, *Faith or Fraud: Fortune-Telling, Spirituality, and the Law* (2020)

Obiora Chinedu Okafor, *Refugee Law after 9/11: Sanctuary and Security in Canada and the United States* (2020)

Anna Jane Samis Lund, *Trustees at Work: Financial Pressures, Emotional Labour, and Canadian Bankruptcy Law* (2019)

Shauna Labman, *Crossing Law's Border: Canada's Refugee Resettlement Program* (2019)

Peter McCormick and Marc D. Zanoni, *By the Court: Anonymous Judgments at the Supreme Court of Canada* (2019)

For a complete list of the titles in the series, see the UBC Press website, www.ubcpress.ca.

Reconciling Truths

Reimagining Public Inquiries in Canada

KIM STANTON

For Natasha
Thanks for reading!
Kim.

UBCPress

1971–2021

30 29 28 27 26 25 24 23 22   5 4 3 2 1

Printed in Canada on FSC-certified ancient-forest-free paper (100% post-consumer recycled) that is processed chlorine- and acid-free.

Library and Archives Canada Cataloguing in Publication

Title: Reconciling truths : reimagining public inquiries in Canada / Kim Stanton.
Names: Stanton, Kim (Kim P.), author.

Series: Law and society series (Vancouver, B.C.)
Description: Series statement: Law and society | Includes bibliographical references and index.

Identifiers: Canadiana (print) 20210272597 | Canadiana (ebook) 20210288019 | ISBN 9780774866651 (hardcover) | ISBN 9780774866668 (softcover) | ISBN 9780774866675 (PDF) | ISBN 9780774866682 (EPUB)

Subjects: LCSH: Governmental investigations – Canada. | LCSH: Truth commissions – Canada.

Classification: LCC KE4765 .S73 2021 | LCC KF5422 .S73 2021 kfmod | DDC 353.4/630971 – dc23

Canadä

UBC Press gratefully acknowledges the financial support for our publishing program of the Government of Canada (through the Canada Book Fund), the Canada Council for the Arts, and the British Columbia Arts Council.

This book has been published with the help of a grant from the Canadian Federation for the Humanities and Social Sciences, through the Awards to Scholarly Publications Program, using funds provided by the Social Sciences and Humanities Research Council of Canada.

Printed and bound in Canada by Friesens
Set in UniversCondensed and Minion by Artegraphica Design Co. Ltd.
Copy editor: Dallas Harrison
Proofreader: Alison Strobel
Indexer: Noeline Bridge
Cover designer: Martyn Schmoll

UBC Press
The University of British Columbia
2029 West Mall
Vancouver, BC V6T 1Z2
www.ubcpress.ca

For my sisters

Contents

Acknowledgments

My first contact with UBC Press was with the late Wes Pue, founding editor of the Law and Society Series, who responded to my inquiry about making a book proposal with the warmth, kindness, and encouragement for which I remembered him from when I was a law student at the University of British Columbia, where he was a professor. My thanks to Senior Editor Randy Schmidt and to the staff and board of UBC Press for their support of this project and to the peer review readers whose responses to my writing inspired me as I finalized the manuscript.

At Goldblatt Partners LLP, my thanks to Beth Lalonde for her patient and invaluable assistance with formatting and logistics, to Emily Denomme for her efficient and careful work on my legion of footnotes, and to Marisa Pollock for using her words as medicine.

Generous and kind friends provided me with beautiful, peaceful places in which to write. At the marvellous home of Elizabeth Shilton and David Mackenzie in southern France, nourished by fresh croissants each morning, loving, intelligent, and stimulating conversation each evening, and unencumbered time and space in between, I rediscovered my joy in my subject. Their extraordinary hospitality enabled me to write the first full draft of this book in July 2019. Stints at Anne Scotton's cabin in eastern Ontario offered reprieves from the city, complete with calling loons and rejuvenating lake swims. Anne's supremely witty and warm company, at a lovely spot amid a birch forest, made for productive writing.

The first reader of my draft manuscript, Marilyn Legge, eloquently reassured me that I was on the right track, giving me the courage to submit the manuscript to peer review. Her unstoppable positivity and the acuity of her reading, along with the boundless support and jazz interventions provided by her and her loving spouse, Michael Bourgeois, buoyed me along in my writing journey. The incisive eyes and towering intellects of Mary Eberts and Heather Ross challenged me to revisit my final text at a crucial time. Their personal courage and feminist mentorship, the strength of their support, and their firm belief in my abilities have been among the great blessings of my life.

Indeed, the steadfast support and honest opinions of my extraordinary women friends have been sustaining threads in my life as a lawyer. What luck I had to meet the incomparable Violet Allard in my first year of law school at the University of British Columbia and the dazzling Kristen Rundle during my doctorate at University of Toronto! Both have done much to give me the confidence to see this project through. I cherish my friendship with each of them and am constantly in awe of their ability to hold me to account while filling me with love and their sparkling company despite the distances between us. A fortuitous trip to Tofino with my dear friend Sandy Ibrahim enabled me to reignite my writing during a period of despair, and I wrote my initial book proposal at a writing retreat organized with characteristic smarts by Andy Paras, whose unwavering friendship and good humour have brightened many a dark day. From pre-pandemic cycling trips with l'équipe de Nathalie Sermet to pandemic sidewalk cuppas and virtual visits, my spectacular women friends near and far have nourished me along the way.

Finally, my everlasting thanks to my parents for their encouragement and to my mother, Dr. Pamela Stanton, for her careful editing of the manuscript. Any errors of course remain mine alone. Although words can never express the love I have for my family or my gratitude for all they have done and for all I have learned from them, I hope they will know that with every word I write, I try to channel their fundamental decency, commitment to the public good, and desire to make the world a better place.

Abbreviations

ADR	alternative dispute resolution
AFN	Assembly of First Nations
AHF	Aboriginal Healing Foundation
AJI	Aboriginal Justice Inquiry of Manitoba
AJIC	Aboriginal Justice Inquiry Implementation Commission
CBA	Canadian Bar Association
CBC	Canadian Broadcasting Corporation
CEDAW	United Nations Committee on the Elimination of Discrimination against Women
CERP	Commission d'enquête sur les relations entre les Autochtones et certains services publics au Québec: Écoute, réconciliation et progrès/Public Inquiry Commission on Relations between Indigenous Peoples and Certain Public Services in Quebec: Listening, Reconciliation and Progress (the Viens Commission)
CFS	Child and Family Services
CJ	Chief Justice
CJC	Chief Justice of Canada
DIA	Department of Indian Affairs
FILUs	Family Information Liaison Units
FSIN	Federation of Saskatchewan Indian Nations

IACHR	Inter-American Commission on Human Rights
INAC	Indian and Northern Affairs Canada
IRS	Indian residential schools
IRSRC	Indian Residential Schools Resolution Canada
J	Justice of a Canadian court
JJ	Justices
JJA	Justices of a Court of Appeal
LEAF	Women's Legal Education and Action Fund
LLP	limited liability partnership
LSC	Legal Strategy Coalition on Violence against Indigenous Women
MMIW(G)	missing and murdered Indigenous women (and girls)
MWI	British Columbia Missing Women Inquiry
NDP	New Democratic Party
NRC	National Reconciliation Commission (Ghana)
NWAC	Native Women's Association of Canada
OPP	Ontario Provincial Police
RCAP	Royal Commission on Aboriginal Peoples
RCMP	Royal Canadian Mounted Police
SCC	Supreme Court of Canada
TRC	Truth and Reconciliation Commission of Canada
2SLGBTQQIA	Two-Spirit, lesbian, gay, bisexual, transgender, queer, questioning, intersex, and asexual
UN	United Nations

Reconciling Truths

Introduction

SETTING THE CONTEXT

One of the most difficult conversations that I have had as a lawyer occurred during my last year as Legal Director of the Women's Legal Education and Action Fund (LEAF) in 2017. It was a call from Meg Cywink, an Anishinaabe woman and advocate for missing and murdered Indigenous women and their families, whose sister, Sonya Nadine Mae Cywink, was murdered in 1994. No one has ever been charged with Sonya's murder. Meg and her family have worked in various ways ever since to address the failings of Canadian law that her family, and well over a thousand other First Nations, Métis, and Inuit families in Canada, have faced.[1]

Meg knew that I had been among the many voices over the years that had advocated for the establishment of the National Inquiry into Missing and Murdered Indigenous Women and Girls (MMIWG),[2] an inquiry that was not shaping up to be the process that we had sought. She and a large group of MMIW families had signed a letter to the Chief Commissioner calling for significant changes to how the inquiry was being run.[3] Meg was calling me to ask whether civil society organizations such as LEAF would support the families like hers that wanted the inquiry to be reset.

During that conversation, which lasted about an hour, I realized that I had never felt so acutely like a *Canadian* lawyer in my life. I had called for a public inquiry with the belief that this mechanism, this Canadian legal mechanism, would be able to identify, name, and address the structural violence that underpins the disproportionate disappearances and deaths of Indigenous girls and women in Canada. I believed that a well-run national inquiry could also engage the wider non-Indigenous public in a way that would ultimately help to shift the narrative in this country away from self-congratulation about Canada's new relationship with Indigenous peoples and our rhetoric about reconciliation and toward a reckoning with our own deeply entrenched systemic racism and sexism that have created and continued this horror in our midst. My academic work on the institutional design of a public inquiry informed my view that such a legal mechanism could work fundamentally to address societal harm and prevent its recurrence.[4] However, the National Inquiry into MMIWG was not turning out to be what many had called for with such fervour and certainty. It appeared instead to be a painful disappointment, in danger of causing further harm to those most affected by the process.

Meg, who had suffered the violent death of her sister without ever seeing any justice done, wanted to know whether I was still prepared to support the inquiry. I said that I thought the inquiry could still be useful, but given the way that it was unfolding, its utility likely would not materialize for a long time. I also told her that even then, it might not help her and her family in any tangible way. In that conversation, I felt every inch a white settler in this country with my three degrees in the colonizer's law and my "expertise" about public inquiries.

My conversation with Meg brought into sharp relief the contrast between my academic understanding of the public inquiry as a legal mechanism and my realization that this mechanism – which I had believed could prompt Canada to address the crisis of violence against Indigenous women and girls – was in danger of failing in its task. Meg told me that she thought the inquiry was just an exercise for academics that was simply retraumatizing families and unlikely to produce anything useful. She wondered what good the inquiry would really do for Indigenous women and girls.

On Becoming a Canadian Lawyer

As a younger woman, I planned to become an international human rights lawyer. Before law school, I worked with Professor Kathleen Mahoney when she was one of the counsel to Bosnia Herzegovina in its genocide case against Serbia Montenegro before the International Court of Justice.[5] I built and coordinated a team to gather affidavits from Bosnian Muslim survivors of human rights violations in Serbian camps during the war in the former Yugoslavia who came as refugees to Canada. The team also sought to gather the evidence to make the case to have rape declared a war crime. During law school, I interned at the United Nations Relief and Works Agency for Palestine Refugees in the Near East in the Gaza Strip, documenting violations of international human rights law by both Israelis and Palestinians. After a couple of years of practising law in Canada, I went to Ghana in West Africa to work with the Center for Democratic Development, funded by a Transitional Justice Fellowship from the Notre Dame Center for Civil and Human Rights. I was an official observer of Ghana's National Reconciliation Commission hearings in 2002–03 on behalf of a civil society coalition that sought to support the work of that truth commission.

These experiences piqued my interest in transitional justice mechanisms: that is, methods for moving countries from autocratic to democratic rule or from war to peace. I returned to Canada with the intention to go to graduate school and write about the truth commission mechanism before returning to international work. During the couple of years between returning to Canada and starting graduate studies, I began to practise Aboriginal law.[6] I had already been struck during my times working overseas by the importance of having local knowledge and insight in order to do effective legal work. I frequently thought that I had gained much more than I had given during my overseas stints, and I often felt distinctly uncomfortable coming to "do good" in Gaza and Ghana from a country that inflicted grave human rights abuses on Indigenous peoples without much self-awareness or acknowledgment of doing so.

Practising Aboriginal law in British Columbia provided me with insights from historical documentation, including by Commissioners appointed to assign territories to Indian bands in the early 1900s.[7] These assignments were made in order to remove the Indigenous peoples from fertile areas on the assumption that white settlers could turn the lands into profitable farms and ranches. The Commissioners' decisions confined the original inhabitants to lands that generally appeared to be rocky outcroppings without water, too small for a viable life of hunting, fishing, and gathering, forcing them to become dependent on social welfare from the state. Their children were forcibly removed to residential schools. Their languages and cultures were diminished or lost. I had known some of the history, but it was eye opening to see it in black and white in the archival documents kept by those who wished to transfer as much land as possible to white settlers. I began to feel much more acutely the hypocrisy of my desire to return to international human rights work when my home context was so fraught with historical and modern human rights violations.

When I began my graduate studies, the massive class action lawsuits against the churches and the government brought by survivors of the residential schools had been under way for years.[8] Provision for a truth and reconciliation commission was part of the settlement agreement being negotiated. When trying to settle on a topic for my doctoral dissertation, I had a serendipitous lunch with retired Senator, first woman Moderator of the United Church of Canada, and first woman President of the World Council of Churches, The Very Reverend, the Honourable Lois Wilson. She pointedly (but not unkindly) told me that, if I wanted to have any credibility as an international human rights lawyer, I had better focus on my own backyard. With Canada's dismal record of human rights violations against Indigenous peoples in mind, I took this advice and wrote my dissertation about the use of truth commissions in established democracies,[9] with a focus on the Canadian Truth and Reconciliation Commission on Indian Residential Schools (TRC) then being negotiated. I pondered what makes a truth commission different from a commission of inquiry and why in Canada we have had hundreds of public inquiries but only one truth commission – and then only because we were forced to include the TRC in a settlement agreement when class action lawsuits were calculated to be too expensive to continue to fight in court. In considering these questions, I repeatedly thought of the Mackenzie Valley Pipeline Inquiry, led by then Justice Thomas Berger. My research on that inquiry led me to conclude that a truth commission is simply a form of public inquiry, and indeed I came to view the Berger Inquiry as Canada's first truth commission. Reaching that conclusion required some unpacking of the terms "truth commission" and "public inquiry."

Commissioning Truth or Merely Inquiring?

In much the same way that I felt hypocritical about seeking to address human rights violations overseas rather than addressing those at home, it seemed to me that my country had the same difficulty. Canada resisted establishing a truth commission to address its practice of removing Indigenous children from their families for over a century in furtherance of its colonial policies, but we in Canada expected that other countries (i.e., African and Latin American countries) should address their own histories of mass human rights violations with truth commissions. What is it about Canadians that makes us think we are somehow exceptional? Our smug self-assurance that we have never been guilty of mass human rights violations seems to be part of the answer.

The symbolism of the legal mechanism's title holds some power. A truth commission and a public inquiry might in fact be similar in operation, but the acknowledgment and intention telegraphed to the world by establishing a truth commission are different from those sent for a commission of inquiry. Why have a commission to tell us the truth when we can have a commission merely to inquire into whether such a truth might exist? Although our narrative of ourselves as "the good guys" in the global sphere persists, a commission of inquiry seems to be a genteel solution for a "civilized" country that does not wish to admit on a global stage to the dirty hands of genocide. Over time, though, the cumulative effect of multiple commissions that present findings about Canada's human rights abuses against Indigenous peoples will chip away at this narrative. After all, we have now been told publicly by the National Inquiry into MMIWG that our country is guilty of ongoing genocide.

For now, it appears that, despite having had the TRC in Canada, we will continue to be much more open to holding commissions of inquiry than we will be to holding truth commissions. We are more likely to continue to inquire into whether there is a truth to be found than to declare that there is a truth that must be addressed. Regardless of what we name a commission, the Canadian public inquiry mechanism, particularly since Berger revolutionized it in the 1970s, is capable of determining the truths that we might wish to ignore. It is a legal mechanism of considerable usefulness and potential, but its utility and promise hinge on key decisions made at the outset.

My work on the Berger Inquiry and the TRC convinced me that the public inquiry mechanism could be used to address fractious issues in our society. I believed that, in the right hands, a truly public inquiry could function as a truth commission to establish an accurate historical record and assist us in preventing future human rights violations. That is why I wholeheartedly joined those who advocated for a national public inquiry to address violence against Indigenous women and girls. However, the potential of a public inquiry to be transformative in society is not easily realized. So much depends on the choices made by those setting up the inquiry – particularly on the people chosen to lead it and the processes chosen to run it. Getting it wrong can revictimize those who have already paid too dearly. As lawyers, as Canadians, we can wring our hands and say "what a shame that the National Inquiry into MMIWG did not go according to plan," but for at least some family members whose questions about their missing and murdered loved ones remain unanswered, going through a $92 million inquiry process that did not run effectively was retraumatizing.[10]

To illustrate how the commission of inquiry mechanism can fulfill or fail to reach its potential, I consider a number of inquiries that have focused on Indigenous people in what is now Canada. The arc of this story follows the evolution of inquiries over time. They began as administrative mechanisms by colonial powers that lacked control on the ground and used Commissioners as *ad hoc* civil servants to assist them in creating and enacting policies on the peoples inhabiting the territories that later became Canada. Berger showed that inquiries could be much more than perfunctory. People in established democracies might cleave to the nomenclature of a truth commission as an exceptional mechanism that addresses mass human rights violations in faraway places, but the public inquiry form has the flexibility to hold a mirror up to the face of our own complicity in such abuses. In the hands of a skilful team, a public inquiry can diagnose the causes of societal ruptures and prescribe appropriate treatments. The inquiry form is adaptable. Over the past few decades, Canadians have seen that an inquiry can be more than a routine handling of a political hot potato. If there is an appetite to hold up that mirror at the start of an inquiry, then it can be run such that it accrues the necessary political will at the finish line for the recommendations to be implemented.

I will enumerate aspects of the institutional design of an inquiry that can lay the groundwork for achieving the implementation of recommendations, but holding up the mirror to our complicity in societal harms will continue to be a challenge. The expectation with a truth commission is that it will create an incontrovertible historical record that can help to put to rest an erroneous narrative about a country perpetuated by its dominant storytellers. This process is not instantaneous. The strong and immediate rejection among white Canadian commentators of the genocide finding in the 2019 report of the National Inquiry into MMIWG[11] illustrates the need to design the public inquiry so as to shift the narrative during its process, thus bringing about the social change necessary to create the path for acceptance of such a conclusion.[12]

This book is an exploration of the Canadian legal mechanism of the public inquiry and its potential to be a transformative means of addressing persistent colonial harms. It is about the ability of this mechanism to shift the dominant Canadian narrative over time and the risks inherent in its use. I have no doubt that the public inquiry mechanism will continue to be employed in Canada as a way to address deep societal challenges, so I seek here to identify how it can be done better.

I begin by providing some history of the origin of the commission of inquiry as a tool of the British government to address contentious issues in its settler colonies before focusing on its use since the 1800s to address "the Indian problem" in what is now Canada. I discuss some similarities and differences between the public inquiry and the truth commission (which is becoming more familiar to us all). I then take the reader to the beginning of the modern commission of inquiry with a chapter recounting the story of the Mackenzie Valley Pipeline Inquiry and its profound impact on the Canadian legal landscape. I trace a trajectory from this inquiry, led by then Justice Thomas Berger in the mid-1970s, which considered whether a pipeline should be built through unceded Indigenous territory, through a number of commissions that have addressed Indigenous issues in the past half century. I touch on various provincial inquiries, many of which have focused on the deaths of Indigenous people such as Helen Betty Osborne and J.J. Harper (the Manitoba Aboriginal Justice Inquiry, 1991), Neil Stonechild (the Stonechild Inquiry in Saskatchewan, 2004), Frank Joseph Paul (the Paul Inquiry in British Columbia, 2007), and Dudley George (the Ipperwash Inquiry in Ontario, 2007). I will also consider national commissions such as the Royal Commission on Aboriginal Peoples (RCAP, 1996) and the TRC (2015).

I provide a history of the residential schools and the search for redress by survivors of those schools and Canada's responses to that search, including the TRC. I include an overview of the negotiations that produced the TRC as well as the other aspects of the Indian Residential Schools Settlement Agreement. I review the mandate and structure of the TRC in comparison to other forms of commission of inquiry in Canada. Having set out the institutional design characteristics that will enable an inquiry or commission to be successful, I analyze the effectiveness of those elements in the TRC. I emphasize that the question of leadership is critical to a truth commission's success, and I consider the challenges that the TRC experienced on that front. I explore how the TRC engaged or failed to engage the public in its task, which I claim was essential to its ability to fulfill its mandate. I also consider comparative information from international examples of truth commission processes.

Although the Canadian context is my main focus, I note that established democracies frequently support truth commissions in transitional states but do not favour them as a mechanism for addressing their own sullied human rights histories. These states prefer instead to appoint commissions of inquiry, which do not begin by acknowledging that a difficult truth must be addressed by society. Rather, they begin by stating that there is a situation that simply requires investigation. I explore the unusual genesis of the Canadian TRC in a legal settlement agreement and conclude that a truth commission is in fact a specialized form of public inquiry. I also explore the potential for public inquiries to perform the function of truth commissions under the right circumstances.

With this background, I then assess the more recent Canadian commissions that have addressed disproportionate levels of violence against Indigenous women: the 2012 Missing Women Inquiry in British Columbia and the 2019 National Inquiry into MMIWG that conflated the public inquiry with the truth commission. The primary work of the book is to analyze the effect that two factors – choice of leadership and process – have on the ability of an inquiry to achieve its mandate and, ideally, have its recommendations adopted. Although I focus here on the Canadian inquiries that have engaged with Indigenous issues, the analysis of how to design an effective public inquiry is intended to be more broadly applicable.

Other books have identified the important day-to-day processes and requirements for running a public inquiry under Canadian law.[13] My focus in this book is on the need for a public inquiry to be well led and properly run if it is to be effective and not perpetuate harm. I provide examples and an in-depth analysis of what this combination of leadership and process must look like for a public inquiry to do more than have its recommendations gather dust on the proverbial shelf.

1

Inquiries in Canada

For many years, colonial governments have favoured establishing commissions of inquiry to formally investigate and address challenging societal problems. Since before Confederation, the public inquiry has been utilized as a legal mechanism to address difficult issues arising from the colonial relationship with Indigenous peoples in what is now Canada. However, the inquiry mechanism has often allowed non-Indigenous governments and their citizens to appear to have paid serious attention to an issue without necessarily taking responsibility for their role in creating the issue in the first place or for preventing its recurrence. Indeed, with some exceptions, the recommendations of numerous investigative and public policy inquiries have gone unimplemented. Why is this? Can it be remedied? Can the public inquiry mechanism contribute to the processes of reconciliation between Indigenous and non-Indigenous peoples now ostensibly under way in Canada? To answer these questions, I consider the particular context of using this colonial mechanism to address the Canadian relationship with Indigenous peoples.

Why Use Public Inquiries?

There can be considerable debate about the utility of any one commission of inquiry. However, in theory, public inquiries are useful for gathering wide-ranging information through their broad investigative abilities in order to provide a comprehensive picture of the facts surrounding an issue or event.[1] They can be an effective mechanism for tackling large and pressing concerns of institutional and policy reform. Their independence from governments and other parties enables them to assess credibly the evidence and report on their conclusions.

An additional trait, one at the heart of my work on public inquiries, makes them a critical legal mechanism for addressing pressing social issues. Former Supreme Court of Canada (SCC) Justice Gerald Le Dain's influential discussion of public inquiries articulates the part that they play in shaping societal attitudes:

> In an inquiry of this kind a commission becomes very much aware of its relationship to the social process. It has certain things to say to government but it also has an effect on perceptions, attitudes and behaviour ... The decision to institute an inquiry of this kind is a decision not only to release an investigative technique but a form of social influence as well.[2]

This potential for social influence makes the public inquiry an appealing mechanism for politicians and advocates alike. Echoing Le Dain's social function thesis, Robert Centa and Patrick Macklem note the investigatory, informative, educational, and social functions of commissions of inquiry. They state that the independent and non-partisan nature of commissions enables them to consider social causes and conditions in a broader fashion than is available to judicial or legislative bodies, thus performing a valuable function in terms of defining public policy. These attributes promote government accountability to the citizenry and help to explain why the public inquiry remains part of the legal order.[3] As Le Dain noted, although an inquiry is accountable to the government, it is ultimately accountable to the public and must speak to the public in its report to the government.[4] Thus, a public inquiry can be an instrument of democracy, or at least it has that potential.

This ability to promote accountability is an important aspect of the commission of inquiry's social function.[5] Unlike a legislative or courtroom process, the public inquiry is not driven by interested parties. Through its hearings and investigative activities, the public inquiry process can precipitate changes in attitudes. The public can become aware of officially recognized problems and begin to seek solutions to them. The inquiry can create pressure on individuals and organizations to account for their acts or omissions, even if they are not legally obliged to do so. "This form of accountability is especially important because it can affect perceptions and behaviour long after the inquiry has ended."[6] Public inquiries can engage in organizational reform through their "greater capacity to engage in quasi-legislative activity by openly articulating new standards of proper conduct and applying them to past events."[7]

These attributes sometimes provoke criticism. A common critique of public inquiries is that they are used as a means of deferring a political problem, given that it can take years to hold public hearings, conduct research, and complete a report.[8] In addition, an inquiry's recommendations are merely proposals for which there is no guarantee of implementation by the government. Commissions of inquiry have no powers to sanction actions of the past, unlike courts, which can issue orders against wrongdoers for their actions.

Another political concern related to commissions of inquiry is that, whereas a government might be able to distance itself from an issue by referring it to a commission, that government can equally refrain from creating a commission. The existence of a commission depends on a government decision to establish it in the first place. Although public inquiries are independent of governments once established, they are dependent on governments for their existence. This means that they are at the mercy of the exercise of political discretion in one crucial sense.[9] Indeed, some commentators have voiced concerns that governments appear to be increasingly reluctant to establish commissions of inquiry when a public crisis might demand it[10] or to grapple with major policy changes that require more time and focus than can be afforded by politicians concerned about election cycles.[11]

A further significant concern about commissions of inquiry relates to procedural fairness, particularly with respect to the coercive powers accorded to some inquiries in their operations (e.g., power of subpoena or power to require testimony under oath). That is, even if a Commissioner might wish to run an inquiry in a manner less adversarial than a court, the parties to the inquiry might feel obliged to participate with an eye on the possible legal consequences for them of the inquiry's findings.[12] An inquiry's investigations or proceedings can unearth information or hear unproven evidence that can harm a party's reputation or provide fodder for future criminal or civil proceedings. Sometimes inquiries have overstepped the bounds of their mandates and become court-like in their processes without ensuring the due process protections available in a courtroom.[13] However, in general, policy-oriented inquiries raise few of the due process concerns of the more investigative inquiry.[14]

All commissions of inquiry, whether investigative or policy oriented, can give rise to criticisms of their costs. The Krever Inquiry into the contamination of the national blood supply with hepatitis C and HIV is often used as an example of the problems with public inquiries.[15] The Inquiry ran over time (it was supposed to take one year and took almost five) and over budget (instead of the $2.5 million initially assigned, it spent $17.5 million),[16] embattled by strenuous legal challenges from those who worried that its conclusions would expose them to massive damages in negligence actions. Justice Krever did not report until the last of the challenges to the Supreme Court of Canada had run its course. The government decided to make changes to the blood system before the release of the report because of the urgency of the matter,[17] rendering the report of questionable value.

Although the financial costs should be an important consideration, it is also vital to ask what the social costs would be of *not* fixing and ensuring the safety of our blood system, of *not* ensuring the safety of a community's drinking water,[18] or of *not* investigating the government's complicity in the denial of fundamental human rights.[19] As noted by Justice John Gomery, "[t]he criticism that commissions cost too much is valid if one takes the position that a price can be put upon the search for truth and justice."[20]

Despite the criticisms outlined above, I still view the public inquiry as a *potentially* useful mechanism. Even if its recommendations are initially ignored, the process of holding a public inquiry opens the possibility for dialogue about issues of public importance and prepares the way for attitudinal change and policy development.[21] As previously noted, a public inquiry has important features, including the ability to consider an issue in its larger context, to use broad investigative powers to assemble a comprehensive factual portrait, and to use its position as an independent, nonpartisan body. Along with their educational potential and their ability to promote accountability, public inquiries can be a valuable public policy tool. However, the utility of an inquiry is tied to the effectiveness of its leadership and to the process used by Commissioners to fulfill their mandate.

Commissions of Inquiry: Some History

The public inquiry mechanism has its roots in the royal commission, which referred to the royal warrant or letters patent issued under the authority of the monarch.[22] Royal commissions can be traced back to at least the Domesday Book of 1086,[23] whereas commissions of inquiry date back to at least the twelfth century, with the exercise of the royal prerogative to appoint citizens to perform duties on behalf of the Crown.[24]

Federal public inquiries in Canada are governed by the *Inquiries Act,* which authorizes the cabinet to "cause inquiry to be made into and concerning any matter connected with the good government of Canada or the conduct of any part of the public business thereof."[25] According to Nicholas d'Ombrain, both royal commissions and commissions of inquiry are established identically as public inquiries under Part I of the *Inquiries Act,* with the same powers and privileges. The decision to call one a royal commission and the other a public inquiry is based on the subject matter of the inquiry.[26] "The Canadian practice has been to reserve the title 'royal' for commissions that are inquiring into matters of policy, loosely defined."[27] Leonard Hallett distinguishes royal commissions of inquiry from other government-appointed advisory bodies because they cease to exist when they make their reports.[28]

The public inquiry mechanism is used in Canada frequently. In his review of the history of Canadian public inquiries, d'Ombrain states that most of the (then) over 350 public inquiries since Confederation have focused on narrow issues, although between the 1930s and the 1960s governments appointed inquiries to gain advice on significant issues of public policy such as dominion-provincial relations and the establishment of the Bank of Canada.[29] The Diefenbaker and Pearson governments brought another round of important national policy inquiries, including those on health, bilingualism, and the status of women, but since then, d'Ombrain asserts, there have been few significant policy inquiries. He comments that "[t]he one major policy inquiry launched by the Mulroney administration, the Dussault-Erasmus commission on aboriginal peoples [i.e., the Royal Commission on Aboriginal Peoples], was more a gesture of puzzled goodwill than a clear-sighted initiative."[30] He states that the Chrétien government "received the report of the commission on aboriginal peoples but with little evident enthusiasm for the ideas contained therein."[31] Although the government's enthusiasm for significant policy inquiries might have declined since the 1960s, the public inquiry is still a prominent tool for investigating incidents that create public concerns.[32]

The Development of the Truth Commission

It is the ability of the commission of inquiry to search for truth and justice that made it suitable for adaptation to the human rights context. The commission of inquiry form has valuable qualities for a truth-seeking commission as well: independence, openness and visibility, the opportunity for the creative framing of issues, a flexible political dynamic through the appointment of Commissioners, the focus on social causes and conditions, and the "social function."[33] The ideas suggested in Le Dain's account of the social function of the public inquiry in Canada in the 1970s likely influenced how some public inquiries were subsequently conducted in Canada. These inquiries began to incorporate elements that mirror features of the truth commissions that arose in the decade that followed. Indeed, the evolution of the commission of inquiry form seen in Canada in the 1970s appears to be prescient when one considers the subsequent development of the truth commission.

The international phenomenon of the truth commission arose largely in the 1980s, and certainly by the 1990s it had become a significant new mechanism in the law's search for accountability for past human rights abuses. A truth commission's very purpose is to have an effect on perceptions, attitudes, and behaviours – it is meant not merely to shed light on a dark period in the country's history but also to help ensure that the mistakes of the past are not repeated. It does so by making recommendations for institutional or structural change and by educating the public about the abuses that occurred. In this way, social influence is the raison d'être of the truth commission. This aspect is akin to the social function of commissions of inquiry, as described above, yet many commentators discuss the truth commission without explicitly connecting it to the commission of inquiry. Commentators who do make the connection try to distinguish the truth commission as a unique mechanism.[34] However, the truth commission is better understood as a specific type of commission of inquiry – it arises in a specific context of addressing human rights violations, and both its process and its goals manifest its social function.

Why did this type of commission of inquiry, the truth commission, arise? Following the Second World War, international law moved toward the development of international human rights law and a focus on individual criminal accountability for violations of the laws of war. Human rights advocates created new ways to address human rights violations. Initially, their innovations took the form of the International Military Tribunal trials in Nuremberg and Tokyo,[35] the formation of the United Nations, and the creation of non-governmental organizations such as Amnesty International.[36] The difficulty in securing accountability for more than a few people and the cumbersome nature of war crimes prosecutions, among other factors, gradually led to a search for other mechanisms that could address past human rights abuses more broadly. The field of transitional justice developed within this legal discourse.

Transitional justice refers broadly to legal mechanisms that address past crimes or abuses in states moving from authoritarian to democratic rule and/or from conflict to post-conflict. That is, the commonly understood notion of transitional justice relates to the desire to resist impunity for human rights violations in countries experiencing profound political upheavals.[37] The later twentieth century saw a debate about the desirability and practicality of accountability in societies recovering from regimes that inflicted massive human rights violations.[38] The discussion of non-prosecutorial options for addressing gross human rights violations arose because of the "political and practical challenges to employing prosecutorial mechanisms."[39] These non-prosecutorial options included a new form of commission – the truth commission – that shifted the focus from punitive justice to "achieving accountability through truth and acknowledgement."[40]

The 1970s saw a wave of nascent democracies arising out of authoritarian rule. These emerging democracies had to decide how to deal with the human rights violations of the past.[41] A desire by new governments to achieve legitimacy and a growing movement to support the rule of law and the dignity of victims combined to create a situation in which governments could not simply ignore the past. The search for politically viable responses and the increasing tendency to seek accountability became the focus of the transitional justice field.[42] Although punishment was still a major focus for many commentators and policy makers in the field of transitional justice, the truth commission model was beginning to gain ground as a valid mechanism for dealing with the past. How a government uses law to frame questions about past injustices shapes how a society formulates its responses to the shadows of its past. According to Martha Minow,

> [a]s a public instrument dealing with the past, law affords lessons about what produces memories for a community or a nation. Legal actors and those who influence them determine what past harms should give rise to a claim and what past violations should constitute a crime.[43]

The truth commission became a viable option because of its less punitive approach to achieving accountability for historical human rights abuses. Whereas many would prefer that human rights violators be prosecuted and punished, the weakness of incoming democratic regimes (e.g., post-Pinochet Chile) often did not allow for a Nuremberg-like response. Another legal mechanism was required to ensure that the search for accountability did not sacrifice the new democracy.[44] When political conditions made trials impossible, truth commissions began to be chosen over prosecutorial responses. It was the overall context, then, rather than "the result of a detached comparison of the merits of one institutional structure against another,"[45] that resulted in the choice of the truth commission.

At first, prosecutorial and truth commission mechanisms were viewed as an either/or proposition, but increasingly they came to be seen as complementary.[46] Truth commissions did often reflect a compromise between punishment and impunity,[47] but as they gained credibility it was argued that they could be a "complex and principled compromise between justice and unity in which central elements of both values are retained."[48] Furthermore, such commissions can provide a "more useful truth" than a trial court,[49] in the sense that the picture might be more complete because of an examination of the larger historical context rather than a focus on guilt or innocence in an individual case. Truth commissions can serve many of the same purposes as prosecutions in countries with histories of massive human rights abuses, including "providing a mandate and authority for an official investigation of past abuses" and establishing a basis for compensation of victims or punishment of perpetrators.[50] Such commissions are viewed as being more adept than trials at advancing restorative justice goals such as acknowledging the suffering of victims.[51]

In countries with limited resources and legal systems that might be in disarray, commissions can carry out their mandates relatively quickly in comparison to the criminal justice system.[52] Although a truth commission is ultimately not viewed as a substitute for the criminal trial for "a true judicial determination of responsibility,"[53] it does enable states to benefit from a detailed historical account of past abuses and recommendations for how institutions can be restructured to avoid such abuses in the future. According to Neil Kritz, "[e]stablishing a full, official accounting of the past is increasingly seen as an important element to a successful democratic transition."[54]

Another reason for the rise of the truth commission was the sheer scale of the human rights violations in many emerging democracies. Prosecutions of all perpetrators would have crippled the legal systems of countries that often lacked the resources to fund their police, court, and penal systems adequately. Ruti Teitel comments on the "advent of the so-called truth commissions" as useful when the scale of the abuses is overwhelming to the criminal justice system:

> The commission of inquiry thus emerges as the leading mechanism elaborated to cope with the evil of the modern repressive state, since bureaucratic murder calls for its institutional counterpart, a response that can capture massive and systemic persecution policy.[55]

Thus, the commission of inquiry became adapted to the context of mass human rights violations in the latter half of the twentieth century, and the developing mechanism became known as the truth commission.

The first historical inquiry referred to as a truth commission occurred in Uganda in 1974.[56] Idi Amin established it under that country's public inquiries legislation with an eye on warding off international criticism of human rights abuses under his rule. The report was not published and its recommendations were not implemented. Despite this inauspicious start for truth commissions, later commissions began to have more in common with what we now think of as truth commissions, including increased transparency and effectiveness. The next truth commissions appeared in the 1980s as a wave of democratization passed through Central and South America. There were truth commissions in Bolivia in 1982, Argentina in 1983, and Uruguay in 1985. Commissions in Chile in 1990 and El Salvador in 1992 followed. A second truth commission occurred in Uganda as well as commissions in Chad and Zimbabwe in the 1980s and into the 1990s.

It was not until the mid-1990s that the use of truth commissions came to significant international attention with the South African Truth and Reconciliation Commission, chaired by Bishop Desmond Tutu. The South African TRC is the best known example of a truth commission to date, created as part of the transition from apartheid to democracy. In 1994, South Africa held its first multiracial elections. The African National Congress candidate, Nelson Mandela, was elected President. South Africa's Interim Constitution called for reconciliation and amnesty, and Parliament passed the *Promotion of National Unity and Reconciliation Act* in response.[57] The South African TRC began operations in 1995 with the aim of producing a report that would document the human rights violations that occurred between 1960 and 1994. The TRC had three divisions: the Human Rights Violations Committee (responsible for collecting statements from victims and witnesses and recording the violations), the Reparations and Rehabilitation Committee (to design a reparations program), and the Amnesty Committee (to process and decide amnesty applications). Controversial and wrenching, the South African TRC brought the truth commission mechanism onto the world stage.[58]

In the 1990s, truth commissions became much more common: "Between March 1992 and late 1993, six truth commissions were established."[59] Transitional justice as a field of legal study also gained traction during the 1990s.[60] Particularly with the South African TRC, the truth commission became accepted as an appropriate possibility for transitional states that seek to address a history of abuses. Although a desire for retributive justice for the most heinous crimes can still create a preference for prosecution instead of truth commissions in some cases,[61] by the end of the 1990s truth commissions had found a place among the array of accountability mechanisms available to emerging democracies.[62]

Transitions toward the end of the twentieth century differed from those in earlier decades partly because of the influence of the human rights movement and the concomitant growth of human rights organizations. Not only was there increased pressure to demonstrate accountability for past abuses, but also the methods used were increasingly scrutinized for their accord with international human rights instruments.[63] The international community has largely accepted that past abuses must be addressed by at least one of a variety of mechanisms, and now "the challenge is to fine-tune and better coordinate the options."[64] There has also been a trend toward universal jurisdiction for human rights violations and thus an expansion of accountability to the international arena: "The drive to curb impunity for massive abuses of human rights has manifested itself not only within countries in transition, but internationally as well."[65]

Increased attention to dealing with historical injustices in the past few decades has given rise to a new variation of the commission of inquiry. The truth commission shares attributes of the public inquiry, such as the ability to look at the larger context and promote social accountability for an issue. However, it also has a symbolic quality that aligns with its explicit social function of public education about human rights violations. I discuss in the next section how the truth commission is an innovation of the old legal mechanism of the public inquiry.

Truth Commissions and Public Inquiries

At a June 2007 conference on the then upcoming Canadian Truth and Reconciliation Commission, National Chief of the Assembly of First

Nations Phil Fontaine adamantly stated that the Canadian commission was not modelled on the South African Truth and Reconciliation Commission. He also insisted that the Canadian commission was not a public inquiry.[66] Executive Director of the Ghana Center for Democratic Development Emmanuel Gyimah-Boadi, speaking about Ghana's National Reconciliation Commission, stated that it did not realize at first that it was not a public inquiry.[67] In Dr. Gyimah-Boadi's opinion, things improved for the commission once it began to act like a truth commission.

The comments by Fontaine and Gyimah-Boadi suggest that there is something qualitatively different about a truth commission compared with a public inquiry. This is because, when a truth commission is sought, something more is wanted than the investigation of the facts and recommendations for future policy that a public inquiry does in its basic form. Establishing a truth commission gives rise to an expectation that historical injustices will be acknowledged and redressed. For those who seek redress, the truth commission cannot simply be a legal exercise; it must be a societal reckoning.

In arguing that a truth commission is actually a form of public inquiry, in no way do I seek to diminish the impulse toward a more expansive role for a truth commission. Rather, I seek to enlarge our understanding of what a public inquiry can do in an established democracy.[68] My point is simply that both mechanisms can perform the social function of acknowledging historical injustices and educating the public to prevent their reoccurrence. The difference is that a truth commission is explicitly expected to perform this function, whereas the public inquiry has the latent possibility to do so.

The desire to distinguish between the two mechanisms stems from a perception of the public inquiry as a formal legal mechanism,[69] which fails to fulfill a social function, a function critical in the context of addressing historical injustices. However, I argue that the truth commission is really a commission of inquiry with certain distinguishing features and objectives. In particular, a truth commission is a specialized form of public inquiry, distinguished by its symbolic acknowledgment of historical injustices and its explicit social function of public education about those injustices.

The scholarly definitions of the two mechanisms suggest important similarities. Consider this definition of a truth commission:

> A truth commission is an *ad hoc*, autonomous, and victim-centered commission of inquiry set up in and authorized by a state for the primary purposes of (1) investigating and reporting on the principal causes and consequences of broad and relatively recent patterns of severe violence or repression that occurred in the state during determinate periods of abusive rule or conflict, and (2) making recommendations for their correction and future prevention.[70]

Compare that definition to this definition of a public inquiry:

> [A public] inquiry is any body that is formally mandated by a government, either on an *ad hoc* basis or with reference to a specific problem, to conduct a process of fact-finding and to arrive at a body of recommendations.[71]

Both conduct reviews of an incident or incidents in a nation's past and contribute to policy solutions for the country's future. Both are temporary bodies that investigate, hear, and report. Both are intended to create historically accurate public records of their topics, and both are expected to make recommendations for remedies of the wrongs investigated in order to ensure that these wrongs are not repeated in the future. However, though they are alike, the two mechanisms can be distinguished by the explicit social function assigned to the truth commission.

Some scholars endeavour to characterize the truth commission as a unique mechanism. Mark Freeman attempts to distinguish truth commissions from various commissions of inquiry.[72] Although he acknowledges that "the Commonwealth commission of inquiry is the closest functional equivalent to a truth commission, and may sometimes be characterized as one even if it is not so titled,"[73] he continues that "there are many significant differences between a truth commission and a typical Commonwealth commission of inquiry." In particular, Freeman notes that truth commissions are victim centred, whereas commissions of inquiry adopt a "more lawyer-driven approach." Commissions of inquiry focus on a specific event or theme, whereas truth commissions often address "thousands of individual cases committed over broad expanses of time and geography."[74]

However, the factors that Freeman lists as distinguishing truth commissions from public inquiries (less lawyer driven, deal with acute violence in the recent past, and focus on victims) do not necessarily sustain his argument. Some truth commissions have had significant legal involvement,[75] some have dealt with historical abuses,[76] and some cannot be said to have been victim centred.[77] Priscilla Hayner contrasts truth commissions to other official inquiries into past human rights abuses that she calls "historical truth commissions."[78] Such commissions investigate abuses that occurred many years earlier in order to clarify historical truths and pay respect to previously unrecognized victims or their descendants. Hayner states that such a government-sponsored inquiry is usually established to investigate practices that affected a minority group about which the wider population was unaware. Thus, such commissions can "have a powerful impact despite the years that have passed."[79] Hayner lists as examples the Australian Human Rights and Equal Opportunity Commission's inquiry into the state's assimilatory practices against Indigenous people, culminating in the 1997 *Bringing Them Home* report, the US Advisory Committee on Human Radiation Experiments, and the US Commission on War-Time Relocation and Internment of Citizens in 1982.[80] She identifies the Royal Commission on Aboriginal Peoples (RCAP) in Canada as a historical truth commission.[81]

This overlap suggests that, rather than trying to draw a sharp distinction between truth commissions and public inquiries, it might be more useful to think of the truth commission as a specialized form of the commission of inquiry, thus recognizing that it has some distinctive features. The most consistent distinguishing features of truth commissions are that they are only struck in the context of addressing human rights violations, and typically they focus on a pattern of human rights abuses over a number of years in the past rather than an isolated and more recent incident.[82] Although some commissions of inquiry can have these features, all truth commissions are expected to have them.[83]

Other features associated with some truth commissions might be shared by commissions of inquiry, depending on how the inquiries are run.[84] For example, a truth commission might be expected to focus on victims rather than perpetrators. Such a focus reinforces the objective of finding a less punitive way to achieve accountability than a criminal law mechanism that focuses on the individual accountability of perpetrators. A truth commission has the prerogative to hear from victims, not for the primary purpose of determining the guilt or innocence of a perpetrator, but as a method of acknowledging the victim's experience. Commissions of inquiry can also choose to hear from victims in order to assist the Commissioners with assembling a public picture of a tragedy.[85] Another feature often associated with truth commissions is that they are frequently led by multiple Commissioners, whereas a sole Commissioner (often a judge) usually – though not always – heads a public inquiry.[86] The appointment of multiple Commissioners provides an opportunity for the representation of different perspectives or, in some cases, societal factions on the panel.

Two main features distinguish truth commissions from other commissions of inquiry. The first feature is that truth commissions involve a state or society trying to repair itself in some way; they "seek to provide an overarching narrative of the historical periods under consideration."[87] Their objectives include encouragement of societal reconciliation and consideration of commemoration and reparation. The objective of encouraging societal reconciliation is not commonly within the ambit of a public inquiry. Promoting reconciliation in a society is a complex process; although both commissions of inquiry and truth commissions can provide acknowledgment of past harms that can sow the seeds of future reconciliation, usually only truth commissions are mandated to promote this goal.[88]

The second feature of a truth commission that distinguishes it from a public inquiry is that the inauguration of a truth commission has a symbolic value. That is, calling a commission a truth commission is an explicit acknowledgment that an injustice has occurred within the state and that the commission's task is to explore and then educate the public about the extent of that injustice. The very existence of a truth commission suggests that there is a truth to be discovered or at least one that needs to be voiced aloud. A commission of inquiry is called only when a government is faced with a problem that needs to be addressed independently. Still, calling a commission a commission of inquiry acknowledges an issue – not necessarily an injustice – and suggests only that it be investigated.

We signal something different by naming a commission a truth commission rather than a commission of inquiry. A truth commission has an explicit social function: education of the public about historical injustice in order to prevent its reoccurrence. A commission of inquiry might well fulfill this social function, and Le Dain's discussion of the social influence of a public inquiry is frequently cited by commentators.[89] However, as with the Mackenzie Valley Pipeline Inquiry, whether a commission of inquiry emphasizes this social function depends greatly on two key factors: the person leading it and the process used to achieve its mandate. A commission of inquiry might proceed with the conscious determination to fulfill a social function, but this intention will become apparent only once the commission is under way. A truth commission signals from its inception to the populace an intention to acknowledge and redress past injustices. Similarly, calling a body a truth commission suggests a more weighty concern about the issues before it as well as the possibility that the truth has somehow been obscured in the past, deliberately or otherwise.[90] It is this symbolic role that can distinguish truth commissions from most public inquiries. However, like a public inquiry, whether a truth commission succeeds in fulfilling its social function will depend on its leadership and its process.

The conceptual framework that I propose here is to recast the truth commission not as a mechanism unique to the transitional justice setting but as a specialized form of a familiar mechanism, the commission of inquiry. Established democracies might be more amenable to addressing historical injustices that continue to divide their populations if they can utilize a mechanism that does not suggest, by its very invocation, that they are human rights pariahs. The truth commission is expected to do explicitly what a commission of inquiry is capable of doing but is not obliged to do: to acknowledge the existence of the historical injustices and to embark on a process that educates the public about those injustices in order to prevent their reoccurrence. My argument is that, whichever form is used, both are capable of fulfilling this social function.

Truth Commissions in Established Democracies

Most commentators address the use of truth commissions "at a transition point in a society" emerging from autocratic rule.[91] Truth commissions in these circumstances are viewed as demonstrating a new era of respect for human rights, national reconciliation, or new political legitimacy,[92] symbolizing a new regime's commitment to the rule of law. But what of truth commissions in established democracies? Despite histories of slavery, colonialism, racism, and other injustices, established democracies have not generally chosen to name the truth commission as the mechanism to address the human rights violations in their pasts. Perhaps established democracies resist using the truth commission since it adverts to the possibility that their democratic stability might have come at a cost to oppressed peoples in their midst and suggests an unwelcome commonality with acknowledged oppressive regimes.[93]

As is evident from the German, Irish, and Australian examples discussed below, the institutions typically created in established democracies to address injustices are human rights commissions and *ad hoc* investigations such as royal commissions or public inquiries. In the American context, Sanford Levinson notes that, though Americans do not have bodies called "truth commissions," their "functional equivalent can be found in investigatory hearings held by certain administrative agencies" and in congressional investigations.[94] Thus, though "truth commissions ... have their counterparts in societies that are both stable and democratic,"[95] it appears that there is a general reluctance in established democracies to call these counterparts truth commissions.[96]

Nonetheless, truth commissions – or bodies that look much like truth commissions – have begun to appear in established democracies. Rather than set up mechanisms explicitly called truth commissions, in recent years Germany, Ireland, and Australia framed commissions of inquiry that, in their operations, acknowledged periods of historical injustice and educated the public about these dark periods. After the reunification of Germany, the German Parliament created the Commission of Inquiry for the Assessment of History and Consequences of the SED [Socialist Unity Party] Dictatorship in Germany, in operation from 1992 to 1994. It was mandated to investigate and document human rights violations under the

East German government between 1949 and 1989. The Commission held public hearings at which testimony was received from selected witnesses and research papers were presented. The papers were included in the 1994 report, which many saw as more of an academic report than one intended to engage the public.[97] Prosecutions were also carried out against former East German officials. Furthermore, as part of the transition to a unified German state, the Gauck Commission, also known as the Gauck Authority, was created. Parliamentarian and former dissident Joachim Gauck was named the Director of the Federal Authority on the Records of the Former Ministry for State Security of the German Democratic Republic. From 1990 to 1993, this commission managed access to the massive archive of surveillance records that the Stasi had kept on citizens and enabled citizens to learn who had informed on them.

Ireland has had two truth commission–like processes, the Independent Commission on Policing for Northern Ireland and the Commission to Inquire into Child Abuse. The Independent Commission on Policing commenced in June 1998, having arisen from the April 1998 "Good Friday Agreement" reached in the multi-party negotiations among the government of the United Kingdom, the government of Ireland, and numerous parties representing the communities of Northern Ireland.[98] Its task after broad consultations was to make recommendations for future policing arrangements in Northern Ireland. The Commission to Inquire into Child Abuse was mandated in 2000 to inquire into the abuse of children in industrial schools. It was to hear from the victims of abuse in the schools, to investigate the abuse, and to make a report to the public, which it did in 2009.[99]

Australia mandated a Human Rights and Equal Opportunity Commission to investigate the removal of Indigenous children from their families. As had Canada's, Australia's policy had been in place from the late 1800s to the latter half of the 1900s. The mandate of the commission was to examine past laws, practices, and policies that led to the forced removal of Indigenous children (known as the Stolen Generation) from their families and to examine current laws, practices, and policies that needed to change to prevent such separations.[100] Established in 1995, the commission held hearings in major cities and smaller communities. Its 1997 report recommended various measures for redressing the harms suffered because of the state's policy of removal. The government of John Howard, elected in 1996, largely rejected the approach recommended by the commission.[101]

These examples show that processes with features associated with the truth commission model have found some expression in established democracies. What might be the reasons for seeking such features for a commission in an established democracy? Perhaps the human rights culture of the past few decades has moved some states to address historical injustices more openly than in the past.[102] The social function of a truth commission holds promise: the tasks of creating an incontrovertible historical record and engaging in public education are intended to help prevent future abuses.[103] Levinson states that the circumstance that generates a truth commission is "the presence within a given social order of deep divisions over basic political questions."[104] If there are societal issues stemming from past injustices, then it might be desirable to find a way to put the past to rest in order to improve relations in the present. This process underscores the distinguishing feature of a truth commission mentioned above: the explicit mandate of reconciliation.

Truth commission–like features might be sought in an established democracy if other legal mechanisms have been inadequate for the task of addressing historical injustices. Levinson notes that "the key question is surely whether *local* institutions, judicial or otherwise, prove willing to address the kinds of issues that are the staple of truth commissions."[105] In Canada, the government repeatedly avoided a public inquiry into the Indian residential schools (IRS).[106] There have been numerous IRS lawsuits in Canada, but the scale of the claims, the cumbersome nature of judicial proceedings, inconsistent rulings, and the awkward fit of the IRS claims with common law doctrines made the court system inadequate for addressing the complex and multi-generational nature of the harms resulting from the IRS experience.[107]

In addition to the inadequacy of conventional legal mechanisms, there is another reason that Indigenous people sought a truth commission to address the IRS legacy. Generally, truth commissions are created in states where the citizenry has a well-founded distrust of the past regime's ability to conduct a fact-finding endeavour with transparency, honesty, and legitimacy.[108] Canada has a history of unfulfilled promises made to Indigenous peoples. There is widespread ignorance among non-Indigenous Canadians about the IRS system and its profound effects on former students and their families.[109] A truth commission's educational aspect can have "unintended secondary effects that result in positive benefits for victims" by increasing public awareness and understanding of the trauma suffered by the victims of human rights abuses.[110] With respect to the Canadian TRC, one of the main objectives set out in the mandate was to "[p]romote awareness and public education of Canadians about the IRS system and its impacts."[111] This mandate tied in with the idea that the truth commission has an explicit social function.

The Canadian TRC, then, was formally called a truth commission and sought in an established democracy. Although I have described the reasons that a process with features associated with a truth commission might be sought in an established democracy, it is rare that such a democracy seeks a body *called* a truth commission. The desire by IRS survivors for a process that explicitly addressed the historical injustice of the IRS system resulted in the TRC. However, it is the commission of inquiry, rather than the truth commission, that typically has been used in Canada to address issues related to Indigenous people.

Commissions of Inquiry and "the Indian Problem"

Where does the story of the public inquiry in Canada begin? Canada is a settler colonial country; thus, the story is a colonial story. After a decline in the use of inquiries in Britain and colonies such as Australia from the late seventeenth century to the end of the eighteenth century, their use was revived during the reign of Queen Victoria.[112] Indeed, the commission of inquiry was a favoured tool of settler societies in the Victorian era.[113] As noted by Miranda Johnson,

> commissions of inquiry were originally used in early modern England to punish opponents of the monarchy. They came into their modern form as inquisitorial aids to policy makers in the [nineteenth century], frequently to investigate the violence perpetrated against colonized peoples in British colonies. In colonial contexts including Jamaica and

South Africa as well as Australia and Canada, scholars have argued that these institutions were used to legitimate the state in moments of profound social conflict.[114]

In Canada, there is a long history of using commissions of inquiry to address issues regarding Indigenous people. In British North America, between 1828 and 1858, six commissions of inquiry – all conducted in response to what was becoming known as "the Indian problem" – laid the foundation for policy on Indigenous peoples before Confederation:

> The first report was somewhat rushed and rudimentary and was prepared in 1828 by Major General Darling, military secretary to the governor general, Lord Dalhousie. It covered both Upper and Lower Canada and led to the establishment of the reserve system as official policy. The second was prepared by a committee of the Lower Canada Executive Council in 1837 and essentially followed the recommendations of the earlier Darling report. In 1839, the third report was prepared by Justice James Macauley and dealt with conditions in Upper Canada. It too generally supported the reserve and civilization policies of the time. A committee of the Upper Canada Legislative Assembly prepared the fourth report in response to Lord Durham's report on conditions in the two Canadas, arriving at conclusions similar to those of the preceding report by Justice Macauley. The fifth, and by far the most important, was the 1844 report of Governor General Sir Charles Bagot, which covered both Upper and Lower Canada. Its recommendations gave a direction to Canadian Indian policy that has endured in many respects right up to the present. A sixth report was prepared in 1858 by Richard Pennefather, civil secretary to the governor general. It too covered both Canadas and was the most thorough report on Indian conditions to that point.[115]

As described by Thomas Lockwood,

> During the early post-Confederation period, the government faced many new difficulties, and to help formulate policies to remedy these situations,

they employed Royal Commissions. Opening and settling of the North-West brought serious problems, [and] one of the most vexing was the treatment of the half-breeds. When open revolt broke out in 1869 the government delegated authority to a commissioner, Donald Smith (later Lord Strathcona). His report did much to put the events which had occurred in that remote area in the proper perspective.[116]

Lockwood adds that "[t]he second Riel Rebellion in 1885 resulted in the issuing of another Commission to attempt to untangle the confused situation."[117] However, according to John Leslie,

[the six pre-Confederation commission reports] were the main instruments of an early Indian policy review process which saw a programme for Indian civilization and advancement devised, evaluated, modified, and reiterated in the four decades prior to Confederation. The philosophical principles and practices enunciated by these six inquiries were adopted by the new Dominion government and applied to Native peoples in other regions of Canada. The legacy of these reports for Canadian Indian policy has been so enduring that, only recently, has the Federal government attempted to break from the long-standing view of Native peoples and society established before Confederation.[118]

Commissions of inquiry continued to be used by federal and provincial governments to address various aspects of "the Indian problem." For example, a dispute between British Columbia and the federal government over the allocation to settlers of reserve lands was referred to a joint federal-provincial commission in 1876, but little progress was made. In 1912, a further joint federal-provincial commission, the McKenna McBride Royal Commission, was appointed to review the issue, with similarly disappointing results for Indigenous peoples.[119] The commission reviewed reserve lands throughout British Columbia and was empowered to increase or decrease the sizes of reserves or eliminate them altogether. The commission's recommendations had significant impacts on reserve lands. Although various recommended reductions in Railway Belt reserves were disallowed by the federal government, and some reserves were added, the commission's recommendations resulted in the cut-off of valuable reserve lands and an overall reduced value of the lands allocated to reserves in the province.[120] The proceeds of lands sold off were to be split between the two governments.[121]

The degree to which the recommendations of the long list of inquiries have been implemented has varied, but governments have continued to resort to the public inquiry mechanism when faced with difficult issues related to Indigenous peoples. Each recent decade has brought at least one major inquiry addressing some aspect of the troubled relationship between Indigenous and non-Indigenous people in Canada. The largest in scope and breadth was the Royal Commission on Aboriginal Peoples, which provided a comprehensive picture of Canada's relationship with Indigenous peoples, including the IRS system.[122]

The five-volume, 3,500-page RCAP report covers 500 years of history between non-Indigenous and Indigenous people in what is now Canada. The Commissioners made 440 recommendations calling for comprehensive changes in the relationship between Canada's Indigenous and non-Indigenous people. The central recommendation called for a complete restructuring of that relationship. There were major recommendations on treaties, governance, the restructuring of federal institutions, and the substantive areas of lands and resources, family, health, healing, housing, education, arts, and culture. The fifth volume of the report laid out a twenty-year plan for renewing the relationship between Indigenous and non-Indigenous people in Canada.[123]

Several provincially appointed inquiries revealed racism as a pervasive factor in Indigenous and non-Indigenous relations. In 1989, the Royal Commission on the Donald Marshall, Jr., Prosecution, created in response to the wrongful conviction of a Mi'kmaq man for murder in 1971, made eighty-two recommendations aimed at improving the administration of justice in Nova Scotia, particularly with respect to racialized communities.[124] The adoption of some key recommendations has begun to change the landscape in Nova Scotia. The Black and Mi'kmaq program at Dalhousie Law School has increased the number of Black and Mi'kmaq lawyers representing Black and Mi'kmaq clients, which in turn will eventually increase the diversity of the bench. These changes are slow in coming but over time can contribute to a more just society in Nova Scotia. The Marshall report prevents anyone in Nova Scotia from honestly saying that racism is not a systemic problem in the province's legal system. Marshall helped to shift the narrative in that province; although the failure to adopt many of the recommendations was itself an indication of how far there is to go, without the Royal Commission findings, there would be much further to go.

The Aboriginal Justice Inquiry of Manitoba provided a historical, cultural, and legal review of the relationship between the Manitoba justice system and the Indigenous peoples of that province in its 1991 report.[125] This was one of the few inquiries that has centred on an Indigenous woman. The Inquiry was appointed to investigate, report on, and make recommendations respecting the relationship between the administration of justice and Indigenous people in Manitoba. In particular, the Inquiry was created to investigate all aspects of the deaths of male Indigenous leader J.J. Harper and Helen Betty Osborne, a young Indigenous woman brutally murdered in 1971 in The Pas by four non-Indigenous men. It was not until 1987 that anyone was tried criminally for her death. At that trial, only two men were tried despite the identities of all four having been widely known in the community within months of the murder sixteen years earlier. J.J. Harper, the Executive Director of the Island Lake Tribal Council, died following an encounter with a Winnipeg police officer. In the manner all too familiar by now, the officer was immediately exonerated by a police department internal investigation. Both incidents had prompted calls for a judicial inquiry into how Manitoba's justice system was failing Indigenous people. The Inquiry reported in 1991, providing a thorough discussion of Indigenous concepts of justice, a history of Indigenous contact with non-Indigenous law, and a discussion of treaty rights. The Inquiry also reviewed Indigenous over-representation in the criminal justice system, a discussion of the court system, Indigenous justice systems, court reform, juries, jails, alternatives to jail, parole, and policing. In the course of its hearings, the Inquiry heard testimony from many Indigenous people about their IRS experiences and wrote about the far-reaching effects of the schools in its report.[126]

In 2000, two young Indigenous men, Lawrence Wegner and Rodney Naistus, froze to death on the outskirts of Saskatoon. Inquests into the deaths of the two men had failed to determine how they had ended up in fields without adequate clothing or shoes in the depths of winter, but that winter, another young Indigenous man named Darrell Night survived after being driven by police to the same area and left there to die. His subsequent allegations of what the police had done sparked a public outcry.[127] The Saskatchewan Commission on First Nations and Métis Peoples and Justice Reform was mandated in 2001 to address concerns raised about the treatment of First Nations and Métis people by the justice system, in particular by police services.[128] The commission partnered with the federal government, the provincial government, the Federation of Saskatchewan Indian Nations (FSIN), and the Métis Nation Saskatchewan and was made up of five Commissioners, two nominated by the FSIN, two by the province, and one from the Saskatchewan Métis community.[129] Submitted on 21 June 2004, the final report identified racism among provincial police forces as a major reason for Indigenous mistrust of the justice system.

Operating at the same time and also reporting in 2004, the Neil Stonechild Inquiry focused on the Saskatoon police practice of dropping off young Indigenous men on the outskirts of the city in the middle of winter and leaving them there to freeze to death. Known as "starlight tours,"[130] the practice continued for more than a decade after Stonechild's body was found in a field outside Saskatoon in 1990, as laid bare by the deaths of Wegner and Naistus. It likely was not just men and boys who were taken on starlight tours, and the practice had been going on for much longer than a decade: in 2003, the new Chief of the Saskatoon Police Service admitted that an officer had been disciplined in 1976 for taking an Indigenous woman to the outskirts of the city and abandoning her there.[131] In any event, Night's survival prompted an investigation into Stonechild's death after a caller to the Saskatoon *StarPhoenix* suggested that reporters check the archives for a March 1991 story about a woman who said that the police had failed to investigate properly her son's freezing death.[132] Although the inquiry formally revealed and documented the reality of the starlight tours, the racism ingrained in the police force that allowed such a horror to become a practice was not adequately addressed. The two police officers linked to seventeen-year-old Stonechild's death were fired, although not for criminal negligence or manslaughter.[133] They were not tried in court for their roles in Stonechild's death.

The BC government appointed a commission of inquiry in 2007 to examine the circumstances surrounding the death in Vancouver of Frank Joseph Paul, a Mi'kmaq man from New Brunswick. In the evening of 5 December 1998, a police officer dragged Paul from a Vancouver Police Department lockup and left him in a nearby alley, where his body was found the next morning. An autopsy concluded that Paul had died from hypothermia because of exposure and alcohol intoxication. The Commissioner, former BC Supreme Court Justice William H. Davies, issued his final report, *Alone and Cold: The Davies Commission Inquiry into the Death of Frank Paul*, on 19 May 2011.[134] Justice Davies strongly criticized the Vancouver Police Department both for its conduct and for the conflict of interest inherent in having investigated its own actions. He recommended the creation of a civilian oversight body to conduct investigations of professional standards. In response, British Columbia created an Independent Investigations Office to investigate cases of serious harm or death in which police are involved.

In Ontario, the Ipperwash Inquiry investigated the death of Dudley George, shot by Ontario Provincial Police (OPP) while he participated in a protest by Indigenous people about a land dispute.[135] During the course of the inquiry, testimony implicated not only members of the OPP but also then Premier Mike Harris in the widespread racism that characterizes police-Indigenous relations in Ontario. Harris was famously quoted as calling on the OPP to "get those fucking Indians out of the park."[136] The Ipperwash Inquiry led to significant recommendations for restructuring provincial government relations with Indigenous peoples in Ontario, including the separation of the provincial ministries of Natural Resources and Indigenous Affairs.[137] The creation of an Indigenous Justice unit of the provincial Ministry of Attorney General as well as the implementation of various recommendations to address police treatment of Indigenous protesters and Indigenous people more generally also emanated from the report.

Of these inquiries, several have managed to have some of their recommendations adopted, whereas others have been less successful. What accounts for the differences? The answers lie in a mixture of factors, including the leadership of the Commissioner(s), the processes used, and the timing – politically – of the reports. For example, several factors might account for the fact that the Ipperwash Inquiry had a number of its recommendations adopted. Commissioner Sidney Linden was well respected in government circles and completed his report in a timely manner. The inquiry had engaged the public and raised awareness of overt racism toward Indigenous peoples by the police and politicians. The family of Dudley George was represented by counsel and garnered sympathy in its search for justice. The political winds had changed by the time the inquiry reported. A Liberal government had replaced the Conservative one that had been involved in the Ipperwash debacle and was eager to contrast itself to its predecessor. Kathleen Wynne was appointed Minister of Aboriginal Affairs and had a keen interest in improving Crown-Indigenous relations, an interest that she carried through to her time as Premier of Ontario.

When I began to think about the role of public inquiries in the Canadian legal order, my thoughts repeatedly turned to the landmark Mackenzie Valley Pipeline Inquiry conducted by then Justice Thomas Berger in the mid-1970s in Canada's North (the Berger Inquiry). Berger had addressed a question of public importance by visiting affected communities, commissioning independent research, communicating the issues to the wider Canadian public, and making bold recommendations to the government. Although not envisioned as such by the government of the day, the Berger Inquiry explored a deep and abiding societal divide between Indigenous peoples of the North and non-Indigenous Canadians of the South. Berger conducted his process in Indigenous communities in a manner considered respectful, and he showed how the process itself could educate the wider public and create positive change. By the time of his report, the inquiry had engendered in Canada a national consciousness-raising process about Indigenous peoples of the Mackenzie Valley and their northern homeland.

In the next chapter, I will discuss the question of which factors make for a successful commission of inquiry (and the question of what success means), beginning with an excursion back in time to the early 1970s in Canada when a fear of running out of oil was top of mind for the federal government and a controversial pipeline was the proposed solution. The federal government had not contemplated the implications of appointing a former Indigenous rights lawyer to lead a commission in a region of the country where Indigenous people formed a majority of the population. What transpired reshaped the legal landscape of Canada.

2

The Mackenzie Valley Pipeline Inquiry

My belief in the potential utility of public inquiries is grounded in my work on the Berger Inquiry.[1] I had witnessed a truth commission in West Africa for a year and returned to Canada with an avid curiosity about the use (if any) of truth commissions in established democracies. I focused on the Berger Inquiry after having become interested in why Western countries do not typically hold truth commissions to address mass human rights abuses in their midst. Although the Canadian Truth and Reconciliation Commission was then under negotiation as part of a legal settlement agreement,[2] it was the first state-sponsored body called a truth commission in an established democracy. The Commission of Inquiry into the Investigation of the Bombing of Air India Flight 182 and the Ipperwash Inquiry were under way, and the Commission of Inquiry into the Actions of Canadian Officials in Relation to Maher Arar was just wrapping up.[3] These inquiries were part of Canada's legal response to significant injustices. In this chapter, I illustrate why I believe that a public inquiry, in the right hands, can be an important pedagogical tool in Canadian society.

It would be difficult to ignore the impact that Thomas Berger had on Indigenous rights law in Canada.[4] In 1971, he argued the *Calder* case before the Supreme Court of Canada. The ruling in that case, released in 1973, became the first acknowledgment of Aboriginal title in Canada. When Berger was appointed to the bench in early 1972, shortly after arguing *Calder*, he was only thirty-eight and the youngest person to be appointed to the BC Supreme Court. Then in 1974, during a period when a Liberal minority government (led by Pierre Trudeau with Jean Chrétien as Minister of Indian Affairs and Northern Development) sought the support of the New Democratic Party (NDP) to maintain power,[5] Berger was appointed Commissioner of a public inquiry into whether a pipeline should be built across the Western Arctic, in the Mackenzie Valley. The government that appointed Berger to run that inquiry certainly did not anticipate the far-reaching process that would result.

The Berger Inquiry was established in the context of the "energy crisis" of the 1970s. Significant oil and gas deposits were identified in the Western Arctic in the late 1960s. Consortiums of industry players formed and submitted proposals for a pipeline from the Beaufort Sea through the Western Arctic and the provinces to the southern Canadian border and into the United States. The federal government had signalled its support for a pipeline with its Expanded Guidelines for Northern Pipelines tabled in 1972. During the same period, environmental activists and Indigenous rights organizations created enough opposition to the proposed pipeline development that the government appointed an inquiry to address their concerns.

The Berger Inquiry was preceded by litigation brought by Indigenous peoples frustrated that a political solution was not forthcoming to the injustices that they saw as perpetrated against them.[6] In the 1970s, Canadian courts had only begun to acknowledge the concept of Aboriginal title, and the government did its best to obstruct a 1973 legal action by Treaties 8 and 11 Chiefs to file a caveat over their lands to protect them from development. The Chiefs, representing the peoples covered by Treaties 8 and 11 in the Northwest Territories, applied to have the Land Titles registry protect their interests in the lands over which they claimed Aboriginal title from having any instruments registered on them until their assertion of rights was settled. The caveat would forbid the transfer of any of the lands until the matter was settled. Lands in the area already subject to fee simple title were excepted. The Chiefs were forced to bring their action for a caveat under the land title system created entirely under the presumption of Crown sovereignty.

Justice William G. Morrow of the Northwest Territories Supreme Court heard the application in April 1973. The Crown initially caused a delay in the proceedings and even went so far as to seek the removal of Morrow J from the case by filing a writ of prohibition in Federal Court to prevent him from proceeding. Justice Morrow stated that

> [t]o me this represents a policy decision by the Government which can only be interpreted as an affront to my Court and to me as the Judge of that Court ... I am certain that this is the first time in the history of Canadian jurisprudence, the first time since Confederation, when one superior Court Judge has been placed under attack by another superior Court Judge of equal status.[7]

The Federal Court judge determined that Morrow J could properly proceed.[8] When the proceedings recommenced in the Supreme Court of the Northwest Territories before Morrow J, the Crown chose not to appear. Justice Morrow appointed independent counsel to assist the Court as *amicus curiae* in the absence of the Crown. After a thorough review of the evidence before him and the authorities (including *Calder*), Morrow J decided that the Indigenous peoples seeking the caveat were "*prima facie* owners of the lands covered by the caveat – that they have what is known as Aboriginal rights," that the government had a "clear constitutional obligation" to protect their legal rights, and that the Aboriginal rights asserted constituted an interest in lands that could be protected by caveat under the *Land Titles Act*.[9]

Although Justice Morrow's decision was overturned on appeal,[10] it was on the ground that unpatented Crown lands in the Northwest Territories in respect to which the Crown has conveyed no interest are not lands within the operation of the *Land Titles Act*, so no caveat could be applied; the appeal was not decided with respect to the arguments about Aboriginal title. The *Calder* decision had opened the door to Aboriginal title, and Indigenous rights groups were beginning to organize opposition to development on their lands. Justice Morrow's decision in the April 1973 interim proceedings to issue a restraining order freezing development of 400,000 square miles of land in response to a petition from representatives of the 7,000 Treaty Indians in the Northwest Territories was a significant wake-up call for the government.[11] His follow-up decision in September

1973 added to the discomfort at the Department of Indian Affairs (DIA) with respect to pipeline development in the Western Arctic. Although the government planned to appeal the decision, and though the litigation approach did not result in a clear victory for the Indigenous peoples seeking to protect their Aboriginal title, the Chiefs' court action had gained some unexpected traction, prompting the government to take their position seriously and forcing a new era of policy considerations for the government.

The government decided on an inquiry as a solution to the growing opposition to the pipeline. The prevailing government assumption was that a pipeline would be built but that an inquiry would assist in determining ways to mitigate its more negative effects. Berger's mandate was to consider the social, environmental, and economic impacts of a gas pipeline and an energy corridor across Canada's northern territories.

From the moment that he took up the task, Berger began redefining the public inquiry mechanism. First, he held preliminary hearings, inviting interested parties to provide information on what they saw as the important issues to be aired and addressed by the inquiry. Then, following these hearings, Berger issued preliminary rulings, including setting out his interpretation of his mandate. He interpreted it broadly to enable him to analyze the overarching narrative of the problem before him, including a consideration of the past.

Any discussion of a public inquiry's work must first look at the mandate provided to the Commissioner, but how the Commissioner interprets that mandate will determine the scope of the inquiry. The Commissioner's interpretation of the mandate is one of the critical factors in whether an inquiry fulfills its social function. One of the controversial aspects of Berger's conduct of this inquiry was his interpretation of his mandate as set out in the order in council.[12] Critics said that Berger wildly expanded the mandate to include Indigenous rights and land claims; others saw his broad interpretation as a necessary way to achieve a holistic view of the issues involved in determining a pipeline's impacts.

During the preliminary hearings, the pipeline consortium attempted to limit the scope of the inquiry, particularly with reference to Indigenous "land claims."[13] Legal counsel for pipeline applicant Arctic Gas stated that determining the terms of use in the proposed energy corridor would not be an infringement on the rights of Indigenous peoples "so long as the compensation for that use is paid to them if it is determined they have rights."[14] The counsel insisted that, since the question of land claims was not explicitly included in the inquiry's order in council, it should not be included in the proceedings. The representations by intervenors at the preliminary hearings made it apparent that Indigenous organizations sought to make submissions regarding land claims before the inquiry. Indeed, every Indigenous organization that appeared at the preliminary hearings took the position that no right-of-way should be granted for the pipeline until its land claim was settled. To Arctic Gas, this represented an unwelcome and unacceptable expansion of the inquiry's terms of reference.

In his preliminary rulings of 12 July 1974, Berger stated that the scope of the inquiry was defined in the order in council and in the Expanded Guidelines for Northern Pipelines: "It is a study whose magnitude is without precedent in the history of our country. I take no narrow view of my terms of reference."[15] Berger concluded his reasons for interpreting his mandate more broadly by stating his conviction that the inquiry "must be fair and ... complete. We have got to do it right."[16] He added that merely studying the pipeline company's proposal without considering the background against which it was made "would be to nullify the basis on which this Inquiry was established."[17]

The interpretation of an inquiry's mandate is an important discretion of Commissioners, as Berger's example shows. Commissioners can decide to limit the scope of their work or expand it by incorporating broader questions under the rubric of discussing a wider problem. If they choose to interpret the mandate expansively, then there is another way in which Berger's example is important. The Berger Inquiry operated under a government that had little interest in acknowledging Aboriginal title, yet Berger rejected the advice of Judd Buchanan, Minister of Indian Affairs, to refuse permission for testimony on the subject of Aboriginal title before the inquiry.[18]

Less than a fortnight after receiving Buchanan's letter seeking to limit his mandate, Berger issued his second set of preliminary rulings. In them, he acknowledged that it was not for the inquiry to decide on the legitimacy of Indigenous land claims. However, given that the position of the Indigenous organizations was that their land claims must be settled before a pipeline could be built, Berger stated that the pipeline supporters should have an opportunity to show that the pipeline could be built without prejudice to those land claims. Accordingly, he decided that the Indigenous organizations should indicate the nature and extent of their land claims.[19] His expansive interpretation of the mandate was but one way in which Berger consistently asserted the inquiry's independence from the government, but it was of fundamental importance.

Flowing from Berger's decision in the preliminary hearings to allow testimony with respect to Indigenous land claims, the inquiry made use of less formal public hearings, in particular, community hearings.[20] The basis of the decision was that the peoples who would be affected by the pipeline should be permitted to argue that such a pipeline would interfere with their assertions of Aboriginal title. Berger thus devised a schedule of community hearings to hear directly from people who would be affected by the pipeline in each community of the Western Arctic. He appointed Michael Jackson as his special counsel to organize the community hearings.[21] These hearings were conducted with a minimum of legal actors, without cross-examination, in the peoples' home communities, and in their own languages.[22] Berger listened with patience and treated people with respect. He observed and participated in their ceremonies. He ensured that the hearings were broadcast and that the larger public was aware of the issues being discussed. Berger encouraged understanding between Indigenous and non-Indigenous people by facilitating education about the issues before him. Instead of choosing to view his mandate narrowly and focus just on the direct effects of a pipeline, he looked at the larger picture and how such a project would directly and indirectly affect ways of life.

The Berger Inquiry managed to gain the cooperation of the parties before it by operating in a non-adversarial manner. Berger's background as an Indigenous rights litigator clearly informed his views as the Commissioner of the Berger Inquiry, yet his approach in some ways was significantly less lawyer driven than might have been expected from a former litigator and then a judge. Still, though the format of the community hearings was informal and did not incorporate legal representation in a dominant manner, behind the scenes Berger made considerable use of legal counsel in order to achieve the goals of the inquiry.[23] For example, counsel for the inquiry held regular meetings between the parties to discuss events or hearings in advance so that potential legal objections were dealt with as much as possible by agreement rather than having counsel make objections during the hearing itself. This was how Berger's special counsel, Michael Jackson, addressed issues that arose with respect to the community hearings, and the method was very effective in keeping those hearings informal and non-adversarial. Thus, though an open, informal image is often projected of the inquiry, it was still a process bound by the law and legal actors.

The community hearings focused on listening to members of the communities that would be affected directly by the pipeline. Berger treated the evidence that he heard in the community hearings with the same respect and gravity as the expert evidence heard in the formal hearings. Also, he decided not to have cross-examination by lawyers in the community hearings, preferring instead to keep legal counsel in the background in order that the community members would feel unfettered in their ability to speak before the inquiry.

Berger brought the attributes of lawyer, politician, and judge to the role of Commissioner. The way that he ran the inquiry, with independent commission counsel, independent research advisers, and vast public hearings, might have served to mitigate the fact that he sat as the sole Commissioner. His choices of key staff contributed enormously to his effectiveness. The independent role of his commission counsel enabled them to assess the evidence before the inquiry and seek to fill the gaps that Berger himself might not have recognized. The strong role played by his special counsel in organizing the community hearings, and the important role played by his Chief Information Officer in implementing the media strategy, provide an image of a closely knit team working with Berger to forward his vision for the inquiry.

Media Strategy

Having a media strategy at all was an innovation for a Commissioner at the time that Berger took up the role, but he employed an extremely effective media strategy from the outset of the inquiry, orchestrated by his Chief Information Officer, Diana Crosbie.[24] She continuously contacted radio, television, and print media outlets to provide information about the progress of the inquiry. Berger instructed commission counsel to brief the editorial boards of major newspapers and maintain a good rapport with reporters.[25] The *Edmonton Journal* and the *Globe and Mail* assigned writers to cover the proceedings on a regular basis. Crosbie and Jackson spoke with Martin O'Malley of the *Globe and Mail* to convince him to come north to cover the community hearings. At the time, he was writing articles that shaped the news of the country. "We had to get him [to cover the hearings]," said Crosbie.[26] They did get him, and eventually he wrote a book about his experience.[27] Rather than grant interviews in the South once the inquiry was under way, Berger told reporters that the inquiry was in the North and that they had to come north to see it.[28] The idea was that the reporters would come and hear what northerners were telling him and, in turn, report what they heard to those in the South.

Berger's approach was that the issues before the inquiry concerned not just northerners but all Canadians. Accordingly, Berger thought that all Canadians should know what was going on in the northern hearings. He and his special counsel, Ian Waddell, met with the head of the Canadian Broadcasting Corporation (CBC) Northern Service in Ottawa.[29] They arranged for the Northern Service to cover the hearings not just occasionally but each evening. Berger also wanted the coverage to be not only in English but also in the local languages so that information about the inquiry would be received in the communities before Berger arrived, and thus all northerners would know what was being said (in their own languages) and what he was hearing. He gained agreement that the Northern Service would provide an hour of nightly prime-time coverage in the Mackenzie Valley of the day's hearings in English and, for the first time ever, in the languages of the Western Arctic.[30] A team of Indigenous reporters covered the sessions: Louis Blondin in Slavey for middle Mackenzie Valley communities and in Hareskin for Fort Good Hope in upper middle Mackenzie Valley; Joe Tobie in Dogrib for lower Mackenzie Valley communities; Jim Sittichinli in Loucheux for northern Mackenzie Valley communities and some communities in the Mackenzie Delta; Joachim

Bonnetrouge in Chipewyan in Fort Liard; and Abe Okpik in Western Arctic Inuktitut dialect (Inuvialuktun) for Inuvialuit communities in Mackenzie Delta and Beaufort Sea and in Eastern Arctic Inuktitut dialect (Inuktitut) for Eastern Arctic communities (now in Nunavut).[31] This extraordinary innovation did not find favour with the Yellowknife City Council, which heard a motion to condemn this use of prime time on the first night of the coverage.[32] Berger also contacted the National Film Board about making a documentary about the inquiry.[33] It was innovative in 1975 to use a film to explain an inquiry to people.[34]

The fact that the hearings were broadcast in Indigenous languages as well as English also meant that other communities could hear that their views were not unique, for virtually all of the Indigenous participants opposed the pipeline and expressed concerns about its negative effects on their land, culture, and people. Berger recognized the importance of engaging the media to convey the proceedings across the Western Arctic and in the rest of Canada. Every major news outlet in Canada covered the inquiry, sending reporters to the community hearings even though they had rarely, if ever, sent anyone north before to cover anything. Prior to the inquiry, there had been virtually no coverage of northern issues, either in print or on radio or television. For the first time, many Canadians saw footage of the North.[35] The Canadian Press assigned a reporter to the northern hearings, and many news outlets in the country picked up the wire reports. Whit Fraser, assigned by Andrew Cowan of the CBC Northern Service to organize its reporting of the hearings, was remarkable for assembling the team of Indigenous reporters and setting up the schedule that would see them report in their own languages each night.[36] He also continuously filed reports to the southern CBC national desk for broadcast on national radio, and someone from the CBC attended every day of the hearings. The extent of the media coverage across the country was completely unprecedented even before the inquiry's widely covered southern hearings.

The media strategy continued right through to the reporting stage of the inquiry. The report was sent under lock and key to financial capitals in the United States and to all Canadian capitals in advance for a simultaneous release.[37] There was a lock-up in Ottawa to which all of the national press gallery came so that they would be briefed to begin reporting as soon as the report was released.[38] It was released on a Monday so that it would not compete in the news cycle with hockey playoffs then in progress. It garnered a special two-hour program on CBC Radio, and CBC Television devoted an hour to its analysis that evening.[39] In addition, it received front-page press coverage and immediately became a bestseller that had to be reprinted only a few days after its publication.[40] Crosbie's phenomenal effort from the outset of the inquiry to fulfill Berger's vision of educating the wider public was successful: "[N]o royal commission in Canadian history received such sustained media attention in spite of its remote location."[41]

The extraordinary attention paid to the inquiry generated public interest in the pipeline proposal and in the North more generally. Sustained media attention, as well as the number and variety of participants in the southern hearings, alerted the federal government to the political currency acquired by the inquiry:

> The release of the Berger report brought into focus the split in the Cabinet over the northern pipeline. When the Berger Inquiry had been set up, the Mackenzie Valley pipeline had been received religion in Ottawa. The pipeline hearings had helped to change these attitudes. In fact, the media had an impact not only on the public but on ministers and civil servants too. They had read about the hearings in the *Globe and Mail*, they had heard reports on the CBC about the pipeline's apprehended impacts, they had seen statements made on television by the native people in their villages and they had been affected by all these things. By the time the Berger report was handed down, many ministers and their deputies had moved a significant distance away from the consensus that had existed in 1974 in favour of the pipeline.[42]

The need for an organized and sustained media strategy and its potential effectiveness were clearly demonstrated by the Berger Inquiry.

Berger's decision to combine different types of hearings (preliminary, community, formal, southern) was very effective, and Berger clearly set out which types of evidence would be heard, from whom, and how the evidence would be weighed. The holding of hearings in the South was an important tool for public education, as was the media coverage generated by the hearings in the North. Berger commented that there were "huge turnouts – people wanted to respond to what they had heard from the northern peoples."[43] Through the design of the inquiry, Berger was able to create dialogue between different parts of Canadian society and Indigenous societies, educating the larger Canadian public as well as the communities through his "teach-ins." The Berger Inquiry process educated the Indigenous population about the scale of the proposed pipeline and its ramifications and provided an opportunity for their political empowerment in the Canadian context.

Indigenous leaders came to prominence through the media coverage garnered by the inquiry, and people both within and outside their communities came to know of their activism. Communities gained confidence by having solidarity with other communities along the proposed pipeline route. Several of the vocal opponents of the pipeline went on to become involved in politics at local and regional levels:

> As a result of its unique procedures, its conscientious efforts at stimulating broad participation and the pervasive importance of the issues the pipeline brought into focus, the inquiry became a giant consciousness-raising exercise and a milestone in the political development of the Dene and the North itself.[44]

However, some critics suggested that the empowerment of Indigenous peoples built before the Berger Inquiry was actually a setback for their struggle for self-determination because their perceived militancy and demands translated into higher projected costs of development for the pipeline companies.[45] The companies' calculations of these costs, in concert with changed market conditions, caused their interest in building a pipeline to wane.[46]

There is no doubt, however, that the inquiry had a profound impact on some of the Indigenous youth who participated in it and have since become the Indigenous and provincial leaders in the North.[47] For example, Nellie

Cournoyea, a member of the Committee for Original Peoples' Entitlement and a resident of Inuvik as the inquiry began, was elected as a Member of the Legislative Assembly for the Western Arctic in 1979 and eventually became Premier of the Northwest Territories from 1991 to 1995. She then served nine consecutive terms as Chair and Chief Executive Officer of the Inuvialuit Regional Corporation between 1996 and 2016. The corporation represents the collective interests of the Inuvialuit and manages the settlement established in the Inuvialuit Final Agreement, a comprehensive land claim agreement signed between the Inuvialuit and the government of Canada in 1984. She also served as the Chief Executive Officer of the Aboriginal Pipeline Group.[48]

Frank T'Seleie, who as a young Chief famously challenged the Foothills Pipe Lines Chief Executive Officer in a community hearing before Berger,[49] eventually became a proponent of a pipeline.[50] After studying at Trent University, he returned to Fort Good Hope. In his second term as Chief, "he became a strong advocate in the new push for a gas pipeline up the Mackenzie, now that most land-claim obstacles have been cleared."[51]

Stephen Kakfwi was a vocal opponent of the pipeline and organized the Dene Nation's presentations to the Berger Inquiry. He became President of the Dene Nation in 1983, guided the Dene-Métis land claims discussions, and led the creation of the Dene Cultural Institute.[52] He was first elected to the Legislative Assembly of the Northwest Territories in 1987, representing the constituency of Sahtu. In 2000, he became Premier of the Northwest Territories and voiced his support for the construction of a Mackenzie Valley pipeline.[53] Kakfwi retired from political office in 2003. He became a member of the National Round Table on the Environment and Economy, and he represented Sahtu communities in 2005 in negotiations with Imperial Oil over the construction of the Mackenzie Valley pipeline. Kakfwi was dropped from the negotiating team because of his proposal that Indigenous communities be allowed to levy property taxes on the pipeline.[54] An IRS survivor, he is married to Marie Wilson, a Co-Commissioner of the TRC.[55]

James Antoine was the twenty-six-year-old Chief of the Fort Simpson Dene, now known as Liidlii Kue First Nation,[56] when he spoke to the Berger

Inquiry in 1975. He assisted in the development of the Dehcho Regional Council and the Dehcho Tribal Council, now called the Dehcho First Nations. Antoine was elected as the Member of the Legislative Assembly for Nahendeh in 1991, and he became a member of the cabinet in 1995. From 1998 to 2000, he was Premier of the Northwest Territories, during which time the Northwest Territories was divided to enable the formation of Nunavut. In 2003, Antoine retired from politics.[57]

Georges Erasmus appeared before the Berger Inquiry as a young leader of the Indian Brotherhood of the Northwest Territories (later re-named the Dene Nation). He wrote a piece entitled "We the Dene" that addressed much of what he had been presenting to the inquiry:

> The main issue facing the Dene is not the proposed Mackenzie Valley pipeline or some such other colonial development. The issue facing us today is the same issue that has confronted us since the first non-Dene arrived in our land. The issue is recognition of our national rights, rec-ognition of our right to be a self-governing people.[58]

Erasmus ran unsuccessfully for the NDP in the 1979 federal election in the Western Arctic riding. He served two terms as National Chief of the Assembly of First Nations from 1985 to 1991, after which he served as Co-Chair of the Royal Commission on Aboriginal Peoples. He then chaired the Aboriginal Healing Foundation. Erasmus is Chief Negotiator for the Dehcho First Nation in its pursuit of a land and self-government agree-ment. It "is the sole aboriginal group in the territory not to announce public support for the latest attempt to build a Mackenzie Valley pipeline."[59]

Public Education

The Berger Inquiry process and its varied hearings meant that the south-ern Canadian population became educated about the existence, concerns, and perseverance of the Indigenous peoples of the North. The evidence of the environmental impacts of a pipeline educated people about those impacts on the land, the wildlife, and the northern peoples. The evi-dence of the social and economic impacts of a pipeline on the Indigenous peoples of the North educated southern people that progress should not be measured just in terms of industrial development or non-renewable resource extraction.

Public education creates awareness that in turn can foster political will to implement policy change. Berger's recommendation about the need to settle land claims had weight behind it at least in part because people became educated about the issues faced by Indigenous northerners. The legitimacy attributed to Indigenous peoples' views through the Berger process is instructive.

Berger also succeeded in having his recommendations accepted at least in part because of the public support garnered by his innovative approach to the conduct of the inquiry. His success with public education can provide practical tools for other inquiries to implement, particularly with respect to his open and transparent approach, comprehensive and effective media strategy, and broader civil society involvement. In addition, his media strategy, brilliantly directed from the beginning to capture a broad audience and to hold their interest throughout the inquiry, was intended to fulfill a public education mandate.[60] Public education leads to understanding and acknowledgment of the realities and existence of different communities.

An effective, accessible report can contribute to the learning process over the longer term. The accessibility of the report format that Berger used contributed to the report's bestselling reception. A concise, readable report is an important virtue for other commissions of inquiry to emulate. Not only does a commission's report create an incontrovertible historical record, but also it can be an extremely effective tool for public education and for shaping national narratives. Issued in Ottawa in April 1977, the Berger Report, entitled *Northern Frontier, Northern Homeland*,[61] became the bestselling publication of the Canadian government,[62] and it has been described as "an international classic on Indigenous-white relations,"[63] "a landmark in Canadian literature, clearly written, well organized, and often visionary,"[64] and "ahead of its time."[65]

The Berger Inquiry generated such broad public interest in the issues that the federal government could not quietly shelve the report. Berger succeeded in educating the public in many respects through both the inquiry and its report: "[T]he Berger Inquiry became a national 'teach-in' and a turning-point in national consciousness. Most importantly it introduced many Northern Indigenous voices and their needs to the Canadian public."[66] The inquiry did so even as it worked within the existing legal framework of the commission of inquiry. The conscious decision to make his inquiry a truly public inquiry paid dividends in its ability to fulfill a social function. Berger's credibility was unimpeachable throughout the inquiry because of his commitment to openness and transparency.

One of the strongest impacts of the Berger Inquiry was its redefinition of Canada's national narrative about the North. The very title of the report – *Northern Frontier, Northern Homeland* – sought to show how the Canadian idea of the North as a vast, empty wasteland of snow and ice belied the fact that it has been the home of diverse and vibrant cultures for far longer than Canada has existed. As Berger stated, "[w]e possess a terrible self-centredness, even arrogance, as a people ... History is what happened to us. We dismiss as a curiosity what has gone before."[67] It was not just his report but also the process that he designed and put into action that addressed the competing narratives brought by all those participating in the inquiry.

There are two significant narratives that the Berger Inquiry and Report address. The first is the mythology of Canada as a northern nation deeply rooted in our vision of ourselves as a country. As illustrated by the national anthem, this is a vision of Canada as "the true North, strong and free." The Berger Report identified the nation-building mythology of non-Indigenous southerners that saw the North as a frontier, just as the West had been seen a century earlier. The report countered this image with the perspective of northern Indigenous peoples who saw themselves as nations too and who had their own ideas of how to build their nations.[68] The report begins this way:

> We are now at our last frontier. It is a frontier that all of us have read about, but few of us have seen. Profound issues, touching our deepest concerns as a nation, await us there.
>
> The North is a frontier, but it is a homeland too, the homeland of the Dene, Inuit and Métis, as it is also the home of the white people who live

there. And it is a heritage, a unique environment that we are called upon to preserve for all Canadians.[69]

Berger is clearly addressing the non-Indigenous public here, a strategy that I view as crucial to any progress to be made by a mechanism that attempts to address historical injustice.

Berger also confronts a second strand of Canadian mythology: Canada as a bastion of tolerance and respect for human rights. This passage of the report addresses Canadians who simply did not see themselves as a nation marked by systemic human rights abuses and a deep societal rift. Canadians at that time would have seen themselves in the image of Lester B. Pearson's Canada: the peacekeeping nation that claimed as its own the drafter of the *Universal Declaration of Human Rights*, a nation with a *Bill of Rights*,[70] a nation on the side of freedom and democracy during the Cold War, the "just society" of Pierre Elliott Trudeau's vision.

The Berger Inquiry was the first indication for many Canadians that Indigenous peoples did not share with non-Indigenous people the same view of the Canadian myth or ethos.[71] The views of Indigenous peoples were passionately articulated before Berger by people such as Gwich'in social worker Phillip Blake, who testified at Fort McPherson on 9 July 1975:

> One-third of Canada is under the direct colonial rule ... One has to read about South Africa or Rhodesia to get a clear picture of what is really happening in Northern Canada. While your newspapers and television talk about sports fishing up here, we as a people are being destroyed.
>
> And it doesn't even merit any coverage.
>
> Look at us. And what we stand for before you accept without further thought that the Indian nation must die.[72]

These sentiments would have shocked many non-Indigenous Canadians when they were spoken before Berger and might do so even today. They reveal a rupture in the Canadian identity as a defender of human rights and a champion of minority rights that values a diverse society of many cultures. These sentiments were echoed by dozens of people through multiple communities along the proposed route of the pipeline.

A Public Inquiry's Social Function

The public inquiry can show itself to be malleable and adaptable under the leadership of someone committed to building a complete picture of the issues presented. The process that Berger used engaged the people who would be immediately affected by the proposed pipeline, but it also engaged the public, resulting in education and awareness. This engagement enabled the Berger Inquiry to contribute to a dialogue in Canada about respectful relations between non-Indigenous and Indigenous people that continues to this day.

In short, Berger's approach was to fulfill what Professor Gerald Le Dain, later Supreme Court of Canada Justice, called the "social function" of a commission: "[O]ne of the most important roles of large-scale public inquiries is their social function. Part of this social function is to ... influence the attitudes and opinions of both policy-makers and citizens."[73] Berger did this by creating awareness of, and public support for, the inquiry process that in turn prompted social accountability with respect to the issues before him.[74] He showed how government disregard for the northern Indigenous peoples' ways of life and aspirations had already created injustices, and he warned against repeating the same mistakes in the future. As a result, Berger recommended a ten-year moratorium so that the government could take the opportunity to settle land claims along the proposed route prior to commencing the pipeline project. All of these decisions create a picture of a commission that differed greatly from prior legal mechanisms, that created a historical record, that educated the wider public, that promoted social accountability for the issues and the outcomes, and finally that fostered a new dialogue between Indigenous and non-Indigenous people in Canada. These are outcomes that can prompt a truth commission to be sought in an established democracy, and the Berger Inquiry addressed these factors in its influential work.

Berger included a paper entitled "The Inquiry Process" as an appendix to the second volume of his report.[75] In this paper, he noted an "emerging function" of the public inquiry discussed by Le Dain in his reflections as Chair of the Royal Commission on the Non-Medicinal Use of Drugs, convened a few years prior to the Berger Inquiry. This function was the opening up of issues to public discussion and the provision of a forum for the exchange of ideas. Berger suggested that "commissions of inquiry have become an important means for public participation in democratic decision-making as well as an instrument to supply informed advice to government."[76] This is a crucial aspect of the social function that the Berger Inquiry performed so well. The fuller interpretation that I attribute to Le Dain's social function is a process that educates the public such that political will is generated to ensure that an injustice is not repeated: that is, a process of creating social accountability. This mechanism of the commission of inquiry is flexible enough that, given leadership that seeks this goal, a public inquiry can fulfill the social function in a manner more commonly expected of a truth commission. The difference is that truth commissions are explicitly mandated to fulfill the social function, whereas whether public inquiries do so depends on their leadership and the processes adopted.

This social function accorded with the mandate of the TRC: that is, acknowledgment of the IRS experiences, impacts, and consequences; provision of a holistic, culturally appropriate, and safe setting for survivors, their families, and their communities; truth and reconciliation events at national and community levels; public education of Canadians about IRS impacts; creation of a historical record of the IRS system and its legacy; support for commemoration of survivors; and production of a report.[77] As noted above, acknowledgment of an injustice, creation of an incontrovertible historical record, and public education about the injustice to prevent its reoccurrence are objectives that make a truth commission a specialized form of public inquiry.

Commissions of inquiry, in their basic form, investigate an issue by gathering a broad spectrum of information in order to see the larger context that gave rise to the problem. They then make policy recommendations to prevent the reoccurrence of the problem. As noted earlier, sometimes a commission, in addition to these essential functions, performs a social function. This involves a process by which the commission includes a wider public than those people directly affected by the issue at hand, openly acknowledges the harm done, fosters a sense of societal identification with the victims, establishes an incontrovertible record, and makes recommendations to help prevent the injustice from happening again. Such a process encourages a form of social accountability. As demonstrated by Berger, the public inquiry form gives a Commissioner the scope to fulfill this social function.

The ability of a public inquiry to fulfill its social function will depend in large part on the inquiry's leadership and the process used for the implementation of the mandate. Berger's leadership was instrumental in making the Berger Inquiry a landmark inquiry in Canada. Berger took an inquiry model that had been around for centuries and made it a process that was truly independent and truly public. His innovations to the public inquiry model provide insights into the qualities that he brought to the public inquiry model, including openness, patience, humility, clarity of vision, and respectfulness.

Conclusion

Thomas Berger's innovations reflect a desire to have a more complete picture than can be provided in a strictly formal adversarial environment when dealing with large and complex policy issues and wide-ranging human rights questions. Berger adopted a contextual approach suited to answering a broadly worded mandate regarding a complex problem at a time when civic participation was viewed as increasingly important. There might also have been some reflection in the format of the Berger Inquiry of an increasing awareness of Canada's multicultural realities, including the fact that many northern inhabitants do not speak English as a first language.

The Berger Inquiry demonstrated how a public inquiry can utilize legal, scientific, and social expertise to synthesize complicated issues. Individual litigation battles can only investigate the evidence that the parties choose to present and reach conclusions within the confines of the common law system. A government department can research issues within the silo of its own jurisdiction and expertise. Berger took advantage of the public inquiry's ability to look beyond the boundaries of any one process or department to explore the causes and nature of a broad issue. He was then able to communicate the process in an extremely effective way to the affected parties and the broader national community. In a paper entitled "Commissions of Inquiry and Public Policy," Berger considered the choice that the government made in opting for a public inquiry rather than deciding to study the impact of a pipeline in house. He suggested that the choice of instrument meant that the issues were publicly canvassed, challenged, and tested and that northerners were consulted.[78] The ability of the public inquiry to make its own rules and procedures and to consult a broad range of sources for the information on which it will base its conclusions sets it apart as a mechanism from other legal mechanisms available in Canada. Adapting the model that Berger initiated for its own purposes can assist a commission with operating differently to address issues regarding Indigenous people.

Finally, Berger's use of the commission of inquiry form displays its flexibility as a legal mechanism for addressing broad social questions. This expansion of an existing legal mechanism is a useful lesson for established democracies that might need to tackle a difficult problem but wish to do so without creating a new institution. An existing mechanism may be used in a new and better way to address a problem.

The Berger Inquiry demonstrates the possibilities inherent in the legal mechanism of a commission given visionary leadership and a considered process. Indeed, Berger blazed a trail that continues to provide useful strategies for the institutional designs of commissions intended to address historical injustices or deep societal divides. A creative approach to the interpretation of the mandate allows consideration of an overarching narrative of the problem at hand. It might also enable a commission to look at the bigger picture of a situation and establish a more accurate historical record. Berger's use of community hearings is instructive. Lawyers played background roles, and affected members of the population were empowered to present their wide-ranging concerns to Berger. His decision to treat the inquiry from the beginning of the process as an opportunity to educate the wider public about the issues before him was enormously important. Berger achieved this by arranging for the proceedings to be broadcast in local languages, during prime time, and by otherwise garnering consistently wide media coverage.[79]

The Berger Inquiry fulfilled the social function that a public inquiry can achieve by creating awareness of the issues that in turn generated social accountability. This process facilitated increased understanding and fostered dialogue between Indigenous and non-Indigenous people. Such dialogue is necessary if a commission seeks to include reconciliation as part of its mandate.

3

Inquiries and Residential Schools

The effectiveness of the Berger Inquiry has had a continuing impact on the Canadian legal landscape. Some of the more effective subsequent commissions have incorporated aspects of that Inquiry into their designs. How does the Canadian Truth and Reconciliation Commission fit into the pattern of commissions in Canada? How does this explicit attempt to reconcile and redress harms inflicted on Indigenous peoples by Canada measure up in terms of institutional design? In this chapter, I consider why the survivors of residential schools specifically sought a body called a truth commission, rather than a public inquiry, as a response to the legacy of the colonial system. I delve more deeply into the failure of other legal responses to that legacy.

When I started graduate school at the University of Toronto in 2005 to follow my interest in truth commissions, over seventy lawyers representing the federal government, churches, and survivors were negotiating the Indian Residential Schools Settlement Agreement.[1] Its terms included provision for a truth and reconciliation commission. The negotiators acting for survivors of the schools specifically called for a truth commission, but it was to be unlike the best known example at the time, the South African TRC.

Canada has been exceedingly slow in coming to terms with its role as a mass human rights abuser. As evident from the swift rejection by many non-Indigenous commentators of the genocide finding of the National Inquiry into MMIWG, many Canadians are in deep denial about Canada's genocidal policies toward Indigenous peoples. There has been some slow reckoning in public inquiries that have acknowledged to varying degrees the forced removal of Indigenous children from their families as a matter of government policy.

We can trace the thread of awareness of the residential schools through commissions in Canada, from their brief mention in the Berger Inquiry's 1977 report, to the chapter of the 1996 Royal Commission on Aboriginal Peoples calling for a public inquiry into them,[2] until the efforts by survivors to gain recognition from Canadian institutions of their experiences finally culminated in the inauguration of the TRC in 2008. To an even greater extent than the Mackenzie Valley Pipeline Inquiry, the TRC was prompted by litigation brought by Indigenous people.[3]

Why Did Canada Have a Truth Commission on Residential Schools?

To understand why residential schools became the subject of a truth commission, it is necessary to know some of the history of the IRS system.[4] For over a century, the Canadian government sought to assimilate Indigenous children into the non-Indigenous culture by promoting and then requiring their attendance at church-run schools. Children were removed from their families and communities and sent away to schools in which they were forbidden to speak their languages, practise their spirituality, or express their cultures. The impacts of this policy as manifested through the residential schools have echoed through the generations. Indigenous people who never attended a residential school have nonetheless suffered from the harms inflicted there because of the interruption of traditional cultural transmission and parenting practice, the loss of skills enabling traditional life on the land, and the pathology and dysfunction now endemic in many Indigenous communities that accompanied the loss of language, culture, and spirituality. It was only in the late 1990s that the government began to acknowledge that its policy of assimilation was harmful.[5] It did so only in response to overwhelming legal pressure. The following historical overview of the IRS system and evaluation of legal mechanisms engaged specifically to address the IRS legacy shed some light on why Canada came to have the TRC.

Historical Overview of the IRS System

Many Canadians might think that a history of the Indian residential schools would begin after Confederation in 1867. However, the relationship in Canada between Indigenous communities and non-Indigenous Canada that led to the schools, and continues to this day, began after contact between settlers and Indigenous peoples. After their initial dependence on Indigenous peoples, followed by a period of economic and political alliances with them, settlers gradually were able to exert power over those who lived on the land before them.[6] The IRS system is one manifestation of this shifting power relationship, reflecting the history and legacy of colonization and, in particular, a government policy of assimilation clearly articulated by the Superintendent of Indian Affairs, Duncan Campbell Scott, in 1920:

> I want to get rid of the Indian problem. I do not think as a matter of fact, that the country ought to continuously protect a class of people who are able to stand alone ... Our objective is to continue until there is not a single Indian in Canada that has not been absorbed into the body politic and there is no Indian question, and no Indian Department, that is the whole object of this Bill.[7]

This policy was asserted through various pieces of legislation, culminating in the *Indian Act* passed by Parliament in 1876.[8] Still in place today, the *Indian Act* is a key feature of the relationship between Indigenous and non-Indigenous peoples in Canada. It defines a person's "Indian status" upon birth and governs an astonishing amount of that person's life before administering the estate upon death. The *Indian Act* charted the policy of assimilation adopted toward Indigenous peoples.[9]

Long before the government instituted the full IRS system, various schools were built for Indigenous children, mainly by churches, beginning with a school near Quebec City operated by missionaries from 1620 to 1629.[10] In 1831, a residential school opened in Brantford, Ontario, and remained open until 1969.[11] In 1842, the Bagot Commission recommended residential schooling in agriculture, and in 1847 Egerton Ryerson recommended religious-based, government-funded, industrial schools for Indigenous children.[12] However, it was following the passage of the *Indian Act* that government policy focused its efforts on schools and on the removal of Indigenous children from their families.[13]

Together with expansionist noises south of the international boundary, the pressure of settlement moving ever westward in the latter half of the nineteenth century prompted the negotiation of treaties in western Canada between representatives of the Crown and First Nations. Additional factors such as disease, warfare, the fur trade, the whisky trade, and the eradication of the bison and resulting starvation shaped the treaties signed in the western prairies during the 1870s. These treaties are referred to collectively as the numbered treaties.[14] In several of the numbered treaties, the government agreed to provide education to Indigenous children. In particular, the government was to provide salaries for teachers to educate the children.[15] The "Report of Commissioners for Treaty No. 8" also indicated that certain assurances concerning education rights were required:

> As to education, the Indians were assured that there was no need of any special stipulation, as it was the policy of the Government to provide in every part of the country, as far as circumstances would permit, for the education of Indian children, and that the law, which was as strong as a treaty, provided for non-interference with the religion of the Indians in schools maintained or assisted by the Government.[16]

Indeed, in recognition of the changing economy and society that came with the settlers, some Indigenous peoples did request schools from the government by the latter part of the 1800s.[17] They sought day schools on the reserves to provide skills training for their children; they wished to be able to communicate through print and telegraph, to learn English, and to read and write, and they anticipated that eventually their children would become teachers.[18] Historians have argued that missionaries saw the treaty clauses about the provision of education as an opportunity to spread their Christian beliefs and began to pressure the government of Sir John A. Macdonald to allow them to operate schools for Indigenous children.[19] In 1879, Macdonald assigned journalist and lawyer Nicholas Flood Davin the task of reviewing the American experience with industrial schools and reporting on their applicability in Canada.[20]

Davin reported that the preferred option would be industrial boarding schools in order to mitigate the "influence of the wigwam."[21] The schools would satisfy the goal of the churches by giving them access to children whom they could save from the "degenerating influence of their home environment."[22] They would meet the government's goals by "civilizing" the children, thus preparing them for participation in the non-Indigenous economy and relieving a financial burden on the state.[23] Frank Oliver, Minister of Indian Affairs in 1908, stated that the schools would "elevate the Indian from his condition of savagery" and "make him a self-supporting member of the state, and eventually a citizen in good standing."[24]

The first Indian residential schools opened in the 1880s in western Canada and expanded into the North and east into Ontario, Quebec, and Nova Scotia.[25] Eventually, they operated in every province and territory except Prince Edward Island, New Brunswick, and Newfoundland. The system was at its height in the 1920s with compulsory attendance under the *Indian Act* and over eighty schools in operation.[26] Most Indian residential schools were run by entities of the Catholic Church,[27] with others run by the Anglican, Presbyterian, Methodist, and later United Churches.

For most of its long history, certain circumstances were prevalent in the IRS system. When Indigenous children were sent to the schools, they were separated from their families and communities, and the cycle of seasonal hunting and gathering was replaced with the Christian calendar.[28] Upon arrival at the schools, their hair was shorn, and their clothes were replaced with European clothing. The Department of Indian Affairs ordered that the use of English (or French) be insisted on, and the use of Indigenous languages was forbidden.[29] Christianity would replace Indigenous spirituality, the expression of which was banned. Throughout the history of the system, there was widespread use of corporal punishment for children who spoke their Indigenous languages.

Part of the stated purpose of the schools was to give the students skills as labourers. For the first few decades, education was limited to half the day, and the balance of the day was spent performing chores that enabled the schools to operate: chopping wood, doing laundry, milking cows, cleaning, sewing, and cooking. Given the remote locations of many of the schools and the low pay, qualified teachers were difficult to attract and retain. The half-day system and the lack of qualified teachers combined to cause dismal levels of student academic achievement, with only a tiny minority of students graduating from the schools.[30] An additional barrier to learning was that both the curriculum and the pedagogy employed failed to take into account the culture of the Indigenous students. Designed by non-Indigenous people for non-Indigenous children, the schools failed to engage the interest of Indigenous children.[31]

In addition to the generally poor quality of education provided, the residential schools themselves were chronically underfunded, and there was inadequate departmental oversight of the conditions at the schools.[32] Poor construction, including inadequate heating, lighting, and ventilation, was compounded by poor maintenance of the buildings.[33] Combined with poor nutrition and clothing, the lack of sanitation, and overcrowding, these conditions were ideal for disease, particularly tuberculosis, which became endemic at the schools.[34] The Department of Indian Affairs was aware early in the operation of the schools of health reports documenting very high rates of death because of these conditions.[35] Children died in the western schools at the shocking rate of between 24 and 47 percent in the early 1900s.[36] The DIA was aware of the mortality rates and the causes of death. Indeed, as early as 1907, its own Chief Medical Officer, Dr. P.H. Bryce, provided a detailed report, the findings of which were reported and deplored in the national press.[37] Despite this report, the DIA and the churches did nothing to address the problems, prompting Dr. Bryce to publish a pamphlet in 1922 calling their administration of the Indian residential schools "a national crime."[38]

The systemic issues arising from chronic underfunding signify another aspect of the IRS system: a lack of care for Indigenous children that ranged from neglect to outright abuse. The schools were marked by widespread mental, physical, and sexual abuse of the children. Reports of abuses were known to the DIA throughout the period of IRS operation.[39] Not only were there many documented incidents of excessive punishment and brutality suffered by the children, but also there were attempted suicides, and hundreds of children ran away from the schools to escape their abusers.[40] Many of these children died of exposure before they could reach their home communities.

As documented in detail by the TRC in each volume of its extensive final report, the litany of abuses suffered by children (and their families and descendants) in the IRS system is truly appalling to read and relay. Although there were caring individuals among the teachers and workers at some of the schools, and some children did receive an education, the overwhelming narrative of the schools reveals the violence inherent in the policy behind the IRS system: to "kill the Indian [to] save the man."[41] Those who escaped physical or sexual abuse still suffered from the loneliness of separation from their families, the confusion of being taught that their culture was inferior, and the loss of their language and spirituality.

In addition to Dr. Bryce, various people over the decades attempted to bring the conditions in the schools to the attention of both church officials and the Department of Indian Affairs.[42] The complaints were met with denials and cover-ups. Some of the complaints were brought by a DIA official. William Morris Graham, Inspector of Indian Agencies for South Saskatchewan, complained to senior DIA officials on multiple occasions about poor teaching, lack of academic studies, terrible sanitary conditions, and neglect of, cruelty toward, and abuse of children in the schools. The DIA refused to act on his complaints "in order to avoid confrontation with politically influential churches."[43]

Indigenous communities in British Columbia voiced concerns in the early 1900s, requesting that day schools be established in their villages so that students could return home at the end of each day.[44] Although a royal commission heard testimony along these lines in 1915–16, it made no recommendation about education.[45] A joint Senate and House of Commons committee on the *Indian Act* between 1946 and 1948 heard from Indigenous peoples that they wanted reform of the schools.[46] By that time, the government knew that the schools were not successful tools of assimilation. This knowledge, combined with shifting ideas about integrated education, led to the gradual phasing out of the schools starting in the 1950s.[47] From the 1950s to the 1970s, the federal government adopted a new policy of educating Indigenous children alongside non-Indigenous children in provincially run schools. The process of adopting this policy was decidedly slow, however, since the government did not withdraw from the partnership with the churches until 1969. At that point, the government took over the IRS system and began to transfer control to Indian bands. In 1970, Blue Quills Indian Residential School was the first such school to be transferred to band control.[48] In 1972, the National Indian Brotherhood released its *Indian Control of Indian Education* policy,[49] emphasizing an approach to education that did not strip the children of their cultural heritage and that stressed Indigenous parents' control of their children's education.[50] The majority of residential schools were closed by the mid-1980s, with a few remaining until the last closure in 1996.

The Search for Redress

As the schools began to close, various factors combined to enable a search for redress for their numerous harms. In general, the 1980s saw an increased rights-based consciousness in Canada with the adoption of the *Charter of Rights and Freedoms* in 1982 and the ensuing rise of rights-based litigation. By the late 1980s, this rights-based focus included the situation of children,[51] as heralded by the adoption in 1989 by the United Nations General Assembly of the *Convention on the Rights of the Child*.[52] Awareness of child sexual abuse in Canada was increased in the 1980s, though at that time such awareness did not include a focus on Indigenous children in residential schools. Both the Badgley Report of 1984,[53] and the Rogers Report of 1990,[54] indicated a widespread problem of child sexual abuse in Canada. The Rogers Report did not specifically refer to the IRS system, but it did note that there must be considerable attention to the "serious and pervasive"[55] problem of child sexual abuse in Indigenous communities.[56]

Despite earlier press reports,[57] and several criminal investigations by police in the late 1980s,[58] the IRS issue did not garner national attention until 1990, when, in the wake of the Mount Cashel Orphanage scandal, Phil Fontaine, then Grand Chief of the Manitoba Chiefs, went public with his own IRS experience of abuse.[59] He called for an apology from the government and the churches. Fontaine's public revelations are considered an important milestone in the history of the IRS system. Church authorities in Manitoba were investigating allegations of sexual improprieties among their priests, and Fontaine called for the investigation to include IRS abuses.[60] His call opened the door for other survivors to begin sharing their experiences. Later in 1990, the Federation of Saskatchewan Indian Nations called for a federal government inquiry into abuses at the schools.[61] The Minister of Indian Affairs stated that an inquiry was not necessary.[62]

Following Fontaine's revelation, Indigenous organizations began to organize and publish on the subject of IRS abuses. For example, the Cariboo Tribal Council published a book in 1991 that interviewed survivors of a Williams Lake residential school, with a significant number reporting having experienced abuses at the school.[63] The First National Conference on Residential Schools was held in Vancouver in June 1991.[64] The Assembly of First Nations published a First Nations Health Commission report cataloguing the damage to Indigenous communities as a result of the IRS system.[65] In general, Canadians began to hear stories in the early 1990s of the abuses of the residential schools, and these stories gained credence with the apologies in 1991, 1993, and 1994, respectively, of the Oblates of Mary Immaculate, the Anglican Church, and the Presbyterian Church for their roles in running the schools.[66] Heightened awareness in Canada of child sexual abuse, in particular because of the Mount Cashel Orphanage scandal, generated calls for the IRS issue to be addressed. The extent of the IRS legacy became known with the establishment of the Royal Commission on Aboriginal Peoples in 1991.[67] During 178 days of public hearings in ninety-six communities, many survivors of the schools gave emotional and troubling testimony recounting the abuses that they had suffered, thus bringing wider attention to the IRS legacy.[68] It is to this commission of inquiry, and its role in the IRS narrative, that I now turn.

The Royal Commission on Aboriginal Peoples

In 1990, an armed standoff between Mohawks of the Kanesatake Reserve and Quebec police arose at the town of Oka because the Club de Golf Oka wanted to renew its lease and expand its golf course on traditional lands of the Mohawk Nation. The lands contained a sacred grove and burial grounds of spiritual importance to the nation, and they covered an area over which the Mohawks had advanced a claim for two centuries.[69] When the town of Oka moved to expand its golf course, members of the Mohawk Nation set up roadblocks, and a tense standoff began. The situation lasted

for several months. Quebec Premier Robert Bourassa requested help from
the Canadian army after a member of Quebec's police force, the Sûreté
du Québec, was shot dead when the police advanced on a Mohawk bar-
ricade. Scenes of townspeople pelting Mohawk women and children with
rocks stirred up considerable anger among Indigenous people across the
country.[70] Scenes of Canada turning its military might on its own people
stirred up considerable attention from the international community.[71] The
Canadian government deployed more than 4,000 troops to support the
Sûreté du Québec, whereas there were 60 people behind the barricades
at Kanesatake: 27 Indigenous men, 16 Indigenous women, 1 teenager, 6
children, and 10 reporters.[72]

In the aftermath of the crisis, the Mulroney government asked former
Chief Justice of the Supreme Court of Canada Brian Dickson to conduct
nationwide consultations with Indigenous leaders and communities to
make recommendations to respond to Indigenous concerns. In his report, Dickson identified sixteen areas requiring attention, and based on
these areas the government ordered a public inquiry with "possibly the
broadest [mandate] in the history of Canadian royal commissions."[73] The
order in council of August 1991 asked the Royal Commission on Aboriginal
Peoples to look into the history, health, education, self-government aspirations, land claims, treaties, economies, cultures, living conditions, languages, spirituality, relationship with the justice system, and the situation
of Indigenous people in general in Canada. On the recommendation
of Dickson, four of the seven RCAP Commissioners were Indigenous.
"[RCAP] was likely the most extensive inquiry into Indigenous relations
ever conducted on a partnership basis in a settler society."[74] Co-chaired
by Justice René Dussault of the Quebec Appeal Court and former National
Chief of the Assembly of First Nations Georges Erasmus, it worked for five
years to address the sweeping mandate.

RCAP held 178 days of public hearings across the country and heard
briefs from over 2,000 people. Public hearings began in 1992 in Winnipeg,
chosen because of its history as a gathering place for trade among
Indigenous peoples and because it had one of Canada's largest urban
Indigenous populations.[75] RCAP's research agenda was extremely broad,
and more than 350 research projects were commissioned.[76] The research

plan identified areas adequately researched and those that represented gaps in knowledge. Guidelines were developed for researchers in order to ensure respect for Indigenous knowledge, and extensive consultation with Indigenous peoples and governments was undertaken.[77]

Processes adopted by RCAP echoed those employed by the earlier Berger Inquiry; it is therefore no surprise that members of the commission consulted Berger at the outset on how to organize and run RCAP.[78] Similarities in procedure included the fact that, prior to the public hearings, the commission held informal consultations with Indigenous leaders, organizations, and federal and provincial politicians responsible for Aboriginal affairs on the mandate, how it would be pursued, and to encourage involvement in the public consultation processes of the commission.[79] Indeed, RCAP emphasized public consultation and utilized various media formats in multiple Indigenous languages to encourage such participation.[80] A program to provide funding and resources to Indigenous groups to facilitate their ability to research and write briefs for the commission was implemented.[81]

Although RCAP engaged in some public education by producing videos, reports, and CD-ROMs of its materials, there does not appear to have been a media strategy to keep the commission in the public eye throughout its work.[82] Thus, despite some responses to interim research reports, the immense project of the commission, stretching as it did over a five-year period, was not a media event and passed unnoticed by much of the Canadian population during its operation.[83]

The Royal Commission on Aboriginal Peoples and Indian Residential Schools

An entire chapter of the RCAP Report is dedicated to the IRS system.[84] The report notes that "[n]o segment of our research aroused more outrage and shame than the story of the residential schools."[85] The chapter is a detailed review of the history of the schools and the government policies behind them. The commission looked at education policy and its development throughout the IRS period. It reviewed the locations, staffing, operations, and conditions of the schools and identified the causes and manifestations of systemic neglect with a thorough review of administrative and financial aspects of the schools. The chapter discusses widespread disease, malnutrition, abuses, and death tolls at the schools. It examines the impacts of the schools on students, their families, their communities, and their descendants and the resulting legacy of the schools.

Despite its own relatively thorough review of the issue, RCAP recommended that a public inquiry into the IRS legacy be created to examine the origins, purposes, and effects of residential school policies, identify abuses, recommend remedial measures, and begin the process of healing.[86] The report notes that there were previous calls for a public inquiry into the IRS legacy from Indigenous leaders and parliamentarians that went unheeded by the government.[87] Indeed, in 1992, Minister of Indian Affairs Tom Siddon stated that "I am deeply disturbed by the recent disclosures of physical and sexual abuse in the residential schools. However, I do not believe that a public inquiry is the best approach at this time."[88]

RCAP's call for a public inquiry came after a review of government responses to the IRS issue that simply put the burden of addressing the IRS legacy back onto Indigenous peoples and communities.[89] The report noted that the government left it to individuals to seek prosecution of perpetrators and failed to consider that "the system itself constituted a 'crime.'"[90] The commission expressed concern that the government's approach tended to deflect attention from the source of the legacy and the government policies that produced the IRS system and focused instead on the future. In contrast, RCAP suggested that a review of the past was necessary in order to move into the future: "Only by such an act of recognition and repudiation can a start be made on a very different future."[91]

RCAP's dissatisfaction with the government's attitude regarding existing legal mechanisms presaged later developments. RCAP concluded that mechanisms that simply focused on individual experiences were insufficient. It noted in its report that the government was also avoiding responsibility for the IRS system by expecting that survivors would take the initiative to deal with their abusers. RCAP recommended a mechanism that would explore the past with an eye to the system as a whole in order to assist with healing individuals, communities, and the nation in the future. This sounds much like the mandate of the TRC. Indeed, RCAP called for a public inquiry but seemed to seek specific features that suggest a truth commission.

Response to the Royal Commission on Aboriginal Peoples

By the time RCAP released its report, Mulroney's government had been decisively defeated. Jean Chrétien, Minister of Indian Affairs when the White Paper of 1969 was tabled,[92] and when the Berger Inquiry was established, was now Prime Minister. Chrétien himself did not respond to the report.[93] His Minister of Indian Affairs, Ron Irwin, suggested that the price tag to implement RCAP's recommendations was too steep given the competing demands on the government's purse.[94] The government might have been emboldened in its lacklustre response to the report by the results of a poll conducted in August 1996. The poll, to determine Canadians' level of interest in RCAP's findings, found that less than 20 percent of Canadians thought that RCAP would find solutions to the problems of Indigenous peoples. "The findings of this poll may have given comfort to the Liberal government as it distanced itself from the final report of the most expensive royal commission in Canadian history as soon as it was released."[95]

The government could afford not to act on the report given that RCAP had not built up public support in order to create pressure to support its recommendations. Although RCAP did attempt to attract media attention to its report and recommendations, the attempts were too little too late since they were not part of a sustained media strategy throughout the life of the commission. The RCAP secretariat sought assistance from interest groups, including the national churches, to educate the public about the report.[96] The Aboriginal Rights Coalition produced a resource kit about the commission's findings and used it to conduct workshops across the country.[97] The National Association of Friendship Centres held panel discussions on the report, and other national Indigenous organizations responded to it. However, the non-Indigenous public showed little interest in the report. The reasons for this lack of interest are suggested by Lorraine Land, who chaired the Aboriginal Rights Coalition during the RCAP proceedings. These reasons included a decline in public sympathy for Indigenous issues because of high-profile land disputes,[98] along with the rise of more conservative political movements,[99] which emphasized the need to treat Indigenous peoples the same as other Canadians, an approach that RCAP "had emphatically shown had been a policy disaster in the past."[100]

Part of the social function of an inquiry is to educate the public, and using the media is an important strategy to achieve this aim. The level of education of the Canadian public achieved by RCAP was very low. As noted by Maurice Switzer, a former editor and publisher of five daily newspapers and a member of the Elders' Council of the Mississaugas of Rice Lake First Nation in Ontario, unless the RCAP Report could generate considerable media attention, it would be relegated to a quiet shelf in history:

> Indian people did not need a royal commission to understand that, statistically, their children stand a greater chance of going to jail than of graduating from high school, or that their [teenagers] are five times more likely to commit suicide than just about anyone else's around the globe ...
>
> But if this is stale news to Indians, their partners in the Canadian confederation need a steadier dose of headlines to awaken them to the reality of what passes for life in Indian country. How else can one hope to overcome the abject ignorance indicated in a recent survey showing that fully 40 per cent of Canadians think Native people enjoy a standard of living as good as or better than theirs? Nothing short of a massive information campaign is required to make Canadians aware that nearly 30 per cent of their Indigenous peoples live in homes without running water, hot or cold.[101]

Not only did a "massive information campaign" not ensue, but also the federal government's eventual response to the RCAP Report addressed only a narrow range of the recommendations and certainly did not adopt its central proposal for a complete restructuring of relations.[102] Rather, the government "continued to conduct its relations with Aboriginal peoples primarily through the top-down, imperialist machinery of the *Indian Act*."[103]

The federal government's narrow response to RCAP was embodied in a new policy with respect to Aboriginal issues entitled *Gathering Strength – Canada's Aboriginal Action Plan,* released in 1998.[104] The policy set out four general objectives that characterized the government's new approach to Aboriginal policy.[105] The policy also outlined a four-point strategy for addressing IRS issues: apology, healing, litigation, and dispute resolution.[106] Of the four, only the strategy for healing received a generally positive assessment from the Assembly of First Nations.[107] One of the major initiatives created from the new policy to address the IRS recommendations of RCAP was the establishment of the Aboriginal Healing Foundation in response to RCAP's recommendation for action to address the loss of languages and cultures caused by the residential schools. Set up as a nonprofit corporation to be run by a mainly Indigenous board of directors, the Aboriginal Healing Foundation was allotted $350 million for an eleven-year mandate ending 31 March 2009 to support community-based, Indigenous-directed healing initiatives that addressed the legacy of physical and sexual abuse suffered in the IRS system, "including intergenerational impacts."[108] The foundation's mandate was extended under the terms of the Indian Residential Schools Settlement Agreement.[109] The foundation was dissolved in 2014 after the Conservative government of Stephen Harper cancelled its funding.[110]

Regarding the other aspects of the four-point response, the government's approach created frustrations, time delays, and burdensome procedures. With respect to the apology, the federal government made what it called a "Statement of Reconciliation."[111] Minister of Indian Affairs Jane Stewart delivered the statement, but for many it fell far short of an apology.[112] The statement referred to the damage to the overarching relationship between Canada and Indigenous peoples caused by attitudes of racial and cultural superiority. The government acknowledged its role in administering the residential schools and noted that some students had experienced "the tragedy" of physical and sexual abuse. The statement said that, "[t]o those of you who suffered this tragedy at residential schools, we are deeply sorry." That is, the statement apologized to those students who had suffered physical and sexual abuse at the schools but not to those students who had experienced other harms (e.g., psychological, cultural, spiritual, or linguistic harm or loss). Furthermore, it was read by the Minister of Indian Affairs – not the Prime Minister – and it was not read in the House of Commons.

The Native Women's Association of Canada formally refused to accept the statement as an apology, and the Inuit Tapirisat of Canada found the statement to be incomplete since it failed to address the wider range of injustices perpetrated by the residential schools.[113] At the time, the government was vigorously defending itself in lawsuits brought by survivors, insisting that the churches, and not the government, were responsible for abuses in the schools. Observers suggested that the government did not issue a full apology because of fear that it would be viewed as an admission of liability that would weaken its legal position in the various court claims being brought by IRS survivors.[114] In contrast, the United Church of Canada issued an "Apology to First Nations" in 1986, and several other church entities followed in its footsteps.[115]

National and international human rights bodies such as the Canadian Human Rights Commission, the United Nations Committee on Economic, Social and Cultural Rights, and the United Nations Human Rights Commission criticized the government's failure to respond adequately to the RCAP recommendations.[116] Ten years later the Assembly of First Nations issued the federal government a failing grade on implementation of the recommendations.[117] In the late 1990s, though, the failure of the government to respond adequately to RCAP, and in particular to address properly the recommendations on the IRS legacy, created enormous frustration among survivors and dashed any hope of a political resolution of the issue:

> It is fair to say that Indian people did not place much faith or hope in the federal response to the Royal Commission's report ... There is no evidence of a new approach to change the wrongs of the past because the federal government expects Indian people to make the changes, but is not itself prepared to do the same. All the old colonial-style extinguishment and assimilationist policies are still dictating the federal government's relationship with Indian peoples.[118]

This frustration with the lack of a political response prompted IRS survivors to turn to legal responses in an effort to seek redress in the courts for the harms that they had suffered, a strategy that ultimately led to a negotiated solution.

Legal Responses to the IRS Legacy

Some of the major mechanisms used in the Canadian legal system to address harms of the IRS system are criminal prosecution, civil litigation, and alternative dispute resolution.[119] An exploration of the forms and limitations of these mechanisms reveals some of the challenges that survivors faced in gaining redress and helps us to understand why negotiators sought a different mechanism in the form of the TRC.

As noted above, a major turning point for Canadians was the Mount Cashel Orphanage scandal of 1989. Several of the Christian Brothers who ran the orphanage were criminally charged for physically and sexually abusing the children in their care. Although the orphanage was not an Indian residential school, the scandal brought considerable national attention to the issue of institutional child sexual abuse and opened the way for Indigenous claimants to turn to the law with respect to their IRS experiences.

Criminal Law

The first significant legal response to IRS abuses came in the form of criminal prosecutions. Criminal charges were laid beginning in the 1980s against former IRS staff for the sexual abuse of Indigenous children.[120] There are few reported decisions, but a relatively early example is *R v Maczynski*. In that case, the appellant sought a reduction in the sentence for twenty-nine convictions of indecent assault, buggery, and gross indecency committed against students when the appellant was a supervisor at an Indian residential school in British Columbia from 1952 to 1961 and from 1965 to 1967.[121] He was sentenced to concurrent and consecutive sentences totalling sixteen years; his appeal was dismissed in 1997. The Court of Appeal noted that the appellant had also been convicted of similar offences in the Yukon and the Northwest Territories and sentenced to

four years in prison.[122] There was a long period between the offences and
the punishment: Jerzy Maczynski was sentenced thirty years after his
employment at a BC Indian residential school ended.

Such lengthy timelines are among the difficulties posed for criminal
prosecutions in IRS cases. The challenges that can often be encountered
in the criminal prosecution process are illustrated in the saga of *R v
O'Connor.* Bishop Hubert Patrick O'Connor was charged in 1991 with four
counts of indecent assault and rape of former students at the Cariboo
Indian Residential School near Williams Lake, British Columbia, where
he was a Roman Catholic priest and school principal in the 1960s.
Procedural wrangling characterized the case. The 1992 trial decision outlined four motions previously brought by the defence seeking a stay of
proceedings of the charges against the accused.[123] A fifth application for a
stay was brought after the trial had commenced and after one complainant
had commenced her evidence in chief. This time the trial judge accepted
a defence argument and stayed charges on the basis that the accused had
not received full disclosure by the Crown of all therapy records of the
complainants. The Crown had disclosed records related to the specific
incidents, but the accused had gained an initial order for access to the
women's complete medical, therapy, and school records. That is, the defence
sought the files of third parties who had treated the complainants. Neither
the complainants nor the third-party record holders had received notice
of the application.[124]

Upon appeal of the 1992 decision to stay the charges, the Court of
Appeal ordered a new trial.[125] O'Connor unsuccessfully appealed that
decision to the Supreme Court of Canada. In a second Court of Appeal
decision, the Court addressed the issue of disclosure of records.[126] This
too was appealed to the Supreme Court of Canada.[127] A majority of the
Court upheld the Court of Appeal decision overturning the stay of proceedings, finding that the non-disclosure had not violated O'Connor's right
to full answer and defence.[128]

At the new trial in 1996, O'Connor was convicted of two counts (rape
and indecent assault) and sentenced to two and a half years of imprisonment. He then appealed the convictions. Ultimately, he served
six months in jail before being released on bail.[129] In 1998, the indecent

assault conviction was overturned, and the Court of Appeal ordered a new trial on the count of rape.[130] The Court of Appeal ordered a new trial based on its finding that the trial judge had erred when he had determined that consent could be vitiated by the exercise of authority. The trial judge had therefore not made a finding about whether the complainant herself had consented to sexual intercourse.[131] The Court of Appeal dismissed the other charge because the complainant had testified that the indecent assault had occurred on a date after the appellant had proved he was no longer at the school.[132] The case was finally resolved by diversion out of the courtroom. The complainants, one of whom had been impregnated by O'Connor, attended a traditional healing circle with him, representatives of the church, and government officials at a community in the traditional territory of the Esketemc people. With the agreement of the complainants, and an apology from O'Connor, the Crown agreed to drop the final charge against him.[133] After seven years of hearings, trials, and appeals, in which the complainants had to give evidence at a preliminary hearing and two trials, this avoided a likely further appeal to the Supreme Court of Canada and a potential third trial.

Although not all other criminal prosecutions have given rise to the prolonged proceedings seen in *O'Connor*, aspects of that case illustrate the limitations shared by many criminal cases.[134] The multitude of pretrial applications brought by the defence in *O'Connor* indicates the lengthy and adversarial nature of the criminal process for all parties.[135] The applications also indicate the vulnerability of complainants to having deeply personal aspects of their lives exposed in court. Unlike a truth commission process in which voluntariness is central to victim participation, a criminal process essentially subjects victims to the coercive disclosure of private information.

The criminal law is the only legal mechanism that can provide retributive justice in the form of sentences for the convicted perpetrators. However, the impact on complainants is another key problem with the criminal process, as illustrated by *O'Connor*. The survivors are not parties to the criminal prosecution but witnesses who can be retraumatized under cross-examination by defence counsel. Furthermore, the trials can be lengthy and stressful for all involved. One of the complainants who had been victimized by O'Connor when she was eighteen years old stated at the age of fifty-one that "she had had enough 'of being victimized by the courts.'"[136]

Prosecutions deal only with aspects of IRS harms that can be captured within the ambit of criminal law: sexual or physical abuse. Criminal law is not able to address the range of other harms that IRS survivors endured, including the loss of culture, spirituality, family, language, and community ties. Also, criminal law cannot compensate IRS survivors in any substantial way for the larger losses that they suffered. For financial compensation, IRS survivors are obliged to launch civil actions for damages. In addition, the criminal justice system deals with cases against individual perpetrators for limited abuses and is incapable of viewing the IRS system as a whole as a crime. The *O'Connor* case shows a system that focuses on the accused and on the credibility of the complainants. Although verdicts convicting individual perpetrators can bring the specific abuses proven in court to the attention of the wider Canadian public, the criminal justice system cannot provide public education on the broader issues and consequences of the IRS legacy.

Another difficulty with criminal prosecution as a legal response to that legacy arises with the inherent difficulties of prosecuting historical institutional child abuse, including the fact that many of the perpetrators are elderly or have died, and the evidence comes from complainants who were children at the time of the abuse. The evidence is likely decades old, and there are problems with memory recall and with finding corroborating witnesses. The accused is of course presumed innocent, and the highest standard of proof is applied (beyond a reasonable doubt) before he or she is found guilty. Thus, there have been few reported prosecutions.[137] These factors tend to discourage Crown counsel from directing resources into pursuing charges and might explain why IRS survivors redirected their energies into the civil litigation process.

Civil Litigation

The first civil litigation claims against the federal government and the churches for abuse in residential schools were filed by survivors in the early 1990s. By 1996, 200 such claims had been received. As of 1 May 2000, a total of 6,324 individual plaintiffs had filed civil suits against Ottawa and the churches.[138] In 2003, there were about 12,000 civil cases filed.[139] Initially, the civil claims made by survivors related to what might be viewed as standard tort claims. That is, the claims were for harms that civil courts are accustomed to hearing: physical assault and sexual assault claims as a result of negligence and breach of fiduciary duty.

Among the earliest claims was *FSM v Clarke*,[140] filed in 1993 by survivors of a residential school in Lytton, British Columbia. Derek Clarke was a dormitory supervisor at the school. By the time of the civil suit, he was in prison, having been convicted of multiple sexual assaults on multiple students. The civil trial judge, Justice Janice Dillon, noted that "[t]his case is not about him."[141] Rather, it was about who was "on watch" at the school.[142] In other words, among the federal government, the Anglican Church of Canada, and the Anglican Diocese of Cariboo, who had responsibility for the children in the school? The plaintiffs alleged negligence, breach of fiduciary duty, and vicarious liability against the defendants. By the time of the judgment, agreement on damages had been reached. The decision was about apportionment of damages since the church and the government each denied responsibility, and each alleged that the other was liable for the entire damages. Justice Dillon found that both the church and the government had failed to protect the plaintiff and that both were vicariously liable.[143] She attributed 60 percent of negligence damages to the Anglican Church.[144] She allowed the Crown's third-party claim against the diocese.[145]

One of the most prominent IRS civil cases, *Blackwater v Plint*, was filed in 1996 by twenty-seven former residents of the Alberni Indian Residential School alleging harms inflicted by a dormitory supervisor.[146] A case history usefully illustrates how handling an IRS action in the civil litigation system was likely to be problematic for addressing the IRS legacy. The civil case followed the criminal prosecution of Arthur Plint, who pleaded guilty in 1995 to sixteen counts of indecent assault on male former students between 1948 and 1953 and (upon his return to the school after an absence of a decade) between 1963 and 1968.[147] Justice Douglas Hogarth of the British Columbia Supreme Court sentenced Plint, aged seventy-seven, to eleven years of imprisonment and stated that

> I do not hesitate to say ... that so far as the victims of the accused in this matter are concerned, the Indian Residential School System was nothing but a form of institutionalized pedophilia, and the accused, so far as they are concerned, being children at the time, was a sexual terrorist.[148]

After the criminal prosecution, the victims of Plint sued him, the school principals during the relevant periods, the United Church that operated the school, and the federal government, on whose behalf the church ran the school for most of its later history.[149] The plaintiffs were between the ages of five and nineteen when they attended the school in Port Alberni. Almost all of the assaults occurred in the dormitory where the children lived or in Plint's adjacent bedroom. At the civil trial, victims of Plint, in addition to those who had been complainants in the criminal charges, testified about the abuses that they had suffered from him. The defendants did not object to their evidence, and the judge accepted that each former student who testified had been assaulted at least once by Plint.

The civil trial was split into two parts. The first part, heard during February, March, and April 1998, addressed the issue of whether the Crown and the United Church were vicariously liable for the assaults on the plaintiffs. To prove that the employers of Plint were vicariously liable for the assaults, the plaintiffs had to prove that Plint had authority over the children and that his ability to assault them was connected to his employment. The Crown and the United Church each said that the other was solely vicariously liable for the assaults: that is, each alleged that the children were in the care and control of the other. Justice Donald Brenner (as he then was) of the British Columbia Supreme Court found that Plint acted in the role of a parent to the children and had that authority conferred on him. He woke the children up each morning, prepared them for school, met them upon their return, supervised their homework, "and in all other respects functioned as their parent."[150] Justice Brenner also found that the connection test had been met.[151] Then the plaintiffs had to prove that the defendants employed Plint. The United Church and the Crown each said that the other was his employer. To determine the identity of his employer, Brenner J had to embark on a lengthy review of the agreements between the United Church and Canada as well as the IRS legislation and the law on vicarious liability. In the end, Brenner J determined that Canada and the United Church were jointly and vicariously liable for assault.[152]

In an interim ruling, Brenner J dismissed an application by the plaintiffs' counsel to admit evidence by John Milloy, an academic expert on the history of the IRS system.[153] At the time of the trial, Milloy had completed a large research project that formed the basis of the IRS chapter of the RCAP Report.[154] The plaintiffs' counsel averred that Milloy would assist the Court by situating "the Church and Canada's policies on residential schools in relation to their overall policy of assimilation" and that his evidence would help the plaintiffs to establish that Canada and the United Church had knowledge of the abuses occurring in the IRS system prior to hiring Plint.[155] Brenner J noted the difference between a commission of inquiry's task to understand the entire IRS system and a court's much narrower task to decide which harms are compensable in law after hearing evidence based on material facts set out in the pleadings.[156] He declined to admit Milloy's report or to hear his evidence.

The second part of the trial was heard over multiple weeks in late 1998, the spring and fall of 1999, and throughout 2000 (by this time, Brenner J had been made Chief Justice of the British Columbia Supreme Court). The second part addressed the remaining liability issues. They included the vicarious liability of the United Church and Canada for perpetrators other than Plint, negligence or direct liability of the defendants, fiduciary duty, non-delegable statutory duty, limitation defences and the third-party claims advanced by the United Church and Canada against each other, and the amount of damages recoverable by the plaintiffs.[157] By the time of the second part of the trial, most of the plaintiffs had settled their claims. Only seven of the initial twenty-three plaintiffs remained.[158] Three years after the first trial decision, the Court released the judgment on the second part of the trial.

In that judgment, Brenner CJ found that both the United Church and Canada were vicariously liable for the damages proved by six of the remaining plaintiffs. He dismissed the claim of one plaintiff. The claims against the defendants for negligence and breach of fiduciary duty were dismissed, and all claims for damages for specific abuses (except those of a sexual nature) were statute barred.[159] He awarded non-pecuniary and aggravated damages for sexual abuse to the remaining plaintiffs in amounts ranging from \$10,000 to \$145,000,[160] and he apportioned liability at 75 percent to Canada and 25 percent to the United Church.

Both Canada and the United Church appealed to the British Columbia Court of Appeal. The appeal was heard in January 2003, and the judgment was released in December that year.[161] The Court largely maintained the damage awards made by Brenner CJ. However, on the issue of liability, the Court applied a doctrine of charitable immunity, exempting the United Church from liability and finding Canada liable for 100 percent on the basis of vicarious liability.[162] Speaking for the Court of Appeal on that issue, Justice William Esson found that, because the plaintiffs could make a full recovery from the Crown, the United Church as a non-profit charitable organization could escape a finding of vicarious liability. This part of the Court's decision was set aside by the Supreme Court of Canada in its unanimous 2005 decision reinstating Brenner CJ's apportionment of liability.[163]

The Supreme Court did not interfere with Brenner CJ's decision regarding the plaintiffs' arguments that harms resulting from loss of language and culture should be recognized. At trial, Brenner CJ had dismissed this argument:

> There is simply no evidence of dishonesty or intentional disloyalty on the part of Canada or the United Church towards the plaintiffs which would make it permissible or desirable to engage the law relating to fiduciary obligations. I include in this conclusion the more general complaints of the plaintiffs relating to linguistic and cultural deprivation. In my view the plaintiffs have failed to demonstrate that either Canada or the Church were acting dishonestly or were intentionally disloyal to the plaintiffs.[164]

The Court of Appeal stated that the loss of culture claim had not been properly pleaded and could not be raised at that stage.[165] Thus, it is unclear how the Court would have dealt with the argument had it (in its view) been properly brought before it.[166] The Supreme Court of Canada acknowledged these arguments in its 2005 decision in *Blackwater v Plint* but noted that the arguments had not been made at trial "other than as contextual background to the circumstances and events at the school," and they were brought by intervenors, based on materials not tested by the courts below.[167]

The deficiencies of this process from a survivor's perspective are clear. In *Blackwater v Plint,* the civil litigation process ended at the Supreme Court of Canada almost a decade after the plaintiffs filed their civil suit and a full decade after Plint was convicted of sexual assault. The plaintiffs who did not settle out of court ended up with a relatively modest amount of money to compensate them for harms inflicted three to six decades earlier. The painful experiences of the abuses suffered were recounted in graphic detail by the plaintiffs in court, but only one type of harm that they suffered (sexual abuse) was ultimately compensated. Most of the arguments made were technical arguments about liability and immunity; one imagines that these arguments did not address the pain suffered by survivors. The defendants aggressively fought the case at every stage; there were appeals and cross-appeals and an extraordinary expenditure of resources in time and legal representation.

Toward the end of the first decade of IRS claims, courts began to receive more civil suits that included claims for cultural harm, loss of language, and intergenerational harm. These were novel arguments in the field of tort law. There are very few mentions of loss of culture or intergenerational harm in the decided IRS cases. One exception is *Bonaparte v Canada,*[168] heard in 2001. This was a class action brought by fifty-six plaintiffs who attended two residential schools near Spanish, Ontario, between 1934 and 1960. These primary plaintiffs were survivors of the schools and made claims for a range of abuses suffered. However, there was also a large group of "secondary plaintiffs," the children of the primary plaintiffs, not yet born when their parents attended the schools. These plaintiffs claimed that the government and the churches had breached their fiduciary duty to protect their Aboriginal rights, including the protection and preservation of their language, culture, and way of life. In addition, the secondary plaintiffs alleged that they had been denied the opportunity to receive their culture from their parents and therefore denied a healthy family life because of their parents' forced attendance at the schools.[169] These 189 secondary plaintiffs claimed damages for breach of fiduciary duty, cultural deprivation, and loss of care, guidance, and companionship pursuant to s 61 of the *Family Law Act*. The Ontario Superior Court motions judge acknowledged that it was only the passage of this law in 1978 that made the action possible since there was no common law cause of action available to relatives for loss of care, guidance, and companionship resulting from the death or injury of a family member.[170]

The defendants (the government and relevant church bodies that operated the schools in question[171]) brought a motion to strike the statement of claim. The motions judge struck the secondary plaintiffs' claim, agreeing with the defendants that these plaintiffs had no reasonable cause of action. The Court of Appeal found that the motions judge was correct in striking the claims, with the exception of the breach of fiduciary duty claim of the secondary plaintiffs, but only as against the federal Crown. The Court determined that it would be inappropriate to decide whether the fiduciary duty extended to the secondary plaintiffs without the benefit of an evidentiary record.[172] There are no further reported decisions in this case. Still, the Court opened the door for arguments about loss of culture to be made should the case proceed. A gloss on this issue is found in a conditional assent to the ratification of the Indian Residential Schools Settlement Agreement in Principle. Chief Justice Brenner of the British Columbia Supreme Court (who had penned the trial decision in *Blackwater v Plint*) stated with respect to the class action cases that

> [a] repeated theme in these cases is the effect that attendance at Indian Residential Schools had on the language and culture of Indian children. These were largely destroyed. However, no court has yet recognized the loss of language and culture as a recoverable tort. Even if such a loss was actionable, most claims would now be statute barred by the *Limitation Act* ... The [Common Experience Payment[173]] can therefore be viewed, at least in part, as compensation for a loss not recoverable at law. In my view, this represents an important advantage to the class.[174]

Thus, Brenner CJ thought that the IRS Settlement Agreement provided acknowledgment of harms for which it would be difficult to recover if the class action proceeded to trial.[175] This exposes both a weakness and a strength of civil litigation for IRS survivors. Some of their losses are not recognized as harms for which they could recover damages, yet the pressure of litigation nevertheless resulted in payments (in the form of the Common Experience Payment) acknowledging those harms.

Alongside the various individual claims made by survivors were a growing number of class action lawsuits across the country. These claims alleged physical, mental, and sexual abuse but also sought to recover damages for the loss of language, culture, and spirituality that class members experienced because of the residential schools.[176] The choice of class actions as an option was not available to plaintiffs until relatively recently. Legislation to enable class actions did not occur in Canada's common law jurisdictions until 1992, when Ontario passed its *Class Proceedings Act*.[177]

Eventually, a National Consortium of Residential School Survivors launched a class action in Ontario on behalf of all survivors of the IRS system across the country as well as parents and children of survivors. The plaintiffs in *Baxter v Canada* sought damages for harms, including physical, emotional, psychological, and sexual abuse; loss of language and culture; deprivation of love and guidance from their families; and inadequate education and living conditions. The class action named the federal government, which then named over eighty church organizations as third parties. Had it proceeded to trial, the sheer number of defendants, and the fact that the period relevant to the class action spanned seventy-five years, would have meant an extremely lengthy and complicated trial. Even to get to trial, a class action must be certified in order to allow it to proceed. *Baxter* was filed in 2002. Third-party notices were filed in 2003. The Ontario Superior Court ruled in 2005 on a motion by the plaintiffs seeking a hearing of the certification motion prior to a multitude of other motions brought by the defendants and third parties.[178] The delays inherent in the process would have meant that many of the elderly plaintiffs would not have lived to see the case go to trial. The class action was certified, and the settlement of it was approved, with conditions, in 2006.[179]

Overall, then, where settlement or success at trial results in compensation for plaintiffs, civil litigation has some positive outcomes. It is capable of achieving monetary awards for survivors of IRS abuses in a process that they initiate in a forum that possesses safeguards of procedural fairness.

An important aspect of the civil process is that it allows for more agency by victims than does the criminal justice system. In a criminal trial, the parties are the Crown and the accused; victims can be called only as witnesses but do not initiate proceedings or instruct counsel. In addition, in a civil case, there is more scope for novel arguments given that both common law and statutory frameworks can be employed. Civil litigation can achieve a degree of perpetrator accountability because the proceedings and the judgment are matters of public record. However, the process is expensive, lengthy, and emotionally draining. Even though the class actions launched with respect to the IRS legacy ultimately produced settlements for individual litigants, their families, communities, and descendants were also affected by the legacy. Litigation is unable to capture adequately the broader harms that the IRS system inflicted. Although the IRS Settlement Agreement acknowledged losses beyond physical harms, such as the losses of culture, language, and spirituality that many agreed were both the aim and the result of the schools, it is not clear that the courts would have acknowledged such losses. Indeed, Jennifer Llewellyn asserted that tort law "appears ill-equipped ... to respond to the intangible harms at issue in residential schools cases."[180]

Furthermore, the litigation process itself can inflict harms. A decision in an IRS case exempting it from mandatory mediation noted the pain and suffering produced for survivors of being in the same courtroom as their abuser.[181] The judge noted that forcing the plaintiffs to discuss the abuse in mediation would be unfair given that there was no reasonable likelihood that the mediation would produce a settlement and that they would be required to provide details of the abuse during examinations for discovery and again at trial if the matter proceeded that far.[182] In addition, as illustrated by the case history of *Blackwater v Plint*, litigation can be a lengthy and convoluted process that ultimately produces limited awards on narrow grounds.

Class action lawsuits, though relieving some of the ongoing costs that individual litigants would need to pay, have also resulted in unseemly behaviour by some law firms that sought to increase the numbers in the class actions without due concern for the psychological repercussions that might be triggered by provoking IRS memories. For example, the Law

Society of Saskatchewan has sanctioned Tony Merchant, one of the primary litigators of IRS class actions, after fielding multiple complaints about how he actively recruited large numbers of survivors for his cases.[183] Lawyers obtained school class lists and band lists and hired people on reserves to organize meetings at which forms were handed out to impoverished survivors asking them to remember the worst things that had happened to them with the promise of financial compensation.[184] Such activities can revictimize and exploit vulnerable survivors, and such tactics prompted rule changes by the Law Society of Saskatchewan with respect to lawyers who pressure vulnerable potential clients.[185]

Civil litigation can provide an opportunity for public education about an issue by bringing institutional defendants' culpability to the fore in a way that criminal law does not. Still, as with the criminal process, civil litigation can find fault with individual parties but cannot rebuke an entire system. Nonetheless, the civil suits brought by survivors created the financial pressure on the federal government and churches that ultimately forced them to negotiate a larger settlement for the IRS legacy. According to the Assembly of First Nations, the sheer volume of claims would have taken the courts an estimated fifty-three years to conclude, at a cost of $2.3 billion to litigate.[186]

Alternative Dispute Resolution

Given the enormous volume of civil lawsuits filed by IRS survivors, and the staggering projected costs of that litigation, the federal government began to search for ways to alleviate the costs of defending the cases. In 1998, the government began consultations with survivors and church representatives on how to address the IRS issue. In response to these "exploratory dialogues,"[187] the government established a number of alternative dispute resolution (ADR) pilot projects across the country.[188] In ADR, complainants participate in a process less adversarial than litigation, with a more flexible approach to evidence and proof. Such processes are intended to deal with claims more quickly and with less cost and stress than litigation.

In 2000, the Law Commission of Canada released a report on institutional child abuse that included recommendations for resolving IRS claims.[189] In 2001, the federal government formed the Indian Residential

Schools Resolution Canada (IRSRC) unit "to centralize resources that are focused on resolving Indian residential school claims, addressing the legacy associated with the schools and encouraging healing and reconciliation."[190] The IRSRC was tasked with creating an ADR process for the mounting number of survivors who sought redress for their IRS experiences. In December 2002, the government announced the creation of a National Resolution Framework, the centrepiece of which was an ADR process to administer and settle sexual and physical abuse claims as an alternative to litigation.[191] The IRSRC launched its ADR process in 2003, the same year as the Court of Appeal decision in *Blackwater v Plint*.[192] The IRSRC made agreements on the apportionment of liability with the Anglican and Presbyterian Churches that year. It was not until early 2004 that the government began receiving applications for alternative dispute resolution.

The ADR process contained two streams for claimants.[193] Category A was for sexual abuse and/or physical abuse that caused harms lasting longer than six weeks and required hospitalization or serious medical treatment. There was a points system – the more severe the abuse, the higher the points allotted, in turn resulting in higher compensation. Category B was for claims of wrongful confinement, abuse that caused harms lasting less than six weeks, and abuse that required hospitalization or serious medical treatment. Once the points were calculated, compensation was awarded based on the total number, the location of the school where the child was abused, and whether the abuse was committed by a person whose religious group had entered into an indemnity or cost-sharing agreement with Canada.[194]

The ADR process set up by the federal government for IRS claims provoked many criticisms. Both the Assembly of First Nations and the Canadian Bar Association published reports critiquing the process as slow, bureaucratic, retraumatizing, and costly.[195] Settlements were unequal (depending on the location of the victim's school and whether the church had an indemnity agreement) and focused on injuries rather than the consequences of those injuries.[196] The costs of administering settlements were triple the amounts of compensation being paid.[197] Like criminal prosecution and civil litigation, the process addressed individual cases. The outcomes of mediated agreements were usually subject to confidentiality agreements, so the opportunity for public education about the broader harms of the IRS system was not available with alternative dispute resolution. In addition to the costs, the Assembly of First Nations and the Canadian Bar Association alleged that the process did not adequately address cultural and intergenerational harms. To address better the bigger picture signified by these harms, both organizations recommended that the government establish a truth and reconciliation process in addition to revising the ADR process.[198]

In 2005, the House of Commons Standing Committee on Aboriginal Affairs and Northern Development concluded after an examination of the ADR process that it was "an excessively costly and inappropriately applied failure."[199] The Committee went on to list its reasons for declaring the process a failure. It also set out criteria for a settlement of the IRS legacy.[200] Indeed, by late 2004, the ADR process had proven to be utterly flawed. From early 2004, when it began receiving applications, to November 2004, over 700 applications had been filed, but only 19 claims had been settled by the process; meanwhile, there were approximately 18,000 litigation claims, and several class action lawsuits pending.[201]

Conclusion

The profound effects of the IRS system on survivors and their families and the more than 100 years of its operation resulted in a legacy experienced in Indigenous communities across most of Canada. Legal structures such as those set up under the *Indian Act* disempowered those communities from seeking redress during most of the period of IRS operation.[202] When at last the voices of survivors began to be heard with respect to the abuses that they suffered at the schools, the IRS system was nearly at the end of its operation. Forums such as that provided by RCAP began the process of educating the public about the IRS legacy but failed to provide redress for survivors. The legal mechanisms that survivors turned to included criminal prosecution, civil litigation, and alternative dispute resolution. Criminal prosecution resulted in some retributive justice for a few aging individual perpetrators of sexual abuse but could not address systemic issues and harms of the IRS system. Civil litigation also resulted in some awards for damages for a few survivors, but the process was lengthy, and again the harms acknowledged by the courts were limited. Alternative dispute resolution was an attempt to remedy the difficulties of civil litigation, but it too ultimately failed to achieve the goal of having a streamlined and effective process to address survivors' needs. Thus, each mechanism offered a measure of assistance in bringing the IRS legacy to public attention, but each failed to address adequately the historical injustices created by the IRS system.

The failure of the ADR approach, attention to the issue from international human rights bodies,[203] calls for a form of commission of inquiry,[204] and, perhaps most importantly, the pressure of the ever-increasing tide of civil litigation combined to cause the federal government to sit down with the parties in 2005 and negotiate a settlement of the IRS issue.[205] Given the inadequacies of criminal prosecution, civil litigation, and alternative dispute resolution discussed in this chapter, the TRC can be viewed as a response to the failure of ordinary legal mechanisms to address historical injustices. In the next chapter, I turn to the negotiations that led to the IRS Settlement Agreement and set out its component parts, including the TRC.

4

Canada's Truth and Reconciliation Commission

In this chapter, I consider the creation, leadership, and process of the Truth and Reconciliation Commission through its first set of Commissioners to its completion in 2015.[1] Survivors and Indigenous representatives in the Indian residential schools settlement negotiations sought a truth commission – not a public inquiry – as part of the settlement. That is, they wanted more than what might be expected from an ordinary public inquiry. They wanted a commission that would acknowledge and witness the IRS system and its impacts and increase awareness – and create a public record – of them. I have proposed that the call for a truth commission might have resulted from the history of promises to Indigenous peoples broken by the Canadian government and the widespread ignorance among non-Indigenous Canadians about the IRS history and legacy. Acknowledgment of an injustice, creation of a historical record, and public education about the injustice to prevent its reoccurrence are objectives that make a truth commission a specialized form of public inquiry. In the previous chapter, I outlined the inadequacy of various existing legal mechanisms to address the IRS legacy. The frustration that survivors experienced with the lack of an adequate political response to the recommendations of the Royal Commission on Aboriginal Peoples fuelled their turning to the courts and contributed to their desire to seek something other than another public inquiry.

Negotiations Leading to the TRC

As discussed in Chapter 3, although RCAP itself did not garner much press, testimony before that commission about the residential schools did attract some national media attention and the attention of the non-Indigenous public. Residential schools became one of the few areas covered by RCAP to gain a response from the federal government. In 1996, RCAP made its recommendation calling for a public inquiry into the IRS system. No such inquiry was established, but that year Indian and Northern Affairs Canada (Indian Affairs) founded its IRS unit. In 1997, Phil Fontaine was elected National Chief of the Assembly of First Nations (AFN) and commenced negotiations with the churches and the federal government for a settlement for IRS survivors. From September 1998 to June 1999, exploratory dialogues were held across the country among the Department of Justice, Indian Affairs, survivors of residential schools abuse, Indigenous leaders, and churches' representatives.[2]

Out of these dialogues, the parties agreed on guiding principles for their settlement discussions.[3] In the meantime, the courts started to decide some of the first IRS civil cases, including decisions such as the 1998 trial decision in *Blackwater v Plint* that apportioned liability at 75 percent for the government and 25 percent for the church.[4] These decisions began to affect settlement discussions.[5] The government released its *Gathering Strength* response to RCAP in 1998. In addition, litigation activities by IRS survivors continued the pressure on negotiators, including *Cloud v Canada (Attorney General)*, a class action lawsuit launched in Ontario in 1998. Additional class action lawsuits soon followed.[6]

In 2000, Matthew Coon Come was elected as National Chief of the Assembly of First Nations. He took a less conciliatory approach to the government than Phil Fontaine, but like Fontaine, Coon Come called for a Truth and Reconciliation Commission on the IRS experience.[7] Also in 2000, the Law Commission of Canada reported on the various possible responses to institutional child abuse in Canada.[8] The mandate of the Law Commission was not specifically on the IRS system, but its report did discuss the residential schools as a special case,[9] concluding that the system not only harmed former students but also harmed their families and communities. Furthermore, in suggesting the importance of redressing these harms, the report stated that any approach to redress must be able to address appropriately "this broader range of harms and this broader range of persons suffering these harms."[10] In its recommendations, the Law Commission set out conditions that would need to be respected if the government chose a public inquiry into the residential schools system as an appropriate response.[11] Its report notably gave consideration to the truth commission model, reviewing how it had been used in transitional justice settings. The report did suggest that such a model could be adapted to address institutional child abuse.[12] The Law Commission recommendations indicated that such a commission must have the power to compel the production of government and institutional evidence, that the information-gathering process must be respectful of survivors, and that it should encourage meaningful apologies.[13] Parties to the IRS negotiations were calling on the federal government to establish a truth commission at that time.[14]

The desire for a mechanism that differed from a public inquiry in the eyes of survivors was driven by perceptions of public inquiries as ineffectual. This is not surprising given the magnitude of the findings produced by RCAP and the relative lack of response by both the government and the public to those findings. The RCAP report in 1996 had been followed by that of the Krever Inquiry in 1997, an inquiry that heightened the criticisms of public inquiries with respect to procedural delays and legal infighting.[15] Although I demonstrate that the truth commission is a form of public inquiry, it is clear that the usual form of public inquiry would not satisfy IRS survivors. They sought the features more obviously associated with a truth commission: symbolism, a focus on victims, public education, and the goal of reconciliation.

As noted above, the pressure of civil suits, including the launch of multiple class action lawsuits, prompted the federal government to form the IRSRC unit in 2001 to institute the alternative dispute resolution program. However, though settlement discussions continued, the Assembly of First Nations signed a memorandum of understanding with a National Consortium of Residential School Survivors to pursue a national class action lawsuit on behalf of all IRS survivors and their families to seek compensation for survivors of sexual, physical, psychological, and cultural abuse:

"The Assembly of First Nations Survivors Working Group takes the position that, although litigation is the least appealing option in the path to healing for those who suffered in these schools, litigation has become the only option as there is a complete absence of any political will by the federal government to properly deal with this issue which includes the issue of cultural genocide," said Vice Chief Ken Young.

The Memorandum of Understanding supports the promotion of a national solution for resolving residential school claims and to develop a fair and expeditious method of determining compensation for residential schools survivors.[16]

This press release displays continued frustration with the lack of a political solution; nonetheless, settlement discussions continued and began to gather momentum. A consensus developed on the AFN recommendations in the 2004 report, which called for a lump sum reparations payment, additional compensation for specific abuses, expedited payments for the sick and elderly, and a truth-sharing and reconciliation process.[17] The report referred to the need for a national mechanism to facilitate reconciliation and healing among the government, churches, survivors, and their communities. The report also envisioned a process designed by the stakeholders to enable survivors to tell their stories, to create public awareness and a public record of the IRS system and its legacy, to create a plan for healing of relationships, to prevent the reoccurrence of a "state-committed atrocity," and to acknowledge and support the need for healing.[18] Then, on 3 December 2004, the Ontario Court of Appeal sustained a class action by survivors of the Mohawk Institute Residential School in Brantford, Ontario, adding to the weight of litigation facing the federal government.[19]

In May 2005, the federal government signed a "political agreement" promising negotiations on a package with the elements contained in the AFN 2004 report as well as compensation for legal fees.[20] The federal government appointed former Supreme Court of Canada Justice Frank Iacobucci to negotiate a settlement on its behalf. On 5 August 2005, the Assembly of First Nations launched a class action lawsuit against the federal government seeking billions of dollars in general, special, and punitive damages for the IRS system. National Chief Phil Fontaine stated that "[t]he Accord has provided a political vehicle to move forward, but a legal vehicle is required to finalize the process with the Assembly of First Nations in a central and representative role, which this action now provides."[21] Then in November that year, the parties reached an Agreement in Principle in the dying days of Paul Martin's minority Liberal government.[22] In October, one month before the Agreement in Principle was reached, the Supreme Court of Canada gave its decision in *Blackwater v Plint*.[23] The unanimous Court reinstated the trial judge's assessment of damages and apportionment of liability for IRS abuses (75 percent to the government, 25 percent to the church) and upheld the Court of Appeal's increase of a damage award for one of the plaintiffs. Given that the Court of Appeal had relieved the churches of liability, the Supreme Court's decision meant that the churches were required to accept responsibility for their roles in running residential schools, thus solidifying the necessity of their participation in the settlement process.

The Agreement in Principle was finalized in May 2006 and approved by the courts later in the year.[24] After the opt-out period passed, the IRS Settlement Agreement came into effect on 19 September 2007. By this time, 14,903 survivors had filed claims against the government. Only 2,805 claims had been resolved through litigation or the ADR process, with total damage awards of more than $110 million.[25]

The Indian Residential Schools Settlement Agreement, 2007

The IRS Settlement Agreement was the largest class action settlement in Canadian history,[26] and it had well over 100 signatories. It set aside $1.9 billion for approximately 80,000 then living survivors of the residential schools. Survivors who did not wish to join the Settlement Agreement but did wish to retain their right to sue the government and the churches had to opt out of the agreement formally by the opt-out deadline of 20 August 2007. Had more than 5,000 survivors opted out of the Settlement Agreement, it would have been void.[27] There were ongoing regional and national administration committees to oversee its implementation.

The IRS Settlement Agreement comprised several mechanisms of redress for survivors of the residential schools. The Common Experience Payment provided for a lump sum to each person who had attended a residential school. An Independent Assessment Process was available to those who claimed damages for harms beyond those suffered simply by attending a residential school (i.e., apart from what the Common Experience Payment compensated). The Settlement Agreement also included a fund for commemorative projects and a fund for healing projects. Finally, it provided for the establishment of the Truth and Reconciliation Commission.

The Common Experience Payment was available to former students still alive on 30 May 2005 (the day that settlement negotiations were initiated) who showed that they had attended a residential school.[28] The Common Experience Payment was $10,000 for the first year that a person attended a residential school and $3,000 for each additional year of attendance. Applicants for the payment did not need to show that they had been abused in order to receive it. The payment was symbolic and intended to acknowledge the fact that simply attending a residential school was a harm. That is, the Common Experience Payment was aimed at redressing the cultural, spiritual, and psychological harms of the schools. As noted in Chapter 3, this part of the Settlement Agreement acknowledged harms for which it would be difficult to recover compensation by way of litigation.[29] These harms included loss of language and cultural transmission. Furthermore, the common law cannot compensate survivors even for some of the harms that it recognizes, such as physical harm, because of the application of limitation periods.[30] Thus, the Common Experience Payment was intended to redress the widespread harms of the IRS system not clearly compensable under the common law system. Accepting the payment meant releasing the government and the churches from all further liability for IRS claims, with the exception of those falling under the Independent Assessment Process described below.

As of 15 March 2010, the government had received 99,756 applications for the Common Experience Payment from the time that it began receiving claims in September 2007. Of this number, 96,817 had been processed, and 75,683 payments had been issued. Applications for reconsideration numbered 24,424, of which 1,324 remained in process.[31] The government also had an Advance Payment Program for survivors sixty-five years or older on 30 May 2005, in acknowledgment that the elderly might not live long enough to see the finalization of the Settlement Agreement. Applications received and verified between May and December 2006 were eligible for an $8,000 advance payment on the Common Experience Payment. As of 31 December 2006, 13,547 elderly survivors had applied for the advance payment, and 10,337 applications were verified and processed.[32]

For the harms ordinarily compensable in the tort system, such as serious physical and sexual abuse, there was an Independent Assessment Process. Those survivors who wished to be compensated for these harms could make a claim under that process, which had a schedule of monetary compensation for a range of abuses depending on their severity.[33] The Independent Assessment Process essentially replaced the ADR system that the IRSRC operated previously in that it incorporated positive elements of dispute resolution, such as providing a more speedy and less adversarial process than litigation. The crucial difference between the Independent Assessment Process and the government ADR program was that it was independent and adjudicative – and intended to be more respectful of survivors.

The IRS Settlement Agreement also made provision for commemoration.[34] There was a $20 million fund for activities that commemorate the children, families, and communities affected by the schools. The fund was intended for projects suggested by survivors or their families and communities. Schedule J states that proposals would be submitted to the Truth and Reconciliation Commission, which would then make recommendations to the IRSRC on which ones to implement.

The Settlement Agreement provided for an additional $125 million over five years to support the projects of the Aboriginal Healing Foundation.[35] In addition, $94.5 million was allocated for the Indian Residential Schools Resolution Health Support program to provide former IRS students and their families with access to "emotional health and wellness support services."[36] This program acknowledged that survivors who engaged in claiming redress available under the Settlement Agreement might experience retraumatization and require health services as a result of disclosing the abuses and impacts caused by the IRS system. Although an official apology was not part of the Settlement Agreement, the government delivered one.[37]

Canada's Truth and Reconciliation Commission, 2008

In addition to the commemoration and compensation components of the IRS Settlement Agreement, the TRC was inaugurated on 1 June 2008. Schedule N of the Settlement Agreement sets out the TRC's mandate. A preamble notes that the TRC process would be part of a "holistic and comprehensive response" to the IRS legacy and a "profound commitment to establishing new relationships." It also states that "[t]he truth of our common experiences will help set our spirits free and pave the way to reconciliation."[38] Schedule N provides the TRC's terms of reference in the form of seven goals.[39] They are acknowledgment of the IRS experiences, impacts, and consequences; provision of a holistic, culturally appropriate, and safe setting for survivors, their families, and their communities; truth and reconciliation events at national and community levels;[40] public education of Canadians about the IRS system and its impacts; creation of a historical record of the IRS system and its legacy; and support for the commemoration of survivors. Finally, the TRC was required to produce a report including recommendations to the government with respect to the IRS system, experience, and ongoing legacy.[41] These recommendations were further delineated in a footnote: "The Commission may make recommendations for such further measures as it considers necessary for the fulfillment of the Truth and Reconciliation Mandate and goals."[42]

The principles on which the TRC would operate reflected the "guiding principles" developed in the exploratory dialogues.[43] These principles included accessibility, victim-centredness, confidentiality (if required by the former student), transparency, accountability, comprehensiveness, and inclusiveness. The process was expected to do no harm, to have concern for the health and safety of participants, and to be open, honourable, educational, holistic, just and fair, representative, respectful, voluntary, flexible, and forward looking in terms of "rebuilding and renewing ... the relationship between Aboriginal and non-Aboriginal Canadians," requiring "commitment from ... the people of Canada."[44]

There were two time frames for the TRC.[45] The first was a two-year period within which the TRC had to complete all national events and produce its report and recommendations. The second was a five-year period for the completion of community events, statement taking,[46] closing ceremonies,[47] and establishment of a research centre.[48] Schedule N also describes the secretariat and its duties for the operation of the TRC,[49] and it calls for the establishment of an Indian Residential School Survivor Committee to assist the TRC in accomplishing its tasks.[50]

Like those of other truth commissions, the TRC's mandate included the creation of a historical record and the making of recommendations. However, aside from the unique mandate and structure that reflect the national context in which the TRC took place, it was distinctive in that it was the only truth commission to be created out of litigation. In other contexts in which truth commissions have arisen, they have been created by a new regime to look into the abuses of a past regime, as in Argentina, Peru, and Chile. Occasionally, a truth commission arises as part of a peace accord brokered between parties to a conflict, as in El Salvador, Guatemala, and Sierra Leone. In Canada, the TRC was a result of negotiations among multiple parties of class action lawsuits. This meant that the TRC needed to prompt Canadians to invest in and take ownership of a process that they did not instigate. That is, the TRC was not created out of a groundswell of concern among the public about IRS survivors; rather, it was agreed to by the federal government's legal advisers in order to settle costly litigation.

A legal settlement is necessarily a compromise with inevitable costs and benefits for each party. The IRS Settlement Agreement had court-supervised implementation, and the TRC was therefore subject to judicial oversight. Thus, if an aspect of Schedule N was being neglected or a party to the Settlement Agreement disagreed with its implementation, then the party had recourse to the courts. Although other truth commissions have also been subject to litigation,[51] the courts had an obligation to oversee the implementation of the Settlement Agreement. Although in some ways this presented a challenge for the TRC, given the potential threats of judicial review by the parties, it also assisted the TRC by enabling it to turn to the courts if the parties disagreed with its approach. In fact, the TRC itself engaged in litigation against the federal government in order to access historical records retained at Library and Archives Canada. The federal government opposed the ability of the TRC to access the records, stating that neither did it have standing to seek the records, nor did the government have the obligation to provide them. The matter was decided in the TRC's favour by Justice Stephen Goudge.[52]

The TRC was like other truth and reconciliation commissions in that it was an official, temporary, non-judicial, fact-finding body set up to investigate a pattern of abuses of human rights committed over a number of years.[53] That is, it was a government-sponsored commission, with a five-year mandate, intended to investigate the IRS system and its legacy. Fitting the definition of a truth commission and substantively fulfilling the goals and functions of a truth commission might not be the same thing. In the remainder of the chapter, I analyze the work of the TRC through a discussion of its leadership, process, and social function. I include comparative information from other truth commissions to help with the assessment.

The Truth and Reconciliation Commission's Leadership

I observed in Chapter 1 that a commission of inquiry can emphasize its social function, but whether it does so depends on two key factors: leadership and process. By process, I mean the interpretation and implementation of its mandate. These aspects are no less critical for a truth commission to succeed as a specialized form of public inquiry.

A common feature of truth commissions is the appointment of multiple Commissioners. Schedule N required that the TRC have three Commissioners – a Chairperson and two Co-Commissioners – and provided guidelines for the process of selecting them.[54] The mandate directed that "[c]onsideration should be given to at least one of the three members being an Aboriginal person" and required that the appointments be made out of a pool of candidates nominated by the constituencies represented in the Settlement Agreement.[55] The decision to have multiple Commissioners indicates that the negotiators of the TRC thought it important to have people with different perspectives lead the commission and hear from those who appeared before them. They required at least one Indigenous Commissioner. The decision not to require all three to be Indigenous implied that it was important to have a non-Indigenous Commissioner as well. The IRS legacy cannot be understood through only Indigenous or only non-Indigenous eyes. It is a part of Canada's shared history, and therefore the leadership of the TRC needed to reflect that by having representation from both Indigenous and non-Indigenous communities. This diversity contributed to the ability of the TRC to fulfill its social function – having Commissioners who were Indigenous and non-Indigenous embodied the fact that each community had a stake in the TRC's work.

Leadership of a truth commission is critical to its effectiveness: "Composition counts. The actual identity of decision makers, including those charged with deciding the truth of contested matters and the consequences that should follow, matters."[56] One can imagine that the South African TRC would have been very different without Bishop Desmond Tutu at the helm; his leadership was integral to the shape taken by the South African process.[57] In Argentina, leading novelist and well-respected author Ernesto Sábato chaired the National Commission on the Disappeared in 1983. The El Salvadoran commission members were chosen as part of UN-brokered peace negotiations, and all three Commissioners and the staff were non-Salvadoran because it was thought that no one from El Salvador would be sufficiently unbiased to conduct the commission's work.[58] The Commissioners included the former President of Colombia, Belisario Betancur, and a former President of the Inter-American Court, Thomas Buergenthal. Hayner notes that in that context "one of the most important qualities of any commissioner is having sufficient personal authority to be able to pick up the phone and get through to almost anyone at any time."[59] Although this image might rely on an outdated paradigm, it will assist the commission's work if the person appointed has a public profile. In any event, whoever leads a commission must be a respected person of integrity so that the country can trust that the Commissioner has the best intentions in undertaking the weighty task.

Indeed, Schedule N reflected an understanding of this by requiring that the Chairperson and Commissioners be "persons of recognized integrity, stature and respect."[60] Finally, the mandate required that the Assembly of First Nations be consulted in the final decision on the appointments.[61] The TRC had two sets of Commissioners. Unfortunately, this was because the first set resigned a few months into their mandate after failing to resolve internal differences between the Chair and the two Co-Commissioners.

The First Panel

Ontario Court of Appeal Justice Harry LaForme, a member of the Mississaugas of the New Credit First Nation, was appointed as the TRC's first Chairperson.[62] He was the unanimous choice of the selection committee co-chaired by Thomas Berger and Marlene Brant Castellano.[63] Called to the bar in 1979, Justice LaForme initially practised law at a large downtown Toronto firm but soon decided to practise Aboriginal law.[64] He was appointed the Commissioner of the Indian Commission of Ontario in 1989.[65] In 1991, the federal cabinet appointed him as Chairperson of the Indian Claims Commission.[66] In January 1994, he was appointed a judge of the Ontario Court of Justice (General Division), now the Superior Court of Justice, Ontario. At the time of his appointment, he was one of only three Indigenous judges ever appointed to this level of trial court in Canada.[67] In November 2004, Justice LaForme was appointed to the Ontario Court of Appeal and became the first (and, when he retired from the bench in 2018, still the only) Indigenous person ever appointed to an appellate court in Canada. Although he did not attend residential school, Justice LaForme says that he was asked by then Grand Chief Phil Fontaine to lead the TRC based on his life experience as an Indigenous person and on the world view that he would bring to the position.[68]

The two Co-Commissioners appointed in 2008 were Claudette Dumont-Smith, who is Algonquin from Kitigan Zibi, and Jane Brewin Morley, a non-Indigenous lawyer based in British Columbia.[69] They were on a list of eight or ten names for the Co-Commissioner positions.[70] Dumont-Smith was the senior health adviser to the Native Women's Association of Canada at the time of her appointment to the TRC.[71] Morley was hired as an adjudicator in the Independent Assessment Process under the IRS Settlement Agreement in 2007.[72]

The Chair of the TRC, Justice Harry LaForme, resigned on 20 October 2008,[73] citing strife between himself and the two Co-Commissioners arising from at least two sources. He stated that there was an "incurable problem" that had led him to conclude that the TRC "as currently constituted" would fail.[74] He alleged that the two Co-Commissioners wanted the TRC run by a simple majority and would not recognize his ultimate authority as Chair to chart its course and shape its objectives.[75] Justice

LaForme said that, despite his efforts, the two Co-Commissioners insisted on majority rule, "thereby ensuring that their restricted vision will be the one consistently sustained."[76] This was not just a case of competing visions, he said, but entailed a compromise in the commission's independence because of the influence on the Co-Commissioners of certain parties to the Settlement Agreement.[77] This led to the second problem, a fundamental difference in how the Commissioners viewed the mandate. According to Justice LaForme, he placed more emphasis on the reconciliation aspect, whereas the two Co-Commissioners were more focused on the truth-telling aspect.[78] This fundamental difference in vision for the TRC ended in his resignation. Minister of Indian Affairs and Northern Development Chuck Strahl's Communications Director, Ted Yeomans, stated that a court-appointed mediator "was not able to reconcile differences between the chair and the two commissioners."[79] Justice LaForme also had concerns about the independence of the TRC because of the administrative structure,[80] and his concerns were echoed by the second panel in their interim report. Furthermore, commission counsel Owen Young, speaking on behalf of Justice LaForme following his resignation, stated that the Chief Commissioner's resignation had resulted from interference by the Assembly of First Nations since the two Co-Commissioners shared AFN National Chief Phil Fontaine's views on the appropriate focus of the commission.[81]

Justice LaForme's resignation was an enormous blow to the TRC. The parties to the IRS Settlement Agreement began meeting soon after his resignation in order to determine the next steps, with retired Supreme Court of Canada Justice Frank Iacobucci acting as the facilitator of their confidential discussions.[82] A new selection committee was finally announced on 30 January 2009.[83] On that day, after calls for their resignation,[84] the two Co-Commissioners resigned effective 1 June,[85] clearing the way for a new panel to be struck. The selection committee set out a new structure with clear definitions of the roles for the Commissioners to clear up some of the concerns flagged by Justice LaForme in his resignation letter.[86]

A statement issued by then Acting Executive Director Aideen Nabigon claimed that it was "business as usual" at the TRC after Justice LaForme's resignation.[87] But this proved not to be the case. The commission's first national event was scheduled to occur in Vancouver in January 2009. The event was cancelled given the uncertainty about the leadership at the TRC, yet as noted by one commentator it is common for a truth commission to experience difficulties in its start-up period, and despite a rough start it was possible for the TRC to succeed.[88]

The Second Panel

After its difficult start, the TRC gained a new slate of Commissioners, and their leadership would be critical to the ability of the commission to fulfill its mandate. The three new Commissioners were appointed one year after the inauguration of the commission. The new Chief Commissioner was Justice Murray Sinclair. When he was appointed an Associate Chief Judge of the Provincial Court of Manitoba in March 1988, he was the first Indigenous judge appointed in Manitoba. He was subsequently appointed to the Court of Queen's Bench of Manitoba in January 2001. He is the son of an IRS survivor.[89]

Justice Sinclair was appointed (along with Court of Queen's Bench Associate Chief Justice A.C. Hamilton) as a Co-Commissioner of the Manitoba Public Inquiry into the Administration of Justice and Aboriginal People (AJI).[90] The AJI Report suggests that Justice Sinclair had a sense at that time of the need to attract broader attention to Indigenous issues:

> The report ... went beyond holding organizations accountable and stressed a sense of social responsibility for the treatment of Aboriginal people ... Although many of the commission's recommendations were directed at "provincial and federal governments," they were in another sense directed at everyone in Canada in an attempt to make known the injustices of the past and create support for Aboriginal self-government in the future.[91]

In addition, this quotation suggests that Justice Sinclair and his Co-Commissioner saw the inquiry as an opportunity to promote social accountability, a feature of the social function of a commission of inquiry. This experience would later be of significant assistance to Justice Sinclair at the TRC. In 1994, he was appointed as the Commissioner for a pediatric heart surgery inquiry, which investigated the deaths of twelve children at the Children's Hospital in Winnipeg.[92] A member of the Three Fires Society, and a third-degree member of the Midewiwin (Grand Medicine) Society of the Ojibway, responsible for passing on traditional knowledge from generation to generation, Justice Sinclair was respected in both Indigenous and non-Indigenous worlds.[93] The TRC completed its work in 2015, and Liberal Prime Minister Justin Trudeau appointed Justice Sinclair to the Senate in 2016.[94]

Justice Sinclair's two Co-Commissioners were Marie Wilson and Wilton Littlechild. Wilson brought a wealth of experience as a journalist and broadcaster, having worked for twenty-five years for the Canadian Broadcasting Corporation in radio and television as regional and national reporter, television program host, and Regional Director for northern Quebec and the territories. At the time of her appointment, she was Vice-President of Operations at the Workers' Safety and Compensation Commission of the Northwest Territories and Nunavut. A non-Indigenous Canadian, she is married to former Northwest Territories Premier and former leader of the Dene Nation Stephen Kakfwi, who first garnered national attention before the Berger Inquiry in the 1970s when he organized Dene opposition to the proposed pipeline. Kakfwi is a residential school survivor.[95]

Littlechild was a Regional Chief of the Assembly of First Nations from Maskwacis Cree First Nation in Alberta. An avid athlete, he has bachelor's and master's degrees in physical education. In 1976, he became the first treaty Indigenous person to receive a law degree from the University of Alberta. He served as the Chairperson of the Commission on First Nations and Métis Peoples and Justice Reform, mandated in 2002 to review the justice system in Saskatchewan.[96] Littlechild had experience in elected federal politics, having served as a Progressive Conservative Member of Parliament from 1988 to 1993 for the riding of Wetaskiwin-Rimbey. He was a parliamentary delegate to the United Nations and served two terms as the North American representative to the UN Permanent Forum on Indigenous Issues. He is an IRS survivor, having lived for fourteen years in residential schools.[97]

All three Commissioners thus exhibited the qualities sought in Schedule N. More than that, their demeanour and actions in the early days of the TRC suggested that they possessed the intangible qualities that make leadership such an important factor in a truth commission's progress.

Justice Sinclair's public speeches displayed an ability to discuss difficult subjects with an engaging combination of respectful solemnity and intelligent humour. His compassion for survivors, and his evident knowledge of and deep commitment to addressing the IRS legacy, complemented a charismatic personality that widened the audience for the TRC's work. Without leadership of considerable profile, political acumen, and media savvy, the TRC could not hope readily to fulfill its public education mandate. Although Indigenous Canadians were well aware of the IRS legacy, non-Indigenous Canadians needed to be educated by the TRC about the policy enacted by their government and the damage that it has done to individuals and communities.[98] The new panel of Commissioners exhibited considerable combined experience with public inquiries, politics (elected, international, and Canadian Aboriginal), and the media, positioning them well for the enormous task ahead. In addition, they were advised by a ten-member Indian Residential School Survivor Committee.[99]

A notable aspect of the TRC structure is that administratively, it was set up as a department of the federal Department of Indian Affairs and Northern Development. Initially, the TRC's Executive Director was appointed as a Deputy Minister of that department. However, upon his appointment as Chief Commissioner, Justice Sinclair became appointed as a Deputy Minister of that department instead.[100] This administrative structure enmeshed the TRC in government bureaucracy, as noted in the TRC *Interim Report*:

> The decision by the parties to the Settlement Agreement to establish the Commission as a federal government department – as opposed to a commission under the Inquiries Act – was made prior to the appointment of the current Commissioners, and is not one with which they would have concurred. That decision has created additional challenges for the Commission. The rules and regulations that govern large, well-established, permanent federal government departments have proven onerous and highly problematic for a small, newly created organization with a time-limited mandate.
>
> Departmental staffing and other processes normally do not apply to federal commissions or special investigations. The requirement that the

Truth and Reconciliation Commission comply with provisions that apply to the operations of a federal department has led to significant delays that will have an impact on the Commission's ability to meet its deadlines. The Commission is required to create an entirely new federal department, subject to, and accountable for, the complete range of federal government statutes, regulations, policies, directives, and guidelines. It has to do this with a comparatively small staff and budget. Meeting these requirements has hampered the Commission's ability to carry out its mandate to implement a statement-gathering process, hold National Events and community hearings, and establish processes for document collection and research activities.[101]

The fact that the TRC was structured administratively as a department of the federal government meant compliance with government oversight, particularly under allowable funding regulations prescribed by law. Red tape abounded and made hiring and other basic decisions subject to federal processes, impairing the TRC's independence in a fundamental way.[102] The fact that the parties decided to set up the TRC as a department rather than under the *Inquiries Act* had far-reaching implications for its ability to subpoena witnesses and require document production, which led to protracted litigation battles between the commission and the government and some of the church parties.[103] However, the decision not to have subpoena power reflected the desire of survivors that the TRC would not be a legalistic process.[104]

The new panel relocated their headquarters from Ottawa to Winnipeg in an effort to assert the independence of the commission from the seat of government and move westward, to where the majority of the schools had operated.[105] In addition to the Survivor Committee, the TRC began to appoint Honorary Witnesses, beginning with then Governor General Michäelle Jean, to raise the profile of and interest in its work and to increase the participation of the wider public.

Staffing changes also followed the change in panels. Bob Watts, former Chief Executive Officer of the Assembly of First Nations and Chief of Staff to National Chief of the Assembly of First Nations Phil Fontaine, during the IRS Settlement Agreement negotiations, served as Interim Executive

Director of the TRC in 2007 while on secondment from the AFN. He was succeeded as Executive Director in 2007 by Aideen Nabigon, whose experience as a federal government bureaucrat might have assisted her with navigating the government's administrative structures.[106] When Justice Sinclair was appointed, he brought on Manitoba lawyer Tom McMahon, who had worked with him on a previous inquiry, as Executive Director. McMahon was replaced by Kimberly Murray, who had distinguished herself as Legal Advocacy Director at Aboriginal Legal Services of Toronto.

McMahon stayed on as general counsel. An earlier appointment by Justice LaForme of Owen Young as counsel had attracted criticism at least in part because as a Crown prosecutor he had sought heavy penalties against the "KI 6," a group of Elders of the Kitchenuhmaykoosib Inninuwug First Nation in its battle against a mining company.[107] The Elders had been part of a group of protesters who had defied a court order and been convicted of contempt of court. They had been sentenced to significant jail terms, as Young had urged in his sentencing submissions. According to a press report, AFN Chiefs had passed a resolution asking Justice LaForme to reconsider the appointment, but he had declined to do so.[108]

Another important staffing change was the resignation of Dr. John Milloy as Research Director in 2010, shortly after the TRC's first national event and a few weeks after he had apologized to church leaders for comments made while expressing frustration about the slow pace of document production by the churches, though he stated that his resignation was unrelated to that episode.[109] Milloy was replaced by Dr. Paulette Regan in the course of the TRC's operations.[110]

The Truth and Reconciliation Commission's Process

In the remainder of this chapter, I consider the TRC's structure and mandate as they appear in Schedule N of the IRS Settlement Agreement, how the TRC sought substantively to fulfill its goals as a truth commission, and some of the challenges that it faced. The goals discussed here follow from the reasons that a truth commission might be sought in a country such as Canada. These reasons include the inadequacy of previously tried legal mechanisms and a desire to set the country on the path to reconciliation.

They also include the impulse to compile a complete historical record and the wish to educate the public about historical injustices. The latter two reasons are related, and I will discuss them under a section exploring how the TRC attempted to fulfill the public education mandate of a truth commission.

One reason that people seek a truth commission in an established democracy is that the usual legal mechanisms have proven to be inadequate. In response to survivors' experiences with criminal and civil litigation processes, it appears from Schedule N that the Settlement Agreement negotiators sought to establish a body that would not mimic a legal proceeding such as a trial. Schedule N specifies the powers, duties, and procedures of the TRC, including receiving statements.[111] The schedule also sets out what the TRC could not do in pursuit of its mandate; it could not hold formal hearings, have subpoena powers, or name names. The TRC's responsibilities with respect to methodology and procedure are enumerated.[112] The factors that the TRC was required to take into account in exercising its duties are set out, including a direction that the Commissioners "shall not hold formal hearings, nor act as a public inquiry, nor conduct a formal legal process."[113]

The prohibition against acting as a public inquiry should be viewed in the context of the whole phrase that also warns against emulating "a formal legal process." This part of the mandate was a caution against repeating past mistakes such as engaging in an adversarial process that revictimized survivors by failing to listen to them and that failed to view the larger picture of the IRS system and its legacy. These concerns flowed from a conceptual idea of a truth commission as separate from a public inquiry. However, as I have argued, a truth commission is better understood as a specialized form of a public inquiry. Here the focus should be on the mandate's expression of a desire not to have a *formal* legal process. With this wording, the negotiators of the Settlement Agreement were likely trying to stress their intention for the TRC not to duplicate criminal or civil court proceedings or the Independent Assessment Process. Nor was the TRC to repeat the perceived difficulties encountered with public inquiries in the past, when adversarial processes overtook the substance of the inquiry. This section of the mandate can be read as eschewing a formal legal process (i.e., an adversarial process) for the TRC. Schedule N emphasizes that the TRC was to be part of a holistic process of reconciliation and healing, with a focus on survivors that would be respectful of Indigenous oral and legal traditions.[114]

One of the difficulties with the criminal and civil legal mechanisms is the hardship that they cause among survivors. In criminal proceedings, the victims of IRS abuses might be called as witnesses, but they are not parties to the proceedings and therefore have no agency in or control of the process. They cannot instruct Crown counsel, and they might simply be sidelined in the court. In civil litigation, the victims as plaintiffs have more agency, but they are still subject to an adversarial process that must fit the abuses suffered into specific legal boxes. The process can drag on for years, with procedural wrangling over legal minutiae overshadowing the search for accountability and redress. This can leave survivors feeling retraumatized, exhausted, and disillusioned. Although witnesses in a criminal proceeding need not pay legal fees, plaintiffs in a civil action can face overwhelming legal costs in a long and contested proceeding.

In response to this negative experience in Canadian courts, the TRC appeared to be structured so that the survivors of IRS abuses would be central to its activities. Indeed, Phil Fontaine stated that the TRC had to be "partial to the interests of the survivors, because the truth commission, this truth commission is about the survivors."[115] The guiding principles stated at the outset of the mandate that the commission would focus on being victim centred and respect the health and safety of participants. The establishment of a Survivor Committee to provide advice to the Commissioners signalled the importance of survivors' involvement in the TRC's work.[116] The TRC's mandate required national and community events, signalling an intention to focus on the community level as well as the broader national community. The mandate stressed that communities themselves would design the community events.[117] In addition, health supports were provided to participants in order to assist them with the difficult process of providing their histories to the commission. The aspects of the mandate focusing on victims and communities were aimed at assisting the TRC to fulfill this central aspect of a truth commission's work.

These aspects acknowledged, and attempted to avoid, the grief and pain among survivors caused by previous legal mechanisms.

Another drawback of criminal prosecution and civil litigation for IRS survivors was the adversarial nature of the proceedings. Court-based legal mechanisms necessarily involve lawyers, and the quality and quantity of legal counsel are central to how these legal processes unfold. Cross-examinations by defence counsel, or tactics such as multiple motions to dismiss the survivors' cases or to seek medical and therapeutic records, make for a highly combative environment that can take a huge toll on survivors.

The TRC was sought as a mechanism that would operate in a non-adversarial manner. In other contexts, truth commissions have been expected to be less lawyer driven than other legal mechanisms.[118] Although all truth commissions do involve lawyers in their activities to varying degrees, the idea that the negotiators of the Settlement Agreement in Canada gleaned from international examples was to emphasize the focus on victims and reduce the focus on the skill of legal counsel to shape the information gained. This reduced focus on legal personnel arose because sometimes truth commissions are established in environments in which the legal system might be in disarray, with few lawyers and judges left in the country (either alive or not part of the prior regime). It might also be because the number of violations is so large that the prosecutorial system is overwhelmed, and another mechanism is necessary to seek accountability.

A truth commission can also be sought in order to elicit truth telling in an environment in which the adversarial approach of a trial, with its tools such as cross-examination, would be inappropriate. In Canada, where the government and the churches acknowledged that IRS abuses had occurred and that the system had been harmful, the evidence presented to the TRC was not to convince the Commissioners that the abuses had occurred. The TRC occurred separately from the reparations process and other elements of the Settlement Agreement. The purpose of the commission as a separate body was to allow a focus on its distinctive goals: acknowledging and witnessing the IRS experience, promoting awareness of the IRS system and its impacts, and creating a public record of the IRS legacy.[119] These goals suggested a desire for a process less adversarial than the court process. Although in some ways the goal seemed to be a less formal and less lawyer-driven process, significant involvement of lawyers was required to ensure that Schedule N's provisions were respected. For example, the schedule provided that Commissioners

> perform their duties in holding events, in activities, in public meetings, in consultations, in making public statements, and in making their report and recommendations without making any findings or expressing any conclusion or recommendation, regarding the misconduct of any person, unless such findings or information has already been established through legal proceedings, by admission, or by public disclosure by the individual. Further, the Commission shall not make any reference in any of its activities or in its report or recommendations to the possible civil or criminal liability of any person or organization, unless such findings or information about the individual or institution has already been established through legal proceedings.[120]

The TRC, like other public inquiries, could not make findings of criminal or civil liability. However, the difficulty that public inquiries have encountered is that, despite not being able to make such findings, they have faced legal challenges by those who wish to protect themselves in other legal processes that might be influenced by the negative findings of a commission.[121]

Schedule N's broad requirements seeking to avoid findings of misconduct or statements about liability presumably required legally trained persons to monitor the commission for compliance. The same applied to a further requirement that the Commissioners

> shall not name names in their events, activities, public statements, report or recommendations, or make use of personal information or of statements made which identify a person, without the express consent of that individual, unless that information and/or the identity of the person so identified has already been established through legal proceedings, by admission, or by public disclosure by that individual.[122]

Furthermore, *in camera* sessions were required to take any statement that contained names in which wrongdoing was alleged unless the person named had been convicted.[123] Given that there had been few successful prosecutions relative to the number of potential perpetrators from over 100 years of the IRS system,[124] this likely would have meant that virtually all statements that alleged wrongdoing against particular perpetrators needed to be conducted *in camera*. The commission was required to gain the express consent of an individual to "provide to any other proceeding, or for any other use, any personal information, statement made by the individual or any information identifying any person."[125] This broad protection could have triggered any number of legal actions. Furthermore, the TRC was required to "ensure that the conduct of the Commission and its activities [did] not jeopardize any legal proceeding."[126]

For a commission intended to be less adversarial, there were significant aspects of the mandate that required monitoring by lawyers and could well provoke court applications by parties who felt aggrieved by the proceedings. This is not to say that the involvement of lawyers necessarily undermines a truth commission, for most such commissions have considerable involvement of lawyers in their operations. However, there was the potential for the non-adversarial goals of the TRC to be affected negatively by the protections for alleged perpetrators set out in the mandate. The proceedings could have been considerably delayed by procedural wrangling over whether a person could tell her or his story without identifying someone or by having to proceed *in camera* at a moment's notice. Such delays were inherent in the IRS litigation and partly why there was a search for a different legal mechanism to respond to the IRS legacy.

Of course, the decision not to name names might also have been an attempt to avoid concerns about due process (the presumption of innocence unless proven guilty is a fundamental tenet of due process) that themselves can cause delays.[127] Another possibility is that the lack of these powers might indicate that the TRC resulted from a carefully negotiated settlement, with lawyers vetting every clause to ensure that their clients were protected. After all, the last school closed in 1996, so some of the people responsible for the system or for specific harms must still have been alive.

The decision not to allow the naming of names might have been intended to assist with garnering participation from presumed or alleged perpetrators, though "it has been repeatedly illustrated that truth commissions do not entice those known to be responsible for brutal activities to tell their stories."[128] Alleged perpetrators had no incentive to participate in the TRC, but perhaps it was thought that they would be more willing to engage in the process if they knew that they would not be subject to any legal proceedings as a result of their participation. However, in the end, it appears that a slim minority of the statements gathered by the TRC were from former staff of the residential schools.[129]

A truth commission is intended to promote public accountability and combat impunity for human rights violations, so a refusal to name names where there is clear evidence of culpability can attract criticism. Yet, though most truth commissions have the power to name perpetrators, few have done so.[130] And in the Canadian context, the institutional nature of the main "perpetrators" – the government and the churches – alters the dynamic. Although it was possible that some would still be alive, many of the people who staffed the schools or directed government IRS policy were dead by the time of the TRC. Thus, there would be more participation of present-day government and church representatives than of individuals who were directly involved with the IRS system. As parties to the Settlement Agreement, the institutions were expected to participate in the TRC process. Given that most of their representatives would not have been perpetrators themselves of specific abuses, perhaps it is not surprising that the TRC had neither the power to subpoena nor the power to name names, two powers commonly allocated to truth commissions.

Schedule N states that "Canada and the churches will provide all relevant documents in their possession and control" to the TRC subject to privacy and access to information legislation as well as solicitor-client privilege.[131] This clause suggests that, because of the cooperation of the parties with respect to document production, the subpoena power for the TRC was unnecessary. However, this cooperation proved to be elusive, and a great deal of litigation emanated from the TRC's decision to seek survivors' statements in the course of the Independent Assessment Process deposited in the National Centre for Truth and Reconciliation Archive.[132]

Truth commissions that have powers of subpoena, search, and seizure do not typically use them, but the fact that they have those powers gives their requests for document production some weight. Truth commissions that have not had these powers, such as in Guatemala, have been described as "extremely weak."[133] Hayner includes Argentina, Chile, and Haiti in the list of truth commissions that had weaker powers of investigation and suggests that broader powers make a truth commission more effective.[134] However, the decision not to provide such powers to the TRC was presumably in keeping with the decision not to emulate a formal legal process. Furthermore, as noted by former Chairperson LaForme, the fact that the courts would oversee the Settlement Agreement added weight to the provisions requiring document production.[135] If a party considered that an aspect of the Settlement Agreement was not being implemented as envisioned, then it could petition a court for review. And of course the churches and the government had an obligation to "provide all relevant documents."[136] However, the TRC itself had to go to court to get disclosure of relevant records. As noted in its final report, "[o]nce the Commission's document-collection processes began, it became increasingly apparent that Canada would not produce numerous documents that appeared to be relevant to the Commission's work."[137] The negotiators had eschewed the powers of search and seizure in favour of a less adversarial process.[138] These aspects were framed as befitting the guiding principles of voluntariness and "do no harm" that informed the negotiations, but depended on the cooperation of all parties, which in the case of Canada proved to be difficult to obtain.

As the foregoing discussion suggests, the TRC's mandate provided a number of opportunities to differ from past legal mechanisms and fulfill the goal of being a less adversarial, more holistic process. However, the TRC had to rely on the cooperation of the parties to realize its potential to avoid the pitfalls of past legal mechanisms.

Creating a Historical Record, Educating the Public

A further reason that survivors sought a truth commission in the IRS negotiations was the widespread ignorance among non-Indigenous Canadians about the IRS system and its profound and continuing effects on

Indigenous communities. The advantage of a truth commission for combatting such ignorance is the ability to create an incontrovertible historical record and enable significant public education. In this section, I consider the challenges and possibilities for the TRC in fulfilling these goals.

Creating a Historical Record

The TRC was tasked with creating a record of the IRS system and its impacts. One of the most important things that truth commissions do is report on what they have heard. A truth commission, by setting out a historical record in its report, makes it very difficult to challenge the human rights violations detailed in the report. Such reports provide official acknowledgment of abuses that thereafter cannot be denied. They also serve as an important tool for public education, creating wide knowledge of the events chronicled. Truth commissions study the overall patterns in the information that they collect through testimony and research. Unlike a criminal trial, they are focused less on what happened in individual cases and more on how individual cases form a bigger systemic picture. For example, in Argentina, the commission amassed and reviewed the complaints of torture of political prisoners to produce a report on the military regime's practices over a fifteen-year period.[139] The Argentinian report, *Nunca Más* (Never Again), was an immediate bestseller, became one of the bestselling books in the country's history, and has been reprinted over twenty times.[140] The Chilean report was released by then President Patricio Aylwin during a televised address to the nation, and the publication of the El Salvadoran report was considered a major political event.[141] Over 2,000 people, "with most in the audience in tears from the impact of hearing the truth finally and authoritatively spoken,"[142] attended the public release of the Guatemalan report.

Although gaining "the truth" about the IRS experience might have been educational for non-Indigenous people,[143] it could often be retraumatizing for survivors. In addition, the truth will be different for each person depending on his or her perspective. Some church or government representatives (and even some survivors) would resist the idea that the IRS system was wholly negative, preferring to focus on the notion that some children did receive an education and that some survivors recall their teachers with fondness.[144] Still, the truth that the IRS system existed and that it has been devastating for Indigenous peoples was already known to them, but this truth was not well known to the majority of Canadians:

> Consensus that residential school experience was injurious in itself, not just in instances of physical and sexual abuse, is shared by only a small proportion of Canadian citizens, in contrast to the view of most First Nations, Inuit and Métis people.[145]

Part of the TRC's challenge was to conduct its work in the face of significant gaps between the knowledge and understanding of the IRS system among many non-Indigenous people compared with many Indigenous people.[146] These gaps arise from long-standing beliefs about the histories and intentions of government policies and the legacies of those policies, such as cycles of dependence and negative social indicators.[147] In other contexts, truth commissions have attempted to create a more complete historical record of a tragic period in a state's history by rounding out the state's version of events with information gained from investigation, records, and testimony.

As with other truth commissions, the TRC was not likely to expose facts that were previously unknown; rather, it could "make an indispensable contribution in acknowledging these facts."[148] In Canada, the facts about the IRS experience might have been publicly available, but the truth was still resisted in the dominant narrative. This narrative said that the schools were created and run with the best intentions and that in hindsight some of the methods used and some of the individuals involved might have been overly harsh or abusive. In conflict with that narrative was an account that viewed the schools as one attempt to obliterate the Indigenous cultures in what is now Canada.[149] The IRS system was only one component of a larger colonial project that continues to be embodied in many aspects of the *Indian Act*. However, as a poll in 2008 indicated, non-Indigenous Canadians would have been largely unaware of the systemic aspect of the IRS legacy.[150] By the end of its mandate, the TRC had managed to raise awareness among non-Indigenous Canadians about the history of Indian residential schools in Canada, if not the systemic aspect of their legacy, with roughly half of Canadians being aware of the TRC's work by 2015.[151] A strong majority of those polled in 2015 agreed with the recommendation that Indigenous history, including the residential schools, be included in standard Canadian school curricula.[152]

At the outset of the TRC's work, the fact that the government issued an unequivocal apology might have helped to refute the myth held by many non-Indigenous Canadians that an Indian residential school was akin to a bad boarding school in which individual teachers were abusive. The apology acknowledged that the IRS system was intended to force the assimilation of Indigenous children – "to kill the Indian in the child."[153] The importance of the work that a commission such as the TRC must do, at the outset, to address these differing narratives cannot be underestimated if the reconciliation aspect of its mandate is to have any chance of success.[154] Despite the enormity of the TRC's task, it is possible that viewing the IRS system as only one component of a larger colonial project made the TRC's mandate more manageable compared with the broader mandate of RCAP. Perhaps RCAP was unable to garner and sustain interest because of the massive scope and overwhelming weight of its mandate, activities, and findings. Perhaps Canadians found that a commission addressing the legacy of residential schools provided a more manageable way to learn about and understand the larger causes of the policy under which the schools were created. Still, given that the TRC was precluded from identifying perpetrators in its report and not permitted to enable survivors to identify anyone by name, the truth that it told about the IRS experience was necessarily incomplete. The TRC Report therefore needed to address the broader truth about the IRS system itself, identifying the structures and institutions that created and perpetuated the toll on Indigenous peoples. The ability to focus on – and provide a detailed view of – the larger picture became a strength of the TRC. Its final report situates the individual stories of survivors in the larger picture of colonial policy and declares at the outset that the policy, with the establishment and operation of residential schools as a central element, amounted to "cultural genocide."[155] There was no requirement for a report at the end of the five-year mandate of the TRC, but the lengthy report produced enabled the commission to assess the material that it had reviewed and heard in order to identify structural or systemic issues.

In its 2011 interim report, entitled *They Came for the Children,* and in its 2015 final report (six volumes), the TRC provided a detailed and convincing historical record of the IRS system in Canada. No one in the country will ever be able to say that these things never happened or that the terrible abuses suffered by Indigenous children were inflicted by a few "bad apples." The reports leave no doubt about the part that the residential schools were intended to play in the destruction of Indigenous languages, cultures, and communities.

Public Education

One of the most important things that a truth commission can do is to engage the wider public with its work. The utility of the commission is lessened if it compiles a history destined to sit silently on a library shelf.[156] Truth commissions are tools for educating a society about a chapter of its past in order to raise awareness and decrease the likelihood of human rights violations being repeated. The public education mandate of a truth commission is central to its social function, particularly its ability to foster social accountability for a shared past. To fulfill this social function, the process requires public support. Gaining that support requires public awareness of a commission's work. A commission must create a narrative that can form the basis of national reconciliation, but the commission must first "manage to penetrate the collective consciousness of the people."[157]

How can this be achieved? Hayner and Freeman set out factors likely to improve the effectiveness of a truth commission. In particular, they note the importance of public support for the establishment of a truth commission; the presence of a vigorous and engaged civil society (in particular strong victims' groups, human rights groups, religious leaders, and intellectuals); widespread social identification with the victims of the abuses; vocal and independent media; and persistent international attention and pressure.[158] The Canadian TRC did not have the benefit of most of these factors. It is unclear how wide public support was for its establishment, since the Canadian public was not formally consulted in the IRS negotiations. Although Canada has strong civil society organizations, there was no organized civil society coalition vocally supporting the TRC's work. There was some positive media coverage while the commission was under way, but the TRC was not ubiquitous in either the domestic press or the international press. It is a testament to the work of the Commissioners and those who engaged in the work of the commission that the Canadian public did become more knowledgeable about the IRS system by the time the TRC had completed its work.[159]

Two areas critical for truth commissions in achieving the kind of support that Hayner and Freeman describe are media engagement and civil society support.

Media Engagement

As acknowledged by one of the TRC staff members, although the IRS experience affected many Indigenous people, most Canadians were ignorant of this reality, so "[o]ne of the big challenges is to raise awareness. We're going to have to be a bit of a megaphone."[160] Unfortunately, at first, the Commissioners came to the attention of Canadians mainly in the process of stepping down.[161] The new Commissioners had to be relentless in gaining media and community attention in order to promote the aims of the TRC.[162] Certainly, in a country as large as Canada, the media were a critical tool in engaging people unable to participate in the TRC's national events because they were so distant from where they lived.

An unusual aspect of the TRC was that its mandate did not direct that it would hold "formal hearings."[163] Rather, Schedule N refers to receiving "statements" and holding "sessions," "consultations," and "public events." Although this distinction was no doubt in part to protect the privacy of survivors, it also could have served to shield the government and the churches from public scrutiny. It meant that the TRC would not be holding an activity that is virtually a hallmark of truth commissions elsewhere. Most people associate truth commissions with the South African TRC, which held nationally televised formal public hearings. It appears that the Canadian TRC held sessions that looked and felt like hearings, in that survivors provided testimony, but the TRC avoided calling these events formal hearings.

The TRC held its first national event in June 2010 in Winnipeg at the National Forks Historic Site. Thousands of people attended and heard survivors speak about their experiences. Subsequent national events were held in Inuvik, Halifax, Saskatoon, Montreal, Vancouver, and Edmonton. In addition, the Commissioners held dozens of smaller community "hearings" and events across the country.

Truth commissions in more recent years often have had televised hearings. In South Africa, public hearings of its TRC were broadcast for over two years. In Ghana, there was daily television and radio coverage of the National Reconciliation Commission hearings. This sort of consistent national coverage provides the public with the opportunity to see and hear testimony. The International Center for Transitional Justice, a New York–based non-governmental organization, has offered media training workshops in various countries undertaking truth commission processes. Such workshops are intended to raise the level of media literacy with respect to the truth commission process and the more victim-centred approach of a truth commission as opposed to a court proceeding. People might expect public hearings with scenes of confrontation between victims and perpetrators rather than the less adversarial process negotiated for the TRC in Canada. Media training can also sensitize members of the media to the issues to be heard by the commission, the appropriate treatment of victims, and the role of the media in public education.

The Greensboro Truth and Reconciliation Commission, a non-governmental project to address a racist incident in Greensboro, North Carolina, held sensitivity training workshops at which guidelines were developed for media outlets planning to cover the proceedings.[164] The Greensboro Commission also had a half-hour weekly talk show on its proceedings.[165] In Ghana, the Civil Society Coalition on National Reconciliation organized media workshops on coverage of the national reconciliation process, including one for media owners and regulators, out of which guidelines were developed for coverage of the process.[166]

·   Other truth commissions have held institutional hearings to focus on the issues arising in certain sectors of the public service or society at large. For instance, South Africa had hearings on the legal profession and the judiciary, and Ghana had institutional hearings on the security sector, media, prisons, the legal profession, and the judiciary. The purpose is to reveal the structural and institutional nature of the human rights violations that occurred in order to recommend ways to prevent future reoccurrences, regardless of the individuals in charge of or working for those institutions.

Although the TRC did not hold institutional hearings in the same way as other truth commissions, it nonetheless reported on the ongoing impacts of government policies on different areas of Indigenous people's lives, including the crucial connection to current child removal policies. As noted by Grand Chief Edward John,

> [t]oday we find that over 50% of all children in government care are aboriginal and in the north region of the province the percentage is a staggering 77% ... It is estimated that there are three times the number of children in government care now than there were children in residential schools at the height of their operations.[167]

The TRC's first Call to Action addressed the need to reduce the number of children in care, but recent census data indicate that 52.2 percent of the number of children in foster care are still Indigenous when they are only 7.7 percent of the population of children in Canada.[168] Naming and making recommendations to address these legacies are necessary if reoccurrences of abuses such as those in residential schools are to be prevented.

The TRC did encourage the public to attend its events and activities, and Commissioners participated in many discussions and events during their tenure in order to raise awareness of the TRC's work.[169] The comprehensive TRC Report will be a lasting record of the IRS history and legacy, and the ninety-four calls to action, which cover a broad range of sectors in Canadian society (business, education, government, sports, the arts, etc.), provide a framework for addressing the damaged relationship between Indigenous and non-Indigenous people in Canada. Calling them Calls to Action rather than the usual "recommendations" echoed the TRC's efforts to engage the public. The Calls to Action do not rely solely on the government to implement many of the recommendations of the TRC; rather, some of them are aimed at community leaders and members of various professions that can make change in different sectors of Canadian society.

Civil Society Involvement

The mandate as set out in Schedule N of the Settlement Agreement, as noted earlier, frames the TRC as part of a process of "rebuilding and renewing ... the relationship between Aboriginal and non-Aboriginal Canadians," requiring "commitment from ... the people of Canada." To work toward reconciliation of Canadian society as a whole, there needs to be active, sustained, and significant outreach to civil society beyond the parties to the Settlement Agreement. Such processes of dialogue and consultation help to generate awareness and then cultivate ownership of the national reconciliation process.

The involvement of civil society – such as student organizations, unions, faith-based groups, cultural organizations, arts groups, and political and human rights organizations – is critical to the success of any truth commission, and it is particularly important for any commission that also purports to be a reconciliation commission. Civil society organizations represent diverse segments of the population and have grassroots networks that can lend useful assistance to a truth commission. Involving civil society is important for gaining citizen participation and support in a truth and reconciliation process. In Ghana, the draft National Reconciliation Commission bill was circulated publicly. The Civil Society Coalition on National Reconciliation, consisting of a broad spectrum of religious, community, academic, and other public interests, was formed to support the project of reconciliation.[170] The coalition and others held a conference to discuss comparative situations in order to determine what Ghana could learn from international experiences and what would be important to include in the Ghanaian context.[171] As in South Africa, in Ghana consultations were held across the country to gain input on the commission's draft legislation before its passage in the Parliament and certainly before inauguration of the commission.

In Canada, a previous example of civil society engagement in a commission of inquiry process was the Coalition for a Public Inquiry into

Ipperwash, formed on 10 December 1997, by a broad base of Indigenous and non-Indigenous partners, including cultural, political, religious, labour, human rights, student, and First Nations organizations and activists. This coalition advocated for a public process to seek the truth about the events surrounding the death of Dudley George, killed by the Ontario Provincial Police during a 1995 unarmed protest at Ipperwash Provincial Park in Ontario. The coalition garnered international attention from organizations such as Amnesty International and from UN bodies.[172] An ongoing example is that of the BC Coalition on Missing and Murdered Indigenous Women and Girls, formed during the BC Missing Women Inquiry (MWI, discussed in the next chapter). This coalition continues to hold the BC government to account with regard to the implementation (or lack thereof) of the MWI's recommendations and has advocated for implementation of the national inquiry's calls for justice.

Although the Canadian TRC resulted from a legal settlement that included parties representing some components of civil society, they were by no means broadly representative of Canadian society as a whole. Some of the major Indigenous organizations were involved in the TRC process, but not all Indigenous organizations were parties to the Settlement Agreement. Large swaths of the non-Indigenous public had no involvement in the TRC. When asked about his goal for the commission, Justice Sinclair stated that

> [a]t the end of the day I want the survivors to be able to say that they were heard. I want the public to say that they heard them. And I want the general society, I want Canadian society, to be able to say that now they know what they can do about it.[173]

Achieving this goal would have been easier if civil society organizations, beyond the parties to the Settlement Agreement, had become involved and supported the work of the TRC. This could have been instigated by outreach from the commission itself, but given its limited resources it would have been useful if the parties to the Settlement Agreement had connected with other civil society organizations to form a broad coalition to support and to increase awareness of the TRC's work. Sadly, this did not occur to the degree that it could have, given the range of civil society organizations interested in the TRC's work in the Canadian context.

The Truth and Reconciliation Commission and National Reconciliation

A final reason that a truth commission can be attractive in an established democracy is the possibility of encouraging societal reconciliation. In Canada, Indigenous legal institutions and systems have often been ignored and devalued.[174] Any attempt at reconciliation in Canada must proceed with an acute awareness of this history and acceptance of it as true. The advice of RCAP must be adopted: Canada should respect the laws of the peoples with whom it hopes to reconcile.[175]

Reconciliation is a concept often discussed under the rubric of restorative justice.[176] Whereas retributive justice emphasizes the punishment of perpetrators, restorative justice focuses on repairing a harm done: "[A] key defining element of restorative justice is its privileging of reconciliation over retribution."[177] Truth commissions, with their focus on victims and communities, are particularly suited to restorative rather than retributive justice approaches to addressing human rights violations.[178] Restorative justice focuses on harms to relationships: "The goal of restorative justice is not a return to the past but rather the creation of a different future founded on relationships of equal concern, respect, and dignity."[179] Respect is an important ingredient if reconciliation is the goal, as noted by Marlene Brant Castellano:

> When violations involve segments of the same society who are destined to go on living together, the goal of reconciliation raises the large issue of relationship between peoples and the establishment or re-establishment of dignity and mutual respect.[180]

The focus of restorative justice on healing the relationship between peoples finds a reflection in the TRC's mandate.[181] In the transitional justice context, mechanisms such as apologies, commemorations, reparations, and truth commissions are viewed as means to achieve restorative justice principles. Restorative justice is a multifaceted process, and often, as in South Africa, truth commissions are expected to address all of its elements.

Canada's TRC was not asked to do all the work of redress because the elements of commemoration and reparation were structured as different parts of the Settlement Agreement. The commission did not need to determine the compensation that survivors should receive or to duplicate the commemorative work already being done by the Aboriginal Healing Foundation (at least until its cancellation in 2014). An additional element critical to the process of reconciliation that the TRC did not have to address was that of an apology.

An apology from the federal government for the IRS system was not part of the Settlement Agreement, though Chief Justice Brenner of the British Columbia Supreme Court took the unusual step of suggesting in his reasons for the decision approving the Settlement Agreement that an apology would be appropriate:

> Although I am making no order and I am issuing no directions, I would respectfully request counsel for Canada to ask that the Prime Minister give consideration to issuing a full and unequivocal apology on behalf of the people of Canada in the House of Commons.[182]

Many who called for an apology referenced the fact that IRS survivors were dying at the rate of five a day and would not live to see a post-TRC apology.[183] As noted in the discussion of RCAP in Chapter 3, the "Statement of Reconciliation" offered by the government in 1998 was not viewed as an apology by many survivors. The Minister of Indian Affairs, rather than the Prime Minister, offered the apology; it was offered at a press conference, not in the House of Commons; and it acknowledged only victims of physical and sexual abuse rather than all of the harms inflicted by the IRS system. In contrast, incoming Prime Minister of Australia Kevin Rudd offered an official apology to the Stolen Generations as the first official order of business in the new Parliament on 13 February 2008.[184] Outgoing Prime Minister John Howard had steadfastly refused to apologize. The symbolism of an official apology is enormous. The person who offers it, and where and when, are all imbued with meaning.

The role of apologies in truth and reconciliation processes is complex. A government or executive might offer an apology after a truth commission has reported, as in Chile. There the new regime accepted responsibility for the violations committed by the prior regime. Such apologies indicate the assumption of public accountability for atrocities, or they might be part of a process of repairing the moral reputations of a state and the victims whose reputations had been attacked by the state under the prior regime.[185] Apologies can be offered as symbolic reparations to victims of atrocities; conversely, they can be withheld in circumstances in which a government might fear opening itself to liability for past actions, or they might be offered only once most victims of state oppression are long dead, as in Canada with respect to the internment of Ukrainian Canadians during the First World War, the imposition of the head tax on Chinese immigrants in the late nineteenth century and early twentieth century, or the internment of Japanese Canadians during the Second World War.

After years of refusal by different administrations, the federal government finally decided to offer a formal apology in Parliament for the IRS legacy. The minority Conservative government of Stephen Harper, elected in January 2006, had resisted making the apology prior to the Settlement Agreement coming into effect. An April 2007 motion by Liberal Member of Parliament Gary Merasty calling on Parliamentarians to apologize preceded a vote in the House of Commons on 1 May issuing an apology for the IRS system. Still, in June that year, at a conference on the TRC at the University of Calgary, then Minister of Indian Affairs Jim Prentice obliquely indicated that the government would apologize only once the TRC concluded its mandate. Quoting Desmond Tutu, he stated that "[y]ou cannot forgive what you do not know."[186]

The IRS Settlement Agreement was finalized in September 2007, and the TRC was inaugurated on 1 June 2008. On 11 June that year, the government gave its long-awaited apology to survivors of the IRS system.[187] In contrast to the 1998 "Statement of Reconciliation" offered by the Minister of Indian Affairs at a press conference,[188] the Prime Minister gave this apology in the House of Commons. Many were present in the gallery of the House of Commons, and many others watched live coverage of the event across the country. The leaders of the other federal parties represented in Parliament also gave apologies. The leaders of five national Indigenous organizations responded from the floor of the House.

The apology received a generally positive response from survivors and the public,[189] and it marked a rare moment of awareness among the general Canadian population. A poll taken just after the apology found an unusually high level of awareness: 83 percent of those surveyed were aware of the apology.[190] Thus, the moment when the government offered an apology to survivors of the residential schools managed to attract the attention of a majority of Canadians. The value of the apology as a tool for public education was considerable, a fact suggesting that the media attention was an effective support to the government's message. The apology was covered live on national television and widely reported in radio, television, online, and print media.

The apology also provided the TRC with a good start, for the government acknowledged the truth of the IRS system's harms, enabling the commission to commence its work without having to convince the country of the IRS legacy. This allowed the TRC to focus on creating the historical record of the IRS system and educating the public to ensure that such an injustice is not repeated. Nonetheless, the commission operated under a Conservative government that did not have a history of strong support for broader political and economic equality for Indigenous peoples.[191] With regard to the other elements of restorative justice, truth commissions are often expected to make recommendations on appropriate reparations for victims, such as financial compensation that might enable them to improve their quality of life. These recommendations are adopted to varying degrees by the state. In the Canadian context, the reparations had already been determined in large part through the Common Experience Payment and Independent Assessment Process. In addition, the federal government made an apology prior to the commencement of the substantive work of the TRC.

The fact that the IRS negotiators decided to have the TRC in addition to and separate from these other aspects of the settlement suggests that there was something to be gained from the commission process itself. That is, the negotiators expected something from the TRC that would differ from the usual truth commission results of making recommendations for commemoration, apology, and reparation. There was something about the *process* itself that was valued, something unique to the Canadian context.

The Role of Public Education

How well a truth commission educates the public about its work determines its ability to garner public support. A high level of public support can bolster a commission's credibility and thus its reputation, which in turn can smooth the way for the commission to access information and address the needs of victims. Also important for maintaining its credibility is a truth commission's management of public expectations about its work. This is another task that does not appear in any written mandate for a truth and reconciliation commission. Such a commission must be extremely conscious of the expectations that it can produce among survivors of human rights violations.[192] In the Canadian context, these expectations would be of an order entirely different from and more complex than those of the non-Indigenous public. Truth commissions have often raised expectations among victims that there will be some resolution to their situation because the very existence of a commission suggests that it will make a difference. Expectations can be even higher when the commission seeks not just truth but also reconciliation.

Another challenge for the TRC was that most of the testimony that it received came from survivors. This fact potentially created the appearance that the TRC would rely on the survivors to do the work to be (re)conciled with or perhaps (re)integrated into Canadian society. The TRC had to be careful not to reinforce the idea (rejected by RCAP) that the government could avoid responsibility by expecting IRS survivors to do the work of healing themselves. The means of reconciliation include truth telling, acknowledgment of past wrongs, reparations for the victims, addressing the structural causes of the wrongs, and rebalancing between societal groups to prevent the harms from reoccurring. The TRC needed to find a way to include the non-Indigenous public such that they would acknowledge that the IRS system was everyone's problem to address. Restorative justice provides a framework for reconciliation,[193] but achieving reconciliation at a societal level rather than a community level is a significant challenge. How can the truth commission mechanism assist in achieving the goal of reconciliation?

One way for a commission to assist with reconciliation in the Canadian context would be to reframe the discussion with respect to who needs to do the reconciling. Although a "hazy" concept,[194] reconciliation in the transitional justice realm refers to repairing "torn relationships between ethnic, religious, regional, or political groups, between neighbours, and between political communities. In short, societal healing."[195] The "societal healing" form of reconciliation found in the transitional justice literature is different from the form that has entered Canadian legal discourse as articulated by the Supreme Court of Canada.[196] In cases such as *Delgamuukw*, the Court developed a concept of reconciliation as a legal process of balancing the fact that Indigenous peoples lived in the territory now called Canada prior to settlers arriving with *de facto* Crown sovereignty.[197] Mark Walters refers to this approach to reconciliation as "a one-sided or mechanical way or as just another way of balancing competing interests."[198] However, this concept of reconciliation became woven into further judgments of the Court in ensuing years.[199] Despite one scholar's view that the Court's conception of reconciliation as enunciated in *Delgamuukw* should be imported into the transitional justice framework, there is much in these decisions that warrants caution.[200] The later "duty to consult" cases, such as *Haida Nation* and *Taku River*,[201] provide a more positive approach to reconciliation insofar as they seem to suggest that it is not that Indigenous peoples must reconcile themselves to the assertion of Crown sovereignty but that Crown sovereignty might not be legitimate unless the Indigenous peoples and non-Indigenous people in question have made a treaty.[202] If the concept of reconciliation found in the Supreme Court's jurisprudence is to inform the process of reconciliation, then it is the approach found in these later cases – emphasizing elements of respect, mutuality, and reciprocity – that would be a more fruitful basis for discussions of reconciliation.[203] The process of reconciliation must be framed as a mutual process to be engaged in by Indigenous and non-Indigenous people alike; it should not be a one-sided process.

Although the IRS Settlement Agreement negotiators emphatically sought to distinguish the TRC from the South African version, it is important to glean from the comparative experience some realistic guidance on what a truth commission can achieve. Not every truth commission has framed its goal as reconciliation of the country, but "[t]hose that have – including South Africa's TRC and the National Commission on Truth and

Reconciliation in Chile – have found it to be a very difficult mission."[204] Reconciliation might or might not occur on an individual or national level; calling the exercise "truth and reconciliation" sets up both concepts as goals. However, no one can declare a person or nation to be reconciled. In addition, it is possible that truth (a slippery concept at the best of times) and reconciliation will be viewed completely differently depending on those asked. Some might see that these objectives have been achieved, whereas others will dispute that perception. The latter might be concerned that those in power appear to support reconciliation for their own political purposes:

> In a political context, those who want nothing done may cynically plan reconciliation merely as a smokescreen. Victims, on the other hand, may perceive and condemn it as a code word for simply forgetting. For those who have to live with their own pain and trauma, the term is indeed extremely sensitive. As a victim of apartheid told the South African Truth and Reconciliation Commission (TRC), "Reconciliation is only in the vocabulary of those who can afford it. It is non-existent to a person whose self-respect has been stripped away and poverty is a festering wound that consumes his soul."[205]

This sentiment could be expressed by an IRS survivor in Canada given the chronic poverty and other negative socio-economic indicators for many Indigenous peoples.

The term "reconciliation" implies that the parties were once whole, then experienced a rift, and now must be made whole again. In colonial settings, this is not the case. The relationship between Indigenous and settler people in Canada was one of nations encountering nations in which one never truly acknowledged the sovereignty of the other and engaged in its oppression and marginalization. Indigenous peoples never agreed to the denial of their sovereignty, cultures, or identities.[206] Thus, Canadian society did not begin with a harmonious relationship of mutual respect and recognition that later fell apart. Here reconciliation must refer to "transformative" as opposed to "restorative" reconciliation. Will Kymlicka and Bashir Bashir describe these two modes of reconciliation – "[t]he restorative dimension seeks to restore and heal a pre-existing 'we,' by closing up a temporary breach, while the transformative dimension seeks to create a new 'we,' which requires opening up new possibilities that did not exist before."[207] Another commentator notes that reconciliation on a national level must be at least in part a political process that includes acknowledgment of the political and legal rights of Indigenous peoples.[208] This highlights the difficulty with public expectations that can be created when a body called a truth and *reconciliation* commission is created. The TRC could not reasonably have been expected to reconcile on its own the entire relationship between Indigenous and non-Indigenous people in Canada. On the face of it, the TRC's mandate was limited to the IRS system: to create a historical record of that system and to educate the public about its legacy. It would be impossible to heal in a few years a wound inflicted over generations.

The Australian context is instructive given the parallels between the countries' treatment of their Indigenous peoples. The Howard government largely rejected the report on the Stolen Generations, though the Rudd government changed course and offered an apology. Erin Daly and Jeremy Sarkin assert that the truths revealed in Australia about the Stolen Generations have "resulted in greater understanding among white Australians of the past experiences of Aboriginals and of their present claims for cultural identity (and social support)."[209] Like Canada, Australia has social factors that might favour reconciliation: The Indigenous population is small, the public is generally liberal, many of the perpetrators are dead, and most people think that racial oppression is unacceptable.[210] But the same factors can work against reconciliation because continued power imbalances will make it difficult for a process of reconciliation to take root properly.[211] When he was Lieutenant Governor of Ontario, James Bartleman, a member of the Chippewas of Mnjikaning First Nation, warned that, unless Canadian society as a whole signalled that it was serious about according equal economic and social rights to Indigenous Canadians, the TRC Commissioners would find that "they have been shod with shoes of clay. There can be no true reconciliation and Canada cannot claim it is a just and equal society unless economic and social equality is accorded to Aboriginal people."[212]

How could the TRC have contributed to a broader sense of reconciliation in a society only prepared to address these power imbalances in an incremental way?[213] As Llewellyn observes, the TRC's mandate did not provide much detail about the reconciliation aspect of its work.[214] Castellano recalls the observation in the RCAP Report that, in the search for reconciliation between peoples, it is extremely important that the leaders of public institutions adopt a more respectful stance.[215] The fact that the mandate did not provide much detail offered an opportunity for the TRC to interpret its possibilities broadly. Although the commission had to exercise caution about what it could reasonably accomplish in the five years that it was granted, perhaps the IRS system could be a springboard for the exploration of broader issues in Indigenous-non-Indigenous relations in Canada. After all, there was a distinction in the TRC's mandate – the commission was expected to address the IRS *system,* but it was also expected to address the IRS *legacy.* The IRS system can be quantified in terms of how many schools, where they operated, for how long, and under which government directives. The IRS legacy is a much more amorphous question. The TRC was able to complete an effective historical study of the IRS system while exploring broader political questions in its discussion of the IRS legacy. This included situating that legacy within colonialism; making connections between residential schools and socio-economic conditions in Indigenous communities; considering the levels of violence, criminalization, marginalization, and discrimination experienced by Indigenous people; and assessing myriad other instances of systemic violence. Again, in addition to the importance of leadership, the process employed in the interpretation of the mandate was critical to the TRC's ability to fulfill that mandate.

Conclusion

The IRS Settlement Agreement and the negotiations that produced it created the unique mandate and structure of the TRC. These negotiations occurred in the Canadian context that had exhibited some of the reasons that a truth commission might be sought in an established democracy: the inadequacy of other legal mechanisms, the desire to create a historical

record, and, in the process, the possibility of educating the public and
fostering national reconciliation. Eduardo Gonzales lists the advantages
that Canada had compared with other states in holding a truth commission,
including the government's apology, the presence of "sophisticated advocacy institutions" that assisted survivors, and the Settlement Agreement
on truth telling and reparations. He also claims that Canada's efforts with
respect to the IRS legacy have garnered "enormous international attention
and support."[216] Gonzales states that, unlike most societies that seek to
inaugurate a truth commission, Canada was not emerging from a period
of prolonged or significant violence that had left legal and governance institutions in disarray.[217] Nonetheless, even if Canada does have certain
advantages compared with other countries establishing truth commissions,
it has some challenges ahead:

> Reconciliation in the context of Indian residential schools presents
> some unique challenges ... Multiple violations of the human dignity of
> Aboriginal peoples over generations and their relative powerlessness in
> the face of public institutions have created distrust that public dialogue
> can bring about change. Past experience in peacemaking and restorative
> justice provides tools for bringing parties together to engage in dialogue,
> but the chemistry that transforms encounter into mutual, hopeful en-
> gagement remains mysterious.[218]

The IRS survivors sought a legal mechanism different from those that
have been tried so far in Canada to address the IRS legacy. In its mandate,
the TRC was designed to fulfill the goals of the parties. However, as with
any public inquiry, much depended on how the Commissioners interpreted and implemented that mandate. The TRC differed from the typical
public inquiry model in several ways. It had multiple Commissioners, one
of whom was not legally trained. The structure included an advisory committee composed of survivors. It lacked the powers of search, seizure, and
subpoena. In addition to compiling a factual record, its mandate focused
on reconciliation and healing. In this, it was able to build on the apology
as well as the reparation and commemoration aspects of the Settlement

Agreement. The TRC explicitly foregrounded its social function as an institution designed to explore the truth of the IRS system and educate the public about its legacy.

In interpreting and implementing the TRC mandate, the Commissioners made connections to the broader picture of Indigenous-non-Indigenous relations beyond the IRS system itself. Like Berger, the TRC Commissioners took a broad approach to their mandate and proceeded with the necessary historical knowledge of and respect for Indigenous cultures to address properly the issues between the parties. They were critically impeded by the commission's administrative structure, created as a department of the federal Ministry of Indian Affairs, a ministry with a long and deeply problematic history in this country. The lack of structural independence, including budgetary constraints and other issues flowing from administrative regulation, inhibited the ability of both sets of Commissioners to carry out their Herculean task within the time period mandated by the terms of the Settlement Agreement.

The TRC had an enormously challenging path given that IRS survivors expected the commission to set the country on a healing journey and that some Indigenous people and non-Indigenous people alike viewed the TRC with skepticism. The very idea of reconciliation through the TRC as I have presented it throughout this book is rejected by some Indigenous scholars, while some non-Indigenous critics suggested that the residential schools provided an education and denied the complicity of the schools in attempted genocide.[219]

The TRC followed decades of other attempts to redress the injustices produced by the IRS experience. Many survivors were engaged in the Settlement Agreement process,[220] and each had to decide whether the potentially traumatizing cost of participation in the TRC's process was worth the potentially healing benefit. Most non-Indigenous Canadians did not have to make the same calculation for their own participation. There was really nothing to prompt them to do so. No part of the Settlement Agreement involved vast numbers of non-Indigenous Canadians, thereby causing them to pay attention to the process. They generally did not see that the process had anything to do with them. Without a significant effort by the TRC to engage them, the wider public would not have realized that there was a benefit to participating in the TRC process and a cost to ignoring it – either helping to reconcile the relationship between Indigenous and non-Indigenous people or consigning it to the heap of failed promises and unresolved issues that litter our shared history.

My discussion of the Berger Inquiry in Chapter 2 included how leaders who exhibit qualities of humility, openness, and respect can positively shape a commission, and the importance of a sustained media strategy for gaining public interest in the commission's work and educating the public about the issues before the commission. Berger paid attention to the importance of process in structuring the operations of his inquiry so that people directly involved in the pipeline question and members of the larger public all took an interest in its development. Of course, the fact that the Berger Inquiry was set up with a modicum of independence not enjoyed by the TRC is a critical aspect of the picture. The elements of leadership and process that shaped the TRC form a basis as well for the following discussion of the National Inquiry into MMIWG.

5

Inquiries and the Crisis of Missing and Murdered Indigenous Women and Girls

My purpose in writing this book is to provide an analysis of the commission of inquiry mechanism in order to improve how these inquiries function in Canada, particularly those established to address issues in relation to Indigenous peoples. At the outset of the book, I described a conversation with Meg Cywink about the National Inquiry into MMIWG. Meg voiced a widening concern about the lack of transparency and apparent dysfunction of the inquiry as it progressed. What went wrong? How does the National Inquiry measure up regarding the leadership and process aspects that I have identified?

In this chapter, I focus on public inquiries (Manitoba's Aboriginal Justice Inquiry, the Oppal Commission in British Columbia, and the National Inquiry into MMIWG), along with a number of other domestic and international processes, that have made recommendations to address the tragedy of MMIW. I explore the dire failure of governments and institutions to implement known methods to prevent violence against Indigenous women and girls.

My experiences as a lawyer trained in Canada who keenly observed a truth commission in West Africa and the TRC in Canada, who has practised Aboriginal law,[1] and who has worked as a women's rights advocate have shaped my views on public inquiries and their ability to address societal ruptures. This background situated me as one of the many advocates who added my voice to those of Indigenous women activists calling for a national public inquiry into the violence against Indigenous women and girls in

Canada that results in murders and disappearances out of all proportion to their percentage of the population.

I joined the call for a national inquiry even after the "debacle" that was the British Columbia Missing Women Inquiry, run by Commissioner Wally Oppal, reporting in 2012.[2] That inquiry was fatally flawed from the outset. Yet I still believed that a well-run national inquiry could move us forward, particularly on the heels of the Truth and Reconciliation Commission. After so many years of advocacy by Indigenous women leaders, in 2015, after the TRC released its report and its Calls to Action that included a call for a national inquiry into missing and murdered Indigenous women and girls, there was remarkable public support for such an inquiry. Indeed, the Liberals made it a part of their election platform, and when elected Prime Minister Justin Trudeau announced that a national inquiry would be established.

With the National Inquiry now complete, I acknowledge the sacrifice and participation of MMIW families in its process and the dedication and difficult work that the staff and Commissioners put into the inquiry as well as the potential utility of the report and its Calls for Justice. However, I view the National Inquiry as a major missed opportunity to shift the narrative in Canada with respect to Indigenous peoples and with regard to violence against Indigenous women and girls in particular. My disappointment arises from the unmet potential for a well-led and properly implemented inquiry to be a pedagogical moment for the country.

This disillusionment is compounded by the fact that only a few years earlier the BC MWI travelled a similar path. Established with the potential to explicate and prevent further tragedy for women in the Downtown Eastside of Vancouver, the MWI process was a frustrating one for various stakeholders. Initially, it operated with the much narrower focus of a hearing commission to investigate a limited range of cases.[3] When it announced that it would broaden its process to include a study commission, it was able to look at broader systemic factors that contributed to the structural violence encountered by marginalized women and girls in British Columbia. There were significant challenges in garnering the trust of the women whom the inquiry sought to study, but the broadening of the mandate offered an opportunity to conduct the process to enable participants to feel that they had been heard and in a manner that would benefit the listeners.

A struggling inquiry (or any inquiry) would do well to draw lessons from the Berger Inquiry to have a clear media strategy, engage the public, hold public hearings not driven by lawyers, conduct them in the witnesses' first languages, go to their communities, have different types of hearings, provide opportunities for civil society engagement, welcome independent research, and make it clear that they will value all of the evidence that they hear. The journey of a public inquiry is just as important as, if not more so than, the destination – that is, the process employed by an inquiry is just as critical as any conclusion that it might reach. Indeed, the ability of a public inquiry to fulfill its social function will depend in large part on its leadership and the process used for the implementation of the mandate. The process does not have to alienate and frustrate those whom it seeks to engage. Rather, it can be conducted in a manner that builds trust, engagement, and social cohesion among communities that have been disheartened by the justice system to date. This in turn can create legitimacy for the commission in the broader community. If this occurs, then the public interest generated in the commission can translate into political will to adopt the inquiry's recommendations.[4]

Unfortunately, the MWI's decisions regarding its work created a process that failed utterly in gaining and maintaining the cooperation of the communities that ostensibly it intended to study and ultimately assist. All of this was on my mind a few years later when I advocated in earnest for a National Inquiry into MMIWG. Litigation, activism, and political action are important and necessary in combination. However, a thoughtfully run public inquiry can provide a sound basis for policy changes and evidence-based solutions years after other actions have come and gone. But it has to be done right.

Background and Context of the Call for a National Inquiry into MMIWG

The fact that Indigenous women and girls are targeted for violence in Canada has been known for decades. Mary Eberts has written about mainstream cultural references to violence against Indigenous women around the time of the 1967 centennial, such as George Ryga's play *The Ecstasy of Rita Joe* and Margaret Laurence's Manawaka cycle.[5] Canadians knew that Indigenous women were being murdered yet did nothing about it, as in the emblematic case of nineteen-year-old Norway House Indian Reserve student Helen Betty Osborne, brutally murdered in The Pas in 1971. Although the Royal Canadian Mounted Police (RCMP) and the people of that small community largely knew within a few months which four white men had committed the crime, there was no trial until 1987 and only one conviction.[6]

Another case that illustrates the failure of the Canadian justice system as well as the broader public to address the devaluing of Indigenous women's lives is that of Pamela Jean George. A Saulteaux woman from the Sakimay First Nation, she was a twenty-eight-year-old single mother of two children who occasionally engaged in survival sex work. Her badly beaten body was found in a ditch west of Regina on the morning of 18 April 1995. She had been picked up off the street by two young white college students, though one had hidden in the trunk of the car when the other approached George. The two men sexually assaulted her and beat her to death. During their first-degree murder trial, Justice Ted Malone of the Court of Queen's Bench reminded the jury that George "indeed was a prostitute" when they considered if she had consented to sex. Her so-called consent was key to the two men being found guilty on the lesser charge of manslaughter. They were sentenced to six and a half years each in prison, a sentence upheld on appeal.[7]

For many years, Indigenous women have tried to draw attention to the disproportionate violence that they experience in Canada. In Vancouver's Downtown Eastside, where many Indigenous women have disappeared and been murdered over the years, a memorial march has been held every 14 February since 1992. The first Women's Memorial March was held after an Indigenous woman from Sechelt was murdered in the Downtown Eastside. Each year the march is held in Vancouver and communities across the country to raise awareness and commemorate MMIW. In Alberta, Muriel Stanley Venne started raising awareness about MMIW through her work with the Institute for the Advancement of Aboriginal Women, established in 1995.

In the past few years, the fact of MMIW has finally attracted the sort of attention that Indigenous women have long called for, but until recently official data on murders and disappearances remained incomplete. Homicide reports did not include missing women or the Indigenous identities of the victims. Some police forces, for example the RCMP, did not collect this information. In light of the incomplete official data, and because of growing concern within Indigenous communities, non-governmental organizations began to collect information about murders and disappearances of Indigenous women and girls. Amnesty International produced an important early report in 2004 called *Stolen Sisters*.[8] In 2005, as President of the Native Women's Association of Canada (NWAC), Beverley Jacobs initiated NWAC's Sisters in Spirit project, which began the work of cataloguing the violence and compiling a database of Indigenous women and girls who had been murdered or had disappeared. The project identified what Jacobs knew to be true: Indigenous women experience violence at many times the rate of non-Indigenous women in Canada.[9] Sisters in Spirit collected information about missing and murdered Indigenous women and girls across Canada, and it constructed an important and reliable database of information drawn from public sources, mainly police and media reports. By 2010, Sisters in Spirit had identified close to 600 cases.[10] Fifty-five percent of the murder cases and 43 percent of the cases of missing women and girls had occurred during or since 2000. The Conservative Harper government cancelled the Sisters in Spirit project funding in 2010, essentially transferring the money to the RCMP.[11] Community database initiatives such as those of Families of Sisters in Spirit and No More Silence took up the mantle of documenting the cases of the murdered and missing.

In 2013, Human Rights Watch produced a report detailing police failures to protect Indigenous women and girls along the Highway of Tears in northern British Columbia, where over a dozen young women had gone missing or been found murdered. The report also detailed violence against Indigenous women and girls by police officers themselves, underscoring the precarity of their lives.

International Inquiries

Canada was not interested in addressing the crisis, so Indigenous women turned to international bodies for assistance. First there was a call for the United Nations Committee on the Elimination of Discrimination against Women (CEDAW) to hold an inquiry. In November 2008, CEDAW requested that Canada report back to the committee within the year on its reasons for failing to investigate the cases of missing and murdered Indigenous women and to correct deficiencies in the system.[12] Canada did not fulfill the UN committee's request for follow-up by November 2009, according to the BC CEDAW Group, which submitted its shadow report to the United Nations in January 2010.[13]

In 2011, CEDAW decided to investigate, having determined that Canada had failed to provide the information requested.[14] The Inter-American Commission on Human Rights (IACHR) also launched an inquiry. Both CEDAW and IACHR issued reports concluding that Canadian governments had fallen far short of their international law obligations with respect to this issue, with CEDAW finding "grave violations" of Canada's commitments under the convention.[15]

UN Special Rapporteur on the Rights of Indigenous Peoples James Anaya, in his 2014 report, recommended that the federal government undertake a comprehensive, nationwide inquiry organized in consultation with Indigenous peoples. Eventually, the growing evidence and awareness of the crisis began to attract broader attention.[16]

The Call for a National Inquiry

Following the release of these reports, NWAC, the Assembly of First Nations, the opposition parties, the Canadian Association of Statutory Human Rights Agencies, women's organizations such as LEAF, and many social justice organizations called for a national public inquiry. In April 2013, Ministers of Aboriginal Affairs from all provinces and territories and leaders from the five national Indigenous organizations attending a meeting on Indigenous issues also joined the call for a national inquiry.

New information came to light that the number of MMIW was much higher than the almost 600 identified by Sisters in Spirit. A doctoral dissertation by Maryanne Pearce documented hundreds more cases.[17] A 2014 report by the RCMP found the number to be almost double that cited by Sisters in Spirit.[18] Then came the murder of Tina Fontaine in 2015. The fifteen-year-old's body was found in the Red River in Winnipeg. She was in the care of Child and Family Services (CFS) at the time of her death. There are more Indigenous children in care now than were in residential schools at the height of the IRS system. Tina was noted as a passenger in a car stopped by Winnipeg police in the night of 8 August. Earlier that day paramedics had picked her up from an alley, where she had been passed out. She had been transported to the Winnipeg Children's Hospital and then released to a CFS worker, who had taken her to a hotel. She had been reported as missing on 31 July.[19] Her body was found on 17 August. So, in the period that Tina was reported missing, she was identified by paramedics, by CFS, and by the police. These institutional actors could have stepped in to alter the course of events. But they did not. The national attention paid to her case added momentum to the call for a national inquiry.[20]

Resistance to a National Inquiry

Despite considerable and mounting evidence of the issue, the Conservative federal government of the day continued to resist the call for a national inquiry, with Prime Minister Harper stating that MMIW should not be viewed as a sociological phenomenon and that individual criminal investigations were sufficient.[21] He later indicated that the call for a national inquiry into MMIW "isn't really high on [his government's] radar."[22] Kellie Leitch, the federal Minister for the Status of Women, stated at a round-table meeting of premiers and national Indigenous organizations that the problem was largely one of domestic violence within Indigenous communities.[23] This was despite the RCMP finding in 2014 that Indigenous women are less likely to be killed by a current or former spouse than non-Indigenous women and NWAC's finding that Indigenous women are almost three times more likely to be killed by a stranger than are non-Indigenous women.[24]

Conservative commentators such as Tom Flanagan and Jeffrey Simpson opined that Canada had spent enough time and money on Indigenous issues and that the problem was really one for Indigenous communities to solve – and of course that inquiries are just a waste of (taxpayers') money.[25]

These commentators helpfully illustrated precisely why an inquiry was needed. Their sheer ignorance in the face of the problem stated the point well: The deeply ingrained attitudes and beliefs in Canada that "we" are not responsible for solving "Aboriginal issues," or that the effects of colonialism are something that Indigenous people should just "get over," contribute to the climate that allows a colossal number of Indigenous women and girls to disappear and be murdered. As for commentators such as Barbara MacDougall, tired of hearing that colonialism is the root cause of the issue,[26] imagine how tiring it would be to hear that we as a society simply do not care to find out why your mothers, daughters, aunties, and sisters are subjected to extreme violence at a disproportionate rate?

When the Inter-American Commission on Human Rights inquired of the government about plans for a national inquiry, the government advised that "money would be better spent on action rather than more recommendations."[27] In support of its argument that "action" rather than further study was required, the federal government pointed to recommendations from over forty-five reports that it said constituted adequate study.[28]

In my role as Legal Director at LEAF, I co-founded an *ad hoc* group of Indigenous and non-Indigenous feminist advocates that we called the Legal Strategy Coalition on Violence against Indigenous Women (LSC). We had come together from across the country (as usual, with no resources and incredibly limited capacity in terms of time and energy) to find ways to support Indigenous women calling for a national inquiry and to provide legal assistance in addressing the crisis of violence against Indigenous women and girls. The group decided to review the reports that the federal government relied on to say that a national inquiry was unwarranted. Indeed, our volunteer researchers went further and reviewed fifty-eight reports, including the forty-five on which the government was relying.[29]

The LSC found that, though the various reports had touched on related issues to varying degrees, none of the reports was from a national commission of inquiry focused on violence against Indigenous women and girls. The root causes were generally agreed on across the reports (e.g., poverty, inadequate housing, colonialism), and consistent themes emerged (e.g., child welfare, policing issues, criminal justice system problems). Most staggering, however, was our finding that the previous reports also consistently made recommendations on how to address and abate the violence. We catalogued over 700 recommendations in those reports and determined that almost none of them had been implemented. The LSC concluded that, though there was consensus on the root causes of violence against Indigenous women and girls, there had been virtually no response to the known measures that could address the crisis.

Why a National Inquiry?

The LSC's work laid bare the need for a national, state-sponsored inquiry to examine why there has been so much resistance to the implementation of known and recommended measures to address the issue.[30] It was not that Canada did not know the root causes or what to do about them. The stark truth was that most Canadians were not interested in doing what they knew needed to be done. Non-Indigenous Canadians like to think of themselves as human rights defenders, the "good guys." They do not like to look at the ugly truths of racism and sexism reflected by the terrifying and callous way that Indigenous women's and girls' lives have been devalued.

A properly run and adequately funded national inquiry could help us to reshape our national narrative into a more honest and less self-serving one. Such an inquiry could teach us about not only the causes of the violence but also how to prevent it from reoccurring.[31] The government's response that action was needed rather than another report reflected a shallow view of the value of a public inquiry. If a national inquiry is provided with strong terms of reference, along with visionary Commissioners who will make it a truly public inquiry, then it is an important action to take. This is because the purpose of such an inquiry is not simply, as the government's response suggests, to make more recommendations. Its purpose is to be a catalyst for real change.

A key assertion of this book is that a commission of inquiry can play an important pedagogical role through its very existence. If properly mandated and conscientiously run, then a public inquiry into why we know that Indigenous women are subjected to violence at a far higher rate than non-Indigenous women, *yet do so little about it*, could educate the wider public about this issue. Hard questions needed to be asked about the resistance of our society to facing honestly the systemic issues that plague it. A well-run commission could stimulate a national conversation about the underlying causes of violence against Indigenous women and girls. That was a conversation that Canadians could not continue to avoid.

When the National Inquiry into MMIWG was announced, I thought about which recommendations to make to those who would create the inquiry.[32] The model that I looked to for the National Inquiry was the Aboriginal Justice Inquiry of Manitoba.[33] The cautionary tale that I looked to was the BC Missing Women Inquiry.

The Manitoba Aboriginal Justice Inquiry, 1988–91

In 1988, the Manitoba government established the AJI to review two cases in detail: Helen Betty Osborne (mentioned above) and Indigenous leader J.J. Harper. A police officer shot and killed Harper in Winnipeg in 1988, three months after the trial in the murder of Osborne. The trial of those charged with Osborne's murder did not occur until sixteen years after her death. The failure of the justice system to do anything for Osborne during all that time, in combination with Harper's death, for which no charges would be laid, sparked the establishment of an inquiry into the treatment of Indigenous people by the Manitoba justice system.

The AJI Mandate

The Commissioners were mandated to investigate, report, and make recommendations to the provincial Minister of Justice on the relationship between the administration of justice and Indigenous people in Manitoba.[34] Although the Commissioners were specifically directed to investigate the Osborne and Harper cases, their mandate allowed for a considerable expansion of their focus. The opening paragraphs of the AJI Report indicate that the Commissioners took a broad view of their mandate and assessed the structural causes of the situations that they investigated:

> The justice system has failed Manitoba's Aboriginal people on a massive scale. It has been insensitive and inaccessible, and has arrested and imprisoned Aboriginal people in grossly disproportionate numbers ...

It is not merely that the justice system has failed Aboriginal people; justice also has been denied to them. For more than a century the rights of Aboriginal people have been ignored and eroded. The result of this denial has been injustice of the most profound kind. Poverty and powerlessness have been the Canadian legacy to a people who once governed their own affairs in full self-sufficiency.

This denial of social justice has deep historical roots, and to fully understand the current problems we must look to their sources ... The mandate of this Inquiry is to examine the relationship between Aboriginal people and the justice system, and to suggest ways it might be improved. In this report we make many recommendations about how existing institutions of justice – the police, the courts, the jails – can be improved. But far more important than these reforms is our conclusion that the relationship between Aboriginal people and the rest of society must be transformed fundamentally. This transformation must be based on justice in its broadest sense. It must recognize that social and economic inequity is unacceptable and that only through a full recognition of Aboriginal rights – including the right to self-government – can the symptomatic problems of over-incarceration and disaffection be redressed.

The problems are daunting and our proposals are far-reaching. But we believe that in the interests of justice, the process of transformation must begin immediately.[35]

The Commissioners embarked on a comprehensive review of the Osborne and Harper cases as well as the larger contexts in which those cases arose.

The AJI Leadership
Two Co-Commissioners – one Indigenous (Justice Murray Sinclair, later the Chief Commissioner of the TRC), one non-Indigenous (Associate Chief Justice Alvin Hamilton) – brought legitimacy and credibility to the inquiry in the eyes of the broader community. Both had experience dealing with Aboriginal law issues, and their broad interpretation of the mandate as well as the report that they produced suggested that they saw the inquiry as an opportunity to promote social accountability.[36]

The AJI Process

In addition to formal hearings on the two primary cases, the AJI held community hearings in thirty-six Indigenous communities, including twenty remote communities, seven other Manitoba communities, and five provincial correctional institutions, with over 1,000 people making informal presentations.[37] The community hearings were open to the public, and written submissions were not necessary. Witnesses were not required to testify under oath, nor were they subjected to examination by commission counsel or cross-examination. Indeed, the inquiry decided not to have lawyers at the community hearing level:

> We took this approach after considerable deliberation. We believed that Aboriginal people already were alienated from, and intimidated by, the formal court system. We wanted to utilize a process that would encourage frank and open expressions of opinion.[38]

In addition to the hearings, AJI staff conducted research and commissioned expert reports. The Commissioners visited tribal courts in the United States, conducted a symposium on tribal courts, and held a conference with Elders.[39] The AJI process thus had some of the hallmarks of the Berger Inquiry in terms of a variety of types of hearings and an open and non-legalistic approach.

Standing

The AJI granted standing (i.e., the right to participate in the inquiry, including the ability to make submissions and cross-examine witnesses, if applicable) as follows:

> We granted standing to: Justine Osborne, the mother of Betty Osborne; the Norway House Indian Band; the Indigenous Women's Collective; and the Royal Canadian Mounted Police. The Swampy Cree Tribal Council also was granted standing on the condition that it, Justine Osborne and the Norway House Band would be treated as one party. Counsel acting for the parties were: John Wilson, for Justine Osborne and the Norway House Band; Monique Danaher, for the Indigenous

Women's Collective; and Hymie Weinstein Q.C. and Craig Henderson, for the RCMP. Commission counsel were Perry Schulman Q.C. and Randy McNicol Q.C.

Limited standing was granted to the Manitoba Métis Federation to make a submission at the close of the proceedings. We rejected the application for standing made by Dwayne Archie Johnston, the only person convicted of the murder of Betty Osborne, because we believed he did not have a direct or substantial interest in the matters we were to examine.[40]

This list of parties granted or denied standing provides an interesting insight into the approach taken by the AJI with respect to the picture that the Commissioners sought to construct from the evidence before them. The convicted killer of Helen Betty Osborne was denied standing, whereas the community and family were granted standing. The Indigenous Women's Collective was granted standing and had its own legal counsel. In contrast, though the later BC Missing Women Inquiry granted full standing (including the ability to make oral submissions and cross-examine witnesses) to some of the women's families and to a number of police officers and to the police departments, it granted only limited standing to a number of organizations representing Indigenous women. These groups had no right of cross-examination, a disadvantage in a hearing run along legalistic lines, although they could take part in the study hearings.

The AJI Report

When it reported in 1991, the Aboriginal Justice Inquiry of Manitoba provided a historical, cultural, and legal review of the relationship between the justice system in Manitoba and the Indigenous peoples in the province.[41] The Commissioners sought to learn about the legal system from the people who had direct contact with it.[42] In addition to its written reports, the AJI produced a video in English, Cree, Ojibway, Island Lake dialect, Dakota, and Dene to make the report more accessible to Indigenous peoples.[43] The report provided a thorough discussion of Indigenous concepts of justice, a history of Indigenous contact with non-Indigenous law, and a discussion of treaty rights. The inquiry reviewed Indigenous overrepresentation in the criminal justice system, discussing the court system,

Indigenous justice systems, court reform, juries, jails, alternatives to jail, parole, and policing. In the course of its hearings, the AJI heard testimony from many Indigenous people about their residential school experiences and wrote about the far-reaching effects of the IRS legacy in its report.[44]

The AJI Report explicitly considered whether systemic racism was a factor in the death of Helen Betty Osborne and in the failure of the police to charge anyone for her death for sixteen years. The inquiry devoted a chapter of the first volume of its report to the subject of Indigenous women,[45] and the second volume focused on the case of Osborne.[46] The AJI reported on the treatment of Indigenous women in Manitoba and took into account racism and sexism in how they are treated by police, the justice system, and society more generally. The inquiry acknowledged how a history of colonialism and the IRS legacy compounded the disproportionate violence experienced by Indigenous women. The Commissioners explicitly stated the fact that Indigenous women are disproportionately targeted for violence in Canada because they are Indigenous and because they are women.

Implementation

An important innovation in Manitoba was the creation of the Aboriginal Justice Inquiry Implementation Commission (AJIC) in 1999 after the failure to implement many of the inquiry's recommendations in the years after its report in 1991.[47] The provincial government created the AJIC with a mandate to review the AJI's recommendations, consult with Manitobans on priority areas for action and on strategies for implementation, and develop an action plan for implementation of the recommendations. Commissioners Wendy Whitecloud and Paul Chartrand (assisted by Elder advisers Eva McKay and Doris Young) circulated proposed recommendations to organizations that would be affected by the recommendations and met with members of relevant government departments. The Minister of Justice and the Minister of Aboriginal and Northern Affairs requested that all government departments provide the AJIC with reports on the status of implementation of the AJI recommendations that pertained to their departments. The Commissioners made quarterly status reports to the ministers responsible and provided a final report with a series of priorities for the government to focus on in implementing the recommendations. This is an unusual mechanism but a useful and important model for governments to consider in ensuring that inquiry reports do not simply gather dust.

The British Columbia Missing Women Inquiry, 2010–12

For many years in Vancouver, dozens of women went missing from the Downtown Eastside, many of whom were Indigenous, poor, and engaged in sex work. Despite their loved ones reporting them missing, and amid tales of a serial killer preying on women and growing alarm among community members about the disappearances, the police resolutely refused to acknowledge any pattern.[48] The Vancouver Police Department and the RCMP finally struck a joint task force in 2001 to look into the cases of missing women. The Joint Missing Women Task Force determined that approximately sixty-five women had disappeared from Vancouver between 1978 and 2001.[49] On 5 February 2002, the task force arrested Robert William Pickton at his Coquitlam farm after an independent weapons search warrant was obtained by a junior RCMP officer.[50] Pickton was convicted in December 2007 and sentenced to life in prison for murdering six women, but another twenty murder charges were stayed, and he boasted in jail of killing forty-nine women to an undercover officer posing as a cellmate on the day of his arrest. DNA evidence has connected Pickton to the deaths of at least thirty-two women.[51] A total of eighteen murders occurred after he was arrested and released for the attempted murder of a sex worker in 1997. Of the women missing from the Downtown Eastside, at least one-third were Indigenous even though they were only 3 percent of the population in British Columbia.[52]

The BC government created the Missing Women Inquiry on 27 September 2010 after Pickton's criminal appeals were exhausted. The inquiry was called to examine and report on the conduct of investigations made between 23 January 1997 and 5 February 2002 by police forces in British Columbia regarding women reported missing from the Downtown Eastside.

During the period that Pickton was murdering women with impunity, many other women, a disproportionate number of whom were Indigenous, disappeared, including those who vanished along a stretch of highway in northern British Columbia now referred to as the "Highway of Tears."[53] According to research conducted by the Native Women's Association of Canada under the Sisters in Spirit initiative, as of March 2010, 580 Indigenous women disappeared or were murdered in Canada over roughly the previous thirty years.[54] In light of these losses, NWAC and other civil society organizations called for a public inquiry to address the heightened level of violence against Indigenous women and the apparent systemic issues underlying the statistics.[55] These systemic issues include poverty, sexism, racism, colonialism, and other root causes of extreme violence against Indigenous women.

The MWI Mandate

When the BC government yielded to calls for an inquiry, it sought to limit the mandate to a relatively narrow investigation of the Pickton case.[56] The civil society organizations that sought an inquiry in order to examine the larger structural issues involved in creating a situation in which dozens of women went missing over a relatively short period of time, and in which many continued to go missing, were skeptical about whether the narrow mandate could seek the answers to the larger questions of how Canadian society views and treats Indigenous women.

The MWI was initially set up as a hearing commission, which under the *Public Inquiry Act* in British Columbia is essentially a fact-finding inquiry. It provides a higher level of procedural protections for participants than what the *Act* calls a study commission.[57] Eventually, the mandate of the inquiry was expanded in March 2011 to include a study component, which provided a more policy-oriented focus. The decision to expand the mandate to include a study commission was a positive one and resulted from pre-hearing conferences that provided community input to the inquiry. Those conferences were a good start since they sought community input on the process of the inquiry. The inquiry heard concerns about the ability to participate if the hearings were too formally legal, the importance of accessibility for and inclusion of vulnerable or marginalized

individuals, and culturally appropriate processes for Indigenous participants.[58] The expansion of the mandate to include a study commission
enabled the MWI to consider the Highway of Tears investigations as well
as those of the Downtown Eastside. The expansion might have provided
an opportunity for the inquiry to delve into the larger systemic issues at
play. However, the progress of the inquiry was marred by several important
factors.

The MWI Leadership

Unfortunately, the inquiry was plagued from the start with criticisms of
illegitimacy. The sole Commissioner, retired BC Court of Appeal Justice
Wally Oppal, was Attorney General of the province from 2005 to 2009.
When Pickton was tried, the trial judge severed twenty of the twenty-six
counts of murder, saying that the jury would not be able to manage a trial
of twenty-six murders. Oppal was Attorney General when the Crown
decided to stay the remaining twenty first-degree murder charges against
Pickton upon his conviction on the initial six charges, determining that
the trial would be superfluous given that he was sentenced to life in prison.
This decision left the families of the twenty women without a sense that
justice was being done. When Oppal was appointed to head the MWI,
these families questioned the choice given that he had been in a position
to create a factual record by ordering a trial for the other murders but chose
not to do so. In addition, the terms of reference required the inquiry to
investigate the Criminal Justice Branch's decision to stay charges of attempted murder, assault with a weapon, forcible confinement, and aggravated assault against Pickton in 1997 for the attempted murder of a woman
who escaped from his farm. Given that Oppal had been Attorney General
at that time, it seemed that the criminal justice system was being charged
with investigating its own. Many saw his appointment as tainted by these
perceived conflicts of interest.[59]

Even more challenging was the fact that, when Oppal was Attorney
General, the Criminal Justice Branch took another inquiry Commissioner
to court to oppose a review of prosecutorial discretion in the course of the
inquiry into the death of Frank Joseph Paul.[60] Indeed, the MWI's terms of
reference specifically took into account the court's determination that the

inquiry should be able to pierce the veil of prosecutorial discretion. Observers of the MWI would recall that it was Oppal who would have been among those who benefited from the ability to remain behind that very veil. Furthermore, while he was Attorney General, Oppal had publicly opposed the calls for a public inquiry into the Pickton investigations. Although Oppal has defended that position as the proper legal position (given that the trial was still under way at the time, and therefore an inquiry should not properly start until after the trial), women's groups heard only his rejection of an inquiry and not the reasons for his objection to it.[61]

Unfortunately, the largest blow to the credibility of the MWI was yet to come.

Standing

On 2 May 2011, Commissioner Oppal delivered his ruling on standing of the various parties that sought to participate in the Missing Women Inquiry.[62] He determined that some parties would have full standing (including the right to cross-examine witnesses and make oral submissions), whereas others would have limited standing. He directed that some organizations with similar interests form coalitions in order to appear before the inquiry. Commissioner Oppal found that eighteen parties (including some coalitions) should have standing at the inquiry. Ten of the eighteen were granted full standing, including the families and the police departments, as well as NWAC and several community-based organizations from the Downtown Eastside, whose presence and participation he found to be essential. Other organizations, including the Union of BC Indian Chiefs and First Nations Summit, were granted only limited standing (i.e., no right of cross-examination, but they could take part in the study hearings). Oppal directed that the thirteen parties granted standing who had requested funding should have publicly funded legal counsel to enable them to participate in the inquiry.

The BC government responded by refusing to provide funds to pay for legal counsel for any of the parties granted limited standing. This was a shocking decision and absolutely unprecedented in the history of Canadian public inquiries. Commissioner Oppal made a public statement to the government,[63] and a large group of highly respected former commission counsel and members of previous commissions of inquiry wrote an open letter calling on the BC government to provide funding to the groups that Oppal had determined he needed to hear in order to conduct the inquiry properly.[64] The government claimed that the decision had been made because of the importance of spending public funds with care in a time of fiscal restraint.[65] Given that the Deputy Attorney General confirmed the funding decision, and that the MWI had a mandate to investigate departments of the Ministry of Attorney General, the optics were not good. It looked as though the government had decided not to provide the means of participation to groups alleging government complicity in the deaths of the women. Furthermore, all three of the police departments and the Criminal Justice Branch of the government were provided with publicly funded lawyers.[66]

This decision left an extremely negative impression on those concerned about the representation of parties other than the police at the inquiry. The parties denied funding withdrew from the inquiry since they did not have the financial means to employ legal counsel to review the thousands of documents involved in the inquiry or to conduct cross-examinations of the many witnesses called to the stand. Although some inquiries are viewed as less formal in terms of legal structure, the MWI was squarely in the legal tradition of a formal hearing to create the factual record, including assessments of credibility of witnesses determined through examination and cross-examination, enormous amounts of documentary evidence, and arguments by counsel. These are not tasks that can be undertaken by non-profit organizations without counsel. Indeed, the inquiry was boycotted by almost every group granted standing because of the denial of adequate funding for legal counsel. It was described as a "sham inquiry" by the Downtown Eastside Women's Centre and Women's Memorial March Committee, two of the groups granted standing but denied funding.[67]

As noted by the many commission counsel who protested the government's funding decision, the groups that withdrew from the Missing Women Inquiry cited the unacceptable interference with its independence that the funding decision represented. Commissioner Oppal had ruled that those groups were critical to the inquiry's ability to fulfill its mandate, and the government had begged to differ. The decision gravely undermined the legitimacy of the inquiry. A further blow came when then Attorney General Barry Penner publicly released a voicemail left for him by Commissioner Oppal pleading for the funding. Penner stated that he publicly released the voicemail out of a concern that Oppal had pre-determined some of the key issues before the inquiry. Penner asked the Criminal Justice Branch to investigate, prompting a response from Commissioner Oppal:

> Responding ... to concerns raised about his impartiality, Mr. Oppal re-ferred to his credentials as a judge for 23 years to back up his insistence that he understands the need not to come to any conclusion before all the evidence and submissions have been heard. The concerns stem from remarks he made that appear to indicate he had already decided that the police had failed to act appropriately. He made the comments while lobbying the government for funding for community groups that he felt should appear at the inquiry.[68]

Instead of acceding to calls for his resignation,[69] Commissioner Oppal decided to appoint two "independent counsel" to represent the interests of the groups denied funding. One, Jason Gratl, was appointed to represent the interests of the Downtown Eastside communities. The other, Métis lawyer Robyn Gervais, was appointed to represent Indigenous interests. At that time, Gervais was relatively junior,[70] not yet an acknowledged expert in the systemic issues that the groups denied funding had sought to raise at the hearings. Nor were those groups that the independent counsel were to represent consulted in their appointment.[71] More importantly, the independent counsel were appointed and funded by the inquiry; accord-ingly, the groups that they were supposed to represent could not in fact instruct them, nor did they have a solicitor-client relationship with them. This was an untenable situation for the groups. As noted in an open letter reacting to the announcement of the two appointments,

> [t]he DEWC and Women's Memorial March Committee as a formal Coalition with a full grant of standing before the Missing Women Commission of Inquiry ... is opposed to the proposal regarding an

independent lawyer to present all the perspectives of the DTES. Our group was not even contacted by the Commission to see if we were amenable to this proposal, rather it was presented as a "fait accompli" and expressions of interests from lawyers were sought within three days.

The latest proposal is a further slap in our face, which comes in light of the BC government's decision to shut out participation of DTES, Women's and Indigenous groups and communities. The purpose of the public inquiry is being whittled away – the adversarial process already makes it highly improbable for vulnerable women to provide their testimonies as they will be subjected to rigorous cross examination by the police's lawyers. This is highly objectionable as it revictimizes and traumatizes survivors of violence in an Inquiry that is supposed to bring some level of justice for them.[72]

Meanwhile, the three police departments (RCMP, Coquitlam, Vancouver) had four to six publicly funded outside counsel each whom they could instruct. The MWI would now receive its factual basis from examinations and cross-examinations of witnesses by the counsel for the police departments along with the lawyer representing a subset of the families of the missing and murdered women. Counsel for NWAC, Katherine Hensel, described this as a "tremendously unfair and discriminatory result" at the inquiry.[73] Indeed, she described the appointment of independent counsel by the inquiry as introducing a new form of discrimination by denying the parties the ability to instruct them and fully engage in the process. NWAC decided that participating would do more harm than good because the result would be unbalanced in favour of the police departments.

The message that Indigenous women received was that they were not considered important enough for the police to investigate their disappearances seriously, nor were they important enough to be heard from at the inquiry investigating police inaction on their disappearances.[74] All of the parties granted standing but denied funding withdrew from the MWI, both because they were unable to participate without legal counsel in a complex, adversarial process and because the decision represented government interference in the inquiry. Amnesty International did have in-house counsel and could have participated, but it withdrew from the inquiry as well because it viewed the independence and integrity of the inquiry as compromised. As a result, none of the organizations with the most insight into the realities for women in the Downtown Eastside was represented at the inquiry. Given that the parties that could have provided a factual record of the affected women were not part of the inquiry, the fear was that the systemic issues would not be addressed adequately as the inquiry moved to the study portion of its mandate.

On 6 March 2012, one of the two independent counsel, Robyn Gervais, resigned, citing the inquiry's failure to provide adequate hearing time for Indigenous witnesses. In fifty-three days of sitting, thirty-nine days of testimony involved police witnesses. The inquiry called for a recess in order to seek "experienced counsel" to take over from Gervais.[75] "Oppal told the inquiry he was adjourning the hearings until Gervais is replaced because aboriginal interests are too important not to have a voice at the inquiry."[76] However, as noted by columnist Ian Mulgrew, "[t]he voice of first nations is being drowned out by the sheer number, [the] collective volume and the aggregate time provided the institutional police voice."[77] With the resignation of Gervais, the First Nations Summit formally withdrew from the inquiry. In an open letter to the Commissioner, the umbrella organization for First Nations involved in the BC treaty process stated that

[w]e want to reiterate our full support for the families of all those women who are missing and murdered. They need to see that justice is not only seen to be done, but that it is done and that the many questions they have are answered fully. The voices of these families and that of our communities must be respected and heard.

We come to the conclusion, given all these developments, together with the conduct of the Inquiry, including your statements to Robyn Gervais today, those voices are not being respected or heard. This continues to reflect what we said in our Statement, a systemic pattern of discrimination. We feel the Inquiry will not be able to fulfill a critical part of its mandate.

Our continued participation has always been subject to review by our Executive and Chiefs. Unfortunately, the fears expressed by our Chiefs and leaders at the outset of this process ... have been confirmed. Given the withdrawal of, and the reasons provided by, the Independent Legal Counsel, Robyn Gervais, today and the withdrawal of all First Nations/ Aboriginal organizations earlier in the process, we feel we cannot continue to participate. Effective today, we withdraw from participation in this Inquiry. We will seek alternative ways for the voices of the families of the missing and murdered women and our communities to be heard and respected.[78]

On 21 March 2012, Commissioner Oppal appointed lawyers Suzette Narbonne and Elizabeth Hunt as independent co-counsel

to present issues related to Aboriginal interests. Commissioner Oppal believes that this role is crucial to ensure that Aboriginal interests are presented at the Inquiry. Both Ms. Narbonne and Ms. Hunt are respected, experienced legal professionals. Commissioner Oppal has every confidence in each lawyer's ability.[79]

Unfortunately, whatever skill Narbonne and Hunt brought to the inquiry, they could not overcome the structural problem that they had been appointed by the inquiry, not by the parties excluded from its process but on whose behalf they were somehow expected to speak.

The MWI Process

The Missing Women Inquiry had some structural components that could have enabled meaningful participation from people who would not otherwise have accessed the inquiry. For example, it held public forums in Vancouver and Prince George to hear from communities affected by the disappearances and murders of Indigenous women. The study commission mandate allowed for hearings that (unlike the hearing commission) did not involve cross-examination in order that people could speak without being questioned by lawyers and without the need for their own lawyers.

However, without the voices of communities well acquainted with the systemic issues that have made Indigenous women invisible in this country, the factual record of the inquiry would be expected to focus instead on the actions or lack thereof of the various police departments regarding the Pickton investigation.[80] The inquiry would not be expected to have the basis on which to make recommendations to address the ongoing colonialism inherent in how police forces treat Indigenous women, how governments direct prosecutorial policy, and how the broader societal community views Indigenous women.

In contrast to the MWI process, the AJI process benefited from considerable participation of Indigenous women. As the AJI Report noted,

> Aboriginal women and their children suffer tremendously as victims in contemporary Canadian society. They are the victims of racism, of sexism and of unconscionable levels of domestic violence. The justice system has done little to protect them from any of these assaults. At the same time, Aboriginal women have an even higher rate of over-representation in the prison system than Aboriginal men. In community after community, Aboriginal women brought these disturbing facts to our attention. We believe the plight of Aboriginal women and their children must be a priority for any changes in the justice system. In addition, we believe that changes must be based on the proposals that Aboriginal women presented to us throughout our Inquiry.[81]

As this overview of the MWI illustrates, and as confirmed by the groups with limited standing that refused to lend their own credibility to the process, the inquiry did not fulfill its potential social function. Instead of being an opportunity for a discussion of the systemic issues that gave rise to the missing and murdered women, the inquiry reinforced the problems. The contrast between the AJI and the MWI illustrates the critical importance of the leadership as well as the process undertaken by an inquiry in achieving the goals of their mandates. In a situation in which the issues to be addressed raise questions about the ability of the community to acknowledge their existence, these factors become vital.

Women's organizations and Indigenous groups had called for an inquiry for years before the MWI was appointed. These bodies sought a process that would reveal the truth of what had occurred in the face of police and government intransigence. The MWI needed to demonstrate that it could fulfill the social function and become a pedagogical process – not just for the police departments and Crown prosecutors but also for the wider society. Instead, the organizations with standing but denied funding stated in a letter to Commissioner Oppal that

> [w]e feel that it is important to state our profound disappointment in how this Inquiry has unfolded. Based on our experiences of exclusion from the Inquiry process, as well as our assessment of events occurring throughout the course of the proceedings, we have no confidence that our participation in the Policy Forums or Study Commission will contribute to the *truth, reconciliation and accountability that we fully expected* when this Inquiry was initiated.[82]

The MWI Report

Although the Missing Women Inquiry has been criticized as a "travesty" and "debacle,"[83] its report overall is a thorough and conscientious document.[84] The MWI Report attempts to do some of the things that the inquiry process did not do. For example, it memorializes the women by composing brief profiles of each one,[85] makes efforts to acknowledge the women, challenges the narrative dismissing them, and refers to the need for reconciliation and healing. The report examines the processes of marginalization and notes that the over-representation of Indigenous women among missing and murdered women in Canada is related to the legacy of colonialism.[86] The framework of analysis for the report is stated to be based on elements that include the contexts of the women's lives and an understanding of equality rights norms applicable in policing.[87]

In the second volume of the MWI Report, Commissioner Oppal reviews the police investigations and draws conclusions about "how we, as a society and through our police forces, failed the missing and murdered women."[88] He states that "[a]mong the questions I have had to consider in the inquiry is whether their status as nobodies also had an impact on the police investigations."[89]

Notwithstanding these positive aspects of the report, its conclusions are problematic since Oppal fails to hold anyone responsible for the harms wrought by the numerous police failures that he identifies: "I focus on systemic failures rather than individual failures. My perspective is foremost oriented to the future: It is aimed at contributing to a safer future rather than attributing blame for past inadequacies and breakdowns."[90] He explains

> that hindsight should not be used to judge past efforts of individuals who did not know what is known today. I fully accept the submissions of the VPD, Vancouver Police Union (VPU) and the Government of Canada on behalf of the RCMP that all of the officers involved in the investigations acted in good faith.[91]

The BC legislation governing public inquiries enables Commissioners to make findings of misconduct.[92] Since there are almost no means in Canadian law to impose accountability for systemic failures, Commissioner Oppal's decision to decline making any finding of individual misconduct prompted criticism: "[T]he police investigations were 'blatant failures,' there were 'patterns of error,' there was an 'absence of leadership,' there were 'outdated policing systems' ... Yet no one was to blame."[93]

Despite the merits of the MWI Report, which obliquely acknowledges some of the failures in the process of the inquiry, in statements such as the "hearing process creates barriers for marginalized individuals,"[94] the flawed process of the inquiry remains a missed opportunity and an injury to the women's families. Moreover, the decision not to hold anyone in particular responsible for the "blatant failures" is an injurious outcome. Yet, in the end, the report does situate the crisis of violence against women in a larger societal framework and identifies its systemic nature. It highlights the disproportionate targeting of Indigenous women within a larger context of marginalization and inequality.[95]

There are two generally acknowledged purposes of a commission of inquiry: (1) to create an accurate historical record of what has occurred, and (2) to offer solutions in order that the tragedy not be repeated.[96] As Canadians know, public inquiries often produce fine reports with valuable recommendations that then appear to gather dust on shelves, but these reports can nonetheless have enduring value. Although some commissions are more successful than others in gaining adoption and implementation of their conclusions and recommendations, all of these processes contribute to the narrative arc about their subjects. Given that the reports might not immediately have the desired effects, it is vital that the inquiries themselves be run in such a way that the process creates positive change through their work. Although the MWI echoed the AJI Report, it did not succeed in its social function because of the failures in its process. Nonetheless, over time, its report might contribute to achieving necessary changes in Canada's treatment of Indigenous women.

The legacy of residential schools and missing and murdered women are connected: "There is broad agreement in the literature that the root causes of the intolerably high levels of violence and vulnerability to violence experienced by Aboriginal women and girls in Canada lie in the colonial policies of historical and contemporary governments."[97] This connection was noted by the AJI:

> The very reason that Betty Osborne was compelled to leave her home and move to The Pas also was rooted in racism. Like so many other Aboriginal young people, she was forced by long-standing government policy to move to a strange and hostile environment to continue her schooling.[98]

This kind of analysis was critical for the MWI to incorporate into its findings and into its process. The community and women's organizations all lost hope that such an outcome was possible based on their experiences with the process of the inquiry. NWAC and others turned to international bodies to investigate the issues of violence afflicting Indigenous women and girls in Canada.

The disappeared and murdered women were not a visible focus of the TRC while it was under way. Nonetheless, the TRC Calls to Action included a call for a public inquiry into the disproportionate violence against Indigenous women and girls and specifically called for an investigation into MMIW. It was this call that the government referenced when it announced the establishment of the National Inquiry into MMIWG in December 2015.

Implementation

Following the release of the MWI Report in 2012, former Lieutenant Governor Steven Point was appointed to oversee implementation of the report's recommendations. He resigned after five months, and the government stopped reporting on its progress in implementing the recommendations in 2014. The Auditor General of British Columbia reported in 2015 that the intent of eight of the sixty-three recommendations had been implemented. The Auditor General made one recommendation: that the government resume publicly reporting its progress on implementation.[99] A coalition of organizations that withdrew from the inquiry because of its flawed process (the Coalition on MMIWG in BC) doggedly continues to call for implementation of the MWI's recommendations and has been active in encouraging implementation of the National Inquiry's recommendations.

The National Inquiry into MMIWG, 2016–19

With these two inquiries in mind, I now turn to the National Inquiry into MMIWG, beginning with a consideration of the two institutional design factors of leadership and process.

First, an effective inquiry must be led by someone with vision, courage, and compassion. He or she must exhibit the qualities of integrity, fair-mindedness, independence, and commitment to openness and transparency. This might seem to be an obvious point, but its importance cannot be understated. Ideally, the person will be capable of commanding the attention of the broader community in order to ensure that the inquiry can fulfill its pedagogical potential.

Second, an inquiry must have a process that lends strength to its work, engages the broader community, and creates knowledge and understanding through its operations so that the result needed from the inquiry is being achieved well before the report is written and the recommendations are made. There are ways to conduct an inquiry that will enable people to feel that they are being heard and that will benefit the listeners. An inquiry process will be effective if it has a clear media strategy, engages the public, holds public hearings that are not lawyer driven, tries to conduct them in the witnesses' first languages, goes to their communities, has different types of hearings (e.g., institutional, community, and expert), provides opportunities for civil society engagement, welcomes independent research, and makes it clear that all of the evidence that it hears will be valued.

Pre-Inquiry Consultation

After the Liberals won the fall 2015 federal election, the government of Justin Trudeau announced the establishment of the National Inquiry into MMIWG. A remarkably thorough and in-depth pre-inquiry consultation phase commenced in which the Ministers of Justice, Status of Women, and Indigenous Affairs travelled the country and heard from various stakeholders. Their staff gathered advice about how the National Inquiry could be shaped and what the scope of the terms of reference might be.[100] A rich array of information was compiled, but in retrospect it is difficult not to wonder about the degree to which it was reviewed by the Commissioners, given the logistical and other challenges that the commission failed to meet. Indeed, a *Globe and Mail* editorial upon the release of the National Inquiry *Interim Report* characterized it as a "frustrating read," noting that the inquiry was characterized by "delays and strife":

> These organizational failures are all the more startling given the fact that the federal government held a "pre-inquiry" from December 2015 to March 2016, with the specific goal of determining how to shape the national inquiry based on the input from the families of victims, Indigenous leaders and the provinces. The commission was given a head start, but managed to turn that into a disadvantage.[101]

The National Inquiry *Interim Report* has a section titled "What Have We Learned from the Pre-Inquiry Process?" indicating that the pre-inquiry community meeting materials were reviewed to identify key issues raised by participants.[102] The section indicates that the Commissioners looked at the federal government's report on the pre-inquiry process of engagement. This latter report is only a slim overview of the wealth of information provided during the six-month pre-inquiry period. The few paragraphs under this heading distressingly omit any mention of the advice gathered during that period about the potential process and scope of the inquiry. A generous amount of information was gathered from past Commissioners, counsel, Research Directors, and other staff of prior commissions of inquiry about what has worked well and what has been less effective. A rich resource was compiled that surely could have been of considerable assistance to the Commissioners in determining how to interpret their mandate and structure the work of the inquiry. There is no mention either of this wealth of information available from the pre-inquiry period or of the Commissioners having reviewed or benefited from it, much less having adopted it.

Calling an inquiry would inevitably heighten expectations among families that they would receive assistance with the investigations of their loved ones' cases. An inquiry investigating systemic causes has limited time and ability to get into the details of any particular file. Establishing an independent cold case investigative task force to operate in parallel to the inquiry and extend past the life of the inquiry would have been apposite. This was not done. The federal government did provide funds for the provinces and territories to set up units to assist families to gain more information on their loved ones' files:

> In response to the pre-inquiry recommendations, the government also announced today $16.17 million over four years for the creation of Family Information Liaison Units [FILUs] in each province and territory and to increase victims services funding to provide culturally-appropriate victims services for families of missing and murdered Indigenous women and girls and survivors of violence.[103]

The FILUs assisted families with accessing available information from government agencies and services about their loved ones, but they were not empowered to reopen investigations. Although the FILUs performed an important role for some families, an ongoing nationally coordinated task force focused on these cases would be a useful mechanism for families who have been unable to obtain answers or closure.

The National Inquiry Mandate

The pre-inquiry phase culminated in the formal establishment of the National Inquiry into MMIWG. In a remarkable feat, the federal government and all provinces and territories passed fourteen orders in council to create a truly national inquiry.[104] On the one hand, this provided the inquiry with a tremendously strong base from which to begin; on the other, it meant that any extension or expansion would require changes to fourteen orders in council down the road. The mandate was also very broad:

a. direct the Commissioners to inquire into and to report on the following:

  i. systemic causes of all forms of violence – including sexual violence – against Indigenous women and girls in Canada, including underlying social, economic, cultural, institutional and historical causes contributing to the ongoing violence and particular vulnerabilities of Indigenous women and girls in Canada, and

  ii. institutional policies and practices implemented in response to violence experienced by Indigenous women and girls in Canada, including the identification and examination of practices that have been effective in reducing violence and increasing safety

b. direct the Commissioners to make recommendations on the following:

  i. concrete and effective action that can be taken to remove systemic causes of violence and to increase the safety of Indigenous women and girls in Canada, and

  ii. ways to honour and commemorate the missing and murdered Indigenous women and girls in Canada.[105]

A broadly worded mandate can be positive in that it gives Commissioners considerable flexibility and scope within which to shape their process, but it also requires that Commissioners immediately temper expectations and define parameters in a manageable way.

The National Inquiry Leadership

Appointing the right Commissioner(s) for the job and shaping the terms of reference in a way that would enable a meaningful inquiry to proceed should have been based on significant consultations with Indigenous women.[106] Unfortunately, though there was a comprehensive pre-inquiry consultation phase, only a small part of it included focused consultations with Indigenous women. Although many of the consultations did focus on topics to be included in the terms of reference, apparently missing was a committee led by Indigenous women at arm's length from the government to develop a short list of possible Commissioners. How such a list was drawn up was opaque, but the decisions made in the Prime Minister's Office appear to have been made without consultation with key long-standing Indigenous MMIW advocates. Such consultation would have ensured appropriate attention to the critical element of leadership.

Indigenous women at the one pre-inquiry roundtable convened on Indigenous law suggested that four Commissioners should be appointed given the significance of the four directions in Indigenous world views.[107] Instead, five Commissioners were appointed (though one resigned partway through). The people named as Commissioners in August 2016 were all accomplished professionals with extensive experience in Indigenous communities, though most were not people known in connection with the MMIW crisis.

Chief Commissioner Marion Buller was the first Indigenous woman to be appointed as a BC Provincial Court judge in 1994, and as of 2006 she ran the First Nations/Indigenous Court in Surrey.[108] She is Cree and a member of the Mistawasis First Nation in Saskatchewan. She was commission counsel for the Cariboo-Chilcotin Justice Inquiry, a lesser-known inquiry that reported in 1993.[109]

Commissioner Michèle Audette is of mixed Québécois and Innu heritage. She is a past President of the Quebec Native Women's Association, the Associate Deputy Minister for the Status of Women in the government of Quebec, and a past President of NWAC.[110]

Brian Eyolfson was Acting Deputy Director in the Legal Services Branch of the Ontario Ministry of Indigenous Relations and Reconciliation. He previously served as counsel to the Ontario Human Rights Commission and was a Vice-Chair with the Human Rights Tribunal of Ontario, on which he adjudicated and mediated human rights applications between 2007 and 2016. Eyolfson practised human rights, Aboriginal, and administrative law as a senior staff lawyer with Aboriginal Legal Services of Toronto, which organization he represented at the Ipperwash Inquiry.[111]

Qajaq Robinson was born in Iqaluit and raised in Igloolik. She is a graduate of the Akitsiraq Law Program (a partnership between the University of Victoria and Nunavut Arctic College). She clerked with judges of the Nunavut Court of Justice and became a Crown prosecutor in Nunavut before joining Borden Ladner Gervais LLP in Ottawa as an associate. Appointed at thirty-six years of age, she was the youngest of the Commissioners.

Notably, there was no one from the Atlantic region, and no Inuk was appointed as a Commissioner despite the epidemic levels of violence against Inuit women in the North.[112] Although Qajaq Robinson grew up in the North and is fluent in Inuktitut, she is not an Inuk. According to Rebecca Kudloo, President of Pauktuutit Inuit Women of Canada, "[i]n 2016 it is not acceptable that the Inuit women of Canada do not have an Inuk as a commissioner."[113]

The fifth Commissioner was Marilyn Poitras, a Métis law professor at the University of Saskatchewan's College of Law who began her career as a Native Court Worker in Regina. She resigned in July 2017, citing irreconcilable differences with the other Commissioners in her letter of resignation.[114] This prompted the Ontario Native Women's Association to withdraw its support from the National Inquiry, amid expressions of concern from various other interested parties and following the resignation of at least four key staff, including the first Executive Director.[115] Sheila North Wilson, the Grand Chief of the Manitoba Keewatinowi Okimakanak, which represents First Nations in northern Manitoba, called for an overhaul of the inquiry and for the federal government to replace Commissioner Buller.[116] The resignation of Poitras came on a day when families of MMIW met with Commissioner Buller to express their concerns about how the inquiry had been unfolding and in particular their perception that it had not been communicating with families since its inauguration the previous September.[117]

Unfortunately, the leadership style of Commissioner Buller – at least the one projected publicly – proved to be problematic. As the National Inquiry seemed to go off the rails, with a multitude of resignations and criticisms, she did not project an air of transparency and openness. Instead, her defensive style and stilted press conferences did nothing to counter the loss of confidence in the ability of the inquiry to do its work. Buller also did not publicly provide a clear vision of the mandate, nor did she proactively set expectations of what could be achieved by the inquiry. Yet, when asked at the November 2017 release of the National Inquiry *Interim Report* if she would have done anything differently to that point, she responded simply: "No."[118]

The National Inquiry Process

The Commissioners failed to communicate effectively an overall vision for the National Inquiry to the public or to those most affected by the tragedy that gave rise to it.[119] A careful review of the wealth of pre-inquiry consultation material gathered would have shown them that a two-year mandate would require them to be realistic in their determination of what could and could not be done in that time. Crucially, they would have had to lower the expectations of families that the inquiry could dig into hundreds of individual cases in order to assess whether they could be solved. A broad mandate and a two-year time frame require efficient planning and allocation of resources, clear communication of choices about what will be addressed and what will not, as well as transparency and competence. Unfortunately, the Commissioners failed to manage adroitly the expectations of those affected by the inquiry, and based on their request for an extension it seems that they had challenges managing the human and material resources available to them.

In addition, decisions about standing, hearings, media strategy, and failures of transparency and communication with parties, witnesses, families, and the wider public all marred the inquiry's work. Had the inquiry rectified its failures with respect to communication, transparency, and accountability as it went along, it would have generated much more goodwill, support, and cooperation from those who desperately wished that it would succeed in its weighty task. Instead, it earned failing grades on these points from the Native Women's Association of Canada and from many who had worked for its establishment.[120]

Standing

The National Inquiry into MMIWG posted a notice advising that parties with an interest in the issues could apply for standing to participate in the inquiry. Ultimately, ninety-eight organizations were granted standing, but the decisions on standing were delivered late, coming only a couple of weeks before the first hearing. Funding agreements were drastically delayed. Resource-strapped parties with standing had to choose whether to attend hearings without any idea if or when reimbursement would follow, and indeed reimbursement took many months to arrive. When the agreements were received, they contained errors. For example, the contribution agreement initially provided to parties with national standing contained wording identifying it as based on the contribution agreement template for the missing salmon inquiry.[121] More problematic were the funding parameters requiring organizations with in-house legal expertise to hire outside counsel in order to qualify for reimbursement, causing unreasonable and unnecessary resource expenditures for small organizations.

Widespread frustration among stakeholders in the National Inquiry because of the lack of transparency about the commission's process and plans led to feelings of being disrespected among those most affected by its work. Although MMIW families were explicitly told that they need not seek standing before the inquiry, a group of families ultimately sought standing because of their frustration with the inquiry's failure to communicate adequately or transparently with them. Their view was that they might have more rights and abilities to engage with the process if represented by counsel.[122] Some groups were granted national standing, whereas others were granted regional standing, but it never became clear what regional standing actually meant. Groups with regional standing ultimately were given no role in the proceedings. Very little information emanated from the inquiry about what groups could expect, what timeline would be followed for hearings, or what role parties with national or regional standing would have at hearings or more generally.

In 2017, there was a troubling level of disorganization with respect to basic logistics. For example, in April, following a first set of community meetings in Whitehorse, the inquiry abruptly announced the indefinite postponement of community meetings planned for the following weeks in Edmonton and Thunder Bay, creating frustration for those planning to attend them.[123] In October, a set of hearings in Yellowknife was cancelled with less than a month's notice.[124] In late November, the inquiry cancelled a hearing in Rankin Inlet planned for the week of 11 December, stating that the chosen venue would not have been able to accommodate the privacy needs of the witnesses. However, inquiry staff would have had the opportunity to make that determination in an August visit to the community hall. Families were told that the hearing might be rescheduled for February 2018 and that staff were considering moving it to Iqaluit or Montreal.[125] The failure to address adequately Inuit women's concerns was exacerbated by this cancellation given that the hearing would have been the first in Nunavut or any Inuit region.

When an inquiry is completed on time and on budget, it contributes to the environment of goodwill that makes acceptance and implementation of recommendations more likely.[126] The importance of engaging individuals with prior inquiry experience is evident in examples such as the Goudge Inquiry, regarding criminal investigations of children's deaths in Ontario, in which the Commissioner, counsel, and staff all had extensive experience with prior inquiries.[127] The National Inquiry lacked many staff with previous inquiry experience, and crucially it lacked people with recognized experience and background in addressing the MMIW crisis. This seemed to stem from a misguided interpretation of independence. Given the importance of building trust, support, and engagement from the affected communities, this was a ruinous approach. Women who had worked to raise awareness and to address the prevalence of MMIW over many years would have been able to provide enormous support to the inquiry. They would have provided their networks in affected communities and their long-standing knowledge of structural violence, positive solutions, and persistent barriers, enabling the Commissioners to determine efficiently the areas with the greatest need of scrutiny. This would have made the most efficient use of limited resources. Any concern about such participation prejudicing the inquiry's work could have been addressed much the way it is in court – the Commissioners could have weighed the information that they received from the sources and made their own assessments. The strict formulation of the Canadian legal concept of independence seemed to be at odds with the claim that the inquiry would not adhere to the usual Western legal process.

The MMIWG *Interim Report* states that, "[f]rom the start, we have sought advice from people, groups, and organizations across the country."[128] Some of the coalitions (LSC, MMIW families) and organizations with national standing (including LEAF) during the period referred to made multiple attempts to connect with the inquiry and were roundly rebuffed for their efforts. Indeed, they attempted to provide constructive feedback to the Commissioners about their lack of engagement with civil society and with families and organizations feeling disconnected from or even unwelcome in the inquiry process. The defensive replies received to letters only deepened these feelings of alienation and collective worry about the direction (or lack thereof) of the inquiry.

Over the first eighteen months, the inquiry went through three Executive Directors and three Communications Directors and lost its chief commission counsel and several commission counsel, a Director of Community Relations, a Manager of Community Relations, and multiple other staff members.[129] In addition, one of the Commissioners resigned. The turmoil evident from these resignations and terminations decreased faith among the public in the operations of the inquiry and certainly decreased its ability to achieve what it had been mandated to achieve with the time and money available. It was disturbing to learn that the inquiry was projecting a deficit for its second year of operation.[130]

Assessing the National Inquiry into MMIWG

No inquiry (or at least no inquiry related to Indigenous issues) has been held in Canada with so much goodwill behind it at the outset, and no inquiry has squandered such goodwill so spectacularly. The National Inquiry into MMIWG had the benefit of a six-month pre-inquiry process that saw roundtables of previous Commissioners, commission counsel, and staff provide their insights into what works and what does not work for an inquiry to succeed.[131] In addition, Indigenous legal experts provided their thoughts on and suggestions for how the inquiry might proceed in a less colonial manner than the Canadian legal mechanism of the public inquiry. Sadly, the National Inquiry became neither an effective Canadian public inquiry nor an effective Indigenous legal mechanism. Although some witnesses praised the inquiry for enabling them to speak their truths, and though the report no doubt will be a valuable educational tool going forward, the inquiry gravely disappointed many of those who had called for its establishment for so many years. Many people worked hard to make the inquiry functional, both inside and outside its structure, but the dysfunction of the leadership and process frustrated their good faith efforts. Furthermore, the extreme trauma experienced by so many families with the deaths and disappearances of their loved ones surely took a further toll on all involved as the families tried to explicate their truths to the broader populace.

Of course, it is also true that the expectations of the National Inquiry were so high that they could never be achieved. Nonetheless, the Commissioners should have been able to run a competent inquiry as a baseline. The inquiry did not seem to succeed even on a simple logistical level, as evidenced by cancellations of hearings because of a failure to engage experts in time to proceed in Montreal and because of a failure to book hotel rooms in advance in Yellowknife.[132] On a procedural level, the National Inquiry retraumatized some families and survivors, counter to the stated intention to operate in a trauma-informed manner. It also managed to create tensions between MMIW families. For example, the paid National Family Advisory Circle members (some of whom were not people known to be engaged in MMIW advocacy prior to the National Inquiry) actively and openly opposed the families who wrote to the Chief Commissioner requesting changes to the course of the inquiry in May and August 2017. Although some families might have had positive experiences with the inquiry, likely because of the efforts of some of the dedicated staff who did their best in the circumstances, many families had negative experiences.

The National Inquiry failed to capture and maintain positive press coverage. Unfortunately, the most press garnered by the inquiry was related to the ongoing turmoil with departing staff. Hearings should have been covered prominently, but instead they passed through cities with few if any reporters present. Press releases were infrequent and not widely circulated. Although the hearings were webcast, there was limited publicity of this positive aspect. In this age of social media, a Communications Director ought to have been able to design and implement an effective and engaging campaign to draw the wider public into the work of the inquiry. It is unclear whether the succession of Communications Directors managed to engage even the people who closely followed the inquiry. I signed up multiple times for the updates promised on the inquiry's website and never received one. This includes the time period when I was Legal Director of a party with national standing before the inquiry.

The National Inquiry did not communicate a vision for the involvement of parties with standing. We received no emails advising us of the role envisioned for the parties, with the exception of a flurry of group emails and calls announcing the first expert hearing in Winnipeg a mere three weeks before it was held.[133] We were advised that only certain parties would be entitled to ask questions in cross-examination and that those questions would be time limited. At the hearing, we discovered that there was seating for only one representative from each party with standing, and the hearing room itself was too small to accommodate everyone comfortably. Despite the extensive knowledge and expertise of the witnesses called (Val Napoleon, Hadley Friedland, and Dawnis Kennedy), the hearing was not framed by a discussion of what their evidence was expected to be and why it was important for the National Inquiry to hear it. Métis law professor Karen Drake of Osgoode Hall Law School, scheduled to appear later in the hearing as an expert witness, opted to cede her time on the stand to the Elders present in order to hold a circle to engage the families in the room. The Elders acknowledged that the inquiry had badly failed to communicate its purpose and agenda to those who had gathered to hear its proceedings, including MMIW family members.

Members of the inquiry publicly blamed the federal government for limiting their ability to succeed by failing to provide the administrative and financial supports necessary to run such a large inquiry.[134] During the pre-inquiry phase, the government had assembled a secretariat of people to address logistical and administrative considerations such as office space, phone lines, and computer support so that the inquiry could hit the ground running. The Commissioners declined to engage the secretariat, citing the need to preserve their independence. There is no doubt that an inquiry must diligently guard its independence, and that it must walk a fine line in order to do so without getting bogged down in logistical and bureaucratic red tape, but it must also be a functional body, able to pursue its mandate. This can be achieved by ensuring that it has the authority and discretion to manage the resources offered to it.

The National Inquiry was uniquely challenging in that it was Canada's first "national" inquiry with orders in council required from each province in addition to the federal government to establish it. This provenance and the inherent trauma of the mandate made for a particularly challenging road for the Commissioners and staff as well as those who would appear before the inquiry or be affected by its work. All the more reason, then, for its leaders to be rigorous in creating a transparent, open, and accountable process in the pursuit of their mandate.

The National Inquiry as Truth Commission

Another problematic aspect of the National Inquiry into MMIWG was its conflation of the public inquiry and truth commission mechanisms. A few months into its mandate, the inquiry began to refer to its process and to its hearings as part of a larger "truth-gathering process." Perhaps the fact that the inquiry attempted to bridge the two types of commission corroborates my thesis that a truth commission is simply a form of public inquiry. Unfortunately, the National Inquiry operated neither as a proficient public inquiry nor as an effective truth commission. The MMIWG *Interim Report* noted that, as a federal public inquiry, it was mandated to hold hearings across Canada, gather witness testimony, conduct independent research and evidence to produce findings of fact, and make recommendations. However, the report states that

> [t]his process is rooted in Western law.
>
>   Because we are working to decolonize the National Inquiry process itself, we have changed the traditional hearing process to one that better reflects Indigenous laws. To differentiate this new format from that of previous inquiries, we have called it the "Truth-Gathering Process."[135]

The *Interim Report* then describes the three types of hearings encompassed by that process. They are community, institutional, and expert hearings, which were types of hearing forged by Justice Thomas Berger as Commissioner of the Mackenzie Valley Pipeline Inquiry in the early 1970s. The MMIWG *Interim Report* notes that "the term 'hearing' is a Western legal one, which may re-traumatize some family members and survivors who have had negative interactions with the legal system."[136] Although this choice of nomenclature echoes that of the TRC, which eschewed the term "hearings" as well, I would say that it is not the term that would retraumatize someone but the process utilized for taking statements. Indigenous people, including family members and survivors, are not so lacking in resilience that the term "hearing" will set them back. Rather, being subjected to a process that does not respect them, their experiences, and their humanity will be a challenge. Changing the name of a process but otherwise not fundamentally changing how it proceeds is not Indigenizing that process. It is merely raising expectations of the people there to "share their truths" and failing to produce a better process.

Suggesting that beginning the process with community hearings stems from a family-first approach, and framing this as an Indigenous conceptualization of the inquiry, belie the fact that inquiries such as those of Air India and Walkerton began by speaking with the families directly affected and injured by the events that gave rise to the inquiries. Respectfully, it is simply a humane place to start when dealing with trauma. Start with the people directly affected so that Commissioners and staff are grounded in that reality for the duration of their work. It will focus their minds on the purpose of the mandate and guide their decision making as the inquiry proceeds.

The National Inquiry into MMIWG struggled to execute its functions as either a "Western" legal mechanism or as something directed by "Indigenous" laws. Some of the difficulty might have arisen from the misguided conception of "independence" that prevented the Commissioners from accessing assistance that would have been critical to their success. It is possible that the internal workings of the inquiry did adhere to Indigenous laws, but the public process of the inquiry did not seem to be vastly different from those of previous commissions, though it did conduct opening and closing ceremonies according to Indigenous laws.

The short time span for the mandate and the wealth of research and recommendations and previous inquiries would have required the Commissioners to make difficult choices about where to focus inquiry resources. In this light, a different route could have been to focus on the failure of various governments and bodies to implement the over 700 known recommendations for addressing violence against Indigenous women.[137] The inquiry could have received testimony about what Indigenous law can tell us about implementing solutions that society is resisting for some reason.

In contrast to the hearings held by the National Inquiry, which were stilted, formal, and unnecessarily legalistic (witnesses were sworn in by commission counsel and cross-examined by counsel for the parties with standing), the Goudge Inquiry deployed roundtables of commission counsel and counsel for the parties to question experts, authors of inquiry research reports, and those knowledgeable about the subject matter of the inquiry to assist the Commissioner in shaping the recommendations.[138] The roundtables proceeded with an informal, interactive format that "led to a sense that the recommendations were based on a consensus involving multiple perspectives."[139] Justice Stephen Goudge focused on implementation from the outset of his inquiry: "His recommendations were intentionally measured, realistic, and proportionate to the problems."[140] Similarly, Justice Dennis O'Connor conducted the inquiry into the Walkerton tainted water scandal with considerable media savvy and high political acuity. His inquiry was on time, on budget, and well run. He engaged with the citizens of Walkerton from the outset, and he and his staff lived in the town throughout the inquiry. They began with four days of hearings with residents to hear the impacts of the tainted water on them. Justice O'Connor believed that broad public participation in the process created great support for his conclusions and recommendations.[141] Although these were provincial inquiries with much more focused mandates and fewer moving parts than a national inquiry, they are nonetheless instructive. Experience from both the Goudge and Walkerton inquiries formed part of the information provided during the National Inquiry's pre-inquiry consultation phase, experience that appeared to fall on deaf ears.

The Extension Request

The National Inquiry into MMIWG requested a two-year extension and an additional budget of up to $50 million in order to complete its mandate.[142] The letter of request dated 6 March 2018 from Commissioner Buller to Minister of Crown and Indigenous Affairs Carolyn Bennett provided a picture of an inquiry that had failed to undertake its mandate expeditiously. At the time they requested a two-year extension, the Commissioners acknowledged that they had not yet held expert and institutional hearings sufficient to ground their final report. The hearings that they subsequently held continued in the disorganized vein of the few held to that point – experts who ought to have been invited were not identified, and those who were identified were not always given sufficient lead time to guarantee their availability or to prepare for appearing before the inquiry.

The letter requesting the extension provided a number of insights into the state of the inquiry:

- A deficit was anticipated for the next fiscal year.
- Only one expert hearing had been held, and no institutional hearing had been held.
- A Métis advisory panel was only then being created, and advisory bodies involving Indigenous youth and 2SLGBTQQIA people had not been created.
- The inquiry had only recently begun to enter data and records into its electronic document management system. (Data entry should have been occurring as data were collected.)
- The lack of research conducted by inquiry staff is highlighted by the stated need to engage contract research if an extension were granted. In addition, the areas listed for research to be commissioned, as well as the original research yet to be conducted by the inquiry's research team, were concerning. These were all areas of research that should have been well under way.

- The letter described ongoing meetings with different stakeholders across the country but did not acknowledge or address the considerable dissatisfaction and concerns raised by various families, coalitions, communities, activists, and parties with standing.

The request for a two-year extension provided a dismaying list of tasks that the inquiry should have been performing but evidently was not. Given the significant staff turnover, the deficient nature of the MMIWG *Interim Report,* the cancellation of hearings, and the turmoil since its inception, the inquiry had questionable ability to manage further activities competently. Its institutional and additional expert hearings had yet to be scheduled. The experience up to that point did not prompt optimism about whether the mandate could be fulfilled. Because of the unique structure of the National Inquiry, each province and territory had to sign off on an extension as well. Minister Bennett said that "the decision to extend the mandate by just six months was made in part because provinces and territories were not unanimously supportive of extending the terms of reference for the inquiry" into the next year.[143]

The two-year extension requested by Commissioner Buller for the inquiry would not have been appropriate to grant given the shocking disarray indicated by its own request for an extension as well as the constant turnover in key staff. Rather, the inquiry needed to be encouraged to wrap up within (or close to) its original mandate period, focusing on properly completing the testimonies of the families that had decided to appear before it, and provide a report of those hearings and what could be learned from the experiences and knowledge of the families. The statements taken up to that point could then have been properly reviewed, analyzed, and reported on by the inquiry within its mandate. The families that chose to participate could and should have been honoured, but it was important to avoid further harm.

If the government was going to expend up to $50 million, then it needed to make a plan, led by and in consultation with respected and credible Indigenous MMIW advocates, for the implementation of a number of the known recommendations for addressing the crisis.[144] If an extension was not granted, then parties with standing, most of which still did not have contribution agreements (promised the previous summer) to facilitate their participation in the inquiry, would not be further inconvenienced, disrespected, and ignored. Rather, they could have been fruitfully engaged in developing an action plan to move forward constructively in addressing the systemic issues that had to be faced. A dynamic group of engaged, knowledgeable, and committed people stood ready to work on these issues. It would have been best to take from the inquiry what it managed to achieve within its original mandate and then proactively to direct energies and resources toward more constructive ways of addressing this horror in our midst.

When the government declined to grant the full two-year extension requested, the Commissioners posted a peevish press release expressing their disappointment, and Commissioner Audette suggested that she might not continue with the inquiry.[145] The Commissioners lamented the short timeline, massive mandate, and failure of the government to provide the longer extension, but the short timeline and broad mandate were known from the outset, requiring an effective plan and wise leadership. One of the commission counsel, Métis lawyer Breen Ouellette, resigned (the sixth commission counsel to leave), stating that he had lost confidence in the inquiry's leadership and alleging government interference.[146] There was no guarantee that, with all the time in the world, the inquiry would have been more effectively run.

Had the National Inquiry been properly run, and had its processes been inclusive of the many activists and organizations that had worked to bring it into existence, it would have been fiercely supported in its operations and in its request for an extension. Instead, the request for an extension met a divided public. Some believed that the inquiry should not be granted an extension because it had proven itself too flawed to be redeemed. Others believed that, despite its evident problems, it would be the only inquiry on MMIWG that Canadians would ever get, so it needed the extra time to try to get it right.

By any measure, the National Inquiry did review a tremendous amount of material to produce its report. There were 2,386 participants in the inquiry, including 1,484 family members and survivors, over the course of fifteen community hearings. A total of eighty-three experts, knowledge keepers, and officials testified at nine expert and institutional hearings.[147] The haphazard nature of the planning and the failure to provide adequate preparation time to parties and witnesses before hearings, and to provide clear rules to all involved,[148] reduced the overall potential and effectiveness of the inquiry.

The National Inquiry Report

The National Inquiry into MMIWG released its final report on 3 June 2019, considerably later than the date to which the inquiry had been granted an extension (April 30). Even the report's release was plagued with confusion and frustration. Although the inquiry headquarters were in Vancouver, the Commissioners decided to have the release in Gatineau on a day when the Prime Minister and many members of his cabinet were slated to be in Vancouver for the international feminist conference Women Deliver. The inquiry arranged for a lock-up of the report to provide it in advance to parties with standing. This was a frustrating failure, for many people waited by their computers across the country for a report that did not arrive on schedule. When it did arrive the following day, it was leaked to the press.[149] This meant that the people with the most knowledge about the inquiry, having participated in it, were unable to comment before the release since they were bound by their confidentiality agreements, but those who received the report via the leak were able to comment on it.

The multi-volume final report begins with dozens of pages of reflections by the Commissioners. There is no mention of the MMIW families until well into the report; rather, it foregrounds the Commissioners and their experiences. However, the report does contain 231 "Calls for Justice" which, though uneven, do build on recommendations made by parties with standing and contained in previous commissions and reports.[150] Since the root causes were known before the National Inquiry began its work, as were a multitude of ways to address those root causes and reduce the violence, the National Inquiry was obliged to incorporate and build on the credible work that preceded it.

Unfortunately, the release of the report was overshadowed by the news from the leaked report that the inquiry had concluded that Canada was committing genocide. Although the inquiry had been wise to commission a supplemental report detailing the reasons for this conclusion, it was not clear at first that the report was even available (the language used in the release suggested that it was to be issued later). The finding of genocide eclipsed any other finding and recommendation in the report. Although this was predictable, the inquiry neglected to devise a media strategy that could account for the massive concentration on that finding. Had the inquiry run with an effective media strategy throughout to engage and educate the public, it could have effectively laid the groundwork for that heavy conclusion to be accepted by commentators and the broader Canadian public. Once again the inquiry failed to operate in a strategic manner, thus sacrificing the biggest opportunity to educate members of the public and bring them on board in order to foment the political will necessary for implementation of its Calls for Justice.

That said, the report is akin to the BC MWI Report, *Forsaken*, in that it is more helpful than would have been predicted from the procedural morass that was the National Inquiry into MMIWG. Although not as well organized or well written as the BC MWI Report, the National Inquiry Report will be useful in the years to come. It contains a wealth of information from the testimonies at the varied hearings and from the research produced by the various researchers employed during its operations. Advocates will be able to cite the information contained therein as they seek improvements in the lives of Indigenous women and girls. Indeed, it is already being cited in trial and appellate court decisions across the country.[151]

But how much more useful could the report have been if the inquiry had been well run, without turmoil and lack of vision and direction, and without the turnover of staff, including Research Directors?

Implementation of Recommendations

Once a commission report is released, the focus shifts to urging governments to implement the recommendations. The National Inquiry into MMIWG recommendations would be analyzed and prioritized ideally in a process led by Indigenous women knowledgeable of the issues. The 1,200 recommendations previously made would also be considered.[152]

A national action plan to address the crisis of MMIW is sorely needed to address the on-the-ground and systemic problems that have been identified by MMIW families, civil society organizations, and activists. The LSC identified a number of measures that came up repeatedly in prior reports, including a national action plan to improve coordination of governments and agencies, Indigenous involvement in program development and delivery, public education, data collection, and more. Some of these measures were already part of the Liberal government's federal strategy in 2017 on gender-based violence, and some will overlap with other current initiatives of the government. A dedicated action plan to pull these threads together into a coherent approach to these systemic problems is necessary. Finally, there is a need for the government to work in concert with MMIW families and communities to design appropriate measures to memorialize and commemorate the disappeared and the dead.

Given the disarray of the National Inquiry, not all of its recommendations are consistent. For example, the criminal justice section calls for harsher sentencing in murder cases in which Indigenous women are victimized.[153] Since Indigenous men are frequently arrested for these crimes, and since there is a severe and well-known problem of over-incarceration, this sentencing recommendation is at odds with the call in the same section for increased restorative justice solutions.[154] Once an analysis is made of the inquiry's report, a set of prioritized recommendations should form the basis of the national action plan. An Implementation Commissioner should then be tasked with ensuring implementation of the recommendations. This would complement Call to Justice 1.10, which calls on the federal government to create an independent mechanism to report annually to Parliament on the progress made by all of those tasked with implementation.

The Viens Commission, 2016–19

While the National Inquiry into MMIWG was unfolding, an entirely separate public inquiry operated in Quebec – the Public Inquiry Commission on Relations between Indigenous Peoples and Certain Public Services in Quebec: Listening, Reconciliation and Progress, known as the Viens Commission after its Commissioner, retired Justice Jacques Viens. After media reports in October 2015 brought to widespread attention the fact that the Val d'Or police had a practice of taking Indigenous women on "starlight tours," dropping them outside town and leaving them to walk back, sometimes after subjecting them to sexual assault,[155] the provincial Liberal government appointed an inquiry in December 2016 with a mandate "to look into discrimination and racism within public services, including health care, youth protection, the correctional system, justice and policing."[156] Initially, the government had declined to appoint an inquiry, citing the existence of the National Inquiry as the appropriate body to address the issues.[157] However, after the Crown declined to lay charges in any of the thirty-seven complaints filed about police conduct, pressure mounted. In addition, the National Inquiry indicated that it would not be looking at the Val-d'Or situation in any detail. The government relented and appointed the inquiry.[158] It included in its mandate a requirement that it share any relevant information gathered with the National Inquiry.[159]

A total of 1,188 stories of interactions with police, hospital staff, and other public services, including youth protection agencies and the justice system, along with expert opinions, were shared over the thirty-eight weeks of hearings. Held mainly in Val-d'Or, the commission also travelled to Mani-Utenam, Mistissini, Montreal, Quebec City, and Kuujjuaq and Kuujjuarapik in northern Quebec. Prominent Indigenous organizations appeared multiple times before the commission, providing testimony on a wide range of issues.[160] By February 2018, the commission had heard from many organizations and experts but not from many individuals about their experiences with the justice system or the public service more broadly. To provide the time to hear from Indigenous people themselves, the government decided to extend the commission's mandate by ten months,[161] stipulating that a report had to be issued by 30 September 2019. Commissioner Viens wrapped up the hearings in December 2018, providing ample time to produce a report.

The inquiry was not without its problems. Minister of Justice Stéphanie Vallée stated at the outset that the purpose was not to lay blame or find culprits but "to reconcile and to progress," which raised concerns from women's organizations about police accountability.[162] There was criticism of the lack of Indigenous leadership and counsel at the inquiry, though it acknowledged this issue.[163] It made unsuccessful efforts to hire

Indigenous counsel but tried to ensure that counsel who were hired did have experience working in Indigenous communities or on Indigenous issues. The inquiry did hire Indigenous staff in a range of roles, in total about a fifth of the staff.[164] Effective September 2018, two lead counsel resigned from the inquiry, one stating that it was "for personal reasons."[165]

Despite the clear focus on Indigenous interactions with the justice system, and the assurance by the Quebec Minister of Justice that the proceedings would be informal,[166] with a white male former judge at the helm and a mandate created under the *Inquiries Act,* the government created what looked from the outset like a typically legalistic inquiry that proceeded in a clearly recognizable and orthodox manner in Canadian law. Several months of hearings with witnesses, legal counsel, and experts ensued. However, the way in which Commissioner Viens ran the proceedings was not a completely standard format for a Canadian public inquiry, though it is becoming more familiar. For example, the commission issued and posted procedural and operational rules providing detailed information about how the inquiry would be run.[167] At the end of the process, Commissioner Viens stated that,

> [i]nspired by the concepts of listening and reconciliation at the heart of my mandate, I endeavoured to give as much leeway as possible to citizens and public service representatives in expressing their reality. For example, I chose to let the witnesses relate the facts as they had lived or experienced them without applying the usual rules for questioning and cross-examination. That decision was motivated by the particularly sensitive character of the events that led to the creation of the Commission, their highly emotional nature and the very real risk of further victimizing individuals who were already in an extremely fragile state.
>
> In other words, I used the prerogatives available to me in terms of processes and rules of evidence to make it easier to shed light on certain events and understand their impacts on the people concerned. Like a hand reaching out – which I like to consider to be a premise for reconciliation – this guideline was reflected in the way our inquiry was conducted, in the support offered to people who came to testify and also in the hearing room.[168]

Regular press releases informed the public about the inquiry's schedule and activities.[169] Commissioner Viens also invited the wider public to participate in the commission's work by inviting briefs to be submitted and presented at public hearings that occurred in major centres and in more remote communities.[170]

Commissioner Viens issued his report on 30 September 2019. He stated that Indigenous peoples in Quebec are subject to systemic discrimination with regard to public services and that it has resulted in poor services or a complete denial of services to entire populations: "In a developed society such as ours this reality is simply unacceptable."[171] He reviewed the colonial history and widespread ignorance as well as prejudices and stereotypes that resulted in this situation, finding that "[w]e all bear collective responsibility for this failure. At times we let our prejudices and our fear of other cultures get the better of our sense of humanity."[172]

Commissioner Viens made 142 calls for action, echoing the TRC's form of recommendations. Stating that "[t]here can be no reconciliation without first acknowledging the mistakes," the first call for action recommended that the Quebec government make a public apology to Indigenous peoples for the harm caused by laws, policies, standards, and practices of public service providers.[173] The release of the report was widely covered in Quebec, though like the commission itself not broadly covered in the rest of Canada. Its release led the news cycles, and within a few days Premier François Legault made an apology in the legislature and vowed to work with Indigenous leaders to implement the recommendations.[174]

Also of note is Commissioner Viens's call for a formal follow-up mechanism independent of the parties involved, recommending in Call for Action 138 that the Quebec ombudsman be mandated to assess and follow up on the implementation of the calls for action until fully executed, with Call for Action 139 recommending that the ombudsman's budget be adjusted to account for these added responsibilities. Call for Action 140 recommends an obligation for the ombudsman to produce a public progress report annually. Commissioner Viens also states the importance of citizen monitoring as an informal mechanism to help ensure implementation. To facilitate this, and in recognition that, "[w]hen it comes to reconciliation and true collaboration between one nation and another," he believes that it is essential for Indigenous peoples to be able to "make the content of the report their own."[175] He therefore recommends translation and distribution of the summary report into all Indigenous languages used in Quebec (Call for Action 141) and distribution in audio form out of respect for those peoples' oral traditions (Call for Action 142).

From the tone of the report and recommendations, it is clear that the process of listening to hundreds of Indigenous people recount their difficult stories had a profound effect on Commissioner Viens. Although he produced a report that is sympathetic and open to Indigenous peoples, it does not provide justice to the courageous women who came forward to disclose publicly the violence perpetrated against them by police officers. Despite acknowledging the useful aspects of the report and recommendations, Indigenous women and organizations in Quebec criticized the report for failing to focus on the situation of the Indigenous women who had prompted the inquiry in the first place.[176] The Quebec police officers association noted that the report was a collection of "hearsay" evidence and therefore that its conclusions were not based on "legal evidence."[177] Thus, the allegations of violence against Indigenous women that had instigated the commission were not seriously addressed.

The long-term impact of the commission remains to be seen, of course, but though not perfect the Viens Commission managed to function in a fairly efficient and purposeful way and made recommendations intended to ensure that their implementation will occur. Like some previous non-Indigenous Commissioners, once Commissioner Viens learned the history and heard the overwhelming evidence (whether hearsay or legal) of structural violence from Indigenous people, he concluded that it is the responsibility of non-Indigenous Canadians to act, noting that "the complexity of the challenge should not stop us from trying."[178]

As a provincial inquiry, the Viens Commission is best compared with the MWI or the AJI rather than the National Inquiry into MMIWG. A provincial inquiry does have the benefit of a less complex jurisdictional environment in which to conduct its work, whereas the National Inquiry had to navigate the federal, provincial, and territorial jurisdictions implicated in its mandate. Nonetheless, the ability to "dance with the one who brung you" is yet another skill required of a Commissioner, no matter the jurisdiction or mandate.

The Nova Scotia Home for Colored Children Restorative Inquiry, 2015–19

Parallel to the ongoing colonialism and genocidal policies directed at Indigenous peoples in what is now Canada has been the racist treatment of the Black population in this land. One of the country's oldest Black populations resides in Nova Scotia, and it is there that we have seen one of the most groundbreaking public inquiries unfold and report.[179] This inquiry obviously did not focus on violence against Indigenous women and girls, but it merits a brief discussion here because of its innovative process.

This inquiry was designed and run in a manner completely unique in the world of public inquiries. Former residents were invited to advise the government in a collaborative design process. Although the inquiry was created pursuant to Nova Scotia's *Public Inquiries Act*,[180] it proceeded in a way that itself would "model the difference it sought."[181] The mandate and terms of reference were determined through a facilitated, collaborative process that lasted ten months and developed relationships that would build a basis for trust.[182] The structure, based on restorative justice principles, included people drawn from the various constituencies most implicated to act as a Council of Parties in the search for a resolution to the decades-long travesty that was the Home for Colored Children. This council formed the group of Commissioners who proceeded on the basis of consensus.[183] Although the inquiry operated independently, it did not view long-standing engagement in and knowledge of the issues as an impediment to that independence. Rather, it viewed that expertise as a strength.[184] It sought to engage the public in its process, thereby educating the wider population about the travesty that the school represented and how that travesty is situated within broader systemic racism in Nova Scotia society.

The report explains how this inquiry differed from a typical public inquiry, while noting that the inquiry model is not set in stone and can be flexible in design and approach.[185] The various innovations and solutions to perpetual inquiry problems are enumerated in the report, and indeed the inquiry appears to have run in the manner that I have suggested in this book is possible and desirable.

Conclusion

Returning to the main focus of this chapter, the National Inquiry into MMIWG, a difficult question remains: Why did a commission that had so much support and goodwill behind it at the outset become such a disappointment in its operation? Despite many stakeholders' efforts to work constructively with the Commissioners and staff to improve its communications, processes, and effectiveness, and despite the genuine efforts of individuals at the inquiry to engage in their work, it is as I feared in 2014:

> While I support the calls for a national inquiry, it is critical to choose the right commissioner(s) for the job, and to shape the terms of reference so as to enable a meaningful inquiry to proceed, or risk the inquiry becoming a wasteful, frustrating, missed opportunity.[186]

It is necessary to take the long view if one is not to become totally disheartened by seeing the enormous resources that go into inquiries and the failure to implement the recommendations from them. These recommendations, hundreds of them, based on evidence, were crafted with forethought and care by innumerable Commissioners of integrity and sincerity. That was the quip about the government response to RCAP: the government called its response *Gathering Strength*, whereas those of us who knew that RCAP's 440 orphaned recommendations sat waiting for adoption on a lonely Ottawa shelf called it "Gathering Dust."

The relatively brief time frame of two years for the National Inquiry into MMIWG to complete its work meant that hard decisions had to be made about its scope and focus. Given the wealth of information previously compiled in dozens of reports and hundreds of recommendations, the inquiry might have examined the phenomenon of non-Indigenous Canadian resistance to doing what we know needs to be done to save women's lives. The entrenched Canadian identity as the "good guy" is what the inquiry needed to dislodge or at least recalibrate. Of course, its conclusion of ongoing genocide will undoubtedly have that effect over time, but the inquiry process was a missed opportunity for Canadians to learn – and, even more importantly, to learn to accept – the truth about violence against Indigenous women in this country and to do something about it. I cannot and would not speak for Indigenous women about whether the National Inquiry was a failure for them, but I can say as a colonially trained Canadian lawyer that it was a missed opportunity to shift fundamentally the narrative in the minds of non-Indigenous Canadians about their complicity in and indeed responsibility for violence against Indigenous women and girls.

Conclusion

Whether a commission (a public inquiry or a truth commission) fulfills the social function of public education about a pressing societal issue depends on its leadership and process. If future inquiries on Indigenous issues adopt – and adapt – the commission model developed in the Berger Inquiry, then the process can build momentum and support through its operations and fulfill its social function of educating the public. However, a failure to engage the non-Indigenous public in the inquiry will impede its ability to fulfill this social function. An inquiry must heed the caution voiced by RCAP about relying on survivors to do the work of reconciliation. An inquiry must shape a narrative that engages Indigenous and non-Indigenous people in a shared process.

The truth commission is a specialized form of public inquiry. Aside from dealing exclusively with human rights and focusing on a pattern of human rights violations rather than an isolated incident, the main distinguishing feature of a truth commission is its symbolic value in acknowledging a historical injustice by its very inauguration. I noted that this symbolic value is operationalized by the explicitly social function of a truth commission to educate the public about the historical injustice in order to prevent any reoccurrence.

The TRC was a response to the failure of the usual legal mechanisms to acknowledge effectively the harms to survivors. In particular, the inability of civil litigation, criminal prosecution, and alternative dispute resolution to capture the systemic nature of the IRS harms prevented these mechanisms from adequately assessing the consequences for people and communities. This hindered the ability of these mechanisms to promote social accountability for the IRS legacy.

One of the most important challenges that the TRC faced was the task of constructing a narrative in Canada that acknowledges Indian residential schools as part of a larger government policy toward Indigenous peoples rather than as a collection of boarding schools with some abusive teachers. Such a narrative contemplates broader harms (cultural, spiritual, linguistic, intergenerational) wrought by the IRS system rather than simply the incidents that happened at certain schools to certain individuals. The point is not to adopt one view to the exclusion of all others but to acknowledge the harms that have occurred in order that Canadian society cannot deny their existence. In this way, a truth commission can promote social accountability. This construction of a national narrative was a critical part of the TRC's mandate of national reconciliation. If Canadians can continue to deny or be ignorant of the IRS legacy, then it will be very difficult to move forward into a respectful future. Thus, the task of creating a national narrative was part of the social function of the TRC.

As demonstrated by the Berger Inquiry, it is possible for a public inquiry to affect significantly the narrative in a country. That inquiry began to educate Canadians about our arrogance in our use of this land and our assumptions about our benevolence as a nation. This shift in narrative was instigated by an inquiry process that interrogated the competing narratives of the North as both frontier and homeland. The work of Indigenous activists to disrupt these Canadian national myths at the time of the Berger Inquiry has continued. Georges Erasmus, in a speech in Vancouver in 2002, stated that

[c]reating and sustaining a national community is an ongoing act of imagination, fuelled by stories of who we are. The narratives of how Canada came to be are only now beginning to acknowledge the fundamental contributions that Aboriginal people have made to the formation of Canada as we know it.[1]

Preaching to the converted does not shift a national narrative – the pedagogical work of an inquiry must engage the broader public if it is to be effective.

The Berger Inquiry coincided with a time when Indigenous organizing with respect to self-determination was developing in Canada and when the concept of public consultation was becoming increasingly accepted.[2] It marks a time when people started to question "progress" and its costs. Concern about the environment began to resonate with non-Indigenous people. Although the Berger Inquiry enabled voices to be heard that would otherwise have gone unheard, the inquiry itself occurred at the whim of a Canadian political system that, during a minority Parliament situation, enables such voices to be heard. A different political balance might have produced a different Commissioner. A different Commissioner undoubtedly would have produced a different report. The significant impact achieved by the inquiry clearly surprised the pipeline's advocates. The idea that the inquiry might have represented "some unavoidable explosion of 'truth'" reinforces the perception that something larger than anticipated from a public inquiry took place.[3]

Why is the Berger Inquiry so important? It represents many aspects of Canada's nationhood. The Berger Report acknowledges the mythologizing by southern non-Indigenous Canadians about the North as well as the pioneering spirit of the explorers – this time for resources in the ground rather than on it. The *Globe and Mail*'s observer of the Berger Inquiry noted its powerful effect on countering the accepted narrative of the North:

> [Berger] described the inquiry in Toronto as "a traveling teach-in" and there is no doubt that, whatever he recommends in his final report, much has been accomplished already by massive consciousness-raising, both in the north and in the south about the north. Not even John Diefenbaker's rhapsodic "northern vision" of 1958 measures up (even though it inspired the greatest political landslide in Canada's history).[4]

Whether or not public inquiries fulfill their social function will depend on their leaders and the processes those leaders adopt. The idea that an inquiry can be a "teach-in" illustrates the pedagogical potential of the commission of inquiry form. It is through this process of consciousness raising that the narrative can be reshaped. The process is the key. Success on the public education front can be achieved through an open and transparent approach, strict adherence to independence, a comprehensive and effective media strategy, and broader civil society involvement. Sustained media attention and the number and variety of participants in the hearings alert the government to the political currency acquired by an inquiry. Public education leads to understanding and acknowledgment of the realities of different communities. This increased awareness in turn can foster political will for implementing policy change. The inquiry process must generate broad public interest in the issues such that the government cannot quietly shelve the report.

Over the decades since the Berger Inquiry, truth commissions have become a commonly used mechanism in addressing deep rifts in societies around the world. Rarely, though, have established democracies employed them. Canada's truth commission to address the legacy of the Indian residential schools is one example. The issue of the schools was raised in a critical way, possibly for the first time, by the Berger Report. In every community that Berger visited in the North, the effects of the schools entered into the testimonies that he witnessed.[5] He became convinced that Indigenous control of the education of Indigenous children would be crucial to the settlement of land claims. Twenty years later the Royal Commission on Aboriginal Peoples dedicated a chapter of its monumental report to residential schools and called for a public inquiry to investigate and document the origin and effects of residential schools policies and practices.[6] Another decade passed before the TRC was negotiated. The thread that links these commissions displays the value of public inquiries in the Canadian legal fabric. The Berger Inquiry was not about residential schools, but its report began to lay the groundwork for their legacy to be discussed in public life.

The public inquiry process can promote social accountability in a way that the courts cannot. A commission can encourage citizens to reflect on their society and acknowledge their own responsibility in creating a greater democratic good. With respect to RCAP, J.R. Miller stated that

[i]t is fitting that a royal commission operating in the name of the people
of Canada is looking into the issue because in a fundamental sense the
party that bears most responsibility for the residential school story is
the people of Canada. Churches and federal bureaucracy no doubt were
the instruments that carried out specific acts or neglected to do what
needed to be done in particular cases. But behind both the churches and
the government stood the populace, who in a democracy such as Canada
ultimately are responsible.[7]

This desire for broader social accountability was part of the genesis of
the TRC. Courts can only provide solutions to individual cases and order
remedies between parties to the litigation; they are unable to address the
collective pain that survivors and their communities endure as a result of
the IRS system. The costs of litigation for individuals, in both financial and
emotional terms, can be prohibitive. The trial process is plagued with
delays, often resulting from arguments about minutiae that do not touch
on the heart of the case. There can be tactical arguments by defence counsel to delay the process or discourage the plaintiffs from proceeding. The
totality of the harms experienced by the plaintiffs might not fall into compensable legal categories, or the time elapsed since the harms occurred
can bar recovery because of limitation periods. There might be no recognition of ongoing and intergenerational harms. Courts are unable to
promulgate societal responsibility for the policies of which the Indian
residential schools were a part. The TRC was negotiated because survivors sought a response that the courts could not provide. In the face of
mass human rights violations, the courts might not be able to deliver
justice. Some measure of healing might result from the acknowledgment
through the TRC process of the injustice that the IRS system caused for
survivors and their communities. The TRC was a critical opportunity to
engage Canadians in ideas about what it means to live in society with one
another.

Berger pointed out the two overarching narratives in the North with
respect to the pipeline, and in doing so he opened the eyes of people to see
how they viewed their country. Some of the work of an inquiry involves
simply teaching Canadians that they have a world view shaped by their

own cultures that might not accord with that of their neighbours. Even to contemplate reconciliation there must be an understanding that the parties might view things fundamentally differently. It is in this process of public education about past injustices that Canada might be able to reach forward into a future that includes a more just relationship between Indigenous and non-Indigenous people.

I have not spoken at length about justice in this book, though in many ways the entire project is about what justice looks like depending on the legal mechanism employed to respond to a grave injustice. The response to past injustice must surely include some kind of justice. The basic impulse behind the concepts of transitional justice and restorative justice is a search for a means of redress for past human rights violations that will acknowledge the harms done and work to prevent their reoccurrence. At the beginning of a speech in Vancouver in 1984, Berger quoted Northrop Frye: "[M]an must seek his ideals through social institutions."[8] Although it was a speech about the Constitution and his idea of Canada, Berger indicated that his approach to the Canadian legal framework links outcomes to processes. If we want the country to exhibit certain values, then our institutions must reflect them. If we are to seek our ideals through social institutions, then a commission of inquiry presents a unique opportunity to do so.

One narrative of Canada tells us that we are a nation of explorers and immigrants, of multiculturalism and tolerance. This standard narrative of Canada is not shared by the Indigenous inhabitants here. With the TRC, Canada embarked on a voyage into a new frontier – an opportunity to formulate a new narrative. The TRC was not a public inquiry in the form so familiar to Canadians. Nor was it entirely like other truth commissions that the world has known. Time will tell whether we have navigated the journey into this frontier any more effectively than in the past.

In considering the inquiries that have addressed the MMIW crisis, I have argued that both the BC MWI and the National Inquiry into MMIWG had challenges flowing from their leadership and processes. A truth commission is simply a form of public inquiry, and, despite my critique of the National Inquiry as a failed hybrid of the two mechanisms, both it and the BC MWI could have been opportunities to conduct transitional justice.

The MWI could have been structured more as a truth commission and less as a formal legal inquiry in that the focus should have been the impact on the women of the structural, systemic issues of policing instead of on the intricacies of police procedure (though the latter should still have been explored). If the process had been led by a person without a taint of conflict of interest, if the government had not frustrated the process for including women's organizations, and if the inquiry had not been dominated by police witnesses and testimonies, then there might have been an opportunity to begin a process of reconciliation for the women and communities traumatized by the events that precipitated the inquiry. If the province had extended funding to all parties with standing, instead of spurning them in the name of cost saving (decidedly not a gesture of reconciliation), then the course of the inquiry would have been different. Instead, whatever the merits of the final report, the inquiry process denied a voice in the proceedings to the very communities silenced by the horrific systemic abuse inherent in Canadian society disproportionately directed at Indigenous women and girls. As lawyer Cameron Ward, who represented the families of twenty-five of the women, told the inquiry during his final submissions,

> [m]y clients are disappointed, discouraged and, most of all, angry at the way this commission has unfolded. They feel this commission has perpetuated the attitude of indifference and disrespect that they themselves first experienced when they reported their loved ones missing.[9]

As for the National Inquiry, the impact and value are still to be assessed, and my observations about its work might not accord with others' experience of it. However, I believe that my reflections might be shared by those with whom I worked to try to ensure that the National Inquiry was not a wasted (and, worse, damaging) opportunity. My purpose here is to try to ensure that, as we continue to utilize the inquiry mechanism, we improve its effectiveness.

The choice of leadership of an inquiry is absolutely critical to the credibility of that inquiry both for the immediate stakeholders and for the broader community. The MWI in British Columbia was hampered from the outset because of the baggage that Commissioner Oppal brought with him to the role. The AJI in Manitoba was bolstered from the outset by the choice of Co-Commissioners with strong reputations for fairness and, it must be said, for the choice of both Indigenous and non-Indigenous Co-Commissioners. The work of Justice Sinclair on the AJI suggests that he was well placed to acknowledge gender dimensions of the IRS legacy in the TRC's work, and indeed the TRC's Calls to Action included a call for a National Inquiry into MMIWG.

The MWI and the AJI are part of a continuum of commissions of inquiry regarding Indigenous issues in Canada. Between them came the Royal Commission on Aboriginal Peoples, which provided a comprehensive picture of Canada's relationship with Indigenous peoples, including the IRS system.[10] RCAP contained a chapter dedicated to issues related to Indigenous women.[11] In many ways, the earlier AJI was a much more effectively run endeavour than the MWI. The fact that the MWI followed the AJI and RCAP yet was plagued with problems does not send a good message about the growth of Canadian society in terms of its ability to address violence against Indigenous women. The tale of these inquiries illustrates the continued and extreme discrimination directed at Indigenous women in Canada and the state's paltry response to it.

The process that an inquiry utilizes has an important role in changing the narrative of a contentious societal issue. A key component of transitional justice is the implementation of processes that deconstruct and reconstruct the national narrative. A dominant Canadian narrative is one of a country that defends human rights and champions the principles of equality and justice for all. Effective transitional justice processes are needed to address the ongoing structural violence created by continued colonialism. Thus, continued use of the commission of inquiry mechanism with regard to Indigenous matters in Canada should incorporate more explicitly aspects that mirror truth commissions in their operations. This would mean acknowledging from the outset the colonialism and racism that no doubt undergird the issue to be addressed rather than suggesting that there is some more palatable context in which to cloak the schism. It would mean adopting a process that is not lawyer driven but survivor centred, trauma informed, and holistic. It would mean treating the process of the inquiry itself as a national teach-in so that the wider public is engaged and educated throughout.

Assessing a commission requires a consideration of factors that include the formal mandate of the inquiry, as expressed in the terms of reference, the budget and time frame of the inquiry, the selection of its leadership, and other measures that a government might have extended, or withheld, that bear on the ultimate success of the endeavour. We need not resign ourselves to holding inquiries whose recommendations gather dust. The factors of institutional design (e.g., pre-inquiry consultations on the terms of reference, an effective media strategy, and public education) included in the inquiry have a strong bearing on the likelihood that its recommendations will be implemented.

The value or success of a public inquiry is not measured solely by the implementation of its recommendations – if it was, then I would wonder why the institution continues to exist given the paltry record of any government in Canada of adopting any inquiry's full set of recommendations. Rather, an inquiry can be measured by the pedagogical value of its process and its ability to create or influence the societal narrative about its subject. Did the public become engaged in the work of the inquiry? Was it therefore truly a *public* inquiry? Did this public engagement translate into support for the inquiry's work? If so, then did this support translate into political will to implement its recommendations? Did the public conversation about the inquiry's topic change as a result of the inquiry's work? Did the wider community become aware of the issue, and did people view the issue differently because of the inquiry? Did the stakeholders involved in the inquiry have to re-evaluate their methods or change their own views of the subject? These questions, if answered in the affirmative, indicate that the inquiry has contributed to the dialogue on an issue, which is a positive measure of any inquiry, given the vagaries of political will and public engagement.

The commission of inquiry and the truth commission share two main goals with respect to addressing past human rights violations: to find out what happened and to prevent its reoccurrence. One might say that in Canada public inquiries have failed miserably on the second goal, particularly with regard to Indigenous peoples. Keep in mind the context of the past number of years – there was the apology in 2008, and the TRC issued its Calls to Action in 2015 – but there still seems to be a massive disconnect between our words and our actions. Indeed, while the TRC was still under way, and while the TRC Interim Report called for increased health supports for Indigenous peoples, the federal government chose to discontinue funding the Aboriginal Healing Foundation and to defund the National Indigenous Health Office as well as the National Centre for First Nations Governance. How can we talk of reconciliation while undermining the very organizations and supports that can help it to occur?

There are two ongoing narratives in Canada – one is of reconciliation, one is of indifference.[12] One way in which the National Inquiry report is important is in making the essential connection to the systemic issues of colonialism, including the IRS legacy, that led to the disproportionate numbers of missing and murdered Indigenous women. This connection must continue to be made forcefully and fearlessly if the narrative of reconciliation is to have any chance of overcoming our indifference to the levels of violence inflicted on Indigenous women in Canadian society. It is our obligation as non-Indigenous Canadians to resist the continued colonial attitudes of our governments, to insist on decolonizing our own minds and actions, to educate ourselves on the work that has been done, and to commit to supporting the work that must come, to name, understand, and challenge violence against Indigenous women and girls.

No single inquiry can fix systemic racism in Canada. This much is obvious. However, a succession of inquiries, if run well, with careful attention to leadership and process, can create awareness, which can chip away at the dominant narrative over time. In this way, Commissioners who utilize the possibilities of the public inquiry model in order to perform a social function provide something of the truth commission for the affected community. Where governments attempt to limit Commissioners from situating their mandates in the larger context in which they exist, Canadian communities are denied the opportunity to learn from or gain some healing from the inquiry process. Governments can show their willingness to undertake the hard work of examining their own human rights behaviour by establishing inquiries with effective leadership and the framework, flexibility, and resources for that leadership to develop an effective process.

This is the post-TRC, post-Marshall, post-so-many-other-inquiries era in which the families of Cindy Gladue and Tina Fontaine have suffered immeasurable harms. We need to connect the dots, and we need to be willing to face uncomfortable truths about ourselves and our society. What is needed is really for non-Indigenous Canadians to face the reality of our deeply entrenched racism and sexism, not only in terms of how we think of and treat Indigenous women but also in terms of structural matters, such as governance, treaty implementation, education, and implementation of countless recommendations from public inquiries such as RCAP. There is a deeper structural issue that must be addressed. Canada is a country based on attempted genocide, and the National Inquiry into MMIWG has found that the genocidal behaviour continues. Our genocidal policies have spawned generations of dysfunction and hurt. Whether we are prepared to own this past and present will determine whether there is any prospect for a future of just coexistence.

Any such self-assessment by non-Indigenous Canadians must include a reckoning about land. The murders and disappearances of Indigenous women are connected in a fundamental way to the loss of the land. Traditional territories are the lifeblood of healthy communities, and the colonial state from the outset has sought to remove Indigenous peoples from their lands. One of the most explicit tools for this policy of the Canadian state has been the *Indian Act*. At the First Nations Summit in Ottawa on 24 January 2012, Prime Minister Harper compared the *Indian Act* to a tree with deep roots and indicated that he had no plan to repeal or rewrite it. According to Satsan (Herb George), President of the National Centre for First Nations Governance (an organization subsequently defunded by the Harper government),

> [t]his government's policy is to perpetuate the *Indian Act* and protect the Department of Indigenous Affairs. Neither instrument is capable of governing First Nations. Canadians are far too familiar with the many examples of how the *Act* and the Department perpetually fails First Nations. This government's decision is to maintain the *Indian Act* in an attempt to keep First Nations people on Crown reserves and separated

from their lands, so that they can move ahead with resource extraction, development and exportation.[13]

Indigenous peoples who have pursued modern treaties typically have removed themselves from the *Indian Act,* and though it might not always have gone smoothly it is generally viewed as a desirable outcome in terms of governance and reclamation of culture, language, and, most importantly, sovereignty.

Despite all that they have been subjected to under our genocidal policies, Indigenous peoples have not disappeared. They assert their rights and cultures through many means, including in the arts, media, and politics. After seven generations of residential schools, the rebirth of Indigenous cultures across what is now Canada is nothing short of amazing. Indigenous legal scholars are actively revitalizing Indigenous law, which they rightly assert pre-existed contact and which they seek to reinstate more openly as part of the governance of their territories. Canadians will see more assertions of sovereignty and self-determination as the Northern Gateway pipeline question looms ahead of us, with the planned path crossing through many First Nations territories in northern British Columbia. Many of the questions and arguments first made publicly in Canada before the Berger Inquiry will be resurrected, and we would do well to adopt the approaches and recommendations of such commissions as we seek to embrace reconciliation in this country. Despite my critiques of some of the commissions that we have had, they form part of an important dialogue in Canada of public inquiries over the years, a dialogue that has sought to address the scarred relationship between Indigenous and non-Indigenous people.

Aside from becoming serious about how to divest themselves from traditional territories, governments must acknowledge that structural violence, stemming from racism and sexism, exists, and we must address the systemic discrimination endemic in our society. This means that known recommendations dating back to the 1970 Royal Commission on the Status of Women, including elements such as a national daycare program and access to education, employment, and housing for women, must be implemented since these changes are needed in order to bring about meaningful equality in Indigenous (and other) women's lives.[14] The answers to some of our difficult societal questions require us to look into our own history and knowledge base.

Finally, we must not forget that all of this talk about inquiries arises from terrible grief, including the loss of well over a thousand women, each of whom should be honoured as a human being with a family, a life, and the right to live without violence. Meg Cywink's sister Sonya was loved and treasured by her family. No inquiry can bring her back or provide all of the answers that her family still seeks. However, if we are to have inquiries in the future, then surely we can do better than to add to their sorrow.

I am by turns fiercely patriotic about and deeply ashamed of my country, Canada. I believe in the possibilities of this country at a time when the world is turning to ideas contrary to the alleged ideas of this one – multiculturalism, fairness, and human rights. I struggle because I know that these ideas are part of the Canadian mythology. I long to find a way to make them less mythological, but I believe that the only way to do so is to have honest conversations about the foundation on which this country was built and still stands. I want us to align our talk with our actions, and our self-image with our truths.

If we are to be the country of our imagining, then we really do have work to do.

Epilogue

On 8 September 2020, as I sat at my friend Anne's cabin working on the final revisions to the manuscript of this book before sending it to UBC Press for publication, I received a call from the federal Minister of Public Safety, Bill Blair. He asked me to accept an appointment as the third Commissioner on the joint federal-provincial public inquiry into the April 2020 mass casualty in Nova Scotia. It was a humbling request, one that would challenge me to implement my own advice on how to design and operate an effective inquiry.

I finished writing this book almost two decades after my opportunity to observe the National Reconciliation Commission in Ghana piqued my interest in such commissions. During this period, many places in the world have leaned toward autocracy and fascism; hatred and war have manifested themselves in new and horrible forms. These threats to democracy have also started to prompt a new awareness and a reckoning of the myriad forms of oppression as well as the culpability of bystanders and democratic institutions in perpetuating them. Reimagining mechanisms of transitional justice to address the root causes of societal ruptures is critical in order to ensure the nourishment of our ability to recognize each other in all of our humanity.

This is not the first book that I had wanted to write from the mass of archival research that I had conducted on past inquiries. That book would have focused entirely on the Mackenzie Valley Pipeline Inquiry, but I thought that this book had a more pressing purpose. The urgency that I felt in writing this book arose from the sense that I described above of a missed opportunity with the National Inquiry into MMIWG. I had joined the call for the inquiry because, from my academic work, I believed that a well-run inquiry could generate the political will to address the terrible indifference of Canadians to violence against Indigenous women and girls. By explaining how institutional design can create positive change, I could indicate how the mechanism of the commission of inquiry could be optimized.

When I worked with the dedicated group of women on the Legal Strategy Coalition on Violence against Indigenous Women, we compiled 700 recommendations that many conscientious people on previous inquiries and investigations had created, based on evidence that they had heard and gathered, that they believed would save the lives of women and girls. And we saw that these 700 recommendations had not been implemented. The deaths and disappearances that finally prompted the National Inquiry did not come out of thin air. They arose in our midst, and those conscientious people on previous inquiries and investigations had identified the root causes. The compounding travesty is that we had 700 ways of preventing egregious harm, and instead we did nothing.

This is the issue that has haunted me and driven me to write this book, which I hope will assist future inquiries, including my own. Having spent a considerable number of years working to address violence against Indigenous women, and given the TRC's Calls to Action and the establishment of the National Inquiry into MMIWG, I saw it as essential to draw out the pedagogical and social potential of public inquiries – to educate the public about injustices in order to prevent their reoccurrence. With all that I have learned about commissions of inquiry, those that have gone well and those that have not, I still believe that they are an important part of our legal fabric. With limited public resources and the need to shore up confidence in public institutions, we must ensure that societal ruptures are addressed in meaningful ways that do not add to cynicism about democratic institutions. Our willingness to look at the hard problems in a conscientious and careful way is vital, and whether or not we succeed in the short term in making the necessary changes, I see commissions of inquiry as instrumental in creating a record that prevents denial and over time will shift our national narrative toward justice.

As I finished writing this book, I realized that, after the past two years of working on it, if I were to begin afresh today, I would write it differently. This book contains my thinking about how commissions can be run in order to ensure that their conclusions do not land silently on a shelf where they remain undisturbed. But that larger question of the systemic reasons that we know what must be done yet do not do it is where I would start if I were to begin writing today. With our continued use of these inquiries, not only must we establish and run them in such a way that recommendations are more likely to be implemented, but also we must ask the right questions of ourselves.

This realization relates to my initial questions about why established democracies do not tend to establish commissions of truth, preferring instead commissions of inquiry, and whether or not the colonial origin of the commission of inquiry mechanism can contribute to reconciliation with Indigenous peoples. It is not so much the name of the mechanism as the society in which it is employed. Can Canada, as a settler colonial country, decolonize itself sufficiently to establish and deploy commissions in a manner that will hold that mirror up to our faces? The foundational work had to be done before I could get to the bigger question of the colonial origin of the mechanism and whether it could ever do the labour of reconciliation – but it is not the mechanism used so much as the ongoing colonialism of the Canadian state that hampers (re)conciliation. In this light, the responsibility for how the National Inquiry into MMIWG unfolded does not lie entirely at the feet of its Commissioners. The decisions made by the government in choosing the Commissioners and assigning and resourcing such a massive mandate must bear considerable scrutiny as well. A colonial government set up a colonial legal mechanism, a public inquiry, to address a crisis created by colonial structural violence. It may be that the heartfelt efforts of the Commissioners and their staff simply could not overcome this truth.

Canada is still a country that decides whether people are members of a particular race through the operation of the *Indian Act*. True, the Liberal government of Justin Trudeau has stated its intention to prioritize its relationship with Indigenous peoples and has initiatives under way in that regard. Its selective implementation of the RCAP recommendations saw the split of Indigenous and Northern Affairs Canada into two new ministries – the Department of Crown-Indigenous Relations and Northern Affairs and the Department of Indigenous Services – but the basis of RCAP's conclusions was that a complete restructuring of the relationship was required. All of the talk of reconciliation is belied by actions that continue to focus on resource extraction from the land; for example, the federal government purchased a pipeline for $4.5 billion, whereas every social indicator for Indigenous peoples continues to be off the charts.

So, I have written a book about how to operate a commission of inquiry in order to improve the likelihood that its recommendations will be implemented, but the underlying question about why we resist implementing recommendations that we know would improve and even save Indigenous lives persists. Perhaps that is a book to be written by a neuroscientist or social scientist since the answer to that question might not lie in the law. Holding inquests and inquiries into Indigenous deaths is a form of performative caring unless we are willing to do the heavy lifting of implementing recommendations. Until then, we will continue to deny the humanity of Indigenous lives.

I suppose that I should not be surprised that it is only in the *process* of writing this book that I can begin to see where I should have started and finished it. And now I will be walking in the shoes of Commissioners before me who have agreed to peer into our society's darkest places and to shine a light into those places. Of course, I fully recognize that I now have a vested interest in my own theories. Doubtless by the time this book has gone to press I will wish I had written it even more differently and will have even more compassion for those Commissioners and others whose work I have critiqued in these pages. I know that I am standing on their shoulders as I undertake the daunting task ahead of me. I expect that those people will offer their own rejoinders, information, and experiences to address any error that I have made. I trust that they will see this book as part of the dialogue on public inquiries in Canada, offered in the spirit of trying fundamentally to improve how we use the public inquiry mechanism. In writing this book, I truly wish to ensure that inquiries do not create more harm than good. I also want to reinforce the importance of a demo-cratic culture in which we not only delve into the shadows with our lanterns but also have the wherewithal to make the changes that we learn we must make in order to exhibit our commitment to equality for all that our Constitution espouses.

My thoughts about the Berger Inquiry will have to wait for another day, at least two years from now, when my work with the Mass Casualty Commission is complete. I am writing this epilogue in November, in a small cabin on the wintry eastern shore of Nova Scotia, during the pandemic, where I am self-isolating for the required fourteen days before meeting my Co-Commissioners in person for the first time. It is a place evocative of reflection, both on the lessons of the past and on the sombre task ahead. My hope as I embark on this journey with my Co-Commissioners is that, by the time we complete our part of the difficult work ahead, we will have asked useful questions and garnered some answers for the people and communities affected by those terrible events. I hope that our leadership and process will contribute to meaningful change. Now the work begins.

Appendix

1828   Report of Major H.-C. Darling, Military Secretary to Governor General Lord Dalhousie

1837   Report of the Committee of the Lower Canada Executive Council

1839   Mr. Justice Macaulay's Report to Sir George Arthur

1844   A Report on the Affairs of the Indians in Canada, Governor General Sir Charles Bagot (this report addressed perceived problems regarding land and recommended the establishment of residential schools)

1858   Report of the Special Commissioners to Investigate Indian Affairs in Canada, Richard Pennefather, Civil Secretary to the Governor General

1869   Dominion Commissioner to Inquire into the North West Rebellion, Donald Smith (later Lord Strathcona)

1876   Joint Indian Reserve Commission

1885   Commission to Inquire into the Second Riel Rebellion

1912   McKenna McBride Royal Commission

1970   Royal Commission on the Status of Women

1973   Royal Commission on the Non-Medicinal Use of Drugs

1977   Mackenzie Valley Pipeline Inquiry (Berger Inquiry)

1989   Royal Commission on the Donald Marshall, Jr., Prosecution

1991   Manitoba Public Inquiry into the Administration of Justice and Aboriginal People (the Aboriginal Justice Inquiry, AJI)

1995   Royal Commission on Aboriginal Peoples (RCAP)

2002   Walkerton Commission of Inquiry

2004   Neil Stonechild Inquiry

2004   Commission of Inquiry into the Actions of Canadian Officials in Relation to Maher Arar

2006   Commission of Inquiry into the Investigation of the Bombing of Air India Flight 182

2007   Ipperwash Inquiry

2011   Davies Commission, Inquiry into the Death of Frank Paul

2012   British Columbia Missing Women Inquiry (MWI)

2015   Truth and Reconciliation Commission of Canada (TRC)

2019   Public Inquiry Commission on Relations between Indigenous Peoples and Certain Public Services in Quebec (Viens Commission)

2019   Nova Scotia Home for Colored Children Restorative Inquiry

2019   National Inquiry into Missing and Murdered Indigenous Women and Girls (MMIWG)

Notes

Introduction

1 The National Inquiry concluded that "no one knows an exact number of missing and murdered Indigenous women, girls and 2SLGBTQQIA people in Canada. Thousands of women's deaths or disappearances have likely gone unrecorded over the decades." National Inquiry into Missing and Murdered Indigenous Women and Girls, *Reclaiming Power and Place: Executive Summary of the Final Report* (2019) at 3 [National Inquiry Final Report, Executive Summary]. See discussion in Chapter 5, below, regarding the estimated numbers of disappeared and murdered women and girls.

2 The inquiry commonly used the acronym MMIWG, and in its report it included First Nations, Métis, and Inuit gender-diverse and non-binary people, represented by the acronym 2SLGBTQQIA (Two-Spirit, lesbian, gay, bisexual, transgender, queer, questioning, intersex, and asexual). National Inquiry Final Report, Executive Summary, *ibid* at 5. I have generally used the acronym MMIW for the sake of simplicity, but I do refer to women and girls throughout this book. I acknowledge that trans, non-binary, queer, intersex, Two-Spirit, and other marginalized people are also disproportionately targeted for violence in Canadian society.

3 The coalition of MMIW families first wrote to the Chief Commissioner in May 2017 to raise concerns about the process of the inquiry (I assisted in drafting the first letter). Their worry increased with the lack of response to their concerns, and they wrote again in August 2017, demanding a reset of the inquiry. In addition, the national organizations with standing before the inquiry, including LEAF, wrote a joint letter to the Chief Commissioner in August 2017 to try to encourage the inquiry to improve its approach, communications, and processes more generally (letters on file with the author).

4 See Kim Stanton, *Truth Commissions and Public Inquiries: Addressing Historical Injustices in Established Democracies* (SJD, University of Toronto Faculty of Law, 2010), online: <https://tspace.library.utoronto.ca/handle/1807/24886>.

5 A professor of law at the University of Calgary, she was later the Chief Negotiator for the Assembly of First Nations in the historic Indian Residential Schools Settlement Agreement.

6 Aboriginal law refers to the area of Canadian law as applied to Indigenous peoples; "Aboriginal" is the term used in s 35 of the *Constitution Act, 1982,* being Schedule B to the *Canada Act 1982* (UK), 1982, c 11. "Aboriginal law" is distinct from "Indigenous law," a general term for the laws of Indigenous peoples (e.g., Haudenosaunee law or Anishinaabe law). I use the following terms: "Indigenous" when referring to the original inhabitants of what is now Canada; "Aboriginal" when referring to concepts in Canadian law such as Aboriginal title, Aboriginal self-government, and Aboriginal rights; "Aboriginal" and "First Nation" when referring to court or government descriptions of Indigenous peoples or people or concepts related to them where the terms refer to legal constructs applied to Indigenous peoples or people; and "Indian" where that is the term used in legislation or policy (e.g., Indian residential schools and Indian bands).

7 See the discussion of the McKenna McBride Commission in Chapter 1, note 121.

8 The term "survivor" refers to former students of the schools and was adopted for use by the TRC Commissioners after initially questioning its appropriateness. See Truth and Reconciliation Commission of Canada, *Survivors Speak* (2015), online: <http://www.trc.ca/assets/pdf/Survivors_Speak_English_Web.pdf> at xii. The Commissioners determined that "[a] Survivor is not just someone who 'made it through' the schools, or 'got by' or was 'making do.' A Survivor is a person who persevered against and overcame adversity." *Ibid* at xiii.

9 By "established democracies," I mean states that generally have stable legislative, judicial, and administrative systems functioning under the rule of law (admittedly a contested concept, particularly by colonized peoples; see, for example, Mark D Walters, "The Morality of Aboriginal Law" (2006) 31:2 Queen's LJ 470 at 478 [Walters, "The Morality of Aboriginal Law"]). I contrast established democracies in this text with "emerging democracies," by which I mean states entering a post-conflict period, undergoing regime change from authoritarian to non-authoritarian rule, where the new regime seeks to create the institutions that would be identified with established democracies.

10 The inquiry's original budget was $53.8 million. An additional $38 million was added when it was granted a six-month extension. See Maura Forrest, "With Federal Government Set to Grant $38M More, MMIW Inquiry Budget Will Hit $92M," *National Post* (14 November 2018), online: <https://nationalpost.com/news/politics/

with-federal-government-set-to-grant-38m-more-mmiw-inquiry-budget-will
-hit-92m>.

11 See Denise Balkissoon, "An Idea: Read the Report on Indigenous Women's Lives
before Dismissing It," *Globe and Mail* (13 June 2019), online: <https://www.
theglobeandmail.com/opinion/article-an-idea-read-the-report-on-indigenous
-womens-lives-before-dismissing/>. The article refers to a number of the kneejerk
responses to the National Inquiry's finding of genocide.

12 As I discuss in Chapter 5, the National Inquiry did not effectively lay the groundwork for this shift in narrative about Canada that would have enabled understanding and acceptance of its primary finding.

13 See, for example, Ed Ratushny, *The Conduct of Public Inquiries: Law, Policy, and
Practice* (Toronto: Irwin Law, 2009); Ronda Bessner & Susan Lightstone, *Public
Inquiries in Canada: Law and Practice* (Toronto: Thomson Reuters, 2017); Stephen
Goudge & Heather MacIvor, *Commissions of Inquiry* (Toronto: LexisNexis Canada
Inc., 2019).

Chapter 1: Inquiries in Canada

1 DH Borchardt, *Commissions of Inquiry in Australia: A Brief Survey* (Bundoora, Vic:
La Trobe University Press, 1991) at 11 [Borchardt], identifies three types of
inquiry:

   1 investigatory – appointed to establish the facts of a situation and to make recom-
     mendations to government on matters of policy;
   2 inquisitorial – set up to determine, in the manner of the police, the facts of an
     incident or of events in the past;
   3 advisory – to formulate the basis of government policy.

2 Gerald Le Dain, "The Role of the Public Inquiry in Our Constitutional System" in
Jacob S Ziegel, ed, *Law and Social Change* (Toronto: Osgoode Hall Law School, York
University, 1973) 79 at 85 [Le Dain].

3 Robert Centa & Patrick Macklem, "Securing Accountability through Commissions
of Inquiry: A Role for the Law Commission of Canada" in Allan Manson & David J
Mullan, eds, *Commissions of Inquiry: Praise or Reappraise?* (Toronto: Irwin Law,
2003) 79 at 80–81 [footnotes omitted] [Centa & Macklem].

4 Le Dain, *supra* note 2 at 82. He states that an inquiry's "function is to inform the
public, to clarify the issues, and to promote understanding of a problem."

5 Roach (a member of my doctoral committee at the University of Toronto Faculty of
Law, along with co-supervisors Mayo Moran and David Dyzenhaus) refers to this
as "social accountability." See Kent Roach, "Canadian Public Inquiries and
Accountability" in Philip C Stenning, ed, *Accountability for Criminal Justice: Selected
Essays* (Toronto: University of Toronto Press, 1995) 268 at 269 [Roach].

6 *Ibid* at 274.

7 *Ibid* at 272.

8 *Ibid* at 268. See, however, John C Kleefeld & Anila Srivastava, "Resolving Mass Wrongs: A Command-Consensus Perspective" (2005) 30:2 Queen's LJ 449 [Kleefeld & Srivastava], who note at 487 that there are also disincentives to calling an inquiry, "such as loss of direction over the inquiry, including its costs and timeline and the surrender of the ability to shape public opinion about a matter under investigation."

9 AR Lucas & EB Peterson, "Northern Land Use Law and Policy Development: 1972–78 and the Future" in Robert F Keith & Janet B Wright, eds, *Northern Transitions* (Ottawa: Canadian Arctic Resources Committee, 1978) at 80.

10 Centa & Macklem, *supra* note 3 at 81. For example, then Prime Minister Stephen Harper infamously refused to establish an inquiry into MMIW because he thought that "another report" was not needed. See Chapter 5, note 21.

11 Nicholas D'Ombrain, "Public Inquiries in Canada" (1997) 40:1 Can Pub Admin 86 at 104–5 [D'Ombrain]:

> Looking back over the sweep of policy inquiries, from Rowell-Sirois to Macdonald, there is no doubt that Canadians have been well served by developing processes that bring Canadians together to examine and develop new ways to deal with known problems. Official Ottawa has benefited from the fresh air and broader view that the inquiry process brings to bear on the policy process. It is disquieting to think that the landmark policy inquiry may be falling into disuse. It cannot be because Canada no longer has need of new ideas.

12 Liora Salter, "The Two Contradictions in Public Inquiries" in A Paul Pross, IM Christie, & John Yogis, eds, *Commissions of Inquiry* (Toronto: Carswell, 1990) 173 at 175 [Salter, "Two Contradictions"].

13 See, for example, *Starr v Houlden*, [1990] 1 SCR 1366, in which the Supreme Court of Canada found that a provincial inquiry amounted to a substitute for criminal proceedings.

14 Michael Trebilcock & Lisa Austin, "The Limits of the Full Court Press: Of Blood and Mergers" (1998) 48:1 UTLJ 1 at 9 [Trebilcock & Austin].

15 *Commission of Inquiry on the Blood System in Canada: Final Report* (Ottawa: Public Works and Government Services Canada, 1997), online: <http://publications.gc.ca/pub?id=9.698032&sl=>. See Trebilcock & Austin, *supra* note 14; Kleefeld & Srivastava, *supra* note 8 at 487–88; John H Gomery, "The Pros and Cons of Commissions of Inquiry" (2006) 51 McGill LJ 783 at para 33 [Gomery].

16 Trebilcock & Austin, *supra* note 14 at 29.

17 *Ibid* at 24.

18 The Walkerton Commission of Inquiry run by Justice Dennis O'Connor made recommendations in 2002 for the future safety of drinking water in Ontario. See Ontario,

Report of the Walkerton Commission of Inquiry (Toronto: Publications Ontario, 2002), online: <http://www.attorneygeneral.jus.gov.on.ca/english/about/pubs/walkerton/>.

19 See, for example, the Commission of Inquiry into the Actions of Canadian Officials in Relation to Maher Arar, *Report of the Events Relating to Maher Arar* (Ottawa: Public Works and Government Services Canada, 2006).

20 Gomery, *supra* note 15 at para 34. Justice Gomery ran the Commission of Inquiry into the Sponsorship Program and Advertising Activities, established by Prime Minister Paul Martin in February 2004.

21 Salter, "Two Contradictions," *supra* note 12 at 182. See Law Reform Commission of Canada, *Administrative Law: Commissions of Inquiry* (Working Paper 17) (Ottawa: Law Reform Commission of Canada, 1977) [Law Reform Commission, Working Paper 17] at 11:

> Some inquiries have been controversial; others have been almost totally ignored. Some have had a substantial impact on government policy; the recommendations of others have been seemingly ignored, although they may have had indirect effects difficult to assess. But it is significant that much of the history of Canada could be interpreted through the work of commissions of inquiry.

22 Law Reform Commission, Working Paper 17, *supra* note 21 at 6. Today the name of a commission does not denote any particular status; the terms "royal commission," "commission of inquiry," and "public inquiry" often are used interchangeably.

23 Leonard Arthur Hallett, *Royal Commissions and Boards of Inquiry: Some Legal and Procedural Aspects* (Agincourt, ON: Carswell, 1982) at 16 [Hallett].

24 Borchardt, *supra* note 1 at 6–7.

25 RS 1906, c I-13, s 2.

26 Salter notes that "[a]lmost everyone agrees that the significance of terminology – inquiries versus Royal Commissions – is of little consequence." Liora Salter, "The Complex Relationship between Inquiries and Public Controversy" in Manson & Mullan, *supra* note 3, 185 at 187 [footnote omitted]. This observation echoes that of the Ontario Law Reform Commission: "It would appear that less emphasis is now given to terminology, and to formal and technical distinctions between royal commissions and other forms of public inquiry." Ontario Law Reform Commission, *Report on Public Inquiries* (Toronto: Ontario Law Reform Commission, 1992) at 144 [OLRC Report]. Although royal commissions "are one of the oldest institutions of government," Hallett determines that, in the Australian context, boards of inquiry were directly related to colonization. He posits that boards of inquiry evolved from the courts of inquiry used by early naval and military colonial governors. Hallett, *supra* note 23 at 16. This relationship between the development of the inquiry mechanism and colonization might warrant further study. There might be a parallel to the

rise of truth commissions in circumstances in which ordinary courts are not workable options.

27 D'Ombrain, *supra* note 11 at 90.

28 Hallett, *supra* note 23 at 1.

29 D'Ombrain, *supra* note 11 at 87 [footnote omitted].

30 *Ibid* at 89.

31 *Ibid.*

32 For example, the Commission of Inquiry into the Investigation of the Bombing of Air India Flight 182 was established on 1 May 2006 by Order in Council PC 2006-293; the Commission of Inquiry into the Actions of Canadian Officials in Relation to Maher Arar was established on 5 February 2004 by Order in Council PC 2004-48.

33 See OLRC Report, *supra* note 26 at 11–12; also see Le Dain, *supra* note 2.

34 See Mark Freeman, *Truth Commissions and Procedural Fairness* (Cambridge, UK: Cambridge University Press, 2006) at 124 [Freeman].

35 Although Nuremberg is viewed by some as a prime example of victors' justice, it is also the initial model for an international attempt to hold individuals accountable for the horrors perpetrated on civilians during the Second World War.

36 Martha Minow, "Innovating Responses to the Past: Human Rights Institutions" in Nigel Biggar, ed, *Burying the Past: Making Peace and Doing Justice after Civil Conflict* (Washington, DC: Georgetown University Press, 2003) 87 at 88 [Minow]. More recently, *ad hoc* international tribunals such as those for the former Yugoslavia and Rwanda, and the permanent International Criminal Court, were developed to respond to mass human rights violations.

37 Ruti G Teitel, *Transitional Justice* (New York: Oxford University Press, 2000) [Teitel]. See also Alexandra Barahona de Brito, Carmen Gonzalez-Enriquez, & Paloma Aguilar, eds, *The Politics of Memory: Transitional Justice in Democratizing Societies* (Oxford: Oxford University Press, 2001) at 320ff [Barahona de Brito, Gonzalez-Enriquez, & Aguilar].

38 Steven Ratner & Jason Abrams, eds, *Accountability for Human Rights Atrocities in International Law: Beyond the Nuremberg Legacy,* 2nd ed (Oxford: Oxford University Press, 2001) [Ratner & Abrams].

39 *Ibid* at 228.

40 *Ibid.* The authors identify the factors that determine the success of such commissions as the presence of sufficient political will, the state of the country's transition, and the available resources.

41 Juan E Méndez, "In Defense of Transitional Justice" in A James McAdams, ed, *Transitional Justice and the Rule of Law in New Democracies* (Notre Dame: University of Notre Dame Press, 1997) 1 at 1. According to Méndez, at 11–12, states with a legacy of human rights violations owe four obligations to victims in their midst: (1) prosecution of the perpetrators; (2) the right to know the truth about the abuses;

(3) reparations; and (4) banning of perpetrators from official roles in the new regime.

42   *Ibid* at 4.

43   Minow, *supra* note 36 at 87.

44   See Jonathan Allen, "Balancing Justice and Social Unity: Political Theory and the Idea of a Truth and Reconciliation Commission" (1999) 49:3 UTLJ 315 [Allen]. He ably assesses the arguments for and against truth commissions as a transitional justice mechanism. His article delves into the legal philosophical underpinnings of transitional justice with respect to the moral defensibility of truth commissions, their utility, and their relationship with justice and the rule of law.

45   Sanford Levinson, "Trials, Commissions, and Investigating Committees: The Elusive Search for Norms of Due Process" in Robert Rotberg & Dennis Thompson, eds, *Truth v Justice: The Morality of Truth Commissions* (Princeton, NJ: Princeton University Press, 2000) 211 at 217 [Levinson].

46   See, for example, the Report of the Secretary-General, *The Rule of Law and Transitional Justice in Conflict and Post-Conflict Societies,* UNSCOR, 2004, UN Doc S/2004/616 [Report of the Secretary-General], which acknowledges truth commissions as "a potentially valuable complementary tool" alongside tribunals and vetting processes, among other transitional justice mechanisms. This was echoed by the UN Office of the High Commissioner for Human Rights in 2006 when it explicitly set out truth commissions as one mechanism among several for returning a country to the rule of law. See UN Office of the High Commissioner for Human Rights (OHCHR), *Rule-of-Law Tools for Post-Conflict States: Truth Commissions,* 2006, HR/PUB/06/1 at 46. Priscilla Hayner, a leading truth commission scholar, was the Principal Consultant for the document; see note 62 below. See also Miriam J Auckerman, "Extraordinary Evil, Ordinary Crime: A Framework for Understanding Transitional Justice" (2002) 15:46 Harv Hum Rts J 39, for a challenge to the primacy of prosecution in response to mass atrocity and a call for goal- and culture-specific responses to mass atrocity.

47   Teitel, *supra* note 37 at 81. See also Barahona de Brito, Gonzalez-Enriquez, & Aguilar, *supra* note 37 at 320ff.

48   Allen, *supra* note 44 at 352.

49   Ratner & Abrams, *supra* note 38 at 238.

50   Neil J Kritz, "Coming to Terms with Atrocities: A Review of Accountability Mechanisms for Mass Violations of Human Rights" (1996) 59:4 Law & Contemp Probs 127 at 127 [Kritz, "Coming to Terms"].

51   See further discussion of restorative justice in Chapter 4, note 176.

52   Ratner & Abrams, *supra* note 38 at 238–39.

53   *Ibid* at 239.

54 Neil J Kritz, *Transitional Justice: How Emerging Democracies Reckon with Former Regimes* (Washington, DC: United States Institute for Peace Press, 1995) vol 1 at xxvi [Kritz, *Transitional Justice*].

55 Teitel, *supra* note 37 at 78.

56 This section relies on Priscilla B Hayner, *Unspeakable Truths: Confronting State Terror and Atrocity* (New York: Routledge, 2001) [Hayner, *Unspeakable Truths*].

57 *Constitution of the Republic of South Africa 1993*, No 200 of 1993 (the "Interim Constitution"); *Promotion of National Unity and Reconciliation Act*, No 34 of 1995. The Interim Constitution was followed by the *Constitution of the Republic of South Africa 1996*, No 108 of 1996, adopted on 8 May 1996 and amended on 11 October 1996 by the Constitutional Assembly.

58 One of the many books written on the South African TRC that gives one a sense of its profound impact is Antjie Krog, *Country of My Skull: Guilt, Sorrow, and the Limits of Forgiveness in the New South Africa* (New York: Three Rivers Press, 2000).

59 Priscilla B Hayner, "Fifteen Truth Commissions – 1974 to 1994: A Comparative Study" (1994) 16:4 Hum Rts Q 597 at 606 [Hayner, "Fifteen Truth Commissions"].

60 Although as noted there were instances of truth commissions prior to the 1990s, transitional justice did not become a significant focus of scholarly attention until the explosion of literature and scholarship that accompanied the South African TRC, established in 1995. See Barahona de Brito, Gonzalez-Enriquez, & Aguilar, *supra* note 37 at 315–51. Barahona de Brito's thorough bibliographical survey notes that the first book to focus on transitional justice was published in 1982 (*ibid* at 316, citing John H Herz, ed, *From Dictatorship to Democracy: Coping with the Legacies of Authoritarianism* [Westport, CT: Greenwood Press, 1982]) but shows that the vast majority of scholarship on the subject commenced in the 1990s. As is evident from Kritz's comprehensive multi-volume set in 1995, transitional justice literature had become a substantial area of scholarship. By then, there had been a considerable number of truth commissions and other transitional justice mechanisms that provided case studies. Kritz, *Transitional Justice, supra* note 54.

61 See Diane Orentlicher, "Settling Accounts: The Duty to Prosecute Human Rights Violations of a Prior Regime" (1991) 100:8 Yale LJ 2537 at 2546, n 32.

62 Ratner & Abrams, *supra* note 38 at 319, with respect to their discussion of Cambodia and the Khmer Rouge. See also Hayner, *Unspeakable Truths, supra* note 56. Her book was the first major text to focus on truth commissions and can be seen as an indication of the growth of their use by 2001. Her book illustrates the degree to which truth commissions had become an accepted mechanism for addressing human rights violations but does not speculate on their utility for established democracies. Aside from providing a definition of a truth commission frequently referenced by virtually all other transitional justice scholars, the book provides a case study of twenty-one

such commissions and explores the questions then being commonly asked by scholars about the best way to deal with cases in which there are thousands of victims and thousands of perpetrators. That is, is it best simply to forget the past and move on, or is it best to address the past? If the latter, the debates on amnesties, truth versus justice, whether truth commissions should name names, and the conflicting choice between truth commissions and trials all require careful attention.

63   Neil J Kritz, "Where We Are and How We Got Here: An Overview of Developments in the Search for Justice and Reconciliation" in Alice H Henkin, ed, *The Legacy of Abuse: Confronting the Past, Facing the Future* (New York: The Aspen Institute and NYU School of Law, 2002) 21 at 24.

64   *Ibid* at 21. See also *ibid* at 43. Although truth commissions are "a relatively recent experiment," their presence over the past two decades means that we "are now entering a period in which retrospective studies are possible in order to begin to evaluate the effect of truth commissions."

65   *Ibid* at 29.

66   Phil Fontaine, "The Long Journey to Justice: The Personal as Political" (lecture delivered at Preparing for the Truth Commission: Sharing the Truth about Residential Schools. A Conference on Truth and Reconciliation as Restorative Justice, University of Calgary, 15 June 2007) [unpublished] [Calgary Conference, 2007]. Fontaine stepped down as National Chief at the AFN annual general meeting in Calgary on 21 July 2009.

67   Conversation with the author, 31 March 2007. The Ghana Center for Democratic Development facilitated the Civil Society Coalition that monitored the commission throughout its mandate (commencing in 2002 and reporting in 2005). As noted by Freeman, *supra* note 34 at 23, n 84, the *National Reconciliation Commission Act, 2002*, Act 611, had to conform to the commission of inquiry provisions of the *Constitution of the Republic of Ghana 1992*, arts 278–83.

68   As noted below, such states are typically reluctant to have bodies called truth commissions.

69   See Chapter 4, note 113.

70   Freeman, *supra* note 34 at 18, citing the UN Secretary-General's definition of a truth commission: "Truth commissions are official, temporary, non-judicial fact-finding bodies that investigate a pattern of abuses of human rights or humanitarian law committed over a number of years." Report of the Secretary-General, *supra* note 46 at 17, para 50. See also Hayner's influential account of truth commissions in *Unspeakable Truths, supra* note 56 at 14 [emphasis in original]:

   (1) truth commissions focus on the *past*; (2) they investigate a pattern of abuses over a period of time, rather than a specific event; (3) a truth commission is a temporary body, typically in operation for six months to two years, and completing its work

with the submission of a report; (4) these commissions are officially sanctioned, authorized, or empowered by the state (and sometimes also by the armed opposition, as in a peace accord).

71 Salter, "Two Contradictions," *supra* note 12 at 175. See Allan Manson & David J Mullan, "Introduction" in Manson & Mullan, *supra* note 3, 1 at 4.

72 Freeman, *supra* note 34 at 56–57.

73 *Ibid* at 124.

74 *Ibid.*

75 See Hayner's comment regarding the difficult and cumbersome process undertaken by the South African TRC to ensure due process for participants. Hayner, *Unspeakable Truths, supra* note 56 at 130.

76 The National Reconciliation Commission of Ghana had the authority to investigate any event from 1957 to 1993 and was not inaugurated until 2002.

77 See the description in Hayner, *Unspeakable Truths, supra* note 56 at 50ff, of the sixteen lesser known truth commissions – many did not appear to focus on victims at all.

78 *Ibid* at 17.

79 *Ibid.*

80 *Ibid* at 17–18.

81 Hayner, *ibid,* suggests that a historical truth commission is a public inquiry into the past but not a truth commission, and Freeman, *supra* note 34, agrees. Yet the National Reconciliation Commission of Ghana fits Hayner's description of historical truth commissions given that it was inaugurated a decade after the end of unconstitutional rule, after a peaceful transfer of power, and with a mandate to investigate a period reaching back to independence in 1957. It is surprising, then, that neither Hayner nor Freeman questions that the Ghanaian commission was a truth commission. Canada's Royal Commission on Aboriginal Peoples came at the same time as Australia's human rights inquiry into its history of residential schools. Although Hayner describes RCAP as a "historical truth commission" (*supra* note 56 at 18), Freeman calls RCAP a "thematic commission of inquiry" (*supra* note 34 at 56). Such commissions of inquiry are not truth commissions in his opinion because they examine controversial "social policy issues" such as racial discrimination (*ibid*) and focus more on policies than on victims. Leaving aside the possibility that Indigenous people might view the issue of "racial discrimination," particularly on the scale exercised under colonization, as much more than a "social policy issue," the implication seems to be that public inquiries address less egregious situations than do truth commissions. Furthermore, their work is "not necessarily focused on the examination of violations committed during periods of abusive rule or armed conflict" (*ibid*). Had RCAP been more victim centred, would Freeman have defined it

as a truth commission? Or, had Indigenous peoples violently resisted the abuses suffered on a larger scale, would that have prompted Freeman to lend the moniker of truth commission to RCAP? Is there an intrinsic failure to recognize that an established democracy such as Canada could be capable of "violations committed during periods of abusive rule"?

82 Thus, a truth commission can comment on systemic patterns rather than determining guilt in individual cases. Kritz, "Coming to Terms," *supra* note 50. Freeman states that truth commissions focus on severe acts of violence or repression, they focus primarily on acts that occurred during recent periods of repressive rule or armed conflict, they focus on violations committed in the sponsoring state, and they operate within the country that establishes them. Freeman, *supra* note 34 at 14–17.

83 Ratner & Abrams review non-prosecutorial options for gaining accountability for human rights violations, including investigatory commissions, civil suits, and immigration measures. With respect to investigatory commissions, they state that

> [m]any nations that have endured serious human rights violations have pursued accountability by establishing an investigatory commission, often referred to as a truth commission or a commission of inquiry. Speaking generally, these panels investigate a past period of human rights abuses (or, in fewer cases, humanitarian law-based crimes) in a particular country, in the end producing an official report ... [The authors list Hayner's criteria for a truth commission.] Aside from these common threads, panels have varied widely; and many of a commission's attributes will depend on its historical, political, and security context.

Ratner & Abrams, *supra* note 38 at 228–29 [footnote omitted].

84 Peter Aucoin, "Contributions of Commissions of Inquiry to Policy Analysis: An Evaluation" in Pross, Christie, & Yogis, *supra* note 12, 197 at 200, states that

> commissions of inquiry are well suited as institutional mechanisms for policy analysis if the following conditions are met:
> - multi-member commissions rather than single member commissions;
> - multi-disciplinary staff;
> - a mixture of experienced administrators and outside expertise;
> - a public hearings process;
> - a diffused and decentralized operational system for research, discussion and deliberation; and
> - public dissemination of studies as well as report.

85 Commissioner John Major of the Commission of Inquiry into the Bombing of Air India Flight 182 devoted the first three weeks of the hearings at the Commission of Inquiry into the Bombing of Air India Flight 182 to hearing the stories of the bombing's victims. Government of Canada, "Public Hearings Begin September 25, 2006,"

(news release, 21 September 2006) online: <https://www.canada.ca/en/news/archive/2006/09/public-hearings-begin-september-25-2006.html>.

86 For example, the Manitoba Aboriginal Justice Inquiry was led by Co-Commissioners; see note 125 below.

87 Freeman, *supra* note 34 at 15.

88 Generally, truth commissions tasked with this mandate are referred to as truth and reconciliation commissions, but not all truth commissions are truth and reconciliation commissions; see Hayner, *Unspeakable Truths, supra* note 56 at 30. Although some emphasize this aspect of their mandates by having the word *reconciliation* in the name of the commission, others set truth seeking as their mandate without attempting overtly to seek national reconciliation.

89 See Roach, *supra* note 5; Salter, "Two Contradictions," *supra* note 12; Le Dain, *supra* note 2 at 85.

90 These sorts of institutional design decisions were noted by the Ontario Law Reform Commission:

> When a government appoints an independent public inquiry with highly respected commissioners to examine a social problem, it does something qualitatively different than when it appoints a less independent task force or advisory body to examine the same problem.

OLRC Report, *supra* note 26 at 13. I also acknowledge that it might not be feasible to determine that a truth is "the truth" in any given circumstance.

91 Ratner & Abrams, *supra* note 38 at 229, citing Hayner, "Fifteen Truth Commissions," *supra* note 59 at 604. Ratner & Abrams conclude at 240 that "[t]he task of investigatory commissions is further complicated by their lack of institutional history and credibility from which well-functioning judicial mechanisms benefit." In my view, had they related truth commissions to the long-standing history of commissions of inquiry, this criticism would fail. The concept that truth commissions are unique to transitional justice has been questioned by some commentators. See David Dyzenhaus & Mayo Moran, eds, *Calling Power to Account: Law, Reparations and the Chinese Canadian Head Tax Case* (Toronto: University of Toronto Press, 2005) at 6. See also Levinson, *supra* note 45 at 211; David Dyzenhaus, "Review Essay: Transitional Justice" (2003) 1:1 Intl J Const L 163 at 174–75 [Dyzenhaus, "Review Essay"]; and Eric A Posner & Adrian Vermeule, "Transitional Justice as Ordinary Justice" (2004) 117:3 Harv L Rev 762. The authors state at 763 that "legal and political transitions lie on a continuum, of which regime transitions are merely the endpoint."

92 See Allen, *supra* note 44 at 319: "Truth commissions are thought to play the symbolic role of making a decisive break with the official sponsorship of human rights violations that characterized the past. They are also intended to demonstrate the importance of justice and respect for the rule of law."

93 See Rose Weston, "Facing the Past, Facing the Future: Applying the Truth Commission Model to the Historic Treatment of Native Americans in the United States" (2001) · 18:3 Ariz J Intl & Comp L 1017 at 1051. Weston advocates for the establishment of a truth commission in the United States to create an official record of human rights abuses and violations experienced by Native Americans that would enable public acknowledgment of the harms. She notes that such an acknowledgment and any resulting apology would allow the United States to avoid the hypocrisy of viewing itself as a defender of human rights in the world community when it has not honestly assessed its own violations on its own territory.

94 Levinson, *supra* note 45 at 216. At 212, he cites as an example the United States Commission on Civil Rights, created under legislation passed in 1957 to investigate and report to Congress on the civil rights situation in America. The commission held hearings throughout the American South with respect to discrimination in voting.

95 Dyzenhaus, "Review Essay," *supra* note 91 at 174, citing Ronald C Slye, "Amnesty, Truth, and Reconciliation: Reflections on the South African Amnesty Process" in Rotberg & Thompson, *supra* note 45, 170 at 170; Levinson, *supra* note 45 at 211.

96 See Hayner, *Unspeakable Truths, supra* note 56, Appendix 1, chart 1 at 305ff. Of the twenty countries that Hayner identifies that held truth commissions (as opposed to historical truth commissions), only one was an established democracy (Germany – Commission of Inquiry for the Assessment of History and Consequences of the SED Dictatorship in Germany, 1992–94) – and it was inquiring into an authoritarian regime. Most of the bodies in established democracies were named as some variation of commission of inquiry, and none used the name truth commission. Appendix 1, chart 2 at 312–13. These commissions were the Commission on Wartime Relocation and Internment of Civilians (United States), 1981–82, created by the Congressional Committee on Interior and Insular Affairs; the Royal Commission on Aboriginal Peoples (Canada), 1991–96, created by the federal government; the Advisory Committee on Human Radiation Experiments (United States), 1994–95, established by the American energy secretary; and the National Inquiry into the Separation of Aboriginal and Torres Strait Islander Children from Their Families (Australia), 1996–97, a special inquiry under the auspices of the permanent Human Rights and Equal Opportunity Commission.

97 *Ibid* at 62. Hayner identifies the German Commission of Inquiry for the Assessment of History and Consequences of the SED Dictatorship in Germany as a truth commission, *ibid* at 61.

98 "The Agreement" (10 April 1998), online: <https://assets.publishing.service.gov.uk/government/uploads/system/uploads/attachment_data/file/136652/agreement.pdf>.

99 Commission to Inquire into Child Abuse, *Final Report* (20 May 2009), online: <http://www.childabusecommission.ie/rpt/pdfs/>.

100 Commonwealth of Australia, Human Rights and Equal Opportunity Commission, *Bringing Them Home: Report of the National Inquiry into the Separation of Aboriginal and Torres Strait Islander Children from Their Families* (Sydney, 1997).

101 Coral Dow, "Sorry: The Unfinished Business of the Bringing Them Home Report," *Parliament of Australia Background Note* (4 February 2008), online: <https://www.aph.gov.au/About_Parliament/Parliamentary_Departments/Parliamentary_Library/pubs/BN/0708/BringingThemHomeReport>.

102 See Jonathan Simon, "Parrhesiastic Accountability: Investigatory Commissions and Executive Power in an Age of Terror" (2005) 114:6 Yale LJ 1419 at 1454:

> The generally positive global media attention to the truth and reconciliation process in post-apartheid South Africa may have increased the aspiration of commissions in stable liberal regimes, including the 9/11 Commission, to achieve new forms of relevance to the democratic process.

103 A truth commission is expected to educate the public on which human rights violations happened in a society, and in its very operation it is expected to emulate a lawful institution, respectful of human rights. This educational value forms an important part of the mandate of a truth commission. Allen, *supra* note 44 at 319. Truth commissions arise in emerging democracies where a state finds it important to demonstrate respect for the rule of law. Re-establishing the rule of law is not a concern for established democracies.

104 Levinson, *supra* note 45 at 220.

105 *Ibid* at 219.

106 As I will discuss in Chapter 3, the report of the Royal Commission on Aboriginal Peoples includes a chapter on the IRS legacy and recommends that a public inquiry be held with respect to that legacy. The government ignored this proposal. See Chapter 3, note 94.

107 Although Canadian precedent allows for historical sexual abuse claims, the statute of limitations for other torts prevented many former students' claims from being addressed in civil actions. Furthermore, significant claims for loss of culture, language, and spirituality did not find an easy home in the common law. In Chapter 3, I will discuss the limitations of civil litigation for addressing IRS harms.

108 See Richard A Wilson, *The Politics of Truth and Reconciliation in South Africa: Legitimizing the Post-Apartheid State* (Cambridge, UK: Cambridge University Press, 2001) at 19: "Truth commissions are one of the main ways in which a bureaucratic elite seeks to manufacture legitimacy for state institutions, and especially the legal system."

109 See "Residential School Survivors Await Start of Truth Commission," *CBC News* (27 July 2007), online: <https://www.cbc.ca/news/canada/residential-school-survivors-await-start-of-truth-commission-1.670219>:

Bob Watts, the commission's interim executive director, said he hopes the commission will make residential schools a well-known part of Canadian history.

"There's never been a forum to allow people to talk about their history and their experience – and this will be that forum that will allow that to happen," he said.

"You can check most school history textbooks and you'll find little to no reference on residential schools," said Watts. "But when you look at the impact on aboriginal communities in Canada, the impact has been severe."

See also *R v Poucette*, [1999] ABPC 52 (overturned on appeal: 1999 ABCA 305). Citing the RCAP Report, Provincial Court Judge John Reilly recounts the harms to Indigenous communities from residential schools in his sentencing decision because he believes that most Canadians do not know about the schools. He states that he was a judge for twelve years before he knew about the IRS system. He became a controversial judge because of decisions such as *R v Twoyoungmen* (1998) 51 CRR (2d) 88 that challenged prosecutorial policies with respect to the Stoney Nation in southern Alberta. See Peter Cheney, "Alberta Judge Upholds Judicial Independence: Critic of Native Reserves Cannot Be Disciplined for Controversial Rulings, Appeal Court Says," *Globe and Mail* (6 September 2000), online: <https://www.theglobeandmail.com/news/national/alberta-judge-upholds-judicial-independence/article4167152/>.

110 Hayner, *Unspeakable Truths, supra* note 56 at 153.

111 Indian Residential Schools Settlement Agreement (8 May 2006), Schedule N, s 1(d), online: <http://www.residentialschoolsettlement.ca/settlement.html> [Settlement Agreement].

112 Borchardt, *supra* note 1 at 7.

113 *Ibid.*

114 Miranda Johnson, *The Land Is Our History* (Oxford: Oxford University Press, 2016) at 82.

115 Canada, Royal Commission on Aboriginal Peoples, *Report of the Royal Commission on Aboriginal Peoples: Looking Forward, Looking Back,* vol 1 (Ottawa: Supply and Services Canada, 1996) at 237, n 11, citing John Leslie, *Commissions of Inquiry into Indian Affairs in the Canadas, 1828–1858: Evolving a Corporate Memory for the Indian Department* (Ottawa: Indian Affairs and Northern Development, 1985) [Leslie]. See also Canada, *Report of the Royal Commission on Aboriginal Peoples: Restructuring the Relationship,* vol 2 (Ottawa: Supply and Services Canada, 1996); Canada, *Report of the Royal Commission on Aboriginal Peoples: Gathering Strength,* vol 3 (Ottawa: Supply and Services Canada, 1996); Canada, *Report of the Royal Commission on Aboriginal Peoples: Perspectives and Realities,* vol 4 (Ottawa: Supply and Services Canada, 1996); Canada, *Report of the Royal Commission on Aboriginal Peoples: Renewal: A Twenty-Year Commitment,* vol 5 (Ottawa: Supply and Services Canada, 1996). The five volumes make up the RCAP Report [RCAP Report, vols 1–5].

116 Thomas J Lockwood, "A History of Royal Commissions" (1967) 5:2 Osgoode Hall LJ 172 at 197.

117 *Ibid* at 198.

118 Leslie, *supra* note 115 at iii.

119 *Report of the Royal Commission on Indian Affairs for the Province of British Columbia* (Victoria: Acme Press, 1916). See RCAP Report, vol 2, *supra* note 115 at c 4. See also Mary Haig-Brown, "Arthur Eugene O'Meara: Servant, Advocate, Seeker of Justice" in Celia Haig-Brown & David A Nock, eds, *With Good Intentions: Euro-Canadian and Aboriginal Relations in Colonial Canada* (Vancouver: UBC Press, 2006) 258 at 259: "[the commission's] focus quickly became reducing the current acreages of reserves and substituting valuable land with less valuable land."

120 Dana McFarland, *Indian Reserve Cut-Offs in British Columbia, 1912–1924: An Examination of Federal-Provincial Negotiations and Consultation with Indians* (MA thesis, University of British Columbia, 1990), online: <https://viurrspace.ca/ bitstream/handle/10613/365/McFarlandIndianReserveCutoffs1990.pdf? sequence=1&isAllowed=y>.

121 Duncan Campbell Scott also suggested that, if the recommendations were accepted by the courts, the title to the lands would be deemed to have been surrendered and extinguished. BC Learning Network, "McKenna McBride Commission," online: <http://bclearningnetwork.com/LOR/media/fns12/pdf/Module2/2.4%20A1%20 McKenna-McBride%20Commission.pdf>.

122 RCAP Report, vol 1, *supra* note 115.

123 Over twenty years later, the Liberal government of Justin Trudeau ostensibly implemented an RCAP recommendation in its decision in 2017 to split Indigenous and Northern Affairs Canada into Indigenous Services Canada and Crown-Indigenous Relations and Northern Affairs Canada. For a discussion of the selective implementation of this RCAP recommendation, see Veldon Coburn, "The Royal Commission on Aboriginal Peoples Recommended Splitting Up the Indigenous Affairs Department 20 Years Ago. The Context Today Is Much Different," *Policy Options* (6 September 2017), online: <https://policyoptions.irpp.org/magazines/september-2017/the -dismantling-of-Indigenous-and-northern-affairs-canada/>.

124 *Royal Commission on the Donald Marshall, Jr, Prosecution* (Halifax: McCurdys Printing and Typesetting, 1989), online: <https://novascotia.ca/just/marshall_ inquiry/>. For an insightful account of the Marshall Inquiry and its ongoing influence, see L Jane McMillan, *Truth and Conviction: Donald Marshall Jr and the Mi'kmaw Quest for Justice* (Vancouver: UBC Press, 2018).

125 Public Inquiry into the Administration of Justice and Aboriginal People, *Report of the Aboriginal Justice Inquiry of Manitoba,* by AC Hamilton & Murray Sinclair (Winnipeg: Province of Manitoba, 1991) [AJI Report]. Co-Commissioner Sinclair later became the Chair of the Canadian Truth and Reconciliation Commission.

126 *Ibid* at 512ff. I take up the ongoing utility of this inquiry and its report in Chapter 5.
127 Betty Ann Adam, "Cold Truths from a Dark Time," *StarPhoenix* (14 January 2015), online: <https://thestarphoenix.com/news/saskatoon/adam-cold-truths-from-a-dark-time> [Adam].
128 Commission on First Nations and Métis Peoples and Justice Reform, *Final Report of the Commission on First Nations and Métis Peoples and Justice Reform. Legacy of Hope: An Agenda for Change* (Saskatoon: Commission on First Nations and Métis Peoples and Justice Reform, 2004) [Commission on Justice Reform Final Report] at 12.
129 Chaired by Wilton Littlechild (later appointed as a Commissioner of the TRC), the others were Joe Quewezance, Hugh Harradence, Glenda Cooney, and Irene Fraser. The credibility of the commission was affected by Commissioner Harradence, who continued to act as defence counsel for one of three men accused of sexually assaulting a twelve-year-old girl from Yellow Quill First Nation during the commission's work. Commission on First Nations and Métis Peoples and Justice Reform, *Working Together – Interim Report* (November 2003), online: <http://www.turtleisland.org/news/jreform.pdf> [Commission on Justice Reform Interim Report] at 5.
130 *Report of the Commission of Inquiry into Matters Relating to the Death of Neil Stonechild* (2004), online: <http://www.publications.gov.sk.ca/freelaw/Publications_Centre/Justice/Stonechild/Stonechild.pdf>.
131 "Saskatoon Police Chief Admits Starlight Cruises Are Not New," *Windspeaker* (1 June 2003), online: <http://www.ammsa.com/publications/windspeaker/saskatoon-police-chief-admits-starlight-cruises-are-not-new>.
132 Adam, *supra* note 127.
133 Joyce Green, "From Stonechild to Social Cohesion: Anti-Racist Challenges for Saskatchewan" (2006) 39:3 CJPS/RCSP 507 at 509. The two officers who left Darrell Night for dead, Dan Hatchen and Ken Munson, were charged, tried, and convicted of unlawful confinement. They were fired and served jail terms. Adam, *supra* note 127.
134 The Davies Commission, Inquiry into the Response of the Criminal Justice Branch, *Alone and Cold: Criminal Justice Branch Response* (Vancouver, 19 May 2011), online: <https://opcc.bc.ca/wp-content/uploads/2017/04/The-Davies-Commission.pdf>. The substantial 12 February 2009 interim report examined the facts surrounding Frank Paul's death and the responses of relevant official bodies, excluding the Criminal Justice Branch, *Alone and Cold, Interim Report*, online: <https://opcc.bc.ca/wp-content/uploads/2017/04/2009-Davies-Commission-Interim-Report.pdf>. The Criminal Justice Branch challenged the commission's authority to inquire into matters of prosecutorial discretion, arguing it was protected from external review. Once the BC Court of Appeal clarified that, with some restrictions, the inquiry into

those matters could proceed, the commission issued a final report just addressing the Branch's response, having dealt with all other aspects of the mandate in the interim report. The Attorney General at the time of the interim report was Wally Oppal, later the Commissioner on the BC Missing Women Inquiry.

135 *Report of the Ipperwash Inquiry: Investigation and Findings,* by Stanley Linden, vol 1 (2007) at 677, online: <http://www.attorneygeneral.jus.gov.on.ca/inquiries/ipperwash/report/vol_1/pdf/E_Vol_1_Conclusion.pdf> [*Report of the Ipperwash Inquiry*].

136 *Ibid* at 360.

137 This decoupling of Crown-Indigenous relations from resource extraction was a positive move toward decolonization, but it is a change that the Conservative government of Ontario elected in 2018 rolled back in its first few weeks in office.

Chapter 2: The Mackenzie Valley Pipeline Inquiry

1 This chapter is based on Kim Stanton, *Truth Commissions and Public Inquiries: Addressing Historical Injustices in Established Democracies* (SJD, University of Toronto Faculty of Law, 2010), online: <https://tspace.library.utoronto.ca/handle/1807/24886> [Stanton, *Truth Commissions*]. Some passages were published in my article "Looking Forward, Looking Back: The Canadian Truth and Reconciliation Commission and the Mackenzie Valley Pipeline Inquiry" (2012) 27:1 CJLS 81.

2 The Indian Residential Schools Settlement Agreement (the "Settlement Agreement") was concluded 8 May 2006 following an Agreement in Principle ("AIP") signed 23 November 2005. Schedule N of the Settlement Agreement, "Mandate for the Truth and Reconciliation Commission" (Schedule E of the AIP), sets out the terms of a truth commission, which forms part of the settlement. The IRS system, briefly stated, was a federal government system of education under which Indigenous children were removed from their families and communities to schools run by churches, with devastating results for the children, their communities, and their cultures.

3 The Commission of Inquiry into the Investigation of the Bombing of Air India Flight 182 was established on 1 May 2006 by Order in Council PC 2006–293. The government of Ontario established the Ipperwash Inquiry to investigate the death of Aboriginal protester Dudley George by Order in Council 1662/2003 on 12 November 2003. The inquiry hearings ran from 2004 to 2006, and the inquiry reported in 2007. The Commission of Inquiry into the Actions of Canadian Officials in Relation to Maher Arar was established 5 February 2004 by Order in Council PC 2004–48.

4 As a litigator, Berger had gained a reputation as an Indigenous rights advocate, first with *R v Bob and White* (1965), 52 DLR (2d) 481 (SCC), a landmark treaty hunting rights case, and then with *Calder v British Columbia (Attorney-General),* [1973] SCR 313, the most significant case by the Supreme Court of Canada on Aboriginal title to that point in the century.

5　At that time, the New Democratic Party held the balance of power, and its election platform in 1972 had included a promise to scrap the Mackenzie Valley Pipeline. The party had also won a seat in the Northwest Territories.

6　Similarly, the pressure of litigation by Indigenous survivors of the residential schools precipitated the TRC.

7　*Re Paulette's Application* (1973), 6 WWR 97 (NWTSC), at paras 6, 8 [*Re Paulette* NWTSC].

8　*Canada (Attorney General) v Morrow (Judge)* (1973), 39 DLR (3d) 81 (FCTD), per Collier J.

9　*Re Paulette and Registrar of Titles (No 2)* (1973), 42 DLR (3d) 8 (NWTSC) at 39–40.

10　*Re Paulette and Registrar of Land Titles* (1975), 63 DLR (3d) 1 (NWTCA).

11　Edgar J Dosman, *The National Interest: The Politics of Northern Development 1968–75* (Toronto: McClelland and Stewart, 1975) at 193.

12　This is the legal instrument that formally sets up a public inquiry.

13　Although I use this term in this section since it was used at the time, the term "land claims" is a misnomer in that it suggests that Indigenous peoples must seek title to their territories from the "rightful" owner (the Crown), whereas in fact the Crown is making the land claims. As Frank Calder has stated, "[t]his is our land. We don't have to go and thank The Queen for giving us this land. This is our land." Frank Calder and Thomas Berger, "Frank Calder and Thomas Berger: A Conversation" in Hamar Foster, Jeremy HA Webber, & Heather Raven, eds, *Let Right Be Done: Aboriginal Title, the* Calder *Case, and the Future of Indigenous Rights* (Vancouver: UBC Press, 2007) 37 at 40.

14　Submission of Michael Goldie, QC, counsel for Arctic Gas, at preliminary hearing in Ottawa (7 May 1974), in Edward L Knowles & Ian G Waddell, eds, *Preliminary Materials* (Yellowknife, NWT: Mackenzie Valley Pipeline Inquiry, 1975) at 119.

15　Mackenzie Valley Pipeline Inquiry, "Preliminary Rulings by the Honourable Mr. Justice TR Berger" (12 July 1974, Yellowknife, NWT) in Knowles & Waddell, *ibid* 156 at 163 [Berger, "Preliminary Rulings I"].

16　*Ibid* at 169.

17　*Ibid.*

18　Judd Buchanan, Minister, Department of Indian Affairs and Northern Development, to Thomas Berger (18 October 1974), Vancouver, UBC Special Collections (Thomas Berger Fonds – Mackenzie Valley Pipeline Inquiry subject files, box 18–5, Correspondence with the Department of Indian Affairs and Northern Development [file] #1 1974–75 [folder one of two]) at 4.

19　Mackenzie Valley Pipeline Inquiry, "Preliminary Rulings by the Honourable Mr. Justice TR Berger" (29 October 1974, Yellowknife, NWT) in Knowles & Waddell, *supra* note 14, 220 at 226 [Berger, "Preliminary Rulings II"].

20 Community hearings were an innovation of the Royal Commission on the Non-Medicinal Use of Drugs, chaired by Gerald Le Dain: *Interim Report of the Commission of Inquiry into the Non-Medical Use of Drugs* (Ottawa: Information Canada, 1970) at 11–14.

21 Following his stint as special counsel for community hearings on the inquiry, Professor Michael Jackson of the University of British Columbia's Faculty of Law continued to focus on Aboriginal rights, particularly, but not exclusively, in the criminal justice system. He was counsel in several landmark Aboriginal law cases before the Supreme Court of Canada, including as co-counsel for the appellants, the Gitksan Hereditary Chiefs et al, in *Delgamuukw* and as co-counsel for the respondents, the Haida Nation, in *Haida Nation*.

22 For a detailed description of Jackson's work as special counsel and of the organization of the community hearings, see Stanton, *Truth Commissions, supra* note 1.

23 They included Michael Jackson as special counsel to Justice Berger for the community hearings, Stephen Goudge as assistant commission counsel, Ian Scott as commission counsel, and Ian Waddell as special counsel for administrative matters.

24 Ian Waddell, interview with Kim Stanton (18 December 2008), Vancouver [Waddell interview]. In 2010, I provided all interviewees (Thomas Berger, Diana Crosbie, Stephen Goudge, and Ian Waddell) with copies of Stanton, *Truth Commissions, supra* note 1.

25 François Bregha, *Bob Blair's Pipeline: The Business and Politics of Northern Energy Development Projects,* new ed (Toronto: J Lorimer, 1979) at 118 [Bregha]. See also Thomas Berger, memo to Ian Scott, Stephen Goudge, Ian Waddell, Michael Jackson, and Diana Crosbie (28 January 1975) suggesting that witnesses could be interviewed post-testimony "to liven up what might otherwise be pretty dull broadcasting" and that "counsel themselves might be interviewed ... from time to time about what they are seeking to establish." Ottawa, Library and Archives Canada [LAC] (Mackenzie Valley Pipeline Inquiry fonds, RG 126, vols 72–77, operational and administrative records created by the inquiry between 1970 and 1977, textual records, box 72, subfile CBC) [CBC subfile].

26 Diana Crosbie, interview with Kim Stanton (21 November 2008), Toronto [Crosbie interview].

27 Martin O'Malley, *The Past and Future Land: An Account of the Berger Inquiry into the Mackenzie Valley Pipeline* (Toronto: P Martin Associates, 1976) [O'Malley].

28 Crosbie interview, *supra* note 26.

29 Thomas Berger, memo to Ian Waddell and Michael Jackson, re 1 November 1974 meeting with Andrew Cowan (5 November 1974), LAC (Mackenzie Valley Pipeline Inquiry fonds), CBC subfile, *supra* note 25.

30 "MVPI – CBC Northern Service Coverage" (press release, 6 February 75), LAC (Mackenzie Valley Pipeline Inquiry fonds), *ibid:*

234 Notes to pages 48–49

The CBC Northern Service will provide extensive coverage of the MVPI ...

The plans are to cover the hearings from beginning to end, as fully as possible, in seven native languages and dialects as well as in English, on radio and television throughout the North. They will also be covered for the rest of Canada in English and French. The CBC regards the MVPI as a matter of major national concern because of the importance of the proposed pipeline to the whole of Canada and particularly to the people of the North.

31 O'Malley, *supra* note 27 at 109; telephone conversation with Diana Crosbie (24 November 2009) [Crosbie 24 November conversation] and email correspondence from Diana Crosbie (26 November 2009).

32 Thomas Berger, interview with Kim Stanton (18 December 2007), Vancouver [Berger interview 1].

33 Thomas Berger to Sidney Newan, Commissioner, National Film Board (2 October 1974), LAC (Mackenzie Valley Pipeline Inquiry fonds), CBC subfile, *supra* note 25. In this letter, Berger advised Newan of his appointment and of the inquiry's mandate and asked him to consider whether the National Film Board would make a film about the issues coming before the inquiry. Berger suggested that such a film could be of use if shown in the communities before or during the hearings. His stated concern was to enable people living in the Mackenzie Valley communities to participate effectively in the work of the inquiry.

34 Waddell interview, *supra* note 24.

35 Crosbie 24 November conversation, *supra* note 31. The rest of the paragraph relies on this conversation.

36 In addition, cameraman Pat Scott and technician David Porter were important members of Fraser's team. Porter went on to become Deputy Premier of Yukon and Founding Chair of Northern Native Broadcasting Corporation. In 2002, he was elected Chair of the Kaska Dena Council. See Indigenous Leadership Initiative, "Dave Porter," online: <https://www.ilinationhood.ca/team/dave-porter>. See also Whit Fraser's memoir, *True North Rising* (Burnstown, ON: Burnstown Publishing, 2018).

37 Crosbie 24 November conversation, *supra* note 31.

38 *Ibid.*

39 Bregha, *supra* note 25 at 122.

40 *Ibid.* A press release (27 May 1977) announced that a second printing of 20,000 copies of the report had been ordered because the first run of 24,000 copies had sold out within days. Ottawa, LAC (Mackenzie Valley Pipeline Inquiry fonds, RG 126, vols 72–77, operational and administrative records created by the inquiry between 1970 and 1977, textual records, box 76, Mackenzie Valley Pipeline Inquiry subfile English Press Releases).

41 Robert JD Page, *Northern Development: The Canadian Dilemma* (Toronto: McClelland and Stewart, 1986) at 100 [Page].

42 Bregha, *supra* note 25 at 126–27.

43 Berger interview 1, *supra* note 32.

44 Bregha, *supra* note 25 at 117.

45 Alain M Cunningham, *Canadian Indian Policy and Development Planning Theory* (New York: Garland, 1999) at 99, citing the decidedly conservative, pro-industry Albertan publication *Western Report.*

46 *Ibid.*

47 Wally Braul makes reference to this in his introduction of Thomas Berger in TR Berger, "My Idea of Canada" (speech, on file with author, delivered at the Citizens for Social Justice annual meeting, Vancouver, 2005). This speech alludes in its title to an essay that Berger wrote in 1981 in tribute to FR Scott: "FR Scott and the Idea of Canada" in Sandra Djwa & R St J Macdonald, eds, *On FR Scott: Essays on His Contributions to Law, Literature and Politics* (Montreal and Kingston: McGill-Queen's University Press, 1983) 179.

48 "Nellie J Cournoyea" in *Canadian Encyclopedia,* online: <https://www.thecanadian encyclopedia.ca/en/article/nellie-j-cournoyea>.

49 John David Hamilton, *Arctic Revolution: Social Change in the Northwest Territories, 1935–1994* (Toronto: Dundurn Press, 1994) at 190 [Hamilton].

50 "Twenty-Five Years after Berger," *The National* (31 October 2001), online: *CBC Digital Archives* <https://www.cbc.ca/archives/entry/twenty-five-years-after-the-berger -pipeline-inquiry>.

51 "The Mackenzie Valley Pipeline: 37 Years of Negotiation," *CBC News* (16 December 2010), online: <https://www.cbc.ca/news/business/mackenzie-valley-pipeline-37 -years-of-negotiation-1.902366> [CBC News, "37 Years"].

52 "Stephen Kakfwi: Straight Talker," *CBC News* (17 November 2005), online: <https:// www.cbc.ca/news2/background/aboriginals/kakfwi.html> [CBC News, "Stephen Kakfwi"].

53 CBC News, "37 Years," *supra* note 51. See also "The Berger Report Is Released," *As It Happens* (9 May 1977), online: *CBC Digital Archives* <https://www.cbc.ca/archives/ entry/the-berger-report-is-released>.

54 CBC News, "Stephen Kakfwi," *supra* note 52.

55 See Chapter 4, "The Second Panel" section.

56 See Liidlii Kue First Nation, "History," online: <https://liidliikue.ca/about/ history/>.

57 See Janine Edklund, "NWT Premier Jim Antoine Lives in 'Interesting Times,'" *Leth-bridge Herald* (1 April 1999) at 1.

58 Georges Erasmus, "We the Dene" in Mel Watkins, ed, *Dene Nation: Colony Within* (Toronto: University of Toronto Press, 1977) 177 at 177–79.

59 Governor General of Canada, "Governor General Announces the Awarding of the Northern Medal to Mr. Georges Henry Erasmus, OC," (22 January 2009), online:

<https://www.gg.ca/en/media/news/2009/governor-general-announces-awarding
-northern-medal-mr-georges-henry-erasmus-oc>.

60   Waddell interview, *supra* note 24; Crosbie 24 November conversation, *supra* note
31.

61   *Northern Frontier, Northern Homeland: The Report of the Mackenzie Valley Pipeline
Inquiry,* by Thomas R Berger (Ottawa: Minister of Supply and Services Canada, 1977)
[Berger Report].

62   Peter A Allard School of Law, "Thomas R Berger, OC, OBC, QC," online: <https://
historyproject.allard.ubc.ca/law-history-project/profile/thomas-r-berger-oc
-obc-qc>.

63   Peter Jull, "'Nations with Whom We Are Connected': Indigenous Peoples and Canada's Political System" (2001) 6:2 Austl Indigenous L Reporter 1 at 13 [Jull].

64   Hamilton, *supra* note 49 at 193.

65   Morris Popowich, "The National Energy Board as Intermediary between the
Crown, Aboriginal Peoples, and Industry" (2007) 44:4 Alta L Rev 837 at para 50. Of
course, there were also critics of the Berger Inquiry. With respect to the report's
principal recommendations, though most Indigenous groups were pleased, some
Métis were concerned that the call for a moratorium on pipeline construction would
decrease their bargaining power for settling land claims since the pressure would be
decreased. "Jubilant Indigenous Leaders Praise Berger's Report," *Our Native Land*
(14 May 1977), online: *CBC Radio Archives* <https://www.cbc.ca/archives/entry/
jubilant-natives-praise-bergers-report>. Two books published in the aftermath of
the inquiry were heavily critical of Berger and the inquiry: Donald Peacock, *People,
Peregrines and Arctic Pipelines: The Critical Battle to Build Canada's Northern Gas
Pipelines* (Vancouver: JJ Douglas, 1977) [Peacock]; Earle Gray, *Super Pipe: The Arctic
Pipeline, World's Greatest Fiasco?* (Toronto: Griffin House, 1979). Both authors were
associated with the pipeline companies, and indeed pipeline applicant Alberta Gas
Trunk Lines funded Peacock to write and publish his book (see Peacock at ix). Gray
was the former Head of Public Affairs for the other applicant. Their two books
prompted Trent University Professor Robert Page to write his book *Northern
Development.* Page participated in both the Berger Inquiry and the National Energy
Board hearings on the pipeline and suggested that Berger was a scapegoat for the
critics when the pipeline applications did not proceed. Although the National Energy
Board reached conclusions similar to those of Berger, he alone was the subject of
attack in the books. Page, *supra* note 41 at xi.

66   Jull, *supra* note 63 at 7.

67   O'Malley, *supra* note 27 at 13.

68   Will Kymlicka & Bashir Bashir, eds, *The Politics of Reconciliation in Multicultural
Societies* (Oxford: Oxford University Press, 2008) [Kymlicka & Bashir], observe at
15 that, "for some commentators, nation-building is the cause of historical injustice

towards Indigenous peoples, not the solution to it. It was precisely in the name of building modern unitary nations that injustices were committed against Indigenous peoples, stripping them of their lands, cultures, and self-governing institutions."

69 Berger Report, vol 1, *supra* note 61.

70 *Canadian Bill of Rights*, SC 1960, c 44.

71 If not the first indication, then an early one, following the notable response to the Trudeau government's 1969 White Paper (see Chapter 3, note 92).

72 Allwest Reporting, Mackenzie Valley Pipeline Inquiry, *Proceedings at Community Hearing* (9 July 1975, Fort McPherson, NWT) at 1077. See also "Statements to the Mackenzie Valley Pipeline Inquiry" in Watkins, *supra* note 58, at 6–7. These sentiments began to be reported in the southern media for the first time with testimony such as this before Berger.

73 Ontario Law Reform Commission, *Report on Public Inquiries* (Toronto, 1992) at 187, citing Gerald Le Dain, "The Role of the Public Inquiry in our Constitutional System" in Jacob S Ziegel, ed, *Law and Social Change* (Toronto: Osgoode Hall Law School, York University, 1973) 79 at 79.

74 The concept of social accountability is discussed in Kent Roach, "Canadian Public Inquiries and Accountability" in Philip C Stenning, ed, *Accountability for Criminal Justice: Selected Essays* (Toronto: University of Toronto Press, 1995) 268 at 269.

75 Berger Report, vol 2, *supra* note 61, at 223ff.

76 *Ibid* at 224.

77 Indian Residential Schools Settlement Agreement (8 May 2006), Schedule N, s 1.

78 Thomas Berger, "Commissions of Inquiry and Public Policy" (address delivered at the School of Public Administration, Carleton University, Ottawa, 1 March 1978), Vancouver, UBC Special Collections (Thomas Berger Fonds – Mackenzie Valley Pipeline Inquiry subfiles, boxes 19–2, 71–9) at 18.

79 Today, of course, this would include all manner of social media engagement.

Chapter 3: Inquiries and Residential Schools

1 Indian Residential Schools Settlement Agreement (8 May 2006).

2 Royal Commission on Aboriginal Peoples, *Report of the Royal Commission on Aboriginal Peoples: Looking Forward, Looking Back,* vol 1 (Ottawa: Supply and Services Canada, 1996); Canada, *Report of the Royal Commission on Aboriginal Peoples: Restructuring the Relationship,* vol 2 (Ottawa: Supply and Services Canada, 1996); Canada, *Report of the Royal Commission on Aboriginal Peoples: Gathering Strength,* vol 3 (Ottawa: Supply and Services Canada, 1996); Canada, *Report of the Royal Commission on Aboriginal Peoples: Perspectives and Realities,* vol 4 (Ottawa: Supply and Services Canada, 1996); Canada, *Report of the Royal Commission on Aboriginal Peoples: Renewal: A Twenty-Year Commitment,* vol 5 (Ottawa: Supply and Services Canada, 1996) [RCAP Report]. RCAP Report, vol 1, c 10.

3   *Re Paulette's Application* (1973), 6 WWR 97 (NWTSC); see also *Canada (Attorney General) v Morrow (Judge)* (1973), 39 DLR (3d) 81 (FCTD).

4   Several books provide much more extensive information about the IRS system than it is possible to provide here. See JR Miller, *Shingwauk's Vision: A History of Native Residential Schools* (Toronto: University of Toronto Press, 1996) [Miller, *Shingwauk's Vision*]; Agnes Grant, *No End of Grief: Indian Residential Schools in Canada* (Winnipeg: Pemmican Publications, 1996); Elizabeth Graham, *The Mush Hole: Life at Two Indian Residential Schools* (Waterloo, ON: Heffle Publishing, 1997); John S Milloy, *A National Crime: The Canadian Government and the Residential School System, 1879 to 1986* (Winnipeg: University of Manitoba Press, 1999) [Milloy]; Roland Chrisjohn, Sherri Lynn Young, & Michael Maraun, eds, *The Circle Game: Shadows and Substance in the Indian Residential School Experience in Canada* (Penticton, BC: Theytus Books, 2006) [Chrisjohn, Young, & Maraun]. See also RCAP Report, vol 1, *supra* note 2, c 10, and of course the TRC Report itself, which contains an extensive history of the schools, the policies that created and sustained them, and the inter-generational harms that resulted and continue to this day.

5   According to Pamela O'Connor, "Squaring the Circle: How Canada Is Dealing with the Legacy of Its Indian Residential Schools Experiment" (2000) 28 Intl J Leg Info 232 at 236, the federal government only recently admitted that the policy purpose of the residential schools was assimilation rather than education. See her note 15. In 1997, John Watson, the highest-ranking federal Indian Affairs official in British Columbia, reportedly made a statement that he described as "the first time that the federal government has acknowledged that the purpose of residential schools was one of assimilation." Stewart Bell, "Ottawa Vows Action on Native School," *Vancouver Sun* (27 June 1997) A3.

6   Georges Erasmus, "Reparations: Theory, Practice and Education" (2003) 22 Windsor YB Access Just 189 at para 190, n 2: "The Two Row Wampum Treaty established the principles of co-existence between Aboriginal Peoples and Europeans. First concluded with the Dutch in 1645, [it was] extended to the British following English conquest of the Dutch in 1664." For more information on the history related in this section, see Brian Rice & Anna Snyder, "Reconciliation in the Context of a Settler Society: Healing the Legacy of Colonialism in Canada" in Marlene B Castellano, Linda Archibald, & Mike DeGagné, eds, *From Truth to Reconciliation: Transforming the Legacy of Residential Schools* (Ottawa: Aboriginal Healing Foundation, 2008) 45 at 49ff; also see Public Inquiry into the Administration of Justice and Aboriginal People, *Report of the Aboriginal Justice Inquiry of Manitoba,* by AC Hamilton & Murray Sinclair (Winnipeg: Province of Manitoba, 1991) 54ff [AJI Report].

7   Ottawa, National Archives of Canada, RG 10, vol 6810, file 470-2-3, vol 7, at 55 (L-3) and 63 (N-3).

8 The *Indian Act* consolidated laws related to "Indians" and designated the Minister of the Interior as the Superintendent General of Indian Affairs. *Indian Act,* SC 1876 (39 Vict), c 18, s 2. Prior legislation included *An Act for the Better Protection of the Lands and Property of Indians in Lower Canada,* SC 1850 (13–14 Vict), c 42, *An Act to Encourage the Gradual Civilization of Indian Tribes in This Province, and to Amend the Laws Relating to Indians,* SC 1857 (20 Vict), c 26, and the *Act for the Gradual Civilization of the Indian,* SC 1869 (32–33 Vict), c 6.

9 RCAP Report, vol 1, *supra* note 2 at 309.

10 "Condensed Timeline of Events" in Castellano, Archibald, & DeGagné, *supra* note 6 at 64–65 ["Condensed Timeline"].

11 *Ibid.*

12 *Ibid.* Ryerson was then the Chief Superintendent of Education for Upper Canada.

13 RCAP Report, vol 1, *supra* note 2 at 309. It was under the *Indian Act* that the government provided for the required attendance of Indigenous children at residential schools. *Indian Act,* SC 1894, c 32, ss 11, 137, 138. The initial power to regulate attendance at school was strengthened in SC 1919–20, c 50, ss 1, 10: "Every Indian child between the ages of seven and fifteen years who is physically able shall attend such day, industrial or boarding school as may be designated."

14 Treaties 1 through 7 were negotiated between 1870 and 1877 in what is now Ontario, Manitoba, Saskatchewan, and Alberta. Treaties 8 through 11 covered northern Alberta, Ontario, and part of the Northwest Territories and were signed between 1899 and 1921. See Sally M Weaver, *Making Canadian Indian Policy: The Hidden Agenda 1968–1970* (Toronto: University of Toronto Press, 1981) at 33 [Weaver].

15 See Hugh Dempsey, *Treaty Research Report: Treaty Seven (1877)* (Treaties and Historical Research Centre, Comprehensive Claims Branch, Self-Government, Indian and Northern Affairs Canada, 1987). See also Dennis FK Madill, *Treaty Research Report – Treaty Eight (1899)* (Treaties and Historical Research Centre, Indian and Northern Affairs Canada, 1986) at 38 [Madill]: Treaty 8 provided that the dominion government was committed to pay the salaries of teachers of Indian children "as the government may deem advisable."

16 Madill, *supra* note 15 at 38, citing Canada, Treaty No 8, at 6.

17 AJI Report, *supra* note 6 at 67–68. Indigenous peoples in eastern parts of the country had requested schooling earlier in the nineteenth century as large numbers of European settlers inundated their territories. JR Miller, "Troubled Legacy: A History of Indian Residential Schools" (2003) 66 Sask L Rev 357 at 361 [Miller, "Troubled Legacy"].

18 Miller, *Shingwauk's Vision, supra* note 4 at 98–100.

19 *Ibid* at 143, and see legislation at note 8.

20 Nicholas Flood Davin, *Report on Industrial Schools for Indians and Half-Breeds.* Report produced for the Minister of the Interior (Ottawa, 1879). Davin became the

founder and editor of the Regina *Leader,* the first newspaper in Assiniboia, before serving as the Member of Parliament for Assiniboia West (now consisting of ridings in both Alberta and Saskatchewan). See Lee Gibson, "Nicholas Flood Davin" in *Canadian Encyclopedia,* online: <https://www.thecanadianencyclopedia.ca/en/article/nicholas-flood-davin>.

21 RCAP Report, vol 1, *supra* note 2, c 10, text accompanying n 6.

22 Milloy, *supra* note 4 at 27.

23 *Ibid* at 36–38.

24 RCAP Report, vol 1, *supra* note 2, c 10, text accompanying n 4. See also c 10, s 1 "The Vision and Policies of Residential School Education," 1.1 "The Vision":

> The tragic legacy of residential education began in the late nineteenth century with a three-part vision of education in the service of assimilation. It included, first, a justification for removing children from their communities and disrupting Aboriginal families; second, a precise pedagogy for re-socializing children in the schools; and third, schemes for integrating graduates into the non-Aboriginal world.

25 See Miller, "Troubled Legacy," *supra* note 17 at 361ff.

26 Miller, *Shingwauk's Vision, supra* note 4 at 142. RCAP Report, vol 1, *supra* note 2, c 10, text accompanying Table 10.1: "In 1931 there were 44 Roman Catholic (RC), 21 Church of England (CE), 13 United Church (UC) and 2 Presbyterian (PR) schools. These proportions among the denominations were constant throughout the history of the system."

27 A majority of the schools were run by orders of the Catholic Church. The church is organized not as one central body but as individual orders. See Canadian Conference of Catholic Bishops, "Apology on Residential Schools by the Catholic Church," online: <https://www.cccb.ca/indigenous-peoples/indian-residential-schools-and-trc/>: "The Catholic community in Canada has a decentralized structure. Each Diocesan Bishop is autonomous in his diocese and, although relating to the Canadian Conference of Catholic Bishops, is not responsible to it."

28 RCAP Report, vol 1, *supra* note 2, c 10, text accompanying ns 1 and 2. The following section relies on the RCAP Report, itself based on archival research by John Milloy of Trent University and by a restricted review of Indian Affairs records made possible only after "protracted and difficult negotiations" (n 1).

29 *Ibid,* text accompanying n 43.

30 Miller, *Shingwauk's Vision, supra* note 4 at 174. See also RCAP Report, vol 1, *supra* note 2 at 319.

31 Miller, *Shingwauk's Vision, supra* note 4 at 57. See also RCAP Report, vol 1, *supra* note 2 at 320.

32 Milloy, *supra* note 4 at 270.

33 *Ibid* at 79ff.

34 *Ibid* at 83ff; RCAP Report, vol 1, *supra* note 2 at 330; Miller, *Shingwauk's Vision, supra* note 4 at 133.

35 RCAP Report, vol 1, *supra* note 2 at 330; see also Miller, *Shingwauk's Vision, supra* note 4 at 304.

36 RCAP Report, vol 1, *supra* note 2 at 331.

37 Miller, *Shingwauk's Vision, supra* note 4 at 134. See also RCAP Report, vol 1, *supra* note 2 at 330–31.

38 RCAP Report, vol 1, *supra* note 2 at 331.

39 *Ibid* at 356.

40 *Ibid* at 351.

41 JA Macrae, Department of Indian Affairs Inspector of Schools for the North West, cited in Milloy, *supra* note 4 at 27.

42 Miller, *Shingwauk's Vision, supra* note 4 at 328.

43 EB Titley, *The Indian Commissioners: Agents of the State and Indian Policy in Canada's Prairie West, 1873–1932* (Edmonton: University of Alberta Press, 2009) at 193.

44 Jo-ann Archibald, "Resistance to an Unremitting Process: Racism, Curriculum and Education in Western Canada" in JA Mangan, ed, *The Imperial Curriculum: Racial Images and Education in the British Colonial Experience* (London and New York: Routledge, 1993) 93 at 99 [Archibald]. See also RCAP Report, vol 1, *supra* note 2 at 312.

45 The McKenna McBride Commission of 1915, struck to review reserve allocations in British Columbia, inquired into schooling of reserve children in the course of its hearings. The Commissioners asked only three questions. How many children attended school? Which school did they attend? If they did not attend, why not? See Archibald, *supra* note 44 at 99.

46 Miller, "Troubled Legacy," *supra* note 17 at 379. See also RCAP Report, vol 2, *supra* note 2, c 4, s 5.1. The special committee recommended the creation of an independent administrative body to deal with Indian grievances, to be modelled on the US Indian Claims Commission, which had begun operations in 1946. The Department of Indian Affairs rejected the recommendation.

47 Miller, "Troubled Legacy," *supra* note 17 at 380.

48 "Condensed Timeline," *supra* note 10 at 65.

49 National Indian Brotherhood, *Indian Control of Indian Education* (policy paper presented to the Ministry of Indian Affairs and Northern Development, Ottawa, 1972).

50 Milloy, *supra* note 4 at 237.

51 See Alison Harvison Young, "Child Sexual Abuse and the Law of Evidence: Some Current Canadian Issues" (1992) 11 Can J Fam L 11 at para 1.

52 *Convention on the Rights of the Child,* 20 November 1989, A/RES/44/25 UNGA (entered into force 2 September 1990).

53   Canada, *Sexual Offences against Children in Canada: Report of the Committee on Sexual Offences against Children and Youth,* by Robin Badgley (Ottawa: Supply and Services Canada, 1984) [Badgley Report].

54   Canada, Special Advisor to the Minister of National Health and Welfare on Child Sexual Abuse, *Reaching for Solutions: The Summary,* by Rix Rogers (Ottawa: Supply and Services Canada, 1990) [Rogers Report].

55   *Ibid,* c 2.

56   *Ibid,* Recommendation 70:

> That the federal government appoint an Aboriginal Expert Advisory Committee on child abuse with a mandate to develop a five-year action plan to address child abuse and related issues in aboriginal constituencies. The Expert Advisory Committee should be made up of aboriginal representatives, including band councils, aboriginal associations, aboriginal workers, child abuse experts and representatives from appropriate government jurisdictions. The Expert Advisory Committee should hold national and/or regional consultations with representatives of aboriginal communities to ensure that the emerging plan reflects the realities and concerns of local communities [footnotes omitted].

Disproportionately high rates of violence against Indigenous women and children are understood to result from a confluence of factors, including the effects of the IRS system. See Native Women's Association of Canada, *Fact Sheet: Root Causes of Violence against Aboriginal Women and the Impact of Colonization,* online: <https://www.nwac.ca/wp-content/uploads/2015/05/Fact_Sheet_Root_Causes_of_Violence_Against_Aboriginal_Women.pdf>.

57   See, for example, a trailblazing article by Maureen Brosnahan, "Indians Recall Bitter School Days," *Winnipeg Free Press* (22 June 1982) 21.

58   Miller, *Shingwauk's Vision, supra* note 4 at 329, citing investigations at Williams Lake and Lytton, British Columbia.

59   Assembly of First Nations, "Residential Schools: A Chronology," online: <http://www.rememberingthechildren.ca/history/>. In 1989, the government of Newfoundland and Labrador established the Royal Commission of Inquiry into the Criminal Justice System (known as the Hughes Inquiry) to examine allegations of cover-up in a police investigation of the sexual abuse of boys living in the Mount Cashel Orphanage in St. John's, run by the Christian Brothers of Ireland in Canada. *Royal Commission of Inquiry into the Response of the Newfoundland Criminal Justice System to Complaints* (St John's: Queen's Printer, 1991), online: <http://www.lewisday.ca/ldlf_files/pdf/Mt.Cashel%20vol%201.pdf>.

60   Miller, *Shingwauk's Vision, supra* note 4 at 328.

61   *Ibid,* n 45, citing reports in the *Globe and Mail* and Saskatoon *StarPhoenix* (11 December 1990).

62 *Ibid,* n 46, citing the *Globe and Mail* (10 November 1990).

63 Cariboo Tribal Council, *Impact of the Residential School* (Williams Lake, BC: Cariboo Tribal Council, 1991).

64 Chrisjohn, Young, & Maraun, *supra* note 4 at 21.

65 Assembly of First Nations, *Breaking the Silence: An Interpretive Study of Residential School Impact and Healing as Illustrated by the Stories of First Nation Individuals* (Ottawa: Assembly of First Nations, 1994).

66 The United Church apologized in 1986. The pope expressed his sorrow about the schools in April 2009. See "Pope Expresses 'Sorrow' for Abuses at Residential Schools," *CBC News* (29 April 2009), online: <http://www.cbc.ca/world/story/2009/04/29/pope-first-nations042909.html>.

67 Miller, "Troubled Legacy," *supra* note 17 at 381.

68 Indian and Northern Affairs Canada, "Backgrounder: Indian Residential Schools" (Ottawa: Indian Residential Schools Resolution Canada, 2005) [Canada, "Backgrounder"].

69 A Mohawk Chief presented documents providing evidence of the dispute at both the 1946–48 and the 1959–61 joint Senate and House of Commons committee hearings into Indian Affairs. RCAP Report, vol 2, *supra* note 2, c 4, s 5. The lands had been the subject of a claim rejected in 1977 under the federal comprehensive land claims policy on the basis that the Mohawks could not prove their continuous occupation since time immemorial. Their specific claim was then rejected in 1986 as not properly falling under the oft-criticized Specific Claims Policy.

70 Searching for details about exactly what happened at Oka, I turned to the RCAP Report, vol 1, *supra* note 2, on the assumption that the incident that prompted the founding of the commission would have warranted a comprehensive account. Curiously, the events at Oka are glossed over in the report, and there is no detailed description of the background or events of that summer.

71 See, for example, Chris Hedges, "Canadian Army Moves in to End a Smoldering Standoff with the Mohawks," *New York Times* (2 September 1990) 3; Judith Gaines, "1500 Police Besiege Quebec Mohawks," *Boston Globe* (14 July 1990); Christine Tierney, "Mohawk Warriors Brace for Canadian Army Invasion," *Reuters News* (28 August 1990), noting the presence of an international observer mission from the International Federation for Human Rights at Kahnesatake; and "Canadian Troops Move In at Mohawk Settlement in Canada," *Associated Press* (1 September 1990). The RCAP Report states that "[t]he sight of Canada's army pitted against its own citizens received attention around the world. Canada's reputation on the international stage, one of promoting human rights and the well-being of Aboriginal peoples, was badly tarnished." RCAP Report, vol 1, *supra* note 2, c 7.

72 Linda Goyette, "Natives Seen through a Kinder Lens," *Kitchener-Waterloo Record* (7 December 1996) A19.

73 RCAP Report, vol 5, *supra* note 2, Appendix C at 296.

74 Peter H Russell, *Recognizing Aboriginal Title: The Mabo Case and Indigenous Resistance to English-Settler Colonialism* (Toronto: University of Toronto Press, 2005) at 338 [Russell].

75 RCAP Report, vol 5, *supra* note 2, Appendix C at 297.

76 *Ibid* at 300.

77 *Ibid* at 300–1.

78 Thomas Berger, interview with Kim Stanton (18 December 2007), Vancouver.

79 RCAP Report, vol 5, *supra* note 2, Appendix C at 297.

80 *Ibid.*

81 *Ibid* at 298.

82 *Ibid*, Appendix C.

83 Bradford W Morse & Tanya M Kozak, "Gathering Strength: The Government of Canada's Response to the Final Report of the Royal Commission on Aboriginal Peoples" in Aboriginal Rights Coalition, *Blind Spots: An Examination of the Federal Government's Response to the Report of the Royal Commission on Aboriginal Peoples* (Ottawa: Aboriginal Rights Coalition, 2001) 32 at 32 [Morse & Kozak]. They state that some of RCAP's interim reports were "highly influential," citing the self-government report as having an impact on the Beaudoin-Dobbie Parliamentary Committee (which called for constitutional reform, including Aboriginal self-government, saying that Aboriginal participation was required, and triggered the Charlottetown round of constitutional negotiations). Morse and Kozak also say that the 1994 report on the High Arctic relocation of Inuit families in the 1950s "led directly to the negotiation of a settlement between the affected families and the federal government." As for media interest, a search of the Factiva database of major North American newspapers produced 229 articles on RCAP in the five years of its operation. The highest proportion of articles was published in the two months following the release of the report.

84 RCAP Report, vol 1, *supra* note 2, c 10.

85 *Ibid*, c 13.

86 *Ibid*, c 10, s 5, Recommendation 1.10.1.

87 *Ibid* at 362.

88 *Ibid* at 363.

89 *Ibid* at 363–64.

90 *Ibid* at 363.

91 *Ibid* at 364.

92 *Statement of the Government of Canada on Indian Policy,* 28th Parl, 1st Sess (1969). The White Paper followed two years of conferences in which the government consulted with Indigenous representatives with respect to restructuring their relationship in order to remove discrimination and improve services and programs. The White

Paper recommended the eventual removal of specific references to Indians in the Constitution; the short-term goal was the repeal of the *Indian Act*. The termination policy under the Liberal government of Pierre Trudeau was bound up with the liberal idea that distinctions based on race should form no part of a democracy. However, this failed to take into account the fact that, though seeking increased autonomy, Indigenous peoples felt strongly that they must maintain their Indian status since the alternative appeared to be assimilation and concomitant loss of culture, language, and land. The response to the White Paper was immediate and unequivocal: Aboriginal organizations felt betrayed because the policy did not reflect the substance of the consultations in which they had participated for the previous two years and because it recommended what were perceived to be assimilationist solutions to their many concerns. According to Weaver, *supra* note 14 at 5, "Indians responded to the policy with a resounding nationalism unparalleled in Canadian history." By spring 1971, the policy was formally withdrawn by Chrétien. The White Paper was a major turning point in Aboriginal policy in Canada, prompting an unprecedented politicization of Indigenous peoples in the country.

93 See Scott Feschuk, "Natives Call for PM's Reaction to Report: Chrétien Has to Say Where He Stands on Royal Commission's Findings, Blondin-Andrew Says," *Globe and Mail* (6 December 1996) A4. Georges Erasmus states in an interview with Dr. Mike DeGagné, President of Nipissing University, and former head of the Aboriginal Healing Foundation (AHF), about the impact of RCAP that he and Dussault met with Chrétien when the report was being released, and it was clear to them that Chrétien would not do anything on the scale of what was needed. They had to do something, so they created the AHF, but they missed an important opportunity to do what was required – investing in Indigenous peoples in a way that would have reduced costs over the long term. Nipissing University, "Georges Erasmus: Reflections on the Royal Commission on Aboriginal Peoples" (2017), online: *Vimeo* <https://vimeo.com/210464622>.

94 Rudy Platiel, "Irwin Seeks Discussion of Proposals for Natives: Suggested Rise in Spending by Government Is Rejected," *Globe and Mail* (23 November 1996) A1.

95 "Aboriginal Commission Fails Poll Test," *Winnipeg Free Press* (9 December 1996) B3.

96 Stewart Phillip, "Federal Government's Response to the Royal Commission on Aboriginal Peoples" in Aboriginal Rights Coalition, *Blind Spots, supra* note 83, 49 at 51 [Phillip].

97 An ecumenical coalition of churches and grassroots groups across Canada, the Aboriginal Rights Coalition was the successor organization to Project North, formed in 1975 to work with Indigenous communities affected by the Mackenzie Valley pipeline proposals.

98 For example, the Gustafsen Lake Standoff in August 1995, where Shuswap people held a sun dance at a sacred ancestral site 350 kilometres north of Vancouver that was also part of a rancher's land. Four hundred police officers held a thirty-one-day siege in one of the largest police actions in Canadian history. See Robert Matas, "Film Suggests Dosanjh Manufactured a Crisis," *National Post* (29 April 2000) A6. Also in September 1995 was the protest by members of the Stoney Point Band at Ipperwash Provincial Park, during which Dudley George was shot and killed by Ontario Provincial Police.

99 For example, Preston Manning's Reform Party, which won sixty seats, all in the western provinces, in the 1997 federal election and formed the official opposition.

100 Lorraine Y Land, "Gathering Dust or Gathering Strength: What Should Canada Do with the Report of the Royal Commission on Aboriginal Peoples?" in Aboriginal Rights Coalition, *Blind Spots, supra* note 83, 56 at 58.

101 Maurice Switzer, "How the News of the Aboriginal Report Is Relayed: It's Not Enough to Publish the Report of the Royal Commission on Aboriginal Peoples. People Have to Be Told about Its Analyses, about the Full Reality of Native Life in This Country," *Globe and Mail* (28 November 1996) A23.

102 Assembly of First Nations, *Royal Commission on Aboriginal Peoples at 10 Years: A Report Card* (2006) [RCAP Report Card]. One of the report's recommendations was that the government call a First Ministers Conference within six months of the release of the report. The government failed to do so, and the lack of response from provincial governments reinforced the federal government's failure to address key aspects of the report. The government did not meet the fiscal targets recommended by RCAP in order to build self-sustaining Indigenous communities, nor did it replace Indian and Northern Affairs Canada (INAC) with a Ministry of Aboriginal Relations, a recommendation key to the goal of creating a partnership relationship to replace the colonial relationship embodied by the *Indian Act* and INAC.

103 Russell, *supra* note 74, at 339–40.

104 Canada, Ministry of Indian Affairs and Northern Development, *Gathering Strength: Canada's Aboriginal Action Plan* (Ottawa: Public Works and Government Services Canada, 1997) [*Gathering Strength*].

105 *Ibid:* (1) "renewing the partnerships" – including the need for reconciliation and healing, and the government offers a "Statement of Reconciliation" for this reason; this portion of the policy also discusses treaty renewal, federal/provincial/territorial/ Aboriginal partnerships, and other aspects of institution building; (2) "strengthening Aboriginal governance" – referring to creating accountable Aboriginal institutions and negotiating land claims; (3) "developing a new fiscal relationship" – improving financial arrangements between federal and Aboriginal governments; (4) "supporting strong communities, people and economies" – including strengthening Aboriginal economic development.

106 Canada, Ministry of Indian Affairs and Northern Development, *Gathering Strength: Canada's Aboriginal Action Plan – A Progress Report* (Ottawa: Minister of Public Works and Government Services Canada, 2000).

107 See Assembly of First Nations, RCAP Report Card, *supra* note 102. The Report Card suggests that the Aboriginal Healing Foundation was created in lieu of the government's implementation of RCAP's recommendation for a public inquiry into the IRS legacy.

108 Aboriginal Healing Foundation, "Frequently Asked Questions," online: <http://www.ahf.ca/faqs>.

109 See Chapter 4, note 35.

110 Funding for the AHF and other Indigenous-focused initiatives, including the Sisters in Spirit Project, the First Nations Statistical Institute, and the National Aboriginal Health Organization, was also cancelled in the 2010 federal budget. See "Aboriginal Healing Foundation," *Voices-Voix* (28 November 2012), online: <https://aboriginal260.rssing.com/chan-9925178/latest.php#c9925178a17?zx=813>; Andre Picard, "Harper's Disregard for Aboriginal Health," *Globe and Mail* (9 April 2012), online: <https://www.theglobeandmail.com/life/health-and-fitness/harpers-disregard-for-aboriginal-health/article4223490/>.

111 *Gathering Strength, supra* note 104, "Statement of Reconciliation: Learning from the Past." Statement read by Honourable Jane Stewart, Minister of Indian Affairs and Northern Development (7 January 1998).

112 Antonio Buti, "Responding to the Legacy of Canadian Residential Schools" (2001) 8:4 Murdoch UEJL at para 36, citing Law Commission of Canada, *Minister's Reference on Institutional Child Abuse: Discussion Paper* (1999) at 15.

113 Morse & Kozak, *supra* note 83 at 36.

114 *Ibid* at 46.

115 Michael DeGagné, "Implementing Reparations: International Perspectives" (paper delivered at "Moving Forward – Achieving Reparations for the Stolen Generations," 15–16 August 2001). This was a national conference in Sydney to facilitate public debate about reparations for the stolen generations hosted by the Australian Human Rights Commission, the Aboriginal and Torres Strait Islander Commission, and the Public Interest Advocacy Centre. DeGagné was then the Executive Director of the Aboriginal Healing Foundation.

116 Mary C Hurley & Jill Wherrett, "The Report of the Royal Commission on Aboriginal Peoples" (Parliamentary Information and Research Service, Library of Parliament, 4 October 1999, revised 2 August 2000), "Commentary."

117 "Ottawa Gets Failing Grade on Response to Aboriginal Commission," *CBC News* (21 November 2006), online: <https://www.cbc.ca/news/canada/ottawa-gets-failing-grade-on-response-to-aboriginal-commission-1.591726>.

118 See Phillip, *supra* note 96 at 54. Carol McBride, "Canada's Response to the Royal Commission on Aboriginal Peoples" in Aboriginal Rights Coalition, *Blind Spots, supra* note 83, 23 at 24, agreed, referring to *Gathering Strength, supra* note 104, and Indian and Northern Affairs Canada, "An Agenda for Action with First Nations" (1998):

> Both of these documents avoid any commitment to fundamental change in the relationship between Aboriginal peoples and the Crown. Instead, they offer incremental change, based on pre-existing federal policies and programs: the very policies and programs which the Royal Commission so thoroughly discredited.

119 Other mechanisms not discussed here include criminal injuries compensation programs, ombudsperson offices, children's advocates, and community-based responses. Also, as a non-Indigenous scholar, I have focused on legal mechanisms under Canadian law. I have not attempted to explore possible mechanisms available under Indigenous law for addressing broad societal problems.

120 RCAP Report, vol 1, *supra* note 2 at 360.

121 *R v Maczynski* (1997), 120 CCC (3d) 221 (BCCA) at para 2.

122 *Ibid* at para 3.

123 This discussion is drawn from the decision of Justice Thackray in *R v O'Connor* (1992), 18 CR (4th) 98 (BCSC). One motion alleged that there had been an unreasonable delay in bringing the matter to trial, thereby impeding the right of full answer and defence. Another application for a stay alleged that the indictment did not contain sufficient particularity. At the hearing of that application, Crown counsel supplied the diary of one of the complainants to the Court, and substantial portions of it were eventually disclosed to the defence. The fourth application for a judicial stay of proceedings alleged abuses of the Court process, that the administration of justice had been brought into disrepute, and that the public would be outraged by the conduct of the Crown and the prejudice created to the accused if the charges were not stayed. This application was also denied. During pretrial motions, the (female) Crown counsel at one point had suggested that the public would rather be appalled by the disclosure order for all of the records of the complainants and attempted to raise a report on gender inequality in the criminal justice system. However, the (male) judge was greatly irritated by the suggestion of gender bias and took a recess, instructing the Crown counsel to reconsider her argument. See John McInnes & Christine Boyle, "Judging Sexual Assault Law against a Standard of Equality" (1995) 29:2 UBC L Rev 341 at 344, n 12.

124 See John A Epp, "Production of Confidential Records Held by a Third Party in Sexual Assault Cases: *R v O'Connor*" (1996–97) 28 Ottawa L Rev 191.

125 *R v O'Connor* (1994), 89 CCC (3d) 109 (BCCA).

126 *R v O'Connor* (1994), 90 CCC (3d) 257 at 261 (BCCA).

127 *R v O'Connor*, [1995] 4 SCR 411.

128 *Ibid.* On the disclosure aspect of the decision, a differently constituted majority of the Supreme Court varied the procedure of the Court of Appeal with respect to applications for disclosure of complainant and third-party records. These decisions were heavily criticized and eventually led to legislative action in the form of Bill C-46, *An Act to Amend the Criminal Code (Production of Records in Sexual Offence Proceedings)*, SC 1997, c 30. The Bill added ss 278.1 to 278.91 to the *Criminal Code*, RSC 1985, c C-46. See Jennifer Koshan, "Disclosure and Production in Sexual Violence Cases: Situating *Stinchcombe*" (2002) 40:3 Alta L Rev 655 at 664ff.

129 Proudfoot JA refused his application for release pending appeal: *R v O'Connor*, [1996] 83 BCAC 4 (CA). McEachern CJ then allowed an application for review of that decision, and Proudfoot JA's order was overturned: *R v O'Connor*, [1997] 89 BCAC 152 (CA).

130 *R v O'Connor* (1998), 159 DLR (4th) 304 (BCCA) at paras 4, 9.

131 *Ibid* at para 5.

132 *Ibid* at para 9.

133 See Tom Hawthorn, "Disgraced BC Bishop Dead of a Heart Attack," *Globe and Mail* (27 July 2007); Douglas Todd, "O'Connor Appeal Dropped after Healing Circle," *Vancouver Sun* (18 June 1998) [Todd, "O'Connor Appeal Dropped"].

134 See, for example, *R v Frapper* (1990), YJ No 163 (Y Terr Ct) (QL); *R v Plint* (1995), BCJ No 3060 (SC) (QL); *R v Maczynski* (1997), 120 CCC (3d) 221 (BCCA); *R v Leroux* (1998), NWTJ No 141 (SC) (QL).

135 As noted by the Law Commission of Canada, "the criminal justice process is still essentially adversarial, reactive and punitive." Law Commission of Canada, *Restoring Dignity: Responding to Child Abuse in Canadian Institutions* (Ottawa: Minister of Public Works and Government Services, 2000) at 134 [*Restoring Dignity*].

136 Todd, "O'Connor Appeal Dropped," *supra* note 133.

137 In May 2006, it was estimated that 80,000 IRS survivors were still alive. See Indian and Northern Affairs Canada, *Backgrounder – Indian Residential Schools* (Indian Residential Schools Resolution Canada, May 2006). A search of reported cases reveals minimal cases prior to 1990 and a few cases per year in the 1990s.

138 Jane O'Hara, "No Forgiving," *Maclean's* (26 June 2000), online: <https://archive.macleans.ca/article/2000/6/26/no-forgiving>.

139 R Murray Thomas, "Can Money Undo the Past? A Canadian Example," (2003) 39:3 Comparative Education 331 at 331. See also Miller, *Shingwauk's Vision, supra* note 4 at 328, citing a *Globe and Mail* report (31 October 1990) [his citation is incomplete].

140 *FSM v Clarke*, [1999] 11 WWR 301 (BCSC) per Dillon J. The decision was released on my first day as her law clerk, 30 August 1999.

141 *Ibid* at para 2.

142 *Ibid* at para 3.
143 Justice Dillon relied at para 135 on *Blackwater v Plint,* a 1998 decision from the same Court with respect to her finding of vicarious liability. *Blackwater v Plint* (1998), 161 DLR (4th) 538. *Clarke* was filed several years prior to *Plint,* but the trial did not proceed until 1998, so the first *Plint* decision was released ahead of the *Clarke* decision.
144 *FSM v Clarke,* [1999] 11 WWR 301 (BCSC) at para 184.
145 *Ibid* at para 204.
146 *Blackwater v Plint* (1998), 161 DLR (4th) 538 (BCSC) per Brenner J (as he then was) [*Blackwater v Plint* (BCSC)]; 2003 BCCA 671; [2005] 3 SCR 3 [*Blackwater v Plint* (SCC)].
147 He was also convicted of additional counts in 1997 and sentenced to an additional year. See *Blackwater v Plint* (BCSC), *supra* note 146 at para 11.
148 *R v Plint* (1995), BCJ No 3060 (SC) (QL) at para 14.
149 The school was founded in the late 1800s by the Presbyterian Church. In 1925, part of the Presbyterian Church combined with two other denominations to form the United Church of Canada. The United Church then ran the school until Canada took over its operation in 1969. Canada continued to run the school until it was closed in 1973.
150 *Blackwater v Plint* (BCSC), *supra* note 146 at para 24, per Brenner J (as he then was).
151 *Ibid* at para 26.
152 *Ibid* at para 151.
153 *Blackwater v Plint* (1998), 165 DLR (4th) 352 (BCSC).
154 RCAP Report, vol 1, *supra* note 2, c 10, based on John Milloy, "Suffer the Little Children: A History of the Residential School System" (research study prepared for RCAP, 25 April 1996). Milloy later served for a time as Research Director of the TRC.
155 *Blackwater v Plint* (1998), 165 DLR (4th) 352 (BCSC) at paras 4, 6.
156 *Ibid* at para 17.
157 *Blackwater v Plint,* 2001 BCSC 997 at para 2.
158 *Ibid* at para 3.
159 That is, the *Limitations Act,* RSBC 1996, c 266, governing the other causes of action had a limitation period that had expired before the case went to court.
160 *Blackwater v Plint,* 2001 BCSC 997 at para 933.
161 *Blackwater v Plint,* 2003 BCCA 671 [*Blackwater v Plint* (BCCA)].
162 *Ibid* at paras 42–50.
163 *Blackwater v Plint* (SCC), *supra* note 146 at para 73, per McLachlin CJC for the Court.
164 *Blackwater v Plint* (BCSC), *supra* note 146 at para 247.
165 *Blackwater v Plint* (BCCA), *supra* note 161 at para 76ff.
166 In its decision in *Blackwater v Plint,* the Supreme Court of Canada recognized at para 74 that "[u]ntangling the different sources of damage and loss may be nigh

impossible. Yet the law requires that it be done, since at law a plaintiff is entitled only to be compensated for loss caused by the actionable wrong." The defendant is liable to the plaintiff for the full extent of the damage that his actions actually caused. He is not required to compensate the plaintiff for "the debilitating effects of the other wrongful act that would have occurred anyway" (para 80). The Court cites *Athey v Leonati*, [1996] 3 SCR 458 at para 32, which Thomas Berger argued before the SCC for the plaintiff.

167 *Blackwater v Plint* (SCC), *supra* note 146 at para 62. The Assembly of First Nations, Women's Legal Education and Action Fund, Native Women's Association of Canada, and DisAbled Women's Network of Canada intervened before the SCC.

168 *Bonaparte v Canada* (2002), 16 CPC (5th) 105 (Sup Ct).

169 *Ibid* at para 4.

170 *Ibid* at para 9.

171 The Attorney General of Canada, Her Majesty the Queen in Right of Canada as presented by the Minister for Indian and Northern Affairs, the Roman Catholic Bishop of Sault Ste Marie, the Roman Catholic Episcopal Corporation of the Diocese of Sault Ste Marie, the Jesuit Fathers of Upper Canada, and the Daughters of the Immaculate Heart of Mary.

172 *Bonaparte v Canada* (2003), 64 OR (3d) (CA) at para 36.

173 This lump sum payment is made, as part of the Settlement Agreement, to each student who shows that she or he attended an Indian residential school. It is intended to acknowledge that simply attending the schools caused harms. See Chapter 4, note 27.

174 *Quatell v Attorney General of Canada*, 2006 BCSC 1840 at para 9.

175 This is echoed in *Ammaq v Canada*, 2006 NUCJ 24, the Nunavut Court of Justice decision ratifying the Agreement in Principle. Kilpatrick J notes at para 45 that "[i]t is argued [by the defendants] that the common law to this point has not recognized loss of culture or language as giving rise to a legal claim of any kind." Kilpatrick J finds that this is one of the "significant risks" facing the plaintiffs in bringing the class action and therefore finds that the settlement is advantageous rather than facing the uncertainties of litigation (para 49).

176 See, for example *Cloud v Canada (Attorney General)* (2004), 247 DLR (4th) 667 (Ont CA).

177 *Class Proceedings Act, 1992*, SO 1992, c 6.

178 *Baxter v Canada*, [2005] OTC 391 (Sup Ct), per Winkler J (as he then was) [*Baxter* (2005)].

179 *Baxter v Canada* (2006), 83 OR (3d) 481 (Sup Ct), per Winkler J. The class action purported to represent 79,000 survivors who resided at a residential school in Canada between 1 January 1920 and 31 December 1996 and were still living as of 30 May 2005.

180   Assembly of First Nations, *Report on Canada's Dispute Resolution Plan to Compensate for Abuses in Indian Residential Schools* (November 2004) at 5 [Assembly of First Nations, ADR Report].

181   *DA v Canada (Attorney General)* (1998), 173 Sask R 312 (QB) at para 7.

182   *Ibid* at para 6.

183   The Law Society fined and reprimanded Merchant in 2002 and 2006 for violating the Law Society of Saskatchewan Code of Professional Conduct by engaging in conduct reasonably capable of misleading recipients in respect of his letters of solicitation to potential residential school survivors. See Jonathon Gatehouse, "Residential Schools Settlement Enriches Lawyer," *Maclean's* (11 September 2006). See also *Law Society of Saskatchewan v Merchant*, [2000] LSDD No 24 (QL). For a discussion of the questions raised about Merchant's controversial billing practices in the IRS cases, see Richard F Devlin & Porter Heffernan, "The End(s) of Self-Regulation?" (2008) 45:5 Alta L Rev 169 at 177ff.

184   Jane O'Hara and Patricia Treble, "Residential Church School Scandal," *Maclean's* (26 June 2000).

185   Law Society of Saskatchewan, "Rule re Solicitation and Marketing Activity Where Prospective Client of 'Weakened State'" (1999). AFN Chief Phil Fontaine contacted law societies across Canada in 1998 to raise concerns about the manner in which some lawyers aggressively solicited survivors of residential school abuse as clients, and about insensitivity shown by some lawyers over the impact of abuse on survivors. Law Society of British Columbia, *Benchers Bulletin* (August–September 1999). For additional responses, see Canadian Bar Association, "Guidelines for Lawyers Acting for Survivors of Aboriginal Residential Schools" (2000); Law Society of Yukon, "Guidelines for Lawyers Acting for Survivors of Aboriginal Residential Schools" (2000); and Law Society of Upper Canada, "Guidelines for Lawyers Acting in Cases Involving Aboriginal Residential School Abuse" (23 October 2003; amended 23 February 2012).

186   Assembly of First Nations, ADR Report, *supra* note 180 at 14.

187   A series of exploratory dialogues among the main parties involved in the IRS issue were held across Canada from September 1998 to June 1999. A summary of these dialogues is published in Canada, *Reconciliation and Healing: Alternative Resolution Strategies for Dealing with Residential School Claims* (Ottawa: Minister of Indian Affairs and Northern Development, March 2000) [Canada, *Reconciliation and Healing*].

188   Indian Residential Schools Resolution Canada, *Report on Plans and Priorities* (Office of Indian Residential Schools Resolution Canada, Treasury Board of Canada Secretariat, 2003–04).

189   *Restoring Dignity, supra* note 135.

190 Indian Residential Schools Resolution Canada, *Departmental Performance Report* (Office of Indian Residential Schools Resolution Canada, Treasury Board Secretariat, 2005).

191 *Ibid.*

192 *Blackwater v Plint* (BCCA), *supra* note 161.

193 This information is drawn from the Assembly of First Nations, ADR Report, *supra* note 180 at 14–15.

194 *Ibid* at 15. If the church responsible for the abuse had an indemnity agreement, then the victim would receive 100 percent compensation; if not, then he or she would receive only 70 percent.

195 *Ibid;* Canadian Bar Association, *The Logical Next Step: Reconciliation Payments for All Indian Residential School Survivors* (February 2005) [CBA Report].

196 Assembly of First Nations, ADR Report, *supra* note 180 at 15.

197 *Ibid* at 14.

198 *Ibid* at 36; CBA Report, *supra* note 195 at 9.

199 House of Commons, Standing Committee on Aboriginal Affairs and Northern Development, *Study on the Effectiveness of the Government Alternative Dispute Resolution Process for the Resolution of Indian Residential School Claims* (March 2005). The committee's report was presented to the House of Commons on 7 April 2005 and adopted on 12 April 2005. This was during the period of Paul Martin's minority Liberal government, elected in June 2004.

200 Legislative committees are another method by which a government can seek to investigate a particular issue. However, they are unsatisfactory for wronged groups because of the partisan nature of the mechanism, lack of transparency, fewer opportunities for participation, and reduced ability to advocate in the legislative arena. The role of paid lobbyists for certain parties can also make for an uneven playing field if aggrieved groups lack the resources to access such avenues. According to the Law Reform Commission report on commissions of inquiry, because of time constraints and partisan considerations, Parliament is not always the best placed to give complex issues the time or the objectivity that they might need, nor is a parliamentary mechanism always the best means for gathering a full range of public opinion. Law Reform Commission of Canada, *Administrative Law: Commissions of Inquiry* (Working Paper 17) (Ottawa: Law Reform Commission of Canada, 1977) at 14–15.

201 Assembly of First Nations, ADR Report, *supra* note 180 at 14.

202 The *Indian Act* also restricted the ability of Indigenous peoples to challenge in the courts the legal structure under which they suffered. After 1880, "Indians" could not access their own band funds without federal government approval. Thus, their ability to travel and meet with one another was hampered. RCAP Report, vol 1, *supra* note 2, c 7, s 2. This in turn made it difficult to formulate a legal strategy. Freedom of

association was restricted by *Criminal Code* provision in 1892. It was an indictable offence for more than three "Indians, non-treaty Indians or half-breeds" to meet together to make demands of civil servants in a riotous or disorderly manner. The *Indian Act* was amended in 1926 to make it illegal for a lawyer to receive fees to represent an "Indian" or a band to commence claims against the Crown. See AJI Report, *supra* note 6 at 70. Between 1927 and 1951, the *Indian Act* prohibited the soliciting of funds to advance "Indian claims" of any kind without official permission.

203   Internationally, *Basic Principles and Guidelines on the Right to a Remedy and Reparation for Victims of Gross Violations of International Human Rights Law and Serious Violations of International Humanitarian Law* were adopted by the UN Commission on Human Rights on 19 April 2005 (HR Res 2005/35). These principles were then reinforced by the adoption on 20 April 2005 of a commission resolution recognizing a right of victims to truth about the causes and conditions of gross violations of international human rights law and encouraging states to consider the use of truth and reconciliation commissions for investigating and addressing gross human rights violations and serious violations of international humanitarian law (HR Res 2005/66). In a December 2004 report, the Special Rapporteur on the Rights of Indigenous Peoples suggested that Canada's response to the IRS legacy was inadequate, noting in particular a failure to address intergenerational harms from loss of culture, identity, and parenting. The report suggested that the continuing IRS impacts on Indigenous communities can be factors in the high rate of Indigenous adolescent suicide. See *Report of the Special Rapporteur on the Situation of Human Rights and Fundamental Freedoms of Indigenous People,* by Rodolfo Stavenhagen, "Mission to Canada," E/CN.4/2005/88/Add.3 (2 December 2004) at para 61.

204   I will discuss these calls in the next chapter.

205   Also in 2005, then Minister of Justice Irwin Cotler called the IRS system "the single most harmful, disgraceful and racist act in our history." "School Abuse Victims Getting $1.9B," *CBC News* (23 November 2005), online: <https://www.cbc.ca/news/canada/school-abuse-victims-getting-1-9b-1.540142>.

Chapter 4: Canada's Truth and Reconciliation Commission

1   This chapter is based on Kim Stanton, *Truth Commissions and Public Inquiries: Addressing Historical Injustices in Established Democracies* (SJD, University of Toronto Faculty of Law, 2010), online: <https://tspace.library.utoronto.ca/handle/1807/24886>, and on some passages previously published in my article "The Canadian Truth and Reconciliation Commission: Settling the Past?" (2011) 2:3 Intl Indigenous Policy J, Article 2, online: <http://ir.lib.uwo.ca/iipj/vol2/iss3/2>.

2   Canada, *Reconciliation and Healing: Alternative Resolution Strategies for Dealing with Residential School Claims* (Ottawa: Minister of Indian Affairs and Northern Development, March 2000).

3 *Ibid.*

4 *Blackwater v Plint* (1998), 161 DLR (4th) 538 (BCSC).

5 The government made agreements with various churches in and around 2003 apportioning liability roughly in the same proportion. Marites N Sison, "Church Eligible for Better Residential Schools Deal," *Anglican Journal* (1 January 2006), online: <https://www.anglicanjournal.com/church-eligible-for-better-residential-schools-deal-3044/>.

6 In addition to the *Cloud* class action in Ontario, *Cloud v Canada (Attorney General)* (2004), 247 DLR (4th) 667 (Ont CA), there were four others within a few years: the *Dieter* class action of students in the western provinces, the *Straightnose* claim from Saskatchewan, and the *Baxter* and *Pauchay* national class actions. See Canada, *Notice of Class Actions* (Indian Residential Schools Alternative Dispute Resolution Process), online: *Assembly of First Nations* <http://web.archive.org/web/20060531010518/http://www.irsr-rqpi.gc.ca/english/dispute_resolution_class_action_notice.html>.

7 Olive P Dickason and David T McNab, *Canada's First Nations: A History of Founding Peoples from Earliest Times,* 4th ed (Don Mills, ON: Oxford University Press, 2009) at 424, citing Lorna Dueck, "Sorry Isn't Good Enough," *Globe and Mail* (31 October 2000) A2.

8 In November 1997, federal Minister of Justice Anne McLellan requested that the Law Commission of Canada conduct research and provide advice on the available processes for addressing institutional child abuse. Law Commission of Canada, *Restoring Dignity: Responding to Child Abuse in Canadian Institutions* (Ottawa: Minister of Public Works and Government Services, 2000), Appendix A at 425–26.

9 *Ibid* at 51–70.

10 *Ibid* at 67.

11 *Ibid* at 259.

12 *Ibid* at 278.

13 *Ibid* at 279.

14 Rick Mofina, "'Truth Commission' Urged: Hearings May Satisfy Victims of Residential School Abuse without Assigning Blame," *StarPhoenix* [Saskatoon] (6 June 2000) front page. In a 2002 article, Llewellyn suggested a restorative justice approach through a truth commission or public inquiry in order to demonstrate that the IRS system affected whole communities and was not simply an individual issue, as denoted by torts litigation. Jennifer J Llewellyn, "Dealing with the Legacy of Native Residential School Abuse in Canada: Litigation, ADR, and Restorative Justice" (2002) 52:3 UTLJ 253 at 260, citing "A Truth Commission Is the Place to Start," *Toronto Star* (10 November 2001).

15 See Chapter 1, note 15.

16 National Consortium of Residential School Survivors, "Assembly of First Nations – Litigation Only Option – Lack of Ottawa's Political Will" (press release), *Turtle Island News* (16 October 2002). The memorandum was signed 4 October 2002.

17 See Indigenous Bar Association to Frank Iacobucci (17 October 2005), on file with the author.

18 Assembly of First Nations, *Report on Canada's Dispute Resolution Plan to Compensate for Abuses in Indian Residential Schools* (November 2004) at 36, online: <https://epub.sub.uni-hamburg.de//epub/volltexte/2009/2889/pdf/Indian_Residential_Schools_Report.pdf>.

19 *Cloud v Canada (Attorney General)*, 2004 CanLII 45444 (Ont CA), a decision penned by Justice Goudge, Catzman and Moldaver JJA concurring.

20 Anne McLellan, Deputy Prime Minister, to National Chief Phil Fontaine (30 May 2005), online: <https://kathleenmahoney.files.wordpress.com/2019/01/a-mclellan_letter.pdf>.

21 That is, the class action would ensure that the Assembly of First Nations would have standing to negotiate a settlement. Assembly of First Nations, "Assembly of First Nations National Chief Files Class Action Claim against the Government of Canada for Residential Schools Policy" (3 August 2005), online: <http://media.knet.ca/node/1528>.

22 The 38th Parliament ended on 29 November 2005. Also in November that year, the federal government, provinces, and Aboriginal organizations reached agreement on the Kelowna Accord, committing the government to spend $5 billion over ten years on education, employment, housing, and other living conditions of Indigenous peoples. The Accord followed eighteen months of negotiations and was considered an important achievement in process and result. After the Liberal government fell in January 2006, the Conservative Harper government refused to honour the Accord, dismissing it as merely a press release with no substance as an agreement and non-binding on the government since the funds were not committed to in the budget. See Canadian Press, "Tories to Avoid Parliament's Kelowna Accord Vote," *CTV News* (22 March 2007), online: <https://www.ctvnews.ca/tories-to-ignore-parliament-s-kelowna-accord-vote-1.234221> ["Tories to Avoid Kelowna Accord Vote"].

23 *Blackwater v Plint*, [2005] 3 SCR 3.

24 See, for example, the 15 December 2006 decision *Quatell v Attorney General of Canada*, 2006 BCSC 1840, per Brenner CJ [*Quatell*]; *Baxter v Canada*, [2005] OTC 391 (Sup Ct), per Winkler J (as he then was); and *Fontaine et al v Canada et al*, 2006 YKSC 63, per Veale J.

25 Indian and Northern Affairs Canada, "Backgrounder: Indian Residential Schools" (Ottawa: Indian Residential Schools Resolution Canada, 2005).

26 Aboriginal Affairs and Northern Development Canada, "Backgrounder: Indian Residential Schools Settlement Agreement" (Gatineau: Aboriginal Affairs and Northern Development Canada, 2008).

27 Indian Residential Schools Settlement Agreement (8 May 2006) at para 4.14 [Settlement Agreement]. Very few survivors opted out: "Valerie Hache, a spokesperson for the federal Indian Residential Schools Resolution Canada, told the *Straight* that some 201 former students have opted out of the settlement." See Carlito Pablo, "After the Settlement Comes Healing, Closure," *Georgia Straight* (6 September 2007), online: <http://www.straight.com/article-108553/after-the-settlement-comes -healing-closure>. See also Federation of Saskatchewan Indian Nations, *Indian Residential School Office Annual Report* (6 September 2007).

28 Settlement Agreement, *supra* note 27, Schedule N, Art 5.

29 See judgment of Brenner CJ in *Blackwater v Plint* (BCSC), *supra* note 4, and Chapter 3, note 166.

30 *Ibid.*

31 Standing Committee on Aboriginal Affairs and Northern Development Concerning the Aboriginal Healing Foundation, *Report of the Standing Committee on Aboriginal Affairs and Northern Development*, "Appendix C: Common Experience Payment Statistics," (House of Commons Canada, June 2010) online: <http://caid. ca/AANO2010Rep2403.pdf>.

32 Indian and Northern Affairs Canada, "Audit of the Advance Payment Program" (4 December 2008) online: <https://www.rcaanc-cirnac.gc.ca/DAM/DAM-CIRNAC-RCAANC/DAM-AEV/STAGING/texte-text/app_1100100011682_ eng.pdf>.

33 Settlement Agreement, *supra* note 27, Schedule D, "Independent Assessment Process."

34 *Ibid,* Schedule J.

35 *Ibid,* Schedule M, s 3.03.

36 Health Canada, "Indian Residential Schools Resolution Health Support Program," online: <http://www.hc-sc.gc.ca/fniah-spnia/services/indiresident/irs-pi-eng.php>.

37 See Chapter 4, note 187.

38 Settlement Agreement, *supra* note 27, Schedule N, preamble.

39 *Ibid,* Schedule N, s 1.

40 They are described further in *ibid,* Schedule N, s 10.

41 *Ibid,* Schedule N, s 1(f).

42 *Ibid,* Schedule N, s 1(f), n 3.

43 See note 2 above. These exploratory dialogues were undertaken to guide the settlement discussions.

44 Settlement Agreement, *supra* note 27, Schedule N, "Principles."

45 *Ibid,* Schedule N, s 8.

46 See *ibid*, Schedule N, s 10(c).

47 See *ibid*, Schedule N, s 10(d).

48 See *ibid*, Schedule N, s 12.

49 *Ibid*, Schedule N, s 6.

50 *Ibid*, Schedule N, s 7.

51 See, for example, the South African case *Azanian Peoples Organisation (AZAPO) v President of the Republic of South Africa*, [1996] 4 SA 671 (S Afr Const Ct).

52 *Fontaine v Canada (Attorney General)*, 2013 ONSC 684. Justice Goudge ran a public inquiry in Ontario in 2008 on forensic pathology. His report included notable recommendations on how coroners fail to serve Indigenous communities. According to a biographical statement by Western University,

> Goudge is best known to the public for leading the Inquiry into Pediatric Forensic Pathology in Ontario in 2008. During that time, he helped shape the use of pediatric forensic pathology related to its practice and use in investigations and criminal proceedings. Following its completion, he was cited as a model of how to lead an efficient, effective, fair and successful public inquiry. Many of his recommendations have since been implemented.

Western University, "The Honourable Stephen T Goudge," online: <https://www.uwo.ca/univsec/pdf/StephenGoudgebio.pdf>. Justice Goudge no doubt drew on his experience as deputy commission counsel on the Berger Inquiry when he took on the role of Commissioner.

53 Based on the definition set out in Report of the Secretary-General, *The Rule of Law and Transitional Justice in Conflict and Post-Conflict Societies*, UNSCOR, 2004, UN Doc S/2004/616, s 17 at para 50.

54 Settlement Agreement, *supra* note 27, Schedule N, s 5.

55 *Ibid*, Schedule N, ss 5(a) and (b).

56 Sanford Levinson, "Trials, Commissions, and Investigating Committees: The Elusive Search for Norms of Due Process" in Robert Rotberg & Dennis Thompson, eds, *Truth v Justice: The Morality of Truth Commissions* (Princeton, NJ: Princeton University Press, 2000) 211 at 223. The Executive Director is also a crucial position. See Priscilla B Hayner, *Unspeakable Truths: Confronting State Terror and Atrocity* (New York: Routledge, 2001) at 215 [Hayner, *Unspeakable Truths*]: "Perhaps more than any other single factor, the person or persons selected to manage a truth commission will determine its ultimate success or failure."

57 South Africa was fortunate to have someone of Tutu's "moral caliber and authority" leading the TRC. Elizabeth Kiss, "Moral Ambition within and beyond Political Constraints: Reflections on Restorative Justice" in Rotberg & Thompson, *supra* note 56, 68 at 91 [Kiss].

58 Hayner, *Unspeakable Truths*, *supra* note 56 at 220.

59 *Ibid* at 216.

60 Settlement Agreement, *supra* note 27, Schedule N, s 5.

61 *Ibid,* Schedule N, s 5(c).

62 Order in Council 2008–794, (2008) C Gaz 1, 1596.

63 Thomas Berger, interview with Kim Stanton (1 April 2009), Toronto [Berger interview 2]. The selection committee chose Justice LaForme from 300 nominations narrowed down to 50 prospects, of which 16 candidates were interviewed. Joe Friesen, "Residential Schools Panel Struggles to Find New Chair. Truth and Reconciliation Always a Difficult Balance, Expert Says," *Globe and Mail* (30 October 2008) [Friesen, "New Chair"]. Marlene Brant Castellano was the Co-Director of Research for RCAP. See also "'Top-Level' Panel to Pick New Truth Commission Head: Lawyer," *CBC News* (14 December 2008), online: <https://www.cbc.ca/news/canada/top-level-panel-to-pick-new-truth-commission-head-lawyer-1.732865>. According to an Indian Residential Schools Resolution Canada government press release, "The Government of Canada Takes a Significant Step towards Launching the Indian Residential Schools Truth and Reconciliation Commission" (28 April 2008), online: <http://media.knet.ca/node/3800> [IRS Resolution Canada press release]:

> Justice LaForme was unanimously chosen to be the Chair of the IRSTRC from the more than 300 submissions in response to a public call for nominations. The selection panel included representatives of national Aboriginal organizations and parties to the Settlement Agreement.

64 Harry LaForme, (untitled lecture presented at the Ethics at Ryerson Speaker Series, Toronto Arts and Letters Club, 13 November 2008) [unpublished] [LaForme].

65 The Indian Commission of Ontario was mandated to assist the governments of Ontario, Canada, and First Nations within Ontario to identify and mediate problem issues of mutual concern, such as land claims, policing, and education.

66 This was also known as the Indian Specific Claims Commission, established under the *Inquiries Act* (per Order in Council PC 1991–1329), to determine the validity of Aboriginal land claims.

67 Court of Appeal of Ontario, "Brief Biographical Note of Justice Harry S LaForme," online: <http://www.ontariocourts.on.ca/coa/en/judges/laforme.htm>. Justice LaForme retired from the bench in 2018.

68 LaForme, *supra* note 64.

69 Order in Council 2008–924, (2008) C Gaz 1, 1755; Order in Council 2008–925, (2008) C Gaz 1, 1755.

70 LaForme, *supra* note 64. The same selection committee process was used to produce a list of names for the Chair and Co-Commissioners. The names were forwarded to Minister of Indian Affairs and Northern Development Chuck Strahl and AFN Grand Chief Phil Fontaine for final determination.

71　Dumont-Smith was a former community health nurse, a member of the Aboriginal Circle of the Canadian Panel on Violence against Women, a Co-Commissioner on the National Aboriginal Child Care Commission, and a member of the Domestic Violence Death Review Committee for Ontario.

72　Morley practised civil litigation for over twenty years until the mid-1990s, when she became a mediator and arbitrator. She held various posts with public organizations such as the Law Foundation of British Columbia, the College of Physicians and Surgeons of British Columbia, the Legal Services Society, the British Columbia Mediator Roster Society, and the British Columbia Dispute Resolution Practicum Society. From 1996 to 2001, she was Chair of the Jericho Individual Compensation Panel, a redress program for victims of institutional sexual abuse at the Jericho School for the Deaf and Blind. From 2003 to 2006, she was the Child and Youth Officer for British Columbia. It is unclear from the public record whether the Chief Commissioner and Settlement Agreement parties had the opportunity to provide input into the selection of Co-Commissioners, though an Indian Residential Schools Resolution Canada government press release suggests that this was so. See IRS Resolution Canada press release, *supra* note 63. The TRC's mandate required that "[t]he Assembly of First Nations (AFN) shall be consulted in making the final decision as to the appointment of the Commissioners." Settlement Agreement, *supra* note 27, Schedule N, s 5(c).

73　This was less than a week after the Conservatives won a successive minority government. The election was held on 14 October 2008.

74　Canadian Newswire Group, "Justice Harry S LaForme Resigns as Chair of the Indian Residential Schools Truth and Reconciliation Commission" (press release, 20 October 2008), citing LaForme's letter to Minister of Indian Affairs and Northern Development Strahl.

75　LaForme, *supra* note 64.

76　*Ibid.*

77　*Ibid.* According to Kevin Libin, "Chairman's Exit Leaves Panel in Disarray. Native Abuses Commission Rudderless," *National Post* (28 October 2008) [Libin, "Chairman's Exit"], "associates of Judge LaForme say he had in mind one political agent in particular: the country's most powerful aboriginal group, the Assembly of First Nations."

78　*Ibid.*

79　Deborah Gyapong, "Truth and Reconciliation Commission Chair's Resignation 'Sad,'" *Catholic Register* (22 October 2008), online: <https://www.catholicregister.org/item/8168-truth-and-reconciliation-commission-chairs-resignation-sad>. The mediator was reported to be Toronto lawyer Will McDowell, dispatched by Ontario Chief Justice Warren Winkler.

80　Norma Greenaway, "Judge Chosen to Lead Commission into Residential Schools Resigns," *Ottawa Citizen* (21 October 2008) A1, A4: "LaForme ... had indicated some unhappiness as early as last July, saying he was worried about possible government interference in the commission's work because it set up an administrative secretariat for the commission as a government department."

81 Joe Friesen, "AFN Meddling Blamed for Exit of Commission's Chairman," *Globe and Mail* (23 October 2008), online: <https://www.theglobeandmail.com/news/national/afn-meddling-blamed-for-exit-of-commissions-chairman/article1064183/> [Friesen, "AFN Meddling"].

82 Canadian Newswire Group, "Iacobucci Updates on Truth and Reconciliation Commission" (press release, 8 December 2008), online: <https://nationtalk.ca/story/iacobucci-updates-on-truth-and-reconciliation-commission>. Iacobucci had also been a lead negotiator for the federal government of the Settlement Agreement.

83 Canadian Newswire Group, "Selection Committee to Begin Immediately to Select Truth and Reconciliation Commission" (press release, 30 January 2009), online: <https://nationtalk.ca/story/selection-committee-to-begin-immediately-to-select-truth-and-reconciliation-commission>. The new selection committee included Frank Iacobucci, Phil Fontaine, and Inuit leader Mary Simon.

84 Ontario's Anishinabek Nation, the Congress of Aboriginal Peoples, and the National Residential Schools Survivors' Society called on the Commissioners to resign. Friesen, "New Chair," *supra* note 63.

85 Although they stayed on with the commission until 1 June, the Commissioners did not conduct any commission work other than writing a memorandum for their replacements. Christine Spencer, "Panel Tab Tough to Reconcile: Aboriginal Abuse Commission Will Cost $3.4M before Hearings Even Begin," *Edmonton Sun* (26 February 2009).

86 "New Job Descriptions for Residential Schools Commissioners," *CBC News* (27 February 2009), online: <https://www.cbc.ca/news/canada/new-job-descriptions-for-residential-schools-commissioners-1.855271>.

87 Truth and Reconciliation Commission on Indian Residential Schools, "It Is 'Business as Usual' at the Truth and Reconciliation Commission (TRC)," press release on file with the author. Nabigon later became the Interim Executive Director of the National Inquiry into MMIWG. See Chapter 4, note 106, as well as Chapter 5, notes 115 and 129.

88 Eduardo Gonzales, "Residential Schools: Give Truth a Chance, Canada," *Globe and Mail* (4 November 2008), online: < https://www.theglobeandmail.com/opinion/give-truth-a-chance-canada/article716723/> [Gonzales]. For example, the National Reconciliation Commission in Ghana got off to a bad start because of a parliamentary walkout by the opposition party over the commission's legislation, but ultimately it managed to fulfill its mandate in a reasonably successful manner. The South African TRC faced multiple court challenges. A commission in Nepal was dissolved soon after it was appointed in 1990 when the two Co-Commissioners resigned in protest

over the appointment of a Chair viewed as a collaborator with the prior regime. See Hayner, *Unspeakable Truths, supra* note 56 at 57.

89 University of Winnipeg, *Justice Murray Sinclair on Campus* (television broadcast, UWinnipeg.tv, 22 September 2009) [University of Winnipeg, *Justice Murray Sinclair on Campus*].

90 I discuss the AJI in Chapter 5.

91 Kent Roach, "Canadian Public Inquiries and Accountability" in Philip C Stenning, ed, *Accountability for Criminal Justice: Selected Essays* (Toronto: University of Toronto Press, 1995) 268 at 288.

92 *The Report of the Manitoba Pediatric Inquest: An Inquiry into Twelve Deaths at the Winnipeg Health Sciences Centre in 1994*, by C Murray Sinclair (Winnipeg: Provincial Court of Manitoba, 2000).

93 Shari Narine, "TRC Back on Track with New Appointments" *Windspeaker* (2009) 27:4, online: <https://ammsa.com/publications/windspeaker/trc-back-track -new-appointments>.

94 Justice Sinclair was appointed in 2017 by the Ontario Civilian Police Commission to investigate the Thunder Bay Police Services Board in relation to the deaths of Indigenous youths in that community.

95 "'Incredible Honour' to Be Named to Truth Commission: Wilson," *CBC News* (11 June 2009), online: <https://www.cbc.ca/news/canada/north/incredible-honour-to -be-named-to-truth-commission-wilson-1.793083>. See also Stephen Kakfwi, "I Accept the Prime Minister's Apology," *Globe and Mail* (12 June 2008) [Kakfwi, "I Accept the Prime Minister's Apology"]. See also Chapter 2, note 52.

96 The commission reported in 2004. Commission on First Nations and Métis Peoples and Justice Reform, *Final Report of the Commission on First Nations and Métis Peoples and Justice Reform. Legacy of Hope: An Agenda for Change* (Saskatoon: Commission on First Nations and Métis Peoples and Justice Reform, 2004).

97 Alberta Order of Excellence, "Wilton Littlechild, IPC, CM, FP, QC, LLD (Hon)," online: <https://www.alberta.ca/aoe-wilton-littlechild.aspx>; see also University of Winnipeg, *Justice Murray Sinclair on Campus, supra* note 89.

98 This is not to say that Indigenous peoples would not have an interest in learning the full truth of what happened to their families under the IRS system. Rather, it refers to the ignorance of many non-Indigenous Canadians about the IRS legacy. See Frank Stirk, "Residential Schools: Truth, Reconciliation – but No Apology Yet," *CanadianChristianity.com* (27 September 2007), online: < https://www. bishop-accountability.org/news2007/09_10/2007_09_28_Stirk_Residential Schools.htm>.

99 Truth and Reconciliation Commission of Canada, "About Us," online: <http://www. trc.ca/about-us/faqs.html>.

100 *Order Designating the Indian Residential Schools Truth and Reconciliation Commission as a Department and the Chairperson as the Deputy Head for Purposes of the Act,* SI/2009–46 (24 June 2009), repealing SI/2008–44.

101 Truth and Reconciliation Commission of Canada, *Interim Report* (TRC, 2012) at 2.

102 The reset of the panel also meant that new orders in council had to be passed to extend the life of the TRC for the year lost because of the resignation of the first panel.

103 This was despite the TRC terms of reference, Settlement Agreement, *supra* note 27, Schedule N, s 11, that required Canada and the churches to provide all relevant documents within their possession or control to the commission.

104 See Settlement Agreement, *supra* note 27, Schedule N, s 2(c).

105 Mark Kennedy, "Truth Seeker: Murray Sinclair's Relentless Quest for the Facts about Residential Schools," *Ottawa Citizen* (22 May 2015), online: <https://ottawa citizen.com/news/politics/truth-seeker-murray-sinclairs-relentless-quest-for-the -truth-about-residential-schools>.

106 "Truth Commission Tied Too Closely to Government," *CBC News* (8 October 2008), online: <https://www.cbc.ca/news/canada/truth-commission-tied-too-closely -to-government-aboriginal-groups-1.699882>. Nabigon previously served as the Director General for Policy, Partnerships, and Communications with Indian and Northern Affairs Canada and the Director General for the Common Experience Payment at the former Office of Indian Residential Schools Resolution Canada.

107 Joe Friesen, Jacquie McNish, & Bill Curry, "Native Leaders Divided over Future of Residential Schools Panel," *Globe and Mail* (22 October 2008), online: <https:// www.theglobeandmail.com/news/national/native-leaders-divided-over-future-of -residential-schools-panel/article661684/>.

108 "Truth and Reconciliation Commission Lawyer Must Quit: Native Leaders," *CBC News* (30 July 2008), online: <https://www.cbc.ca/news/canada/truth-and -reconciliation-commission-lawyer-must-quit-native-leaders-1.752399>.

109 Bill Curry, "Research Director Resigns from Reconciliation Commission," *Globe and Mail* (12 July 2010), online: <https://www.theglobeandmail.com/news/national/ research-director-resigns-from-reconciliation-commission/article1378802/>. According to Ry Moran, shortly after the Winnipeg national event, the national events planning team also resigned. Ry Moran, "Truth and Reconciliation Commission" in *Canadian Encyclopedia* (24 September 2015), online: <https://www.thecanadian encyclopedia.ca/en/article/truth-and-reconciliation-commission>.

110 Both wrote books on the IRS system: John S Milloy, *A National Crime: The Canadian Government and the Residential School System, 1879 to 1986* (Winnipeg: University of Manitoba Press, 1999); Paulette Regan, *Unsettling the Settler Within: Indian Residential Schools, Truth Telling, and Reconciliation Canada* (Vancouver: UBC Press, 2011).

111 Settlement Agreement, *supra* note 27, Schedule N, s 2.

112 *Ibid,* Schedule N, s 3.

113 *Ibid,* Schedule N, s 2(b).

114 *Ibid,* Schedule N, ss 4(e), (a), and (d), respectively.

115 Friesen, "AFN Meddling," *supra* note 81.

116 Settlement Agreement, *supra* note 27, Schedule N, s 7. The IRS Survivor Committee was established on 15 July 2009. The committee had ten members: seven First Nations, two Inuit, and one Métis. Truth and Reconciliation Commission of Canada, "About Us," online: <http://www.trc.ca/about-us/meet-the-survivor-committee.html>.

117 Settlement Agreement, *supra* note 27, Schedule N, s 10(b).

118 Mark Freeman, *Truth Commissions and Procedural Fairness* (Cambridge, UK: Cambridge University Press, 2006) at 124.

119 See Settlement Agreement, *supra* note 27, Schedule N, s 1.

120 *Ibid,* Schedule N, s 2(f).

121 Michael Trebilcock & Lisa Austin, "The Limits of the Full Court Press: Of Blood and Mergers" (1998) 48:1 UTLJ 1 at 22.

122 Settlement Agreement, *supra* note 27, Schedule N, s 2(h).

123 *Ibid,* Schedule N, s 2(i).

124 See my discussion of the criminal law response to the IRS legacy in Chapter 3.

125 Settlement Agreement, *supra* note 27, Schedule N, s 2(j).

126 *Ibid,* Schedule N, s 2(k).

127 Not naming names also means that people who might be viewed as perpetrators are denied the opportunity to clear their names, at least before the TRC (they might have the opportunity to do so in the Independent Assessment Process). Although Schedule N does not explicitly provide for immunity from prosecution, it does so implicitly through the parts of s 2(f)–(k). The possibility of prosecution arose only through the admission or public disclosure by the individuals themselves. There is no protection against self-incrimination in the TRC mandate.

128 Elizabeth Stanley, "What Next? The Aftermath of Organised Truth Telling" (2002) 44:1 Race & Class 1 at 3.

129 Truth and Reconciliation Commission of Canada, *Honouring the Truth, Reconciling for the Future: Summary of the Final Report of the Truth and Reconciliation Commission of Canada* (Ottawa: Truth and Reconciliation Commission of Canada, 2015) at 26 [TRC, *Honouring the Truth*].

130 Hayner, *Unspeakable Truths, supra* note 56 at 107.

131 Settlement Agreement, *supra* note 27, Schedule N, s 11.

132 *Canada (Attorney General) v Fontaine,* 2017 SCC 47.

133 Commission to Clarify Past Human Rights Violations and Acts of Violence that Have Caused the Guatemalan People to Suffer, in operation from 1997 to 1999. See Charles

O Lerche, "Truth Commissions and National Reconciliation: Some Reflections on Theory and Practice" (2000) 7:1 Peace and Conflict Studies 1 at 8.

134   Hayner, *Unspeakable Truths, supra* note 56, Appendix 1, Chart 8 at 336.

135   Harry LaForme, "Remarks by Justice Harry S. LaForme" (remarks at the Assembly of First Nations 29th Annual General Assembly, Quebec City, 15 July 2008) [unpublished]:

> [T]he ... commitment [of the parties to the Settlement Agreement] to the truth and reconciliation process has been given legal effect through court judgments.
>
> This gives real force to the commitment of the government and churches to provide access to their Indian residential school archives.

136   Settlement Agreement, *supra* note 27, Schedule N, s 11.

137   TRC, *Honouring the Truth, supra* note 129 at 27. See also the reference to Goudge JA's decision, *supra* note 52.

138   Even some commissions of inquiry have been unwilling to use their powers of subpoena. Several scholars wrote an open letter to urge RCAP to use its judicial powers to advance its research objectives, noting that its willingness to do so "will certainly be seen as an important test of RCAP's degree of commitment to pursue unrelentingly the basic truths essential to the fulfillment of its extensive mandate." The signatories included Patricia Monture-Okanee, John Milloy, Brian Slattery, Marvin Storrow, and Blair Stonechild. See Anthony Hall, "RCAP's Big Blind Spots" in Aboriginal Rights Coalition, *Blind Spots: An Examination of the Federal Government's Response to the Report of the Royal Commission on Aboriginal Peoples* (Ottawa: Aboriginal Rights Coalition, 2001) 66 at 71–72.

139   Hayner, *Unspeakable Truths, supra* note 56 at 21, referring to the National Commission on the Disappeared (Comisión Nacional sobre la Desaparición de Personas, CONADEP) report, *Nunca Más: Informe de la Comision Nacional sobre la Desaparicion de Personas* (20 September 1984).

140   *Ibid* at 34.

141   *Ibid* at 37, 39.

142   *Ibid* at 153.

143   I acknowledge that there is no one truth to be found or uncovered but a record to be constructed based on the information gathered by the truth-seeking process.

144   JR Miller, *Shingwauk's Vision: A History of Native Residential Schools* (Toronto: University of Toronto Press, 1996) at 341–42.

145   Marlene Brant Castellano, "A Holistic Approach to Reconciliation: Insights from Research of the Aboriginal Healing Foundation" in Marlène B Castellano, Linda Archibald, & Mike DeGagné, eds, *From Truth to Reconciliation: Transforming the Legacy of Residential Schools* (Ottawa: Aboriginal Healing Foundation, 2008) 383 at 386 [Castellano, "A Holistic Approach to Reconciliation"].

146   For polling information on this point, see Environics Research Group, *Final Report: 2008 National Benchmark Survey* (prepared for Indian Residential Schools Resolution Canada and Truth and Reconciliation Commission, 2008) at 13ff [Environics, *Benchmark Survey*].

147   The differing perceptions are evident in the stereotypes visible in mainstream media coverage of the Settlement Agreement. See, for example, Jack Branswell & Ken Meaney, "Residential School Cash Has Deadly Fallout: Suicides, Drug Abuse Attributed to Compensation," *Calgary Herald* (26 January 2009) A7; Canadian Press, "Racist Overtones Surround Residential School Payments: National Chief," *Guelph Mercury* (20 September 2007) A6.

148   Pablo de Grieff, "Justice and Reparations" in Jon Miller & Rahul Kumar, eds, *Reparations: Interdisciplinary Inquiries* (Toronto: Oxford University Press, 2007) 153 at 161–62.

149   Roland Chrisjohn, Sherri Lynn Young, & Michael Maraun, eds, *The Circle Game: Shadows and Substance in the Indian Residential School Experience in Canada* (Penticton, BC: Theytus Books, 2006) at 4–5. The authors describe the dominant narrative as a "standard" account of the IRS system and the conflicting narrative as an "irregular" account. By "irregular," they appear to mean the dissident or minority account.

150   A poll conducted for Indian Residential Schools Resolution Canada and the TRC in May 2008 found that six in ten Canadians were unable to cite any long-term consequence for survivors of having gone through the IRS system. Environics, *Benchmark Survey, supra* note 146 at 20.

151   Angus Reid Institute, "Truth and Reconciliation: Canadians See Value in Process, Skeptical about Government Action" (9 July 2015), online: <http://angusreid.org/aboriginal-truth-and-reconciliation/> [Angus Reid Institute poll].

152   *Ibid.*

153   Prime Minister Stephen Harper, "Statement of Apology to Former Students of Indian Residential Schools" (Ottawa, 11 June 2008), online: < https://www.rcaanc-cirnac.gc.ca/eng/1100100015644/1571589171655> [Harper, "Statement of Apology"].

154   Erin Daly & Jeremy Sarkin, *Reconciliation in Divided Societies* (Philadelphia: University of Pennsylvania Press, 2007) at 145 [Daly & Sarkin] that,

> where there is no consensus on the morality of the fundamental questions (*Was it a war or a genocide? Was everyone equally guilty of excess or can the victim class be reliably distinguished from the perpetrator class? Was torture widespread or was it exceptional?*), then the truth that is officially revealed is unlikely to bring people together. Instead, it may foster deeper divisions.

155   TRC, *Honouring the Truth, supra* note 129 at 1.

156 Neil J Kritz, "Where We Are and How We Got Here: An Overview of Developments in the Search for Justice and Reconciliation" in A Henkin, *The Legacy of Abuse* (New York: The Aspen Institute and NYU School of Law, 2002) 21 at 38.

157 Daly & Sarkin, *supra* note 154 at 110.

158 Priscilla B Hayner and Mark Freeman, "'Truth-Telling' in International Institution for Democracy and Electoral Assistance" in David Bloomfield, Teresa Barnes, & Luc Huyse, eds, *Reconciliation after Violent Conflict: A Handbook* (Stockholm: International IDEA, 2003) 122 at 128–29.

159 Angus Reid Institute poll, *supra* note 151.

160 Misha Warbanski, "Truth and Forgiveness," *McGill Daily* (24 January 2008), online: <https://www.mcgilldaily.com/2009/08/truth_and_forgiveness/>. Warbanski cites then TRC staff member Seetal Sunga.

161 See note 84 above.

162 The Environics poll conducted in April and May 2008 found that most Canadians who had heard about the Settlement Agreement had done so via mass media. Environics, *Benchmark Survey, supra* note 146 at 27. Overall, awareness among Canadians of the Settlement Agreement was "fairly low" – only four in ten had heard of the Common Experience Payment, and two in ten or fewer had heard of the other elements of the Settlement Agreement. *Ibid* at 25.

163 Settlement Agreement, *supra* note 27, Schedule N, s 2(b).

164 See Greensboro Truth and Reconciliation Commission, "Public Hearings – News Media," online: <http://www.greensborotrc.org/hearings_news_media.php>.

165 See Greensboro Truth and Reconciliation Commission, "News and Events – TRC Talk," online: <http://www.greensborotrc.org/trc_talk.php>.

166 Ghana Journalists' Association, "The Spirit of Akosombo: Guiding Principles for Media Coverage of the National Reconciliation Process" (June 2002), on file with the author.

167 Edward John, "From Apology to Action: A Response to the Residential Schools Apology," *Vancouver Sun* (12 June 2008). Edward John is Grand Chief, Tl'azt'en Nation.

168 Canada, First Nations Child and Family Services, "Reducing the Number of Indigenous Children in Care," online: <https://www.sac-isc.gc.ca/eng/154118735229 7/1541187392851>.

169 TRC, *Honouring the Truth, supra* note 129 at 32.

170 I was an official observer of Ghana's National Reconciliation Commission hearings during 2002–03 on behalf of the Civil Society Coalition. I attended the NRC's hearings and reported regularly to the coalition, whose members would deliberate on how best to support the work of the truth commission. Sometimes this meant sending a delegation of eminent leaders to meet with the Commissioners to make

recommendations on the effectiveness of the NRC's work. Sometimes it meant organizing things such as street theatre in communities to which the NRC was travelling in order to educate the local population on the NRC's mandate and process. The coalition was an enormously conscientious effort by civil society leaders to ensure the success of the NRC.

171   Ghana Center for Democratic Development, *National Reconciliation: International Perspectives. Report of an International Conference on National Reconciliation in Ghana, June 20–21, 2001* (Accra: CDD-Ghana, 2001).

172   For example, the UN Human Rights Committee criticized Canada for not conducting a public inquiry into the death of Dudley George: "The Committee strongly urges a public inquiry into all aspects of the matter, including the role and responsibility of public officials." United Nations Human Rights Committee, *Consideration of Reports Submitted by States Parties under Article 40 of the International Covenant on Civil and Political Rights, Concluding Observations: Canada, 7 April 1999*, 99–09927 (E) 070499 (1999). An inquiry was established in 2003, began hearings in 2004, and reported in 2007.

173   CBC Radio, "Reconciliation," *The Current* (16 June 2009).

174   See Law Commission of Canada, ed, *Indigenous Legal Traditions* (Vancouver: UBC Press, 2007) [Law Commission of Canada, *Indigenous Legal Traditions*]; James Tully, *Strange Multiplicity: Constitutionalism in an Age of Diversity* (New York: Cambridge University Press, 1995) at 21.

175   See Marlene Brant Castellano, "Renewing the Relationship: A Perspective on the Impact of the Royal Commission on Aboriginal Peoples" in Aboriginal Rights Coalition, *Blind Spots, supra* note 138, 1 at 12 [Castellano, "Renewing the Relationship"].

176   A useful definition of restorative justice appears in Julian V Roberts & Kent Roach, "Restorative Justice in Canada: From Sentencing Circles to Sentencing Principles" in A Von Hirsch et al, eds, *Restorative Justice and Criminal Justice: Competing or Reconcilable Paradigms?* (Oxford: Hart Publishing, 2003) 237 at 238–39:

> Restorative justice is an informal and non-adjudicative form of dispute resolution that brings offenders, victims and their supporters and other members of the community together ... to discuss and decide what should be done with respect to a crime. Restorative justice has been described as a ... model of justice ... that sees crime as a violation of a relationship involving the victim, offender and the community.

The Supreme Court of Canada endorsed the principles of restorative justice as appropriate in criminal sentencing practices in 1999 in a case that specifically dealt with the unique circumstances of Indigenous offenders in Canada: *R v Gladue*, [1999] 1 SCR 688. Restorative justice is intended to incorporate Indigenous approaches to criminal behaviour, but it has not been without controversy. See, for example, Sandra Goundry, *Restorative Justice and Criminal Justice in British Columbia: Identifying Some Preliminary Questions and Concerns* (Vancouver: BC Association of Specialized Victim Assistance and Counselling Programs, 1998); Annalise E Acorn, *Compulsory Compassion: A Critique of Restorative Justice* (Vancouver: UBC Press, 2004); EJ Dickson-Gilmore and Carol LaPrairie, *Will the Circle Be Unbroken? Aboriginal Communities, Restorative Justice, and the Challenges of Conflict and Change* (Toronto: University of Toronto Press, 2005).

177 Kiss, *supra* note 57 at 79.

178 Naomi Roht-Arriaza & Javier Mariezcurrena, *Transitional Justice in the Twenty-First Century: Beyond Truth versus Justice* (Cambridge, UK: Cambridge University Press, 2006) at 4.

179 Jennifer Llewellyn, "Bridging the Gap between Truth and Reconciliation: Restorative Justice and the Indian Residential Schools Truth and Reconciliation Commission" in Castellano, Archibald, & DeGagné, *supra* note 145, 185 at 188–89 [citations omitted] [Llewellyn, "Bridging the Gap"].

180 Castellano, "A Holistic Approach to Reconciliation," *supra* note 145 at 385–86, citing Marlene Brant Castellano, *The Final Report of the Aboriginal Healing Foundation*, vol 1 (Ottawa: Aboriginal Healing Foundation, 2006) at 177–79. Castellano was the Co-Director of Research for RCAP and a researcher and writer for the Aboriginal Healing Foundation's final report.

181 See Settlement Agreement, *supra* note 27, Schedule N, preamble.

182 *Quatell, supra* note 24 at para 35.

183 Leighann Chalykoff, "Conservatives Won't Say 'Sorry' for Residential School," *Yukon News* (31 March 2007), online: <https://www.yukon-news.com/news/conservatives-wont-say-sorry-for-residential-school/>. See also Assembly of First Nations, *Report on Canada's Dispute Resolution Plan to Compensate for Abuses in Indian Residential Schools* (November 2004) at 20.

184 Prime Minister Kevin Rudd, "Apology to Australia's Aboriginal Peoples" (13 February 2008), online: <https://info.australia.gov.au/about-australia/our-country/our-people/apology-to-australias-indigenous-peoples>.

185 Ruti G Teitel, *Transitional Justice* (New York: Oxford University Press, 2000) at 140.

186 Jim Prentice, "Truth and Reconciliation as Nation Building" (lecture delivered at Preparing for the Truth Commission: Sharing the Truth about Residential Schools. A Conference on Truth and Reconciliation as Restorative Justice, University of Calgary, 15 June 2007) [unpublished].

187 Harper, "Statement of Apology," *supra* note 153. The minority Conservative government was evidently spurred on by the leader of the New Democratic Party of Canada, Jack Layton, whose efforts to achieve the apology were acknowledged by

Prime Minister Harper in his speech. Also, members of his own caucus convinced Harper that an apology would help with their party's initiatives on Aboriginal matters. Bill Curry & Brian Laghi, "Mounting Sense of Urgency Was Apology's Catalyst: Pleas by Two Cabinet Ministers, a Senator and NDP Leader Persuaded Harper That Statement Should Precede Work of Commission," *Globe and Mail* (13 June 2008) A4 [Curry & Laghi]. See also Courtney Jung, "Canada and the Legacy of the Indian Residential Schools: Transitional Justice for Indigenous peoples in a Non-Transitional Society" (8 April 2009) at 16, online: *Social Science Research Network* <http://ssrn.com/abstract=1374950> [Jung]. Jung refers to the pressure on the caucus to pass Bill C-44, the *Act to Amend the Canadian Human Rights Act* (the amendment would remove the exemption shielding federal and Indigenous governments from human rights complaints).

188   See Chapter 3, note 111.

189   Matthew Coon Come, "Victims Hail Harper's Healing Words: I Choose to Accept the Apology and Move On, Forgiving Those Who Sexually and Physically Abused Me in the Quebec Residential School," *Gazette* [Montreal] (13 June 2008) A17; Daniel Nolan, "Six Nations Welcomes Federal Apology," *Hamilton Spectator* (13 June 2008) A3; Kakfwi, "'I Accept the Prime Minister's Apology,'" *supra* note 95. But see Beverley Jacobs, "Response to Canada's Apology to Residential School Survivors" (2008) 26:3–4 Canadian Woman Studies 223 at 223–25, where she recounts her response to the apology as President of the Native Women's Association of Canada: "Words must turn into action."

190   Omar El Akkad, "School-Abuse Apology Widely Backed," *Globe and Mail* (14 June 2008) A4, citing an Innovative Research Group poll conducted between 11 and 13 June.

191   For example, the Harper government refused to honour the Kelowna Accord, a $5.1 billion program for Indigenous health, education, and housing, negotiated in 2005 and ignored a House of Commons vote requiring the government to fulfill its obligations under the Accord. See "Tories to Avoid Kelowna Accord Vote," *supra* note 22. The Harper government also reversed Canada's position and refused to endorse the *United Nations Declaration on the Rights of Indigenous Peoples,* which the General Assembly adopted by a vote of 143 to 4 on 13 September 2007. General Assembly, "General Assembly Adopts Declaration on Rights of Indigenous Peoples: 'Major Step Forward' towards Human Rights for All, Says President" (news release), UNGAOR, 61st Gen Plen, 107th and 108th Mtgs, UN Doc GA/10612 (2007). The Harper government might have been more open to making the apology given that it was a minority government. See Curry & Laghi, *supra* note 187.

192   Sam Garkawe, "The South African Truth and Reconciliation Commission: A Suitable Model to Enhance the Role and Rights of the Victims of Gross Violations of Human Rights?" (2003) 27 Melbourne UL Rev 334 at 351:

> Perhaps one overall lesson to be learnt from the [South African] TRC from a victim perspective is the importance of being realistic and clear from the beginning about possible achievements for victims, and ensuring that victims are made aware of the limitations of what a truth commission can accomplish.

193 Chris Cunneen, "Reparations and Restorative Justice: Responding to the Gross Violation of Human Rights" in Heather Strang & John Braithwaite, eds, *Restorative Justice and Civil Society* (Cambridge, UK: Cambridge University Press, 2001) 83 at 88 [Cunneen].

194 Hayner, *Unspeakable Truths, supra* note 56 at 6.

195 *Ibid* at 133.

196 See Kim Stanton, "Reconciling Reconciliation: Differing Conceptions of the Supreme Court of Canada and the Canadian Truth and Reconciliation Commission" (2017) 26 J L & Soc Pol'y 21. The discussion in this section is drawn from this article.

197 *R v Van der Peet*, [1996] 2 SCR 507. This was one case in a trilogy of cases related to Aboriginal commercial rights. The other two cases were *R v NTC Smokehouse Ltd*, [1996] 2 SCR 672, and *R v Gladstone*, [1996] 2 SCR 723. In *Van der Peet*, at para 31, Lamer CJC also discussed the purpose of s 35 (the section of the 1982 Constitution recognizing "existing Aboriginal and treaty rights"):

> [W]hat s. 35(1) does is provide the constitutional framework through which the fact that aboriginals lived on the land in distinctive societies, with their own practices, traditions and cultures, is acknowledged and reconciled with the sovereignty of the Crown. The substantive rights which fall within the provision must be defined in light of this purpose; the aboriginal rights recognized and affirmed by s. 35(1) must be directed towards the reconciliation of the pre-existence of aboriginal societies with the sovereignty of the Crown.

> *Delgamuukw* was before the courts for thirteen years and was finally decided by the Supreme Court of Canada in 1997. *Delgamuukw v British Columbia*, [1997] 3 SCR 1010 [*Delgamuukw*]. The case was brought by thirty-eight Gitksan Houses and twelve Wet'suwet'en Houses seeking ownership and self-governance of 58,000 square kilometres of land in British Columbia. The Court's judgment addressed Aboriginal title but did not allocate ownership. Instead, it called for a new trial. Lamer CJC wrote at para 186 that,

> [b]y ordering a new trial, I do not necessarily encourage the parties to proceed to litigation and settle their dispute through the courts ... Ultimately it is through negotiated settlements, with good faith and give and take on all sides, reinforced by the judgments of this Court, that we will achieve ... the reconciliation of the pre-existence of aboriginal societies with the sovereignty of the Crown. Let us face it, we are all here to stay.

198   Mark D Walters, "The Jurisprudence of Reconciliation: Aboriginal Rights in Canada" in Will Kymlicka & Bashir Bashir, eds, *The Politics of Reconciliation in Multicultural Societies* (Oxford: Oxford University Press, 2008) 165 at 190 [Walters, "The Jurisprudence of Reconciliation"].

199   Walters notes that the Court's introduction of "reconciliation" into its Aboriginal rights decisions coincided with the release of the RCAP Report in 1996: "[T]he Royal Commission reintroduced reconciliation into Canadian political discourse." *Ibid* at 176.

200   Jung, *supra* note 187 at 23, states that "the Supreme Court has interpreted reconciliation as an obligation to reconcile Canadian and aboriginal legal systems." This is perhaps too generous a view of the Court's decision. Rather, the Court saw reconciliation as a process of recognizing that Indigenous societies pre-existed Crown sovereignty but that they are now part of a broader Canadian society, and therefore their rights are subject to limits that make them consistent with the goals of that society. See *Delgamuukw, supra* note 197 at para 165, per Lamer CJ. For a thoughtful analysis of the Court's conception of s 35 rights and the limits of its approach to reconciliation, see Dawnis Kennedy, "Reconciliation without Respect? Section 35 and Indigenous Legal Orders" in Law Commission of Canada, *Indigenous Legal Traditions, supra* note 174 at 75.

201   *Haida Nation v British Columbia (Minister of Forests)*, 2004 SCC 73 [*Haida Nation*]; *Taku River Tlingit First Nation v British Columbia (Project Assessment Director)*, 2004 SCC 74. In these cases, the Supreme Court developed the concept of the honour of the Crown and deepened the government's duty to consult with First Nations about land use in their traditional territories. In *Haida Nation,* the Crown argued that there is no legal duty to consult or accommodate a First Nation with respect to land use until the scope and content of its Aboriginal title is finally determined. This argument was rejected by the Court. The judgment of a unanimous Court was delivered by McLachlin CJC, who stated at para 32 that

> the duty to consult and accommodate is part of a process of fair dealing and reconciliation that begins with the assertion of sovereignty and continues beyond formal claims resolution. Reconciliation is not a final legal remedy in the usual sense. Rather, it is a process flowing from rights guaranteed by s. 35(1) of the *Constitution Act, 1982.* This process of reconciliation flows from the Crown's duty of honourable dealing toward Aboriginal peoples, which arises in turn from the Crown's assertion of sovereignty over an Aboriginal people and *de facto* control of land and resources that were formerly in the control of that people.

202   See Mark D Walters, "The Morality of Aboriginal Law" (2006) 31 Queen's LJ 470 at 501 [Walters, "The Morality of Aboriginal Law"], and Walters, "The Jurisprudence of Reconciliation," *supra* note 198 at 178.

203 Walters suggests that this form of "reconciliation through negotiation" is "about establishing the legal and moral authority of the Canadian state." Walters, "The Jurisprudence of Reconciliation," *supra* note 198 at 186. Jung, *supra* note 187 at 23, states that "one implication of reconciliation is negotiation among equals, which has been interpreted as a duty to consult that imposes on the Canadian government an obligation of good faith." She suggests that this aspect of the Canadian courts' form of reconciliation can be useful in the transitional justice context.

204 Priscilla Hayner, "Same Species, Different Animal: How South Africa Compares to Truth Commissions Worldwide" in Charles Villa-Vicencio and Wilhelm Verwoerd, eds, *Looking Back, Reaching Forward: Reflections on the Truth and Reconciliation Commission of South Africa* (Cape Town: University of Cape Town Press, 2000) 32 at 39.

205 Bloomfield, Barnes, & Huyse, *supra* note 158 at 22, para 2.1.3.

206 Indeed, as noted by McLachlin CJC in *Haida Nation, supra* note 201 at para 25, "[p]ut simply, Canada's Aboriginal peoples were here when Europeans came, and were never conquered."

207 Kymlicka & Bashir, *supra* note 198 at 19.

208 Cunneen, *supra* note 193 at 90.

209 Daly & Sarkin, *supra* note 154 at 146.

210 *Ibid.*

211 *Ibid.*

212 James Bartleman, "The Importance of Truth Telling in a Just Society" (lecture delivered at Preparing for the Truth Commission: Sharing the Truth about Residential Schools. A Conference on Truth and Reconciliation as Restorative Justice, University of Calgary, 15 June 2007) [unpublished].

213 Indeed, Indigenous people who did not support the IRS settlement and TRC process viewed the concept of reconciliation as a way for the Canadian government to appear to address an issue without actually addressing it. See Roland Chrisjohn & Tanya Wasacase, "Half-Truths and Whole Lies: Rhetoric in the 'Apology' and the Truth and Reconciliation Commission" in Gregory Younging, Jonathan Dewar, & Michael DeGagné, eds, *From Truth to Reconciliation: Response, Responsibility and Renewal – Canada's Truth and Reconciliation Journey* (Ottawa: Aboriginal Healing Foundation, 2009) 217; also see Taiaiake Alfred, "Restitution Is the Real Pathway to Justice for Indigenous Peoples" in Younging, Dewar, & DeGagné, *ibid* 179 at 184 [Alfred]. The TRC would have had to be prepared to encounter this cynicism since it is based on a long history of mistrust between Indigenous peoples and the government.

214 Llewellyn, "Bridging the Gap," *supra* note 179 at 186.

215 Castellano, "Renewing the Relationship," *supra* note 175 at 12.

216 Gonzales, *supra* note 88. Gonzales consulted for the TRC when he was a Senior Associate with the International Center for Transitional Justice.

217   *Ibid.* See also Jung, *supra* note 187, who subtitles her 2009 article "Transitional Justice for Indigenous People in a Non-Transitional Society." This assessment might not accord with perspectives of Indigenous communities whose legal and governance institutions have been severely damaged by colonization and that might consider that a transition is under way.

218   Castellano, "A Holistic Approach to Reconciliation," *supra* note 145 at 386.

219   See Alfred, *supra* note 213. Non-Indigenous views expressing skepticism about the TRC include Libin, "Chairman's Exit Leaves Panel in Disarray," *supra* note 77, quoting Tom Flanagan, University of Calgary political science professor and an architect of Stephen Harper's 2004 and 2006 election campaigns, as saying that the TRC is "mostly 'political theatre'"; RA Clifton, "Residential Schools: Another View: 'Most of These Students at Least Learned Modern Skills that Would Help Them Participate More Fully in Both Aboriginal and Canadian Society,'" *National Post* (31 May 2008) A25.

220   See note 27 above; almost 100,000 people applied for the Common Experience Payment.

Chapter 5: Inquiries and the Crisis of Missing and Murdered Indigenous Women and Girls

1   As explained in note 6 in the Introduction, "Aboriginal law" is the term used to describe the law of the Canadian state as applied to Indigenous peoples; "Aboriginal" is the term used in s 35 of the *Constitution Act, 1982*. As a Canadian lawyer, I do not practise "Indigenous law" since that term refers to the various legal traditions of Indigenous peoples themselves.

2   See Gary Mason, "The Debacle over B.C.'s Missing Women," *Globe and Mail* (20 October 2011), online: <https://www.theglobeandmail.com/opinion/the-debacle-over-bcs-missing-women/article4199587/> [Mason].

3   The *Public Inquiry Act*, SBC 2007, c 9, provides for the establishment of both hearing commissions and study commissions.

4   This paragraph is drawn from an 11 April 2011 unsolicited memorandum (on file with the author) that I sent to MWI Assistant Commission Counsel Karey Brooks upon the announcement of the study commission. I subsequently met with commission counsel to discuss the lessons of previous inquiries. Policy Counsel Dr. Melina Buckley acknowledged the potential for inquiries to fulfill a truth and reconciliation function in "From Report to Substantive Change – Healing, Reconciliation and Implementation" (April 2012) at 2, but she stated that the ability of the MWI to promote social accountability was constrained by its "more limited terms of reference."

5   Mary Eberts, "Victoria's Secret: How to Make a Population of Prey" in Joyce Green, ed, *Indivisible: Indigenous Human Rights* (Winnipeg and Halifax: Fernwood Publishing, 2014) at 146.

6 The Aboriginal Justice Inquiry's review of the case in Public Inquiry into the Administration of Justice and Aboriginal People, *Report of the Aboriginal Justice Inquiry of Manitoba*, by AC Hamilton & Murray Sinclair (Winnipeg: Province of Manitoba, 1991) [AJI Report], which I discuss later in this chapter.

7 *R v Kummerfield*, [1998] 9 WWR 619 (SKCA).

8 Amnesty International wrote a report on the issue in 2004. Amnesty International, *Stolen Sisters: A Human Rights Response to Discrimination and Violence against Indigenous Women in Canada* (October 2004), online: <http://www.amnesty.ca/sites/default/files/amr200032004enstolensisters.pdf>.

9 Statistics Canada data from 2017 show that the homicide rates of Indigenous women and girls were six times higher than those of non-Indigenous women and girls. Statistics Canada, *Homicide in Canada, 2017*, by Sara Beattie, Jean-Denis David, & Joel Roy, Catalogue No 85–002-X (Ottawa: Statistics Canada, 21 November 2018).

10 Native Women's Association of Canada, *What Their Stories Tell Us: Research Findings from the Sisters in Spirit Initiative* (2010), online: <https://www.nwac.ca/wp-content/uploads/2015/07/2010-What-Their-Stories-Tell-Us-Research-Findings-SIS-Initiative.pdf> [NWAC 2010].

11 Jorge Barrera, "Moon Setting on Sisters in Spirit?" *APTN News* (4 November 2010), online: <https://aptnnews.ca/2010/11/04/moon-setting-on-sisters-in-spirit/>.

12 BC CEDAW Group, "Nothing to Report: A Report on Implementing Priority Recommendations Made by the Committee in Its 2008 Concluding Observations on Canada" (January 2010), online: <https://povertyandhumanrights.org/wp-content/uploads/2010/04/nothing-to-report.pdf> at 3. The BC CEDAW Group is a coalition of BC women's and human rights organizations that has been monitoring the status of women's equality in the province since 2001.

13 *Ibid.*

14 See Committee on the Elimination of Discrimination against Women, *Report of the Inquiry Concerning Canada of the Committee on the Elimination of Discrimination against Women under Article 8 of the Optional Protocol to the Convention on the Elimination of All Forms of Discrimination against Women* (30 March 2015), CEDAW/C/OP.8/CAN/1 [CEDAW Report].

15 Inter-American Commission on Human Rights, *Missing and Murdered Indigenous Women in British Columbia, Canada* (21 December 2014), OEA/Ser.L/V/II. Doc.30/14 [IACHR Report]; CEDAW Report, *supra* note 14.

16 *Report of the Special Rapporteur on the Rights of Indigenous Peoples: The Situation of Indigenous Peoples in Canada*, UNGAOR, 27th Sess, UN Doc A/HRC/27/52/Add.2 (2014).

17 Maryanne Pearce, *An Awkward Silence: Missing and Murdered Vulnerable Women and the Canadian Justice System* (LLD, Common Law Section, University of Ottawa, 2013).

18 Royal Canadian Mounted Police, "Missing and Murdered Aboriginal Women: A National Operational Overview," CAT NO: PS64–115/2014E-PD (2014) [RCMP 2014].

19 "Tina Fontaine Died Because Police, CFS Failed Her, Family Says," *CBC News* (25 September 2014), online: <http://www.cbc.ca/news/canada/manitoba/tina-fontaine -died-because-police-cfs-failed-her-family-says-1.2777606>.

20 The older white man accused of her murder was acquitted in 2018. No one else has been charged in connection with her death.

21 Alex Boutilier, "Native Teen's Slaying a Crime, Not a 'Sociological Phenomenon,' Stephen Harper Says," *Toronto Star* (21 August 2014), online: <https://www.thestar. com/news/canada/2014/08/21/native_teens_slaying_a_crime_not_a_sociological_ phenomenon_stephen_harper_says.html>. Harper made these comments following the death of Tina Fontaine.

22 "Full Text of Peter Mansbridge's Interview with Stephen Harper," *CBC News* (17 December 2014), online: <https://www.cbc.ca/news/politics/full-text-of-peter -mansbridge-s-interview-with-stephen-harper-1.2876934>.

23 Gloria Galloway & Kathryn Blaze Carlson, "Tories Suggest Missing Aboriginal Women Related to Domestic Violence," *Globe and Mail* (26 February 2015), on-line: <https://www.theglobeandmail.com/news/politics/tories-suggest-missing -aboriginal-women-related-to-domestic-violence/article23222654/>.

24 RCMP 2014, *supra* note 18; NWAC 2010, *supra* note 10. NWAC also found that only 53 percent of murder cases involving Indigenous women and girls have led to charges of homicide. This is dramatically different from the national clearance rate for homi-cides in Canada, last reported at about 89 percent (RCMP 2014), and in contrast to the RCMP's assertion that the clearance rate is not dramatically different.

25 Tom Flanagan, "A Federal Inquiry Was Never Going to Accomplish Much," *Globe and Mail* (28 August 2014), online: <https://www.theglobeandmail.com/opinion/ a-federal-inquiry-was-never-going-to-accomplish-much/article20227821/>; Jeffrey Simpson, "Posturing Is the Only Reason for a Missing Women Inquiry," *Globe and Mail* (27 August 2014), online: <https://www.theglobeandmail.com/opinion/ posturing-is-the-only-reason-for-an-inquiry/article20211559/>.

26 Barbara McDougall, "We Need Real Action, Not More Information, on the Tragedy of Aboriginal Women," *Globe and Mail* (25 August 2014), online: <https://www. theglobeandmail.com/opinion/we-need-real-action-not-more-information-on-the -tragedy-of-aboriginal-women/article20189539/>. McDougall was the Minister Responsible for the Status of Women in Brian Mulroney's cabinet from 1986 to 1990.

27 IACHR Report, *supra* note 15 at para 295.

28 *Ibid* at para 299.

29 Pippa Feinstein & Megan Pearce, "Review of Reports and Recommendations on Violence against Indigenous Women in Canada" (Legal Strategy Coalition, February

2015), online: <https://www.leaf.ca/legal/legal-strategy-coalition-on-violence -against-indigenous-women-lsc/> [LSC Report]. The National Inquiry into MMIWG relied on the LSC's work for its literature review in its *Interim Report*. See note 102 below.

30 See Kim Stanton, "Putting a National Inquiry on the Radar," *Blogging for Equality* (16 January 2015), online: <http://www.bloggingforequality.ca/2015/01/putting -national-inquiry-on-radar.html>. Text from this post is included in this section. Unfortunately, this blog, originally posted by University of Ottawa Law Professor Angela Cameron, is no longer online.

31 See Kim Stanton, "A National Inquiry on #MMIW? Yes, but Do It Right," *Rabble* (2 October 2014), online: <http://rabble.ca/blogs/bloggers/views-expressed/2014/10/ national-inquiry-mmiw-yes-do-it-right>.

32 The federal government invited me to participate in the pre-inquiry consultations conducted in early 2016 along with other people with knowledge of previous public inquiries in order to assist it in drafting the terms of reference. For example, at a roundtable on 6 February 2016 organized by Ronda Bessner and Mary Eberts under the auspices of Osgoode Hall Law School, I provided an overview of my thesis on the pedagogical potential of public inquiries, the need for an effective media strategy, and other lessons from my academic work. Status of Women staff followed up with me after the roundtable for further discussion on 12 February 2016.

33 AJI Report, *supra* note 6.

34 *An Act to Establish and Validate the Public Inquiry into the Administration of Justice and Aboriginal People*, SM 1989–90, c 1, s 3(1).

35 AJI Report, vol 1, *supra* note 6, "Introduction."

36 This discussion of the AJI draws from Kim Stanton, *Truth Commissions and Public Inquiries: Addressing Historical Injustices in Established Democracies* (SJD, University of Toronto Faculty of Law, 2010), online: <https://tspace.library.utoronto.ca/ handle/1807/24886> [Stanton, *Truth Commissions*], and, along with the following discussion on the MWI, from Kim Stanton, "Intransigent Injustice: Truth, Recon- ciliation and the Missing Women Inquiry in Canada" (2013) 1:2 Transitional Justice Rev, Article 4, online: <https://ir.lib.uwo.ca/tjreview/vol1/iss2/4/>.

37 AJI Report, vol 1, *supra* note 6 at 5.

38 *Ibid.* See also Kent Roach, "Canadian Public Inquiries and Accountability" in Philip C Stenning, ed, *Accountability for Criminal Justice: Selected Essays* (Toronto: University of Toronto Press, 1995) 268.

39 AJI Report, *supra* note 6.

40 *Ibid,* vol 2, c 1, "The Mandate of the Inquiry."

41 AJI Report, *supra* note 6.

42 *Ibid,* vol 1 at 5.

43 *Ibid* at 14.

44   *Ibid* at 512ff.

45   *Ibid* at c 13.

46   The third and final volume related to the death of J.J. (John Joseph) Harper.

47   Aboriginal Justice Implementation Commission, *Final Report* (Winnipeg: Aboriginal Justice Implementation Commission, 2001), online: <http://www.ajic.mb.ca/reports/final_summary.html>. This model and the failure to implement many past recommendations prompted a clause in the Saskatchewan Commission on First Nations and Métis Peoples and Justice Reform terms of reference requiring it to recommend "short and long term implementation strategies and identify a vehicle to oversee implementation of its recommendations." Commission on First Nations and Métis Peoples and Justice Reform, *Final Report of the Commission on First Nations and Métis Peoples and Justice Reform. Legacy of Hope: An Agenda for Change* (Saskatoon: Commission on First Nations and Métis Peoples and Justice Reform, 2004) at 12. In its *Interim Report* in 2003, the commission recommended that a justice reform implementation vehicle be created to come into effect immediately upon the release of its final report. Commission on First Nations and Métis Peoples and Justice Reform, *Working Together – Interim Report* (November 2003), online: <http://www.turtle island.org/news/jreform.pdf>.

48   British Columbia Missing Women Inquiry, *Forsaken: Report of the Missing Women Commission of Inquiry. The Women, Their Lives, and the Framework of Inquiry: Setting the Context for Understanding and Change*, vol 1 (Vancouver: British Columbia Missing Women Inquiry, 2012); *Forsaken: Report of the Missing Women Commission of Inquiry. Nobodies: How and Why We Failed the Missing and Murdered Indigenous Women*, vols 2A & 2B (Vancouver: British Columbia Missing Women Inquiry, 2012); *Forsaken: Report of the Missing Women Inquiry. Gone, but Not Forgotten: Building the Women's Legacy of Safety Together*, vol 3 (Vancouver: British Columbia Missing Women Inquiry, 2012); *Forsaken: Report of the Missing Women Commission of Inquiry. The Commission's Process*, vol 4 (Vancouver: British Columbia Missing Women Inquiry, 2012) [*Forsaken*]. *Forsaken*, vol 1, at 4–5; vol 2A, at 141.

49   Missing Women Inquiry, *Status Report on Commission Progress* (3 March 2011), online: <https://missingwomen.library.uvic.ca/wp-content/uploads/2010/10/Status -Report-March.pdf> [MWI Status Report].

50   *Forsaken*, vol 2A, *supra* note 48 at 20, 182–83.

51   *Forsaken*, vol 1, *supra* note 48 at 33.

52   *Forsaken*, vol 1, *supra* note 48 at 94.

53   At least eighteen and potentially over thirty women disappeared from the stretch of highway between Prince George and Prince Rupert over roughly the same period. All but one were Indigenous. Lheidli T'enneh First Nation, Carrier Sekani Family Services, Carrier Sekani Tribal Council, Prince George Nechako Aboriginal

Employment and Training Association, and Prince George Native Friendship Center, *The Highway of Tears Symposium Recommendation Report* (2006) at 9, online: <https://www.highwayoftears.org/uploads/Highway%20of%20Tears%20Symposium%20Recommendations%20Report%20-%20January%202013.pdf>. National media attention ensued when a non-Indigenous tree planter named Nicole Hoar disappeared from the highway in 2002.

54 NWAC 2010, *supra* note 10 at i. Unfortunately, the federal government decided in the fall of 2010 to end funding to Sisters in Spirit.

55 Native Women's Association of Canada, "NWAC Reinforces the Call for a National Public Inquiry" (press release, 12 November 2012), online: <https://nationtalk.ca/story/nwac-reinforces-the-call-for-a-national-public-inquiry>.

56 *Public Inquiry Act*, OIC 605/2010 (2010).

57 See *Taser International v British Columbia*, 2010 BCSC 1120 at para 40.

58 MWI Status Report, *supra* note 49 at 11.

59 In addition, Oppal lost his bid for re-election in the 2009 provincial election in the riding of Delta South by thirty-two votes after having given up the seat that he won in 2005 in the riding of Vancouver-Fraserview. That seat was viewed as safe for Oppal, but he changed ridings to enable another party member to gain a seat (that MLA, Kash Heed, subsequently resigned amid investigations of election irregularities). Some critics viewed Oppal's appointment as a Commissioner as a partisan consolation by the Liberal Party. See Suzanne Fournier, "Liberal Insider Denies 'Baggage' Handicap, Vows Even-Handed Approach," *The Province* [Vancouver] (29 September 2010), online: <http://www.pressreader.com/canada/the-province/20100929/281590941907071>. "[Grand Chief Stewart Phillip] was critical of the appointment, noting that Oppal was a government 'insider' owed a favour for giving up his Vancouver seat in the last election, only to lose himself when he ran in Delta South."

60 The government of British Columbia appointed a commission of inquiry in 2007 to examine the circumstances surrounding the death of Frank Joseph Paul, led by former BC Supreme Court Justice William H. Davies QC. The two reports of the Davies Commission are discussed in Chapter 1; see note 134.

61 "Oppal Says He Won't Resign from Pickton Inquiry," *APTN National News* (1 October 2010), online: <https://www.aptnnews.ca/national-news/oppal-says-he-wont-resign-from-pickton-inquiry/>.

62 Missing Women Inquiry, *Ruling on Participation and Funding Recommendations* (2011), cited in *Forsaken,* vol 4, *supra* note 48, Appendix G-1, online: <https://missingwomen.library.uvic.ca/wp-content/uploads/2010/10/Forsaken-Vol-4-web-RGB.pdf>.

63 Commissioner Wally Oppal to the Honourable Barry Penner, Attorney General of British Columbia (30 June 2011), no longer available online; referenced in "Statement

by Missing Women Commission of Inquiry Commissioner Wally Oppal," (29 August 2011), online: <https://missingwomen.library.uvic.ca/wp-content/uploads/2011/08/2011-08-29-Statement-of-the-MWI-Commissioner.pdf>.

64 Letter to Shirley Bond, Attorney General of British Columbia (7 September 2011), on file with the author.

65 It is difficult to reconcile this sentiment with the fees reportedly paid by the province to commission counsel. These fees included, in the fiscal year ending 31 March 2012, $483,741 billed by Commission Counsel Art Vertlieb; $482,139 by Associate Counsel Karey Brooks and her firm; $324,267 by Commissioner Oppal; $203,134 by first-year lawyer Jessica McKeachie; $236,606 by an unnamed third-year lawyer; and $299,807 by Executive Director John Boddie. In contrast, Cameron Ward, who represented twenty-five murdered women's families, billed $60,000 for the same period. See Brian Hutchinson, "Missing Women Inquiry Workers Paid More than B.C.'s Longest-Serving Judges," *National Post* (10 August 2012), online: <https://nationalpost.com/news/canada/missing-women-inquiry-workers-paid-more-than-b-c-s-longest-serving-judges>.

66 Although the police lawyers numbered around two dozen, one lawyer, Cameron Ward, represented twenty-five families of the missing women.

67 Women's Memorial March, "Downtown Eastside Women's Centre and Women's Memorial March Committee Announce Non Participation in Sham Inquiry," online: <http://womensmemorialmarch.wordpress.com/2011/10/03/non-participation-sham-inquiry/>; also see statement regarding independent counsel: Women's Memorial March, "Downtown Eastside Women's Centre and Women's Memorial March Committee Object to Missing Women's Commission's Latest Amicus Proposal," online: <http://womensmemorialmarch.wordpress.com/2011/08/05/amicusproposal/>.

68 See Robert Matas, "Pressure on Oppal Mounts as Integrity of B.C. Missing Women Hearings Doubted," *Globe and Mail* (30 August 2011), online: <https://www.theglobeandmail.com/news/british-columbia/pressure-on-oppal-mounts-as-integrity-of-bc-missing-women-hearings-doubted/article592682/> [Matas]: "[T]he criminal justice branch of the Attorney-General's Ministry is closely reviewing remarks by Mr. Oppal that have raised concerns about his impartiality."

69 Gary Mason of the *Globe and Mail* noted that the ensuing loss of credibility prompted calls for Oppal's resignation: "It's hard to recall a major inquiry that has been as badly botched as the one looking into the missing women of British Columbia." Mason, *supra* note 2.

70 Commissioner Oppal also appointed two senior lawyers, Bryan Baynham QC and Darrell Roberts QC, as *pro bono* support for her. Missing Women Inquiry, "Missing Women Commission Appoints Two Independent Lawyers: Two Others to Participate Pro Bono," online: <https://missingwomen.library.uvic.ca/media-releases/page/3/

index.html>. According to MWI spokesperson Chris Freimond, "the *pro bono* attorneys will assist Gervais because she is less experienced than Gratl and has a broader mandate to tackle," adding that the Aboriginal female community that she would represent is "extremely large and complex." Carrie Swiggum, "Missing Women's Inquiry Adds Four Lawyers to Represent Advocacy Groups" (10 August 2011), *The Tyee*, "The Hook," online: <http://thetyee.ca/Blogs/TheHook/Rights-Justice/2011/08/10/Missing-Women-Inquiry-Lawyers/>. Baynham was then the Chair of Vancouver firm Harper Grey LLP's Condo Litigation and Defamation, Media and Privacy Law Practice Groups. Roberts practised commercial litigation, professional malpractice, estate litigation, major personal injury, class actions, environmental law, construction litigation, defamation, Aboriginal law, products liability, estate and property law litigation, and constitutional law, according to the profile on his then firm's website (Miller Thomson). It is unclear what expertise they were able to provide related to Indigenous women.

71 "Letter: First Nations Summit Withdrawal from Missing Women Commission of Inquiry" (7 March 2012), online: <https://thenelsondaily.com/news/letter-first-nations-summit-withdrawal-missing-women-commission-inquiry-17553> [FNS Withdrawal Statement].

72 Downtown Eastside Women's Centre and Women's Memorial March Committee, "Open Letter" (5 August 2011), online: <http://womensmemorialmarch.wordpress.com/2011/08/05/amicusproposal/>. See also Mason, *supra* note 2.

73 Katherine Hensel (untitled presentation delivered at SPINLAW Conference, Panel on the Missing Women Inquiry, University of Toronto Faculty of Law, 3 March 2012) (attended by the author).

74 *Ibid.*

75 Neal Hall, "Missing Women Inquiry Adjourned to April 2 to Allow Appointment of Aboriginal Counsel," *Vancouver Sun* (12 March 2012), online: <https://vancouversun.com/news/missing-women-inquiry-adjourned-to-april-2-to-allow-appointment-of-aboriginal-counsel>: "Art Vertlieb, counsel for inquiry, told Oppal that he has contacted an experienced, well-respected lawyer to take over the role of representing aboriginal interests."

76 "Missing Women Inquiry Adjourned to Replace Lawyer," *CBC News* (12 March 2012), online: <http://www.cbc.ca/news/canada/british-columbia/story/2012/03/12/bc-missing-women-inquiry.html>.

77 Ian Mulgrew, "Oppal Misses Opportunity to Make Inquiry Meaningful Process," *Vancouver Sun* (12 March 2012).

78 FNS Withdrawal Statement, *supra* note 71.

79 Missing Women Inquiry, "Appointment of Independent Counsel Presenting Issues Related to Aboriginal Interests Announced" (press release, 21 March 2012), online: <https://missingwomen.library.uvic.ca/media-releases/page/2/index.html>.

Narbonne is a sole practitioner whose practice includes criminal and human rights law. According to her webpage, she began practice as a legal aid lawyer in The Pas, Manitoba (site of Helen Betty Osborne's death) and later practised in Prince Rupert, in northern British Columbia, before moving to the BC coastal community of Sechelt. Narbonne Law Office, "Suzette Narbonne, Lawyer," online: <http://narbonnelawoffice. com/bio.html>. Elizabeth Hunt is a member of the Kwakiutl Nation who practised with Secwepemc and Tsilhqot'in communities in central British Columbia before returning to practice on Vancouver Island. CR Lawyers, "Elizabeth Hunt," online: <https://www.crlawyers.ca/about#ElizabethHunt>.

80 Counsel for twenty-five of the women's families, Cameron Ward detailed his concerns regarding the lopsided evidentiary record in his closing submissions to the MWI. Missing Women Commission of Inquiry (final submissions on behalf of the families of Dianne Rock et al), online: <http://www.cameronward.com/wp-content/ uploads/2012/08/Missing-Women-Inquiry-Closing-submissions-of-the-Families -public.pdf>.

81 AJI Report, *supra* note 6, c 13, "Aboriginal Women – Introduction."

82 "Open Letter: Non-Participation in the Policy Forums/Study Commission" (10 April 2012), online: <https://secureservercdn.net/198.71.233.229/62d.179.myftpupload. com/wp-content/uploads/1970/01/OpenLetterstoMWCI_041012.pdf?time= 1620239656> [emphasis added].

83 Matas, *supra* note 68; Mason, *supra* note 2.

84 *Forsaken, supra* note 48. This is in no small part because of the work of Policy Counsel Dr. Melina Buckley, a respected feminist legal practitioner in Vancouver who has written extensively on systemic discrimination against women, including the landmark report of Supreme Court of Canada Justice Bertha Wilson on women in the legal profession. Canadian Bar Association, *Touchstones for Change: Equality, Diversity and Accountability, Report on Gender Equality in the Legal Profession* (Canadian Bar Association, 1993).

85 *Forsaken,* vol 1, *supra* note 48, part 3.

86 *Ibid,* vol 1, part 4 at 94.

87 *Ibid,* executive summary at 21. It is apparent that the inquiry benefited from having staff capacity to consider the systemic issues driving the reasons that so many Indigenous women have gone missing without a massive mobilization of police resources. In addition to Melina Buckley, mentioned above, associate commission counsel was Karey Brooks, actively involved in feminist legal work in Vancouver (a former board member of West Coast LEAF, one of the women's organizations that withdrew from the inquiry) as well as a partner at the law firm of Janes Freedman Kyle, where she practises Aboriginal law. One of the interim policy papers released by the inquiry in February 2012 cites significant scholarship on the systemic reasons

for the extreme violence toward Indigenous women in Canada, and it is evident that some members of the inquiry staff were aware of the larger context of the inquiry. Melina Buckley, *Police Protection of Vulnerable and Marginalized Women* (Missing Women Inquiry, February 2012) online: <https://missingwomen.library.uvic.ca/wp-content/uploads/2010/10/POL-1-Feb-2012-MB-Police-Protection-of-Vulnerable-and-Marginalized-Women.pdf>. The press release regarding the four reports is available at Missing Women Inquiry, "Missing Women Commission of Inquiry Releases Study Reports" (press release, 21 February 2012), online: <https://missingwomen.library.uvic.ca/media-releases/page/2/index.html>. However, without the Commissioner's leadership that interprets the mandate and structures the operations of the commission (appointment of outside counsel, which witnesses to prioritize at hearings, etc.) to prioritize these contextual factors, the value brought to the inquiry by such qualified counsel will necessarily be thwarted.

88   *Forsaken, supra* note 48, executive summary at 24.

89   *Ibid*, vol 2A at 2.

90   *Ibid*, vol 2A at 3.

91   *Ibid*, vol 2A at 4.

92   *Public Inquiry Act*, SBC 2007, c 9, s 21(1)(d).

93   Ian Mulgrew, "Oppal's Report Leaves the Missing Women Forsaken Once Again," *Vancouver Sun* (17 December 2012), online: <http://missingwomen.blogspot.com/2012/12/#467111321890152281>.

94   *Forsaken, supra* note 48, executive summary at 13, referring to vol 4b.

95   *Ibid* at 7.

96   Stanton, *Truth Commissions, supra* note 36.

97   Tracy Byrne, *Stopping Violence against Aboriginal Women – A Summary of Root Causes, Vulnerabilities and Recommendations from Key Literature* (prepared for the government of British Columbia, 23 February 2011) at 7. NWAC has made the link between the IRS legacy and the increased likelihood that Aboriginal women will experience violence. Native Women's Association of Canada, *Community Resource Guide: What Can I Do to Help the Families of Missing and Murdered Aboriginal Women and Girls?* (Ottawa: Native Women's Association of Canada, 2010), online: <https://www.nwac.ca/wp-content/uploads/2015/05/2012_NWAC_Community_Resource_Guide_MMAWG.pdf > at 70ff. An MWI policy paper identifies the IRS legacy as one factor that makes Aboriginal women vulnerable to systemic racism. Melina Buckley, "Police Protection of Vulnerable and Marginalized Women" (Missing Women Commission of Inquiry, February 2012) at 10; online: <https://missingwomen.library.uvic.ca/wp-content/uploads/2010/10/POL-1-Feb-2012-MB-Police-Protection-of-Vulnerable-and-Marginalized-Women.pdf>. See also Beverley Jacobs & Andrea J Williams, "Legacy of Residential Schools: Missing and Murdered

Aboriginal Women" in Marlene B Castellano, Linda Archibald, & Mike DeGagné, eds, *From Truth to Reconciliation: Transforming the Legacy of Residential Schools* (Ottawa: Aboriginal Healing Foundation, 2008) 121 at 138.

98 AJI Report, vol 2, *supra* note 6, c 9.

99 Office of the Auditor General of British Columbia, *Follow-Up on the Missing Women Commission of Inquiry* (2016), online: <https://www.bcauditor.com/sites/default/files/publications/reports/FINAL_MWCI_2.pdf>.

100 Government of Canada, "Pre-Inquiry Design Process" (3 August 2016), online: <https://www.rcaanc-cirnac.gc.ca/eng/1449240082445/1534527468971>.

101 "Inquiry into Missing and Murdered Indigenous Women Can Still Make a Difference," Editorial, *The Globe and Mail* (3 November 2017), online: <https://www.theglobeandmail.com/opinion/editorials/globe-editorial-inquiry-into-missing-and-murdered-indigenous-women-can-still-make-a-difference/article36827702/>.

102 National Inquiry into MMIWG, *Interim Report: Our Women and Girls Are Sacred* (2017), online: <https://www.mmiwg-ffada.ca/wp-content/uploads/2018/03/ni-mmiwg-interim-report.pdf> at 29 [National Inquiry into MMIWG, *Interim Report*]. Unfortunately, the *Interim Report* suggests that the pre-inquiry phase did cause heightened expectations and confusion among MMIW families. The National Inquiry called on the federal government to share the families' contact information and/or to inform the families of how to participate in the inquiry. National Inquiry into MMIWG, *Interim Report* at 74, 81.

103 Dennis Ward, "Commissioners Named for National Inquiry into Missing and Murdered Indigenous Women and Girls," *APTN News* (3 August 2016), online: <https://aptnnews.ca/2016/08/03/commissioners-named-for-national-inquiry-into-missing-and-murdered-Indigenous-women-and-girls/>.

104 National Inquiry into MMIWG, "Legal Notices and Records," online: <https://www.mmiwg-ffada.ca/legal-notices/>.

105 National Inquiry into MMIWG, "Terms of Reference," online: <https://www.mmiwg-ffada.ca/wp-content/uploads/2018/06/terms-of-reference.pdf>.

106 BC MWI Commissioner Oppal, in reflecting on pre-inquiry conferences in which he heard frustrations with the narrow terms of reference that he had been appointed under for the MWI, stated that "[i]n the future I would strongly urge the government to consult with key stakeholders when developing its terms of reference, particularly on matters that engage complex social issues." *Forsaken*, vol 4, *supra* note 48 at 5.

107 Roundtable on Indigenous Law and Legal Knowledge, INAC office, Toronto (12 March 2016). I was present at the roundtable. See Government of Canada, "Full Summary of What We Heard: Final Report of the Pre-Inquiry Engagement Process" (19 May 2016), online: <https://www.rcaanc-cirnac.gc.ca/eng/1463677554486/1534775555263#sec3_2>.

108 National Inquiry into MMIWG, "Meet the Commissioners," online: <https://www. mmiwg-ffada.ca/meet-the-commissioners/> ["Meet the Commissioners"].

109 Complaints by Indigenous peoples of the Cariboo-Chilcotin region of British Columbia about the way that police, lawyers, and judges dealt with them prompted the provincial Attorney General to call the inquiry and to appoint Justice Anthony Sarich as Commissioner. *Report on the Cariboo-Chilcotin Justice Inquiry* (1993), online: <https://www.llbc.leg.bc.ca/public/pubdocs/bcdocs/149599/cariboochilcotinjustice. pdf>. The inquiry heard about matters that included the profound effects on the people of the residential school near Williams Lake and of the lingering memories of the Chilcotin war in 1864. In 2018, Prime Minister Justin Trudeau apologized in Tsilhqot'in territory for the hanging of six Chiefs in the war. Amy Smart, "Trudeau Apologizes to Tsilhqot'in Community Members for 1864 Hanging of Chiefs," *CBC News* (2 November 2018), online: <https://www.cbc.ca/news/canada/british -columbia/trudeau-apologizes-to-tsilhqot-in-community-members-for-1864 -hanging-of-chiefs-1.4890486>.

110 "Meet the Commissioners," *supra* note 108.

111 *Ibid.*

112 "Government Ignored List of Inuk Candidates in Favour of Its Own for National Inquiry: Source," *APTN News* (8 August 2016), online: https://aptnnews.ca/2016/ 08/08/government-ignored-list-of-inuk-candidates-in-favour-of-its-own-for -national-inquiry-source/; Pauktuutit Inuit Women of Canada, *Nipimit nanisiniq – Finding Voice: Report on the Pre-Inquiry Consultation* (February 2016) at 4, online: <https://www.pauktuutit.ca/wp-content/uploads/2016-03-31-Nipimit-Nanisiniq -Finding-Voice-Pre-Inquiry-Consultation-Report-FINAL.pdf>; Sima Sahar Zerehi, "Qajaq Robinson No Substitute for Inuk on Inquiry Commission, Says Inuit Women's group," *CBC News* (4 August 2016), online: <https://www.cbc.ca/news/canada/north/ qajaq-robinson-no-substitute-for-inuk-mmiwg-commissioner-1.3706650>.

113 Nikki Wiart, "For the Record: Indigenous Leaders Speak on the MMIW Inquiry," *Maclean's* (3 August 2016), online: <https://www.macleans.ca/news/canada/for -the-record-indigenous-leaders-on-the-mmiw-inquiry/>.

114 Kathleen Harris, "Missing and Murdered Inquiry to Forge Ahead Despite Resignation of Key Commissioner," *CBC News* (11 July 2017), online: <https://www.cbc.ca/news/ politics/poitras-commissioner-resignation-1.4199126>.

115 *Ibid.* Following the resignation of the National Inquiry's first Executive Director, Québécoise lawyer Michèle Moreau, Aideen Nabigon became the Executive Director. She was followed by Skownan First Nation member Debbie Reid, a former AFN adviser. Director of Operations Calvin Wong stepped in as Interim Executive Director when Reid resigned. Jennifer Moore Rattray, a member of the Peepeekisis First Nation in Saskatchewan, took on the role in 2018.

116   Gloria Galloway, "Indigenous Women's Group Pulls Support from Missing and Murdered Inquiry as Commissioner Resigns," *Globe and Mail* (11 July 2017), online: <https://www.theglobeandmail.com/news/politics/mmiw-commissioner-marilyn -poitras-resigns-in-another-blow-to-inquiry/article35653097/>.

117   *Ibid.* According to participants in the meeting, the resignation was not mentioned to the families.

118   Native Women's Association of Canada, *Report Card #3 on the National Inquiry, May 2017–March 2018,* online: <https://www.nwac.ca/wp-content/uploads/2018/05/ NWAC-MMIWG-Report-Card-3-May17-Mar18.pdf> [NWAC *Report Card #3*].

119   A National Inquiry *Research Plan* dated October 2017 stated that the inquiry's reports "must reflect the Commissioners' philosophy and vision," but nowhere are they enunciated. National Inquiry into MMIWG, *Research Plan* (2017) at 6, online: <https://www.mmiwg-ffada.ca/wp-content/uploads/2018/04/research-plan-1.pdf>.

120   See, for example, NWAC *Report Card #3, supra* note 118.

121   The Cohen Commission into the collapse of the salmon stocks in the Fraser River in British Columbia got under way in 2010.

122   Toronto lawyer Suzan Fraser represented the families.

123   Clare Clancy, "Frustration after Edmonton Meetings Cancelled by Inquiry into Missing, Murdered Indigenous Women and Girls," *Edmonton Journal* (23 June 2017), online: <https://edmontonjournal.com/news/local-news/activists-frustrated-after -edmonton-meetings-cancelled-by-inquiry-into-missing-murdered-Indigenous -women-and-girls>; "Inquiry into Missing and Murdered Indigenous Women Postpones Edmonton, Thunder Bay Meetings," *CBC News* (14 April 2017), online: <https://www.cbc.ca/news/canada/edmonton/mmiwg-advisory-meetings-postponed -1.4071117?fbclid=IwAR1hB6X5mvsScAOsCKa55fsA0x0081f5JcNUg3dp89ZFT -8dEkDHcw1GmYY>.

124   "Yellowknife Hearings for MMIWG National Inquiry Postponed," *CBC News* (20 October 2017), online: <https://www.cbc.ca/news/canada/north/mmiw-national -inquiry-postponed-1.4364525>.

125   Sarah Rogers, "MMIWG Inquiry Cancels December Nunavut Hearing," *Nunatsiaq News* (24 November 2017), online: <https://nunatsiaq.com/stories/article/65674 mmiwg_inquiry_cancels_nunavut_hearing/>. The hearing was ultimately rescheduled in Rankin Inlet in February 2018.

126   Lorne Sossin, "The Goudge Inquiry: Anatomy of Success for an Inquiry to Change Policy?" in Gregory J Inwood & Carolyn M Johns, eds, *Commissions of Inquiry and Policy Change: A Comparative Analysis* (Toronto: University of Toronto Press/IPAC, 2014) 244 at 258 [Sossin].

127   *Ibid* at 255. *Report of the Inquiry into Pediatric Forensic Pathology in Ontario,* by Stephen T Goudge (Toronto: Queen's Printer for Ontario, 2008), online: <http:// www.attorneygeneral.jus.gov.on.ca/inquiries/goudge/index.html>.

128 National Inquiry into MMIWG, *Interim Report, supra* note 102 at 30.

129 See Nancy Macdonald & Meagan Campbell, "Lost and Broken: The Inquiry into Missing and Murdered Indigenous Women Is Crumbling amid Defections, Bureaucratic Chaos and Personal Conflict. Inside the Meltdown – and the Desperate Bid to Turn Things Around," *Maclean's* (13 September 2017), online: <https://www.macleans.ca/lost-and-broken/>.

130 Commissioners of the National Inquiry into MMIWG to Honourable Carolyn Bennett (6 March 2018), online: <http://www.mmiwg-ffada.ca/wp-content/uploads/2018/04/extension-request-letter-and-workplan.pdf>.

131 Although this process predated the appointment of the Commissioners, the ministerial staff compiled notes and materials from the meetings, and according to their *Interim Report* the data and meeting materials from the pre-inquiry process were available to them once appointed. National Inquiry into MMIWG, *Interim Report, supra* note 102 at 29, 69.

132 I was asked by the inquiry to provide expert evidence on international law at the expert hearing to be held in Montreal only a few weeks later. I demurred since that is not my field of expertise, but in any event the hearing was then postponed as the inquiry found that experts were not available on short notice.

133 At that point, LEAF did not have a contribution agreement and had to make the difficult financial decision to expend its scarce resources on travel and accommodation in Winnipeg without any assurance of recompense. Indeed, over a year later, none had been received, although LEAF was eventually reimbursed.

134 National Inquiry into Missing and Murdered Indigenous Women and Girls, *Reclaiming Power and Place: Executive Summary of the Final Report* (2019) at 8.

135 National Inquiry into MMIWG, *Interim Report, supra* note 102 at 57.

136 *Ibid* at 58.

137 LSC Report, *supra* note 29. According to the National Inquiry into MMIWG, *Interim Report, supra* note 102 at 32, the number of prior recommendations exceeded 1,200.

138 Sossin, *supra* note 126 at 251–52.

139 *Ibid* at 251.

140 *Ibid* at 254.

141 Carolyn M Johns, "The Walkerton Inquiry and Policy Change" in Inwood & Johns, *supra* note 126, 214 at 214ff. The Ipperwash Inquiry built on the Walkerton public engagement model in its policy phase, using a combination of research papers, expert panels, roundtables, community dialogues, and an advisory committee. *Report of the Ipperwash Inquiry: Investigation and Findings,* by Stanley Linden, vol 3 (2007), online: <http://www.attorneygeneral.jus.gov.on.ca/inquiries/ipperwash/report/vol_3/index.html>, c 11 at 53.

142 See note 130 above.

143 "MMIW Commissioners Slam Decision to Grant Shortened Extension," *Global News* (5 June 2018), online: <https://globalnews.ca/news/4253549/mmiw-inquiry -granted-extension/>.

144 Some sentiments expressed in this section echo those in my editorial "MMIWG Inquiry Process Needs to Improve," *Law Times* (16 April 2018), online: <http://www. lawtimesnews.com/article/mmiwg-inquiry-process-needs-to-improve-15597/>.

145 National Inquiry into MMIWG, "Commissioners Express Profound Disappointment. Short Extension Injustice to Families, Survivors and Canada" (press release, 5 June 2018), online: <https://www.mmiwg-ffada.ca/wp-content/uploads/2018/06/EN_- PressRelease_June-5-2018_VF.pdf>; Jorge Barrera, "MMIWG Inquiry Commissioner May Quit after Ottawa Grants Limited Extension," *CBC News* (5 June 2018), online: <https://www.cbc.ca/news/Indigenous/inquiry-extension-ottawa-1.4691903>.

146 Kathleen Martens, "National MMIWG Inquiry 'Speeding towards Failure' Says Latest Lawyer to Resign," *APTN News* (3 July 2018), online: <https://www.aptnnews.ca/ national-news/national-mmiwg-inquiry-speeding-towards-failure-says-latest -lawyer-to-resign/>.

147 National Inquiry into MMIWG, "Reclaiming Power and Place: The Final Report of the National Inquiry into Missing and Murdered Indigenous Women and Girls" at "Fast Facts," online: <https://www.mmiwg-ffada.ca/>.

148 A document entitled "Legal Path: Rules of Respectful Practice for the National Inquiry into Murdered and Missing Indigenous Women and Girls" was belatedly posted in draft form and never finalized. National Inquiry into MMIWG, "Legal Path: Rules of Respectful Practice for the National Inquiry into Murdered and Missing Indigen- ous Women and Girls," online: <http://www.mmiwg-ffada.ca/wp-content/ uploads/2018/04/legal-path-rules-of-respectful-practice.pdf>.

149 Jorge Barrera, "National Inquiry Calls Murders and Disappearances of Indigenous Women a 'Canadian Genocide,'" *CBC News* (31 May 2019), online: <https://www. cbc.ca/news/Indigenous/genocide-murdered-missing-Indigenous-women -inquiry-report-1.5157580>.

150 See, for example, the work of the volunteer-based Legal Strategy Coalition on Violence against Indigenous Women, on which the National Inquiry relied in its *Interim Report,* that identified the common themes and recommendations from prior reports. National Inquiry into MMIWG, *Interim Report, supra* note 102, c 3, n 3.

151 See, for example, *R v TLC*, 2019 BCPC 314; *R v Berg*, 2019 ABQB 541; *R v Emile*, 2019 NWTTC 9; *R v A(M)*, 2020 NUCJ 4; *Saskatchewan v Durocher*, 2020 SKQB 224; *R v Doering*, 2020 ONSC 5618; *R v LP*, 2020 QCCA 1239; and *R v Sharma*, 2020 ONCA 478.

152 See note 137 above.

153 See, for example, Call to Justice 5.19.

154 See, for example, Call to Justice 5.11. For a thoughtful assessment of the National Inquiry Final Report, see Val Napoleon, "An Imaginary of Our Sisters: Spirits and Indigenous Law" in *Indigenous Spiritual and Religious Freedom,* ed. Beverley Jacobs, Jeffery Hewitt, & Richard Moon (Toronto: University of Toronto Press, forthcoming).

155 CBC Radio-Canada's *Enquête* program on 22 October 2015 triggered the events that led to the inquiry. *Public Inquiry Commission on Relations between Indigenous Peoples and Certain Public Services in Quebec: Listening, Reconciliation and Progress. Summary Report* (Quebec City: Government of Quebec, 2019) at 7 [CERP, *Summary Report*]; *Final Report* (2019), online: <https://www.cerp.gouv.qc.ca/fileadmin/Fichiers_clients/ Rapport/Final_report.pdf>. Sée also Julia Page & Catou MacKinnon, "'Their Stories Must Not Be Forgotten': Viens Commission Closes with Pleas for Val-d'Or Women," *CBC News* (14 December 2018), online: <https://www.cbc.ca/news/canada/montreal/ viens-commission-end-1.4945426> [Page & MacKinnon].

156 Page & MacKinnon, *supra* note 155. Also see the full inquiry mandate: CERP, "Mandate," online: <https://www.cerp.gouv.qc.ca/index.php?id=11&L=1> [CERP, "Mandate"].

157 Jonathan Montpetit, "What's Next for the Indigenous Women of Val-d'Or?" *CBC News* (19 November 2016), online: <https://www.cbc.ca/news/canada/montreal/ val-dor-Indigenous-women-1.3858658>.

158 Melissa Fundira & Jonathan Montpetit, "Quebec Premier Announces 2-Year Inquiry into Treatment of Indigenous People," *CBC News* (21 December 2016), online: <https://www.cbc.ca/news/canada/montreal/quebec-public-inquiry-Indigenous -people-1.3906091> [Fundira & Montpetit].

159 CERP, "Mandate," *supra* note 156 at s 8.

160 For example, the Quebec Native Women President appeared four times (Page & MacKinnon, *supra* note 155), and the Cree Health Board, of the Grand Council of the Crees (Eeyou Istchee), appeared eighteen times and presented a brief that included attention to health and housing issues. Cree School Board, "Brief of Kathleen Wootton, Chairperson" (24 January 2018), online: <https://www.cerp.gouv.qc.ca/ fileadmin/Fichiers_clients/Documents_deposes_a_la_Commission/P-341_M-006. pdf>. Both organizations were granted full participant standing in the inquiry. CERP, "The Quebec Inquiry Grants Standing to 13 Full and Limited Participants" (11 May 2017), online: <https://www.cerp.gouv.qc.ca/fileadmin/Fichiers_clients/ Press_release_Standing_applications_2017–05–11.pdf>.

161 Sidhartha Banerjee, "Boushie Case Looms over Quebec Indigenous Inquiry as Montreal Hearings Begin," *Canadian Press* (12 February 2018), online: <https://www. ctvnews.ca/canada/boushie-case-looms-over-quebec-Indigenous-inquiry-as -montreal-hearings-begin-1.3800186 >; "Inquiry into How Indigenous People Are

Treated by the Public Service Gets 10-Month Extension," *CBC News* (9 February 2018), online: <https://www.cbc.ca/news/canada/montreal/inquiry-into-how -Indigenous-people-are-treated-by-the-public-service-gets-10-month-extension -1.4529649>.

162 Fundira & Montpetit, *supra* note 158.

163 Jaela Bernstien, "'White Judge, White Lawyers': Quebec Inquiry into Discrimination Lacks Indigenous Voices, Critics Say," *CBC News* (15 March 2018), online: <https:// www.cbc.ca/news/canada/montreal/Indigenous-representation-quebec-inquiry -1.4575750>.

164 *Ibid.*

165 Christian Leblanc and Marie-Josée Barry-Gosselin served as chief counsel and assist-ant chief counsel of the Viens Commission, respectively. "Main Prosecutors Quit Viens Commission on Quebec's Treatment of Indigenous People," *CBC News* (6 September 2018), online: <https://www.cbc.ca/news/canada/montreal/viens -commission-counsel-resignations-1.4813068>. See also the inquiry's press release: CERP, "Me Suzanne Arpin Appointed Chief Counsel and Spokesperson of the Quebec Inquiry Commission" (6 September 2018), online: <https://www.cerp.gouv. qc.ca/fileadmin/Fichiers_clients/Communiques/Press_release_September_6.pdf>.

166 Fundira & Montpetit, *supra* note 158.

167 CERP, *Procedural and Operational Rules* (2018), online: <https://www.cerp.gouv. qc.ca/fileadmin/Fichiers_clients/Documents_site_web/Regles_de_procedures__ ANG.pdf>.

168 CERP, *Summary Report, supra* note 155 at 8.

169 CERP, "Media Relations," online: <https://www.cerp.gouv.qc.ca/index.php?id= 15&L=1>.

170 CERP, *Summary Report, supra* note 155 at 9.

171 *Ibid* at 11.

172 *Ibid* at 16.

173 *Ibid.*

174 "Quebec Premier Apologizes to First Nations, Inuit for Discrimination," *APTN News* (2 October 2019), online: <https://aptnnews.ca/2019/10/02/quebec-premier -apologizes-to-first-nations-inuit-for-discrimination/>.

175 CERP, *Summary Report, supra* note 155 at 93.

176 Quebec Native Women, "Indigenous Women Forgotten by the Public Inquiry Commission Report" (30 September 2019), online: <https://www.faq-qnw.org/en/ news/Indigenous-women-forgotten-by-the-public-inquiry-commission-report/>; Benjamin Shingler & Kamila Hinkson, "Quebec Should Apologize for Systemic Discrimination in Treatment of Indigenous Women, Viens Report Says," *CBC News* (30 September 2019), online: <https://www.cbc.ca/news/canada/montreal/quebec -treatment-Indigenous-viens-commission-report-1.5297888> [Shingler & Hinkson].

177 *Ibid.*

178 CERP, *Summary Report, supra* note 155 at 32.

179 *Journey to Light: A Different Way Forward. Final Report of the Restorative Inquiry – Nova Scotia Home for Colored Children* (Province of Nova Scotia: Nova Scotia Home for Colored Children Restorative Inquiry, 2019), online: <https://restorativeinquiry.ca/> [*Journey to Light*].

180 *Public Inquiries Act,* RSNS 1989, c 372, as amended 2015, c 50.

181 *Journey to Light, supra* note 179 at 19.

182 *Ibid* at 21; Restorative Inquiry: Nova Scotia Home for Colored Children, "Terms of Reference," online: <https://restorativeinquiry.ca/terms-of-reference.html>.

183 *Journey to Light, supra* note 179 at 38.

184 *Ibid* at 33.

185 *Ibid* at 28–29.

186 See my *Rabble* op-ed, *supra* note 31.

Conclusion

1 Georges Erasmus, Third LaFontaine-Baldwin Symposium Lecture (Vancouver, 2002), published as "Conversation Three" in Rudyard Griffiths, ed, *A Dialogue on Democracy in Canada: Volume 1 of the LaFontaine-Baldwin Lectures* (Toronto: Penguin Canada, 2002), 127.

2 Peter Puxley, "A Model of Engagement: Reflections on the 25th Anniversary of the Berger Report (the Report of the Mackenzie Valley Pipeline Inquiry, 1977)" (August 2002), online: *Canadian Policy Research Networks* <http://cprn3.library.carleton.ca/documents/14369_en.PDF>.

3 JC Stabler & MR Olfert, "Gaslight Follies: The Political Economy of the Western Arctic" (1980) 6:2 Can Pub Pol'y 374 at 385, citing Judith Timson, "Berger of the North," *Maclean's* (10 January 1977) 30.

4 Martin O'Malley, *The Past and Future Land: An Account of the Berger Inquiry into the Mackenzie Valley Pipeline* (Toronto: P Martin Associates, 1976) at 223. His reference to Diefenbaker's speech is somewhat ironic. The campaign speech, "A New Vision," delivered in Winnipeg on 12 February 1958, outlined his vision of the North as the new frontier, ripe for development. John Diefenbaker, "John Diefenbaker's Northern Vision" (8 March 2009), online: *Who Owns the Arctic? Arctic Sovereignty and International Relations* <http://byers.typepad.com/arctic/2009/03/john-diefenbakers-northern-vision.html>. Diefenbaker went on to win the largest landslide to that date in Canadian political history, winning 208 of 265 seats. "Total Triumph," *CBC News* (6 April 1958), online: <https://www.cbc.ca/archives/entry/total-triumph-for-diefenbaker-tories-in-1958>. It was Diefenbaker who began construction of the Dempster Highway. He was also the Prime Minister who introduced the Bill of Rights and extended voting rights to Indigenous peoples.

5 *Northern Frontier, Northern Homeland: The Report of the Mackenzie Valley Pipeline Inquiry,* by Thomas R Berger (Ottawa: Minister of Supply and Services Canada, 1977) at 90–92.

6 Royal Commission on Aboriginal Peoples, *Report of the Royal Commission on Aboriginal Peoples: Looking Forward, Looking Back,* vol 1 (Ottawa: Supply and Services Canada, 1996); Canada, *Report of the Royal Commission on Aboriginal Peoples: Restructuring the Relationship,* vol 2 (Ottawa: Supply and Services Canada, 1996); Canada, *Report of the Royal Commission on Aboriginal Peoples: Gathering Strength,* vol 3 (Ottawa: Supply and Services Canada, 1996); Canada, *Report of the Royal Commission on Aboriginal Peoples: Perspectives and Realities,* vol 4 (Ottawa: Supply and Services Canada, 1996); Canada, *Report of the Royal Commission on Aboriginal Peoples: Renewal: A Twenty-Year Commitment,* vol 5 (Ottawa: Supply and Services Canada, 1996) [RCAP Report], RCAP Report, vol 1, c 10.

7 JR Miller, *Shingwauk's Vision: A History of Native Residential Schools* (Toronto: University of Toronto Press, 1996) at 434.

8 Thomas Berger, "The Constitution, the Charter and the Idea of Canada – From a Canadian Perspective" (address presented to the Canadian Bar Association, Vancouver, 24 March 1984), Vancouver, UBC Special Collections (Thomas Berger Fonds – Speeches 1977–84, box 71-2 Canadian Bar Association – Address, meeting of 24 March 1984 [folder one of two], Berger Address to Provincial Council, BC Branch, CBA, Vancouver, 24 March 1984) at 1.

9 James Keller, "Families of Pickton Victims Denounce 'Missing-Evidence' Inquiry," *Globe and Mail* (4 June 2012), online: <http://www.theglobeandmail.com/news/british-columbia/families-of-pickton-victims-denounce-missing-evidence-inquiry/article4231153/>.

10 RCAP Report, *supra* note 6.

11 RCAP Report, vol 4, *supra* note 6, c 2. See also RCAP Report, vol 3, *supra* note 6, c 2.3.2.

12 Joyce Green, "From Stonechild to Social Cohesion: Anti-Racist Challenges for Saskatchewan" (2006) 39:3 CJPS/RCSP 507.

13 Centre for First Nations Governance, "Feds Cut NCFNG Nation Rebuilding Services" (16 April 2012), online: *Centre News* <http://media.knet.ca/node/21898>.

14 The Royal Commission on the Status of Women highlighted discrimination against Indigenous women in its report and recommended amendment of the *Indian Act* to allow an Indigenous woman upon marriage to a non-Indigenous man to retain her status and transmit it to her children. *Report of the Royal Commission on the Status of Women* (Ottawa: Information Canada, 1970) at 238.

Selected Bibliography

Books and Reports

Aboriginal Rights Coalition. *Blind Spots: An Examination of the Federal Government's Response to the Report of the Royal Commission on Aboriginal Peoples* (Ottawa: Aboriginal Rights Coalition, 2001).

Amnesty International. *Stolen Sisters: A Human Rights Response to Discrimination and Violence against Indigenous Women in Canada* (October 2004), online: <http://www.amnesty.ca/sites/default/files/amr200032004enstolensisters.pdf>.

Assembly of First Nations. *Report on Canada's Dispute Resolution Plan to Compensate for Abuses in Indian Residential Schools* (Assembly of First Nations, November 2004).

Barahona de Brito, Alexandra, Carmen Gonzalez-Enriquez, & Paloma Aguilar, eds. *The Politics of Memory: Transitional Justice in Democratizing Societies* (Oxford: Oxford University Press, 2001).

Bessner, Ronda, & Susan Lightstone. *Public Inquiries in Canada: Law and Practice* (Toronto: Thomson Reuters, 2017).

Borchardt, DH. *Commissions of Inquiry in Australia: A Brief Survey* (Bundoora, Vic: La Trobe University Press, 1991).

Buckley, Melina. "From Report to Substantive Change – Healing, Reconciliation and Implementation" (Missing Women Commission of Inquiry Policy Discussion Report, April 2012).

Canada. *Sexual Offences against Children in Canada: Report of the Committee on Sexual Offences against Children and Youth,* by Robin Badgley (Ottawa: Supply and Services Canada, 1984).

Castellano, Marlene B, Linda Archibald, & Mike DeGagné, eds. *From Truth to Reconciliation: Transforming the Legacy of Residential Schools* (Ottawa: Aboriginal Healing Foundation, 2008).

Chrisjohn, Roland, Sherri Lynn Young, & Michael Maraun, eds. *The Circle Game: Shadows and Substance in the Indian Residential School Experience in Canada* (Penticton, BC: Theytus Books, 2006).

Daly, Erin, & Jeremy Sarkin. *Reconciliation in Divided Societies* (Philadelphia: University of Pennsylvania Press, 2007).

Djwa, Sandra, & R St J Macdonald, eds. *On FR Scott: Essays on His Contributions to Law, Literature and Politics* (Montreal and Kingston: McGill-Queen's University Press, 1983).

Foster, Hamar, Jeremy HA Webber, & Heather Raven, eds. *Let Right Be Done: Aboriginal Title, the* Calder *Case, and the Future of Indigenous Rights* (Vancouver: UBC Press, 2007).

Freeman, Mark. *Truth Commissions and Procedural Fairness* (Cambridge, UK: Cambridge University Press, 2006).

Graham, Elizabeth. *The Mush Hole: Life at Two Indian Residential Schools* (Waterloo, ON: Heffle Publishing, 1997).

Grant, Agnes. *No End of Grief: Indian Residential Schools in Canada* (Winnipeg: Pemmican Publications, 1996).

Green, Joyce, ed. *Indivisible: Indigenous Human Rights* (Winnipeg and Halifax: Fernwood Publishing, 2014).

Haig-Brown, Celia, & David A Nock, eds. *With Good Intentions: Euro-Canadian and Aboriginal Relations in Colonial Canada* (Vancouver: UBC Press, 2006).

Hallett, Leonard Arthur. *Royal Commissions and Boards of Inquiry: Some Legal and Procedural Aspects* (Agincourt, ON: Carswell, 1982).

Hayner, Priscilla B. *Unspeakable Truths: Confronting State Terror and Atrocity* (New York: Routledge, 2001).

Inwood, Gregory J, & Carolyn M Johns, eds. *Commissions of Inquiry and Policy Change: A Comparative Analysis* (Toronto: University of Toronto Press/IPAC, 2014).

Johnson, Miranda. *The Land Is Our History* (Oxford: Oxford University Press, 2016).

Kritz, Neil J. *Transitional Justice: How Emerging Democracies Reckon with Former Regimes* (Washington, DC: United States Institute for Peace Press, 1995) vol 1.

Krog, Antjie. *Country of My Skull: Guilt, Sorrow, and the Limits of Forgiveness in the New South Africa* (New York: Three Rivers Press, 2000).

Kymlicka, Will, & Bashir Bashir, eds. *The Politics of Reconciliation in Multicultural Societies* (Oxford: Oxford University Press, 2008).

Law Commission of Canada. *Restoring Dignity: Responding to Child Abuse in Canadian Institutions* (Ottawa: Law Commission of Canada, 2000).

–, ed. *Indigenous Legal Traditions* (Vancouver: UBC Press, 2007).

Leslie, John. *Commissions of Inquiry into Indian Affairs in the Canadas, 1828–1858: Evolving a Corporate Memory for the Indian Department* (Ottawa: Indian Affairs and Northern Development, 1985).

Manson, Allan, & David J Mullan, eds. *Commissions of Inquiry: Praise or Reappraise?* (Toronto: Irwin Law, 2003).

McAdams, A James, ed. *Transitional Justice and the Rule of Law in New Democracies* (Notre Dame: University of Notre Dame Press, 1997).

Miller, JR. *Shingwauk's Vision: A History of Native Residential Schools* (Toronto: University of Toronto Press, 1996).

Milloy, James S. *A National Crime: The Canadian Government and the Residential School System, 1879 to 1986* (Winnipeg: University of Manitoba Press, 1999).

Native Women's Association of Canada. *What Their Stories Tell Us: Research Findings from the Sisters in Spirit Initiative* (2010), online: <https://www.nwac.ca/wp-content/uploads/2015/07/2010-What-Their-Stories-Tell-Us-Research-Findings-SIS-Initiative.pdf>.

O'Malley, Martin. *The Past and Future Land: An Account of the Berger Inquiry into the Mackenzie Valley Pipeline* (Toronto: P Martin Associates, 1976).

Ontario Law Reform Commission. *Report on Public Inquiries* (Toronto: Ontario Law Reform Commission, 1992).

Pross, A Paul, IM Christie, & John Yogis, eds. *Commissions of Inquiry* (Toronto: Carswell, 1990).

Ratner, Steven, & Jason Abrams, eds. *Accountability for Human Rights Atrocities in International Law: Beyond the Nuremberg Legacy*, 2nd ed (Oxford: Oxford University Press, 2001).

Ratushny, Ed. *The Conduct of Public Inquiries: Law, Policy, and Practice* (Toronto: Irwin Law, 2009).

Regan, Paulette. *Unsettling the Settler Within: Indian Residential Schools, Truth Telling, and Reconciliation Canada* (Vancouver: UBC Press, 2011).

Roht-Arriaza, Naomi, & Javier Mariezcurrena. *Transitional Justice in the Twenty-First Century: Beyond Truth versus Justice* (Cambridge, UK: Cambridge University Press, 2006).

Rotberg, Robert, & Dennis Thompson, eds. *Truth v Justice: The Morality of Truth Commissions* (Princeton, NJ: Princeton University Press, 2000).

Russell, Peter H. *Recognizing Aboriginal Title: The Mabo Case and Indigenous Resistance to English-Settler Colonialism* (Toronto: University of Toronto Press, 2005).

Teitel, Ruti G. *Transitional Justice* (New York: Oxford University Press, 2000).

Tully, James. *Strange Multiplicity: Constitutionalism in an Age of Diversity* (New York: Cambridge University Press, 1995).

Watkins, Mel, ed. *Dene Nation: Colony Within* (Toronto: University of Toronto Press, 1977).

Weaver, Sally M. *Making Canadian Indian Policy: The Hidden Agenda 1968–1970* (Toronto: University of Toronto Press, 1981).

Younging, Gregory, Jonathan Dewar, & Michael DeGagné, eds. *From Truth to Reconciliation: Response, Responsibility and Renewal – Canada's Truth and Reconciliation Journey* (Ottawa: Aboriginal Healing Foundation, 2009).

Ziegel, Jacob S, ed. *Law and Social Change* (Toronto: Osgoode Hall Law School, York University, 1973).

Inquiry Reports

Aboriginal Justice Implementation Commission. *Final Report* (Winnipeg: Aboriginal Justice Implementation Commission, 2001).

Australia. *Bringing Them Home: Report of the National Inquiry into the Separation of Aboriginal and Torres Strait Islander Children from Their Families* (Sydney: Human Rights and Equal Opportunity Commission, 1997).

Berger, Thomas R. *Northern Frontier, Northern Homeland: The Report of the Mackenzie Valley Pipeline Inquiry* (Ottawa: Minister of Supply and Services Canada, 1977).

British Columbia Missing Women Inquiry. *Forsaken: Report of the Missing Women Commission of Inquiry* (Vancouver: British Columbia Missing Women Inquiry, 2012).

Commission on First Nations and Métis Peoples and Justice Reform. *Final Report of the Commission on First Nations and Métis Peoples and Justice Reform. Legacy of Hope: An Agenda for Change* (Saskatoon: Commission on First Nations and Métis Peoples and Justice Reform, 2004).

The Davies Commission. Inquiry into the Response of the Criminal Justice Branch. *Alone and Cold: Criminal Justice Branch Response* (2011), online: <https://opcc.bc.ca/wp-content/uploads/2017/04/The-Davies-Commission.pdf>.

Goudge, Stephen T. *Report of the Inquiry into Pediatric Forensic Pathology in Ontario* (Toronto: Queen's Printer for Ontario, 2008).

Hamilton, AC, & Murray Sinclair. *Report of the Aboriginal Justice Inquiry of Manitoba* (Winnipeg: Province of Manitoba, 1991).

Linden, Stanley. *Report of the Ipperwash Inquiry* (Toronto: Queen's Printer for Ontario: 2007).

National Inquiry into Missing and Murdered Indigenous Women and Girls. *Reclaiming Power and Place: The Final Report of the National Inquiry into Missing and Murdered Indigenous Women and Girls* (Ottawa: National Inquiry into Missing and Murdered Indigenous Women and Girls, 2019).

Public Inquiry Commission on Relations between Indigenous Peoples and Certain Public Services in Quebec: Listening, Reconciliation and Progress. Final Report (Quebec City: Government of Quebec, 2019).

Report of the Commission of Inquiry into Matters Relating to the Death of Neil Stonechild (Saskatoon: Commission of Inquiry into Matters Relating to the Death of Neil Stonechild, 2004).

Report of the Royal Commission on Indian Affairs for the Province of British Columbia (Victoria: Acme Press, 1916).

Report of the Walkerton Commission of Inquiry (Toronto: Publications Ontario, 2002).

Restorative Inquiry – Nova Scotia Home for Colored Children. *Journey to Light: A Different Way Forward. Final Report of the Restorative Inquiry – Nova Scotia Home for Colored Children* (Province of Nova Scotia: Nova Scotia Home for Colored Children Restorative Inquiry, 2019).

Royal Commission on Aboriginal Peoples. *Report of the Royal Commission on Aboriginal Peoples* (Ottawa: Supply and Services Canada, 1996).

Royal Commission on the Donald Marshall, Jr, Prosecution (Halifax: McCurdys Printing and Typesetting, 1989).

Sarich, Anthony. *Report on the Cariboo-Chilcotin Justice Inquiry* (Victoria: Cariboo-Chilcotin Justice Inquiry, 1993).

Truth and Reconciliation Commission of Canada. *Honouring the Truth, Reconciling for the Future: Summary of the Final Report of the Truth and Reconciliation Commission of Canada* (Ottawa: Truth and Reconciliation Commission of Canada, 2015).

Index

Aboriginal Healing Foundation (AHF), 52, 75, 99, 128, 203, 245n93, 247n107

Aboriginal Justice Inquiry (AJI), 106, 148–53; about, 35; BC Missing Women Inquiry compared to, 162, 201; Berger Inquiry compared to, 150; community hearings, 150; and criminal justice system, 151–52; establishment of, 148; implementation, 152–53; Implementation Commission (AJIC), 152–53; Indigenous women's participation, 162; leadership, 149, 201, 225n86; mandate, 148–49; process, 150, 162, 201; and racism, 152; Report, 106, 148–49, 151–52, 162; on residential schools and missing/murdered women, 165; and sexism, 152; and social accountability, 106, 149; standing, 150–51; Viens Commission compared to, 190; visits to USA tribal courts, 150

Aboriginal Rights Coalition, 73

Aboriginal title, 41–43; Berger Inquiry and, 44; *Calder* and, 40, 42; federal government and, 44. *See also* land(s)

accountability: criminal law vs. less punitive processes and, 26; human rights movements/organizations and, 22; for human rights violations, 18; National Inquiry into MMIWG and, 172; police, 187; public inquiries, and government and, 13; public inquiries and, 16; transitional justice and, 19; truth commissions and, 17, 22; victim- vs. perpetrator-focused inquiries and, 26; Viens Commission and, 187; for violations of laws of war, 18. *See also* social accountability

Advance Payment Program, 98–99

adversarial process: Berger Inquiry and, 45–46; criminal prosecution/civil litigation and, 113; and larger/more complete picture, 58, 111; and revictimization of survivors, 111; and survivor hardship, 112; toll on

Universal Declaration of Human Rights,
    55
Unspeakable Truths (Hayner), 221*n*62
Uruguay, truth commissions, 21
US Advisory Committee on Human
    Radiation Experiments, 25
US Commission on War-Time Reloca-
    tion and Internment of Citizens, 25

Vallée, Stéphanie, 187
Van der Peet, R v, 271*n*197
Vancouver Police Department, 37, 153
Venne, Muriel Stanley, 142–43
Victoria, Queen, 31
Viens, Jacques, 186, 188
Viens Commission (Public Inquiry
    Commission on Relations between
    Indigenous Peoples and Certain
    Public Services in Quebec), 186–91;
    report, 187, 189–90
violence against Indigenous women
    and girls: BC Missing Women Inquiry
    and, 140–41; calls for national public
    inquiry into, 139–40, 144–45; col-
    onialism and, 146, 152, 165; commis-
    sions of inquiry and, 201; criminal
    justice system and, 143; cultural ref-
    erences to, 142; failure to prevent,
    139; federal government and, 144;
    implementation of recommenda-
    tions and, 208; indifference toward,
    208; international inquiries into, 144,
    165; knowledge about, 141–43; like-
    lihood, vs. non-Indigenous women,
    283*n*97; LSC and national inquiry
    into, 146–47; national inquiry into,
    3–4; National Inquiry into MMIWG

and, 193; non-Indigenous Canadian
    resistance to remedying, 192–93;
    numbers of cases, 143, 144–45;
    racism and, 205; reasons for inquiry
    into, 147–48; recommendations for
    addressing, 180; residential schools
    and, 152, 165, 242*n*56; resistance to
    national inquiry, 145–47; sexism
    and, 205; as structural, 205–6; sys-
    temic factors underlying, 140–41,
    154; TRC Calls to Action and, 165;
    unimplemented report recommen-
    dations regarding, 146–47; Viens
    Commission and, 190. *See also* BC
    Missing Women Inquiry (MWI);
    missing/murdered Indigenous
    women and girls; National Inquiry
    into MMIWG

Waddell, Ian, 47
Walkerton Inquiry, 179, 180, 217*n*18
Walters, Mark, 132
Ward, Cameron, 199, 280*nn*65–66,
    282*n*80
Watts, Bob, 109–10, 228*n*109
Wegner, Lawrence, 36
Weston, Rose, 226*n*93
White Paper of 1969, 73, 244–45*n*92
Whitecloud, Wendy, 152
Williams Lake residential school, 69
Wilson, Bertha, 282*n*84
Wilson, Lois, 6
Wilson, Marie, 51, 107
Women's Legal Education and Action
    Fund (LEAF), 3, 214*n*3
Women's Memorial March, 142, 157,
    158–59